$11.

4.4.78

AN ECONOMIC HISTORY OF THE LOW COUNTRIES 800–1800

An Economic History of the Low Countries 800–1800

J. A. van Houtte

ST. MARTIN'S PRESS
NEW YORK

All rights reserved. For information, write:
St. Martin's Press, Inc., 175 Fifth Avenue, New York, N.Y. 10010
Printed in Great Britain
Library of Congress Catalog Card Number: 77-81397
ISBN: 0-312-23320-5
First published in the United States of America in 1977

Contents

2008710

vi / *Contents*

Preface

This work concerns the economic and social development of the Low Countries between the High Middle Ages and the end of the early modern period.* The political past of these countries has been a very troubled one. As the Carolingian Empire dissolved, feudal principalities emerged, extending over the area of the Low Countries and encroaching into what is now northern France. Almost all of these principalities were united under the House of Burgundy in the course of the fifteenth and sixteenth centuries. The state that was thus created was soon to disintegrate again, during the Dutch Revolt, and by the late sixteenth century it had been divided between the Dutch Republic, or United Provinces, in the north and the Catholic Netherlands in the south, which remained subject to the Habsburgs – Spanish until 1713, and Austrian from then until the end of the *ancien régime*. The prince-bishopric of Liège had avoided annexation by Burgundy, and remained independent until the French Revolution, when Belgium was annexed to France (1794) and the United Provinces were turned into a satellite state, the Batavian Republic (1795).

In the centuries which this book covers, the Low Countries formed a political unity only for a short period, and even then Liège was not included. However, the Low Countries as a whole did have an essential unity, for their economic and social character

---

* 'Low Countries' is here, and throughout the work, used (as in the past) to denote the area of today's Benelux countries, i.e. Belgium, the Netherlands and Luxembourg.

vii

was quite different from that of the neighbouring territories that were to develop into France and Germany. I hope that these pages will bear out this assertion, for it is fundamental to the framework of the book.

The chronological limits of the work have been set at the ninth century and the end of the eighteenth century. The first of these dates marks the emergence of a recognizably distinct character in the Low Countries, which earlier had been indistinguishable in the melting-pot of Frankish society. As the thousand years which this book covers began, the Low Countries had acquired a clear lead in the economic life of the North Sea countries, an area rivalled in economic matters only by the Mediterranean until the end of the Middle Ages. They developed and retained this lead until the end of the seventeenth century, and gradually lost it only in the eighteenth. However, by this time Belgium was becoming ready to take up a new role in the continent's economic history – as a pioneer in the Industrial Revolution, although of course the lead here belonged to Great Britain rather than to the Low Countries. This turning-point marks the end of the book, which thus traces the rise and decline of the Low Countries as a leading economic power in a thousand years of European history.

The book falls naturally into four periods: the rise and waning of the Middle Ages, the Golden Age and the search for a new structure. In each of these periods, the various aspects of economic and social history have been investigated in turn, on a deliberately classical model, so that particular subjects may be more easily accessible to the reader. The book is inevitably based only to a small degree on my own research, and owes a great deal to my predecessors; but I believe that it is important to take stock of recent advances in knowledge and arrive at a synthesis. I hope, of course, that this work will be of service in prompting further research.

Among many debts of gratitude, I should particularly like to acknowledge the help and encouragement given to me by Professor C. H. Wilson, FBA, Professor of Modern History at Cambridge and Chairman of the Department of History at the Institute of European Studies in Florence, who commissioned the work, followed its progress with great interest and awaited its completion with more than due patience. I am also grateful to Mr Norman Stone, of Jesus College, Cambridge, for his help with the translation. As has been true in the case of all my earlier work, this one would never have seen the light of day had it not been for the peace and happiness that I owe to my family.

J. A. van Houtte
Louvain, October 1976

PART ONE

The Growth of Economy and Society in the Middle Ages *800–1300*

1 *The Rural Economy*

1 GROWTH AND PROGRESS IN AGRICULTURE

Even in Carolingian times, some parts of the Low Countries had an exceptional density of population. The Frisian coastlands were always threatened by the sea, and human beings could survive only on man-made mounds, the *terpen*. By 900 so many farms existed on them that there must have been from four to twenty people per square kilometre, compelled to import at least some of what they needed from outside. Indeed, the polyptych of St Bertin's Abbey in Saint-Omer suggests that even fifty years before there had been thirty-four people per square kilometre, which is almost as many as there are today, the region having remained agricultural. Such density is surprising, given that agricultural yields were very low. In the Lille area, around 810, the estate of a son-in-law of the future emperor Louis the Pious yielded only from 2.6 to 3 times the weight of grain that had been sown, and this was the staff of life. As the relationship of demand and supply was so precarious, there would have to be great economic changes if the population grew.

This population growth was probably a fairly recent phenomenon, for the end of the Western Empire and the Merovingian period had been marked by stagnation and even decline, and the Norman invasions of the ninth century probably also arrested population growth. But after the turbulence had subsided, between 1000 and 1300, the population again increased. In two noble families in Namur, for instance, the average numbers of children reaching maturity were 5.75 and 4.3 respectively, and if

3

the nobles of Artois and French Flanders had many children, there is nothing to suggest that the lower orders were any less fertile, though of course our sources do not enable us to examine their genealogies. If the new surplus population were to live from agriculture, farming would have to become either more intensive, deriving higher yields from existing land, or more extensive, carried out over a larger area. Both changes apparently occurred at the same time.

We do not know much about agricultural techniques in the Low Countries at this time. They probably varied a great deal from place to place, and even within individual localities. In many cases our information comes only from a later period, but we can assume that the primitive methods which are revealed went back to a distant past. There was, for instance, burn-beating in the Ardennes forest zone. This enriched the land with vegetable ash, and it would then be tilled for several years in succession until it failed to yield enough. In the eastern provinces of the Netherlands some fields were cultivated permanently and were extensively manured with clods of humus taken from lands only intermittently cultivated. The great discovery of Carolingian times was the three-field system, which was more productive than any other method of soil utilization and which suggests that the population was growing. Its advantage was that work could be spread out over the year, while tilling was more frequent, manure more effective and weeding more thorough. Work was divided between three or more fields, alternately sown with winter and spring cereals and then left fallow in the third year of the cycle. The three-field system was used in the Scheldt basin and the estates of Prüm Abbey in the Eifel in the ninth century. Peasants were soon obliged to deliver both cereals to their lords and, though we have no details, the system presumably soon became common.

We know very little of the peasants' tools and techniques; detailed study of iconography might be revealing on this matter. The *Viel Rentier d'Audenarde*, a summary of peasants' obligations in the later thirteenth century, is among our most interesting sources. The earth was turned by two-handled ploughs with a coulter, ploughshare and mould board. Oxen were used to pull them at first, but when an effective harness had been invented horses increasingly took their place. Ploughing was done in stretches, originally of only four furrows, according to a tradition that probably dated from a period of wetter climate. Hammers were used to break up clods that were too large and the soil was enriched by liquid manure, marl or clumps of grass. Sowing was done by hand, the grains being taken from a fold in the peasant's clothing or a basket. A particularly early reference to the harrow for covering the seed can be found in the land register of Cambrai Cathedral around 1275. At the harvest it was only the ears of the corn that were cut, with a sickle or scythe, for the straw had to be burnt to enrich the soil. Sometimes green plants such as peas or lupins were sown, for they could be buried under the plough to increase humus. The harvested grain was threshed with a flail and ground in mills driven by horse- or water-power.

Perhaps this intensification of farming was prompted by the threat of rural over-population. However, clearances of large areas of land seem to have been a much more effective response to this threat, and they were virtually universal throughout Europe from about 1000 onwards. The Low Countries were outstanding in this respect partly because of the originality of their methods of draining.

The coastal plains on the North Sea had been flooded increasingly since Roman times, because there was more rainfall and the sea-level rose. People could live only on a few areas of high ground, and even these had to be raised repeatedly to keep them dry. But gradually the sea withdrew and as the rivers silted up with sand or clay the shallows surfaced. Dykes were built to hasten the process of draining, and the incoming water was collected and released through primitive locks. By about 960 a Norwegian chieftain who ravaged Friesland noted that there were ditches around the fields and pastures; by 1020 the Rotterdam region presented a similar picture, and thirty years later Count Baldwin v of Flanders was praised because he had made rich pasture out of his barren coastal lands. To start with such salty plains would be used exclusively for grazing sheep, and only after they had lost their high salinity was it possible to use them for other animals or as arable land – even so, the land has remained mainly under grass to this day. Once the sea had been pushed beyond the dunes and a relatively continuous coastline established, attempts were made, from about 1150, to reclaim land from the sea wherever conditions allowed. It was, as far as we can tell, in Flanders that the first polders were created, possibly in response to the danger of a new flooding. As late as the twelfth and thirteenth centuries this danger caused the natives to build mounds as refuges, or to add to them, and it was then, too, that a huge tidal wave created the Zuiderzee.

In Flanders Benedictine and Cistercian monasteries were prominent in creating the polders. They levied tithes and so had an interest in creating new land which, like their older properties, could provide them with an income. Such extensions of their lands were leased out, distributed as fiefs in return for a service, or directly exploited. In this last case, *granges* (barns) would be set up, in which monks directed the labour of lay-brothers or peasants. The great barn of Ter Doest at Lissewege, north of Bruges, has survived to this day as a testimony to the scale of these enterprises. Secular lords behaved in much the same way, though as they were less apt to record things in writing, we know less about them. In the thirteenth century the bourgeoisie of Flemish towns, especially Ghent, joined in, for the purposes of land speculation, the production of peat (an important fuel) or sheep farming for wool and meat. The peasants' role is obscure but it was probably not negligible, especially in Friesland where free peasantry was the rule.

Along the lower reaches of the great rivers, and throughout the county of Holland, stretches of land alternated with extensive marshes and flood waters created as incoming tides caused the rivers to overflow. Men began to build dykes along the Meuse and the Rhine about 1000. The counts of Holland and the bishops of Utrecht, who claimed the land recovered from the sea, leased it, while it was being drained, to entrepreneurs who would recruit the necessary labour, or to groups of peasants. For a small rent such colonists would get pieces of land called *copen*, which were of uniform dimensions – 85 metres broad and 960 long, though on occasion the length might be double that. On their narrow side they ran along the dyke, and they were surrounded by drainage ditches, some of which can still be seen. In the thirteenth century the supply of land clearly diminished, though demand for it kept up, and Count William I of Holland (1203–22) pressed ahead with damming at the river mouths. By the later thirteenth century this may have resulted in the rise of *copen* rents and the abandonment of land reclamation for almost two hundred years thereafter.

Whoever had started the draining, the actual upkeep of the ditches and dykes was obviously a matter for the local proprietors and tenants. In Flanders, Zeeland (where Flemish influence remained dominant until about 1200), and for a time in Friesland as well, such work was undertaken by the sovereign, through his agents in collaboration with local experts. The polders were administered by drainage syndicates, the *wateringues* or *waterschappen*. The authority of the oldest of these was very extensive, but by the thirteenth century the polders thus drained became smaller, and the new *wateringues* were on a correspondingly reduced scale. Both types are still in existence. In the polders of Holland and Zeeland it was the peasant communities that undertook the draining, through an elected council, the *heemraden*. When William I started draining he put these councils under superior ones, the regional *hoogheemraden*, perhaps because experience in Flanders had shown him that the work ought to be more centralized. This enabled him to drain marshes far inland, for which some central authority was needed, because watercourses had to be dug over long distances and across many farmers' lands. This reform may have contributed to the fall of the water-level. Later, when the princes were less powerful, the *hoogheemraden* won more independence.

Striking and original as the Low Countries' war with the sea was, in fact much more land was gained by clearance of forest and heath. This process has not been much studied recently, presumably because there was nothing unusual in it. Here too the monasteries seem to have been the leaders, though again perhaps only because our sources are so often of ecclesiastical origin. Monks sought solitude, and they were often given large areas of uncultivated land which princely benefactors wanted to see civilized rather than left to outlaws. The monasteries also set up *granges*, either to exploit the land directly or to collect rents payable on it by tenants. Sometimes they took more than their due. In 1196 Premonstratensians, who had been given lands near Bois-le-Duc with rights of usage over the commons, soon parcelled out these commons as well, and forged a charter to prove that they were in the right. Less is known of the activities of secular lords and peasants in this respect. Sometimes peasants squatted on lands that belonged to an absent lord and cleared them for their own benefit. Countless place-names date from this period and it is not just the increase in written sources for the eleventh century that is responsible for this. Dutch names ending in *-rade* or *-rode*,

and Walloon ones ending in *-ster* or *-sart* bear witness to their
origins in land clearance.

It was not only to land clearance that the surplus population
turned for subsistence. There was also a flight to the towns, and
the part played by men from the Low Countries in the Norman
Conquest (1066), the Crusades (1096–1270) and the siege of Lisbon
in 1147. After Hastings the Conqueror gave great estates to his
Flemish companions and other lesser Flemings were established in
Northumberland to guard the Scottish border. A generation later
they were transferred to Pembrokeshire, to guard against the
Welsh, and some of their idioms are said to have entered the local
speech. In the twelfth and thirteenth centuries bands of marauding
knights, known as the *Brabanciones*, roamed France. Their name
was derived from the Brabant origins of part (probably the oldest
part) of this force.

Besides such adventurers, many peasants seeking a peaceful
livelihood emigrated, chiefly to Germany. The Ottonian conquest
of lands beyond the Elbe, and the entry of Poland, Bohemia and
Hungary into the European community opened eastern-central
Europe to emigration from the West. Local lords tried to increase
their yields by clearances and by advanced techniques that were
unknown to the natives. They therefore brought in foreign
colonists, most of them from the Low Countries, which were probably denser in population than any other part of Europe except
Italy. Besides Flemish and Dutch skill in marsh draining was soon
famous, and the predominance of such emigrants in the movement
as a whole was illustrated by the terms 'Flemish law' or 'Dutch
law' to describe the personal status of such immigrants and their
descendants, wherever they had come from. To this day there is a
region sixty kilometres south-west of Berlin called Fläming. The
Dutch and the Flemish were in the forefront wherever marshes
were drained, as in Holstein, or where river-courses had to be
changed, as with the Elbe and many of its tributaries. When
forests and moorland were cleared in Brandenburg, Pomerania and
other parts of Germany, the Zips in the Slovak Tatra, and the
Transylvanian Alps, it was probably colonists from Brabant and
the Meuse or Walloon regions who did most of the work.

They would usually be recruited by an entrepreneur (*locator*)
whom a local lord had told to supply labour. The colonists would
be attracted by promises of abundant lands and a hitherto unthink-

able personal liberty. This, along with other factors such as the rise of towns, created throughout most of the Low Countries a highly individual and virtually free class of peasants, in great contrast to that dominated by the old manorial system.

2 THE DECLINE OF THE MANORIAL SYSTEM

In the ninth century rural life in almost all western Europe was dominated by great estates. For centuries kings, great nobles and abbeys had owned vast lands, and the struggle among Charlemagne's descendants, like the Norman invasion, allowed the large owners to acquire more because their less powerful neighbours had to cede their lands in exchange for protection. The peasants themselves lived mostly in a state of personal subjugation, which required them to render to their lord various services. The troubles of the age and the decline of trade strengthened this system, and brought the manor to its classic form. It probably penetrated parts of the Low Countries that hitherto had hardly known it – northern Brabant, the Veluwe, Overijssel, Drenthe and Holland. Only Friesland, which had maintained a well-developed commerce, continued in the main to resist.

Property, in the archetypal manorial system, was divided in two. The produce of a demesne covered at least part of a lord's own needs, while a number of tenements gave subsistence to the peasants who held them, and enabled them to discharge their obligations to the lord. There were also serfs without tenements, who were attached to the lord's household and were kept by him, but there were not enough of them to cultivate the demesne. Ploughing, carting and harvesting for the lord had to be done by the peasants, unpaid, whether they were 'free' or serfs, a distinction which probably went back to a past that had known slavery, but which lost its original significance as slavery declined. The corvées of serfs were generally heavier, however, than those of free men. On an estate belonging to St Bertin's Abbey at Saint-Omer, for instance, the serfs were expected to work three days a week for their lord, the free men only two. All villeins, whatever their status, had to supply the lord with cereals, especially rye, but also barley and malt for brewing, and hay for the lord's horses. Pigs, sheep, hens and eggs were also specified, for even the upper classes' standard of living was not high. Deliveries of wool and flax were frequent: they were worked by women of the estate, either at home or in the lord's residence (in a workshop that our sources call the *gynaeceum*). Quitrents which were stipulated in cash were often added to these obligations, and the peasant had also to pay a tithe for the spiritual services he received from the church – a source of income that the lords often took for themselves.

The relative importance of demesne and tenement varied a great deal, and villeins could to some extent make use of the vast forests, pastures and uncultivated land that a demesne might contain. Demesne land accounted for almost three-quarters of a Carolingian estate at Somain, near Valenciennes, but it was heavily wooded, whereas the demesne of St Peter's Abbey in Ghent was limited to one-fifth of the total area of the estate. For as far back as we know, landed property covered a wide area. St Bertin's Abbey set aside almost 11,000 hectares to supply its monks and had the abbot's revenues as well, though we do not know how large they were. This estate extended over twenty-four different places. The property of Lobbes Abbey on the Sambre stretched out over at least 137, and perhaps as many as 184, villages. One cause of this dispersion of ecclesiastical property was the need for wine for the celebration of Mass. As commerce declined, vine-growing spread, probably in Charlemagne's day towards the north as far as Flanders, but the low quality of the wines produced in such unfavourable climes encouraged many monasteries to buy vineyards in the Rhineland or Île-de-France.

The extension or dispersion of the estates often prompted their division into several different units, described as *villae* or *curtes*. These, too, varied a great deal in size, according to the nature of the soil or its natural covering. In the tenth century a highly wooded estate situated west of Brussels had no fewer than 18,600 hectares, whereas early in the ninth century four others in northern France had between 1,400 and 2,850, the *villa* of St Peter's in Ghent only 450 and another belonging to St Bertin's only about a hundred. The arable land of the demesne as well as that of the tenements seldom, if ever, lay in a single continuous tract, being scattered, rather, over the various areas belonging to an estate.

Services due from the villeins were fixed, as a rule on the basis of a messuage, the *manse*, which was usually a combination of arable and garden land with, occasionally, some pastures and woods. There were usually between ten and forty of these per manor, but there were exceptional cases with as few as four or as many as 118. The obligations attached to *mansi* varied not only from manor to manor, but sometimes from one to another in the same *villa*, differences due perhaps to variations in the size of the *mansi* or to the fact that some *mansi* had been attached to the manor later than others and had kept their original status. Some of them bore responsibility for military services or were given to persons with an office in the manor, such as forester or steward. Wherever the manorial system prevailed, the personal liberty of the peasant, free or serf, was heavily curtailed. He was bound to the soil, was subject to *merchet* (i.e. he could not marry without his lord's permission) so that his descendants would not escape the lord's power, and he could not bequeath his property because of mortmain.

There were really very few serfs, but the 'free' villeins, the great majority of the rural population, were just as powerless against lords with an armed band to enforce obedience. Not counting ecclesiastics, who owed their authority and property to the protection and generosity of other large landowners, it was the landowning lords who constituted the military class in Carolingian society. Many of them had received their fiefs from the Frankish kings for a military purpose: since the eighth century the kings had used this method to get help in what remained of the administration and defence of their kingdoms. To start with it had been a relationship of personal loyalty but as royal authority declined feudalism developed on *de facto* hereditary lines.

Gradually changes took place that profoundly shook the manorial system. Tenements were simply usurped – the ecclesiastical ones were in special danger because in general churchmen were forbidden to bear arms. In a world of violence they were often forced to hand over their defence to a secular protector (*avoué*) who was, of course, in a good position to seize the lands he was supposed to protect. This was also true of stewards administering a property. The steward of Halen manor, near Diest, which belonged to St Truiden Abbey, only sixteen kilometres away as the crow flies, expropriated a large part of it in the first half of the twelfth century. The abbot, after failing in repeated efforts to recover the property, had to put up with it and enfeoff the steward. Many *mansi* were also occupied by more than one tenant from the ninth century on. In 893, in a manor of the Ardennes, 114 peasant families held thirty-four *mansi* and this became more general as the population grew. It became increasingly difficult to apportion the services owed for a single *manse*, and it was quite impossible once new tenements were formed out of lands that had earlier belonged to several *mansi*. In the Ardennes and Namur, the *manse* was replaced as a unit of account by a new unit, the *quartier*, which probably marked an attempt to keep the old services in existence, and new tenements were even formed on this basis. But by the thirteenth century *quartiers* in turn had more than one tenant, and in the end the term only meant a certain (variable) area of land, as happened in Brabant with the term *manse*.

As the *mansi* dissolved, the demesnes followed suit. The Halen steward had taken over both demesne and tenements. There were obvious dangers for lands far from their owner's residence. Traditional methods of farming were threatened still more by the effects of clearances. Colonists were attracted by the promise of corvées of a few days annually instead of as many weekly. Such generous conditions and the rise of new towns tempted many peasants to escape from their manors. The lords were unable to stop them. Many of them had been weakened because their properties had been split up at the whim of inheritance and in any case the monarchies, whose power grew as their vassals' declined, were in no way inclined to help the nobles recover fugitives. Since the peasants could now get away, they were more and more reluctant to render all the services they were supposed to, and as the *manse* declined the obligations became difficult to determine anyway, which encouraged many peasants to evade them.

There was only one thing the lords could do, and that was to end the system on the best terms they could get. They too reduced corvées, and could thus no longer command the labour they needed for the demesne. This could also happen when tenements were lost to a manor after a usurpation. Corvées having lost their significance, both lord and peasant agreed to commute them into rents of goods or cash. As regular markets for agricultural goods started up in the towns, the cash for these rents became available. Corvée had always produced poor returns, and now that the system was breaking up the villeins took every opportunity to refuse services, particularly where the lord's power of constraint was weakened by distance. Some lords even encouraged their villeins to buy their freedom for they no longer needed such labour now that there was a market to supply them with whatever they required. By the thirteenth century at the latest the entire system of forced labour had virtually disappeared and the peasant worked on his own account. This proved in the long run to be even better for him than he could have imagined at the start. The rent he owed in cash was fixed for all time, but its real value fell with inflation; and if the rent were in goods, it was again he who would profit, because it represented a diminishing share of output as agricultural productivity rose.

Since the demesne could no longer be cultivated by corvée, the lords sometimes found it profitable to lease it. Sometimes the steward would take it for a quitrent, and quite often would then hire his own steward to farm it, while he himself joined the idle class of an emerging nobility that included *ministeriales* of recent fortune as well as old families. Most often the demesne was divided into tenements farmed out either to household serfs or newcomers. Much the same happened after clearances on uncultivated land. As for the church's estates, the declining number of lay brothers forced the abbots to stop farming their *granges* and lease the land. This happened in Flanders by the twelfth century, perhaps because of the clearances that were especially widespread there, and extended all over the Low Countries in the following century. The *granges* were rented out as farms, although they continued to entail certain obligations – a function that, in the Veluwe at least, had always been their primary one.

The land was originally let for a quitrent, fixed in perpetuity according to custom. When the owners saw that they were losing as money gradually declined in value, they became concerned to keep up the value of their share of the agricultural income. Sometimes they went in for share-cropping (*métayage*), especially when they had kept the less valuable land which would be worked temporarily by peasants with insufficient capital. This method took too much of the yield to attract peasants who had the resources to clear virgin land. At the same time, late in the twelfth century, temporary leases appeared, first of all in Flanders. Tenure being traditionally hereditary, a temporary lease was the only way for lords to recover their lands from time to time and take their share of rising agricultural prices. Some leases were originally fixed for life, but it became customary for them to be limited to a number of years. Originally the figure was quite arbitrary, but gradually the habit formed of choosing a multiple of three years, in accordance with the three-field system – particularly twelve or fifteen, at the term of which the peasant was to marl the fields. The lease gained in popularity from the thirteenth century onwards.

Businesslike owners tried to regroup their properties. Distant manors which were particularly exposed to seizure were costly and they were often sold, the money being reinvested in land nearer at hand. Many monasteries abandoned their far-off vineyards now that wine could be bought on the market, and though Nivelles Abbey bought a vineyard in the Rhineland early in the fourteenth century, and let it out to share-croppers, that was an exceptional event. The monks who visited it annually to supervise the harvest and take their share were absent for over a month.

Villeins enjoyed rights of use over uncultivated land. They used it as pasture, or to supply wood for fuel or for the framework of their wattle huts, for furnishings, tools and the like. When the lords gave up cultivating the demesne, their tenants, whose numbers and farms had grown, were careful to extend their rights over uncleared land. For some time many lords tried to retain the pasturage for themselves, for, though they had given up farming, they still kept horses. Haying was often one of the last services to go, sometimes one of the few to be perpetuated. In the end many pasturages went the way of the arable land, leased to peasants.

Sometimes the uncultivated lands were divided between lord and peasants, who might also rent the lord's share, but usually the lord gave it up in return for cash or a quitrent. In any event, exploitation of uncultivated lands led to new regulations, for the increased numbers of users meant that some supervision of tree-felling, grass-lifting or pasturage became necessary. The peasants who had rights of usage would elect a council to exercise control, and this council, often after bitter disputes with neighbouring villages, would fix the boundaries. These were the *meenten* of northern Brabant and the Belgian Campine, the *marken* in the eastern provinces of the Netherlands, the *masuirs* and *waréchaix* of the Walloon area. Many historians of the previous century imagined that these were vestiges of primitive agrarian communism, but in reality they began only in the thirteenth century and reflected one of the many changes that rural life was then undergoing.

These changes eventually affected the peasants' personal status.

Colonists were no longer subject to serfdom on new lands, so the lords had to abandon it for their remaining subjects also. In many cases, the *hospites* who worked on clearances were freed *en masse*, and 'laws' were made for them by local lords, which served as models for other villages: the 'law' of Prisches near Avesnes (1158) was adopted for some thirty villages in Hainault and the Vermandois, and that of Beaumont in the French Ardennes (1182) was the model for several clearances in Luxembourg. In the mid-twelfth century, ninety villages of the Bruges area were freed at a stroke, and in 1252 the countess of Flanders abolished serfdom throughout her principality, which weakened her noble vassals still further. In the twelfth century the bishops of Liège ceased to apply the right of mortmain, and it was also abolished in Brabant in 1247. In Hainault, serfdom also declined.

Serfs who did not benefit from measures of collective manumission were able to buy their personal liberty. Villeins could also improve their lot because of urban markets. At the very least, they were now free to marry as they liked and, for a small sum, to pass on their property to heirs. By the later thirteenth century villeinage had virtually disappeared in the greater part of Flanders, Brabant, Holland and Zeeland, as serfdom had done. Friesland had never known it to any degree. Where it survived, it had ceased to be burdensome.

Villeinage also had its advantages, for the villein enjoyed hereditary tenure. The villeins' descendants could now mortgage lands or lease them to third parties with the lord's permission, which could not be withheld if the new occupants were his subjects. In practice a class of peasant proprietors arose and gained a large part of the land, both where villeinage survived and where there was a free peasantry. On the other hand, by the early thirteenth century, the urban bourgeoisie was also taking an interest in landed property. The nature of such property had become quite different since the ninth century, when virtually all of the land had belonged to the church or to great vassals.

The kings of France and Germany had quite soon ceased to count for much as landowners in the Low Countries. Their manors had been ceded to vassals, given to the church or seized by usurpers. But once the more powerful of these had taken over such estates, they were able to set themselves up as princes over large areas. Although they, too, gave away considerable portions of their lands over the centuries, these feudal princes still had great estates at the end of the thirteenth century. The church was certainly the principal beneficiary of their generosity, but it had also suffered heavy losses, both through seizure and through more or less voluntary enfeoffment, and these losses outweighed the new donations. Gifts of whole manors became rare, and after the eleventh century the church received only fractions of manors. A century later the gifts would be limited to a certain stretch of demesne or forest, to a single church, together with the right to dispose of its benefice (i.e. religious functions attached to the donation, and the revenues relating to them), or merely a mill. By the late thirteenth century, gifts of land virtually ceased.

The secular lords had in any case gradually lost their earlier wealth. Their properties had been split up among successive heirs, and the remnant had become too small to be further divided without diminishing the standard of living of the nobles, old or new. In some regions in the thirteenth century there were large numbers of impoverished noblemen, some of whom relapsed into the peasantry. Others sold off their manors, either as a whole or gradually, and some such lands were bought up by prosperous members of the urban bourgeoisie who wished to acquire the prestige that a seignorial position could give, although it no longer conveyed serious power.

Apart from collecting his rents, the new type of lord could at most levy tithes and gather the income from a communal mill or a brewery that the peasants were forced to use; most often, the lords maintained some kind of jurisdiction. Such income no longer counted for much and rural incomes ceased to predominate. Other opportunities were open to the servants of the sovereign who could share the exercise and profits of his authority, now gradually being substituted for the political splintering and military anarchy of the lesser feudal lords. Monarchical service, which was open to commoners, might also provide opportunities for the more capable among the nobles. Lords could consider themselves lucky if their fief allowed them to levy a toll on the passage of goods, for, parallel with the shifts in political power, the rise of towns based on trade and industry had created a new economic and scoial balance.

2 *The Revival of Towns and Trade*

THE DEVELOPMENT OF TRADE

Trade in Carolingian Europe was generally in a state of profound lethargy, but it was still active in the Frisian lands between the Dutch river delta and the Danish peninsula. The inhabitants were forced to trade, because of their high population density: they had taken refuge on ridges where arable land was scarce and animal raising predominant, and natural conditions were such that they could survive only if they imported grain. Scarcity of land also impelled them, since agriculture offered so few possibilities, towards seafaring and trade, although the two were not necessarily connected. Frisian sailors, for example, supplied crews for Charlemagne's fleets, and in the ninth century they helped both the Danes who sacked England and Alfred the Great who resisted later Danish incursions.

In exchange for what they bought, the Frisians could in part offer goods from their own lands. They certainly sold animal skins, although their dairy produce was not mentioned at this time. Frisian cloth was of greater importance, and Charlemagne thought it fine enough to present some to Haroun-ál-Rashid, the Caliph of Baghdad and hero of the *Arabian Nights*. The origins of this cloth have been heatedly debated, since written reference to it is hardly clear. Some historians, considering that Friesland had no real wool industry later on, believe that it could not have had one at this time, and in their opinion, the adjective 'Frisian' must apply to the merchants trading with the cloth, and not to the area that produced it, which was more likely to have been England or

Flanders, as a prelude to the renown their wool industries were to have. Other historians have claimed that the *pallia frisonica* really did come from Friesland. Archaeology has revealed nothing about Flanders, but in England and Friesland searches have shown the remains of both fine and coarse cloth strikingly similar to cloth discovered in the Scandinavian archaeological sites, which did have ties with Friesland. Many spinning and weaving tools have been found in the Frisian mounds, and the area may well have had quite a developed industry, though this does not preclude the possibility that other areas on the North Sea also produced cloth for export.

Frisian ship owners and merchants also acted as middlemen for other goods. They had their own quarters in Rhenish towns such as Xanten, Birten (the Roman *Vetera Castra*), Duisburg, Cologne, Mainz, Worms and Strasbourg, while on the Meuse, Maastricht owed something of its prosperity to them. Five centuries after the fall of the Roman Empire that had caused their growth, these areas were still the chief centres north of the Alps for vine growing and the ceramic, iron and arms industries. The Frisians also attended the fairs at Saint-Denis, outside Paris, which was the centre of another vine-growing region. They were, however, chiefly active in the North Sea – which contemporaries accurately described as the Frisian sea – and the Baltic, especially along the trade route that linked Anglo-Saxon England, Quentowic on the Canche (probably Étaples in the Pas-de-Calais), the mysterious Witla which was somewhere in the Zeeland islands, Dorestad, which lay opposite the modern town of Wijk-bij-Duurstede, where the Lek divides from the Rhine, Stavoren, Emden, Haithabu in the Schleswig area and Birka on Lake Mälar in Sweden.

At Birka, it led into another artery of trade, that through Russia to the Black Sea and the Caspian, which at this period was the main link between Europe and the Byzantine and Arab East, the threshold of Asia. From Asia came the spices that were so much in demand for cooking or medicine and as aphrodisiacs, and the Chinese silks that were still treasured although the silkworm had recently been introduced into the Mediterranean lands. Our sources are silent on this, but Frisians probably helped distribute such goods in the North Sea area. Scandinavia and Russia supplied them with their own products, especially furs, which were important in the fashions of the rich throughout the Middle Ages and later. These goods were all luxuries for which Frisians trading in the North had to pay in precious metal, as is clear from the many discoveries of Frisian coins made in eastern Europe. There was no gold or silver in the Low Countries, so perhaps Irish gold, brought out through Anglo-Saxon middlemen, was used. The West lost more and more gold, especially through Norman looting during the whole of the ninth century, and the Frisians had to make do with exports of silver, probably from the Harz mountains.

In this chain of market-places, Dorestad, in Friesland itself, was a major Carolingian customs post. Looted several times by the Normans, it never recovered from the final sacking in 863. Its place was taken mainly by Emden, which arose late in the eighth century and grew rapidly thereafter, and by Stavoren, which was rich enough to attract a Viking raid even in the later tenth century. Most Frisian merchants, however, lived in the country, and not in the market-places. Like the Danes, Swedes and Gotlanders of this pre-urban era, they combined agriculture, trade and even piracy in a way that seems incredible to the modern observer. Friesland itself was a particular victim of Viking raids, and it is hardly surprising that both the first and last references to Viking raids in Carolingian Europe (810–1007) apply to Friesland, where the greatest plunder was to be had.

It has often been claimed that these raids, and especially the destruction of Dorestad, ruined Frisian commerce. Nevertheless other markets did succeed Dorestad. They may have been just as prosperous, though we cannot tell, partly perhaps because our written sources for the post-Carolingian period are so meagre, and partly because these places have been lived in continuously ever since, so that there has never been the opportunity for the kind of revealing archaeological discoveries that were possible in Dorestad itself, which ceased to exist as a town. The decline of Frisian commerce by the end of the tenth century seems to have resulted rather from the erosion of the markets and routes with which it was linked. The arrival of the wild Petchenegs and Polovtsians in the Ukraine and their wars with the Varangian principality of Kiev cut communications between Scandinavia and the Near East, and strangled the system of which they were a vital component.

The end of the Frisian phase in the history of north-western trade was a product of the fundamental reversal of the economic

balance of Europe. The Mediterranean now resumed its traditional function as chief link between East and West, and the centre
of gravity in the European economy shifted from north to south.
Formerly, Mediterranean trade between East and West had been
weakened by the struggle of Byzantium and Islam for control of
the sea, and the adverse balance of payments that had gradually
stripped Europe of its gold. Relations between the Mediterranean
and the Low Countries had, however, never been wholly severed.
The oriental goods that reached the Carolingian Empire could
have come via either the Mediterranean or the Scandinavian
routes. In the ninth and tenth centuries, moreover, Verdun was
an important collection point for slaves brought, partly by
Frisian traders, from England and the Slav lands beyond the Elbe,
and sent off, under the direction mainly of Jewish dealers, to Arab
Spain and the whole Moslem world, as far away as Persia and
Afghanistan.

Although trade with Arab Spain was important for the West, it
was soon overtaken when Italy recovered her economic supremacy. The prosperity of tenth-century Byzantium had a considerable effect on the Italian towns that had always preserved a
modest trade with the Greek East. Venetian traders wandered,
especially into Lombardy and the eastern Alps, and set up trading-
posts like Regensburg or the Rhineland ones, so that an alternative route was established for the carriage of oriental goods to
the Low Countries. Moreover Genoa and Pisa on the Tyrrhenian
coast profited from the decline of the naval power of Arab Spain,
and were able to expel the Saracens from their fortified points on
the coasts of Provence and Languedoc. With the development of
their Mediterranean trade, they were able to send goods over the
western passes of the Alps and along the valleys of the Rhône and
its tributaries. Italian merchants travelling to England along the
French routes are mentioned at the very end of the eleventh
century, at Saint-Omer, and they probably visited Flanders as
well, though our sources do not refer to them until 1127.

At the same time the Frisian and other merchants had revived
trade elsewhere in the Low Countries. Full participation in trade
required profound social change. The growth of population in
this period created a surplus labour force, beyond the needs of
manorial subsistence production, which was available for the production of goods to be bartered against foreign ones. By 983

cloth, metal objects and animal skins that had been produced at least partly in the neighbouring regions were being sold at the Visé fairs, half-way between Liège and Maastricht.

It was not the Frisians alone who lived on trade. Our oldest source for this, a list of the dues payable in London by foreigners that dates back to 991–1002, mentions merchants of Flanders, Huy and Liège on the Meuse, and 'Emperor's men', who are generally supposed to have come mainly from the Rhineland, especially Tiel on the Waal, the English connections with which are stressed in many of our sources around 1000. When Frisians occupied the lower Waal in 1018, the Tielers complained to the emperor, on the grounds that their links with England would suffer from the new circumstances. Tiel was the final stage on the journey to the North Sea for traffic coming along the Rhine, the essential artery in a system that included central Europe and Italy, with their connections to the East. Tiel's prosperity survived until about 1100. In the twelfth century the counts of Holland took over the area of the lower Waal, and the river also ceased to be the main branch of the Rhine delta, so that trade was diverted towards the Lek and the lower Rhine. Moreover, as Cologne's commerce with England grew, it no longer needed middlemen, whilst the arrival of Italian merchants along the French routes to Flanders may also have reduced the Rhine's role in trade between the Mediterranean and the North Sea.

In a register of the Coblentz tolls drawn up in 1104 to record the taxes levied on foreigners within living memory – i.e. within a generation, or since about 1070 – the merchants have much the same origins as had been the case in London a century earlier, with the addition of men from Antwerp and the Meuse towns, especially Namur and Dinant. At the end of the eleventh century we find those from Liège and Huy clashing over taxes with Cologne, which they had to go through to reach Westphalia and Saxony, obviously in search of the Harz copper ore they needed for their brass industry. In Coblentz's trade, the lower Rhine was represented, as before, by merchants from Tiel, from neighbouring places such as Heerewarden, where ships could go from the Meuse to the Waal, and Zaltbommel, and from Deventer and Utrecht. Little is known of Deventer's trade in this period. It was probably mainly with the north, as Utrecht's certainly was. Just after 1000 Groningen, like these other places, had a toll and a mint, evidence of at least some trading there. Frisians continued to trade in the north: in Sigtuna cemetery in Sweden, two tombs with runic inscriptions exist, erected in the first half of the century to the memory of dead compatriots. But the Frisians had lost their lead in northern trade to the Danes, who now came in larger numbers to the markets of the Low Countries.

Like England, the Rhineland and the north, France also attracted traders. They accompanied the villeins who went to Soissons in 1066 to assist with the wine harvest, and they probably brought back wine in exchange for cloth which, according to a contemporary poem, was sent from Flanders to France. This was the beginning of Flemish commerce with the south, although as yet merchants from the Meuse had not appeared in France, probably because they were too greatly involved in Germany before 1100 to take much interest in matters elsewhere.

2 THE REVIVAL OF THE TOWNS

It was impossible for trade, however modest, to continue without markets, for even pedlars had to have their source of supply. In western civilization, markets were the nuclei of towns. In Roman times, the towns of Gaul had prospered because of trade, although later on the commercial economy had been weakened and in the Carolingian period little survived of the Roman towns in the Low Countries. In the market-places that had developed in Friesland, the merchants, strongly attached to the land as they remained, still needed labour to load and unload or maintain their carts and ships; while artisans could also set up there, to sell their output directly to foreign merchants. Dorestad, the chief Frisian market, extended for almost a mile on both sides of a branch of the Rhine, with a market-place at the edge of the settlement, and a Carolingian fortress. The town was surrounded by a mound and palisade. In this turbulent era, men had to provide defences for a place where looters were certain of finding great riches stored, and even so Dorestad succumbed.

Markets came into existence along the routes of Frisian commerce. The name *vicus* in the ninth century could be applied to any settlement at all, but *portus* certainly indicated some trading activity, and it was used in connection with Deventer, where the bishops of Utrecht had their residence from the mid-ninth to the mid-twelfth century, and where their comparatively sophisticated demand stimulated urban growth. On the Meuse, Maastricht was frequently visited by traders, as we learn from Charlemagne's biographer, Eginhard, while up-river Huy, Namur and Dinant were all known as *portus*. On the Scheldt the term was used for Ghent, Tournai and Valenciennes, and on the Scarpe, a tributary of the Scheldt, for what is today the village of Lambres, near Douai. Most such places had the same combination of characteristics as Dorestad: a good situation for trading, and the relative safety of fortifications. Deventer lay at a point where the road to Saxony crossed the IJssel, and the bishop's court must have been fortified somehow, as was the custom; Maastricht possessed the only bridge over the Meuse in the Low Countries, and an old Roman road went over it: Tournai and Valenciennes had bridges over the Scheldt, and the remnants of a Roman wall. The towns up-river on the Meuse were dominated by rocky heights where the people could hide and defend themselves. There was a ford over the Meuse at Huy, and Namur lay at the confluence of the Sambre and the Meuse. Ghent, where the Lys joined the Scheldt, was often described as *castrum*, and Antwerp from the eighth century onwards as *castellum*, both words implying fortification.

Like Dorestad the other *portus* were destroyed by Normans, but unlike it they rose again rapidly, and developed. The old Ghent, for instance, was ravaged in 851 or in 879–80, at the same time as the abbeys protecting it, but a new Ghent was created early in the tenth century not far from the old one, under the walls of the recently built count's castle. There were other similar cases, and the growth of trade encouraged the development of many new centres for trade in the Low Countries. Almost all of the modern towns date back to the tenth, eleventh, twelfth or, at the latest, thirteenth centuries.

The Rhine and Meuse valleys, the oldest theatres of the revival of trade, and Flanders were the first to experience the vigorous growth of towns. In Friesland, Stavoren led the way by about 900, at the latest, while just after 1000 Groningen had its church of St Walpurga, a favourite patron of merchants. On the IJssel there was only Deventer until the thirteenth century, when their economic growth caused Kampen, Zutphen and Zwolle to attain urban rank. In the same period Leeuwarden and other, lesser, places on the Zuiderzee in modern Friesland were transformed from peasant or fishing villages. After the bishop of Utrecht had

E.H.—2

returned to his residence the Arab traveller Ibrahim-al-Jacoub, who visited it in 973, described it as a large town, and he must have been comparing it with the towns of the German Rhine he had just passed through. It remained for many years the most important of the Dutch towns because of its Rhenish trade (in which it succeeded Tiel) and the traffic through it between Flanders and the north. Changes in the river beds and consequently also in the trade routes along the branches of the Rhine delta conferred on Nymegen, where the Waal splits off, and Arnhem, near the confluence of the Rhine and the IJssel, the full status of towns.

On the middle Meuse Dinant, Namur, Huy, Liège and Maastricht formed from that time a group of towns; downstream, Ruremonde and Venlo were added in the thirteenth century, while Maastricht became an important junction for trade by land between Germany and the North Sea, partly, no doubt, because of progress made in harnessing techniques. It was thought for many years that the towns of Brabant came into existence in the second half of the twelfth century because of trade along this route: but it would seem rather that other routes were responsible, those linking the upper Meuse, the lower Scheldt and the Dutch archipelago, which avoided the long detour of the middle Meuse. From Namur, Antwerp could be reached through Nivelles, where there was a large abbey, and Brussels, where the Senne became navigable, or along the valley of the Dyle through Gembloux, which had another abbey, Louvain, where boats could be unloaded, and Malines, which also had a monastery.

The new route from the Rhineland to Flanders left the now abandoned Roman road to Bavai at Maastricht, and continued either through the domain of the abbey of Saint-Truiden through Zoutleeuw and Tienen, both of which lay on tributaries of the Scheldt, to Louvain and Brussels, or through Hasselt, Diest and Aerschot towards Malines or again Louvain. All of these places had become towns by the twelfth or thirteenth centuries, if not before. Godfrey I, duke of Brabant (1095–1139), and his successors perhaps deliberately fostered the growth of the towns by founding abbeys or chapters in the less populous parts of their dukedom. Bois-le-Duc, certainly, was favoured by its closeness to the Meuse when it received the legal status of town in 1185, through the award of an individual magistracy distinct from that of the surrounding countryside. But in most cases such initiatives failed. The little towns of the Campine moors and north Brabant had to wait for several centuries before they became anything other than country markets.

Apart from the Carolingian places that were restored after the invaders' ravages, other towns appeared in the Scheldt basin from the tenth century on: Douai, for instance, succeeded Lambres, which did not recover, and Cambrai. On the Dendre, the obvious route out of Hainault, Alost emerged because it marked the crossing of the road from Brussels, and Termonde because it was similarly placed for the Malines road. Both routes led to Ghent and Bruges. Bruges, first mentioned in 892, became an important centre for trade under the protection of a count's castle. The *portus* was originally separated from the sea by shallows that could be negotiated only at high tide, but a tidal wave, probably in 1134, opened up a wide bay, the Zwin, which allowed ships to come within three miles of the town in deeper water. Watercourses, some of which were artificial, linked it with Bruges and Ghent, fostering the growth of trade and the towns. The same tidal wave may also have made the little town of Aardenburg into a temporary trading-place. In western Flanders, Saint-Omer on the Aa and Arras were further centres of internal and maritime trade.

Until about 1050 the Flemish coast was separated from the upper Scheldt by wild moorland. To link them, Count Baldwin v (1035–67) apparently founded a set of towns, many of which had a fair. Ypres, Messines, Lille, Cassel, Aire and other places in inland Flanders owed their existence to him, and his example seems to have persuaded the dukes of Brabant to follow suit in the next century. Count Philip of Alsace (1168–91) founded at least four new towns in Flanders: Gravelines at the mouth of the Aa, Nieuport at the mouth of the Yser, Damme as an entry port for Bruges at the point where the Zwin came furthest inland and Biervliet in Flemish Zeeland, where peat extraction and stock raising had advanced far enough to need a port.

Mons, at first merely one of many religious settlements in Hainault, became a town only in the thirteenth century, when the counts shifted their capital from Valenciennes. In Luxembourg, which had a small population and vast forests, only the town of Luxembourg itself had the social and economic standing of a town; other places were simple country markets. Zeeland, with nothing but its cattle and fisheries, generally remained quite as rural. Its only town of any importance was Middelburg, which had probably started off as part of a chain of forts erected against the Vikings but profited from the urbanizing policy of the counts of Flanders when they dominated the region in the eleventh century. In Holland the oldest town was Dordrecht, which was on the confluence of several rivers and caught some of Tiel's trade when the area was taken over by the counts of Holland. Its prosperity grew still more when the inland waterways of Holland were used for trade with the north, which turned it into an important junction. Most of the other later Dutch towns, such as Haarlem, Delft, Leyden and Gouda were mere centres of manorial and county administration until the thirteenth century, and Amsterdam was just a fishing village.

What, in general, were the determining factors in the siting and growth of towns? The remnants of Roman settlements, most of which became fortified refuges in Merovingian times, could shelter trade, especially at Maastricht and Tournai. Elsewhere a Carolingian palace, as at Nymegen, or, more often, a count's castle would play the same role. At Liège and Utrecht a bishop's residence, and at Nivelles and Malines an abbey formed the nucleus of the town. When the Norman invasions had ceased these refuges, whatever their origin, attracted a population that lived more or less from trade. *Portus*, soon frequently known as *suburbia* or suburbs, developed under the walls of fortresses where the people could flee with their goods when danger threatened. Often there would be a market-place under the very walls of a *castrum*.

When the population grew the pre-urban fortifications would not be large enough to shelter all the people in moments of danger, and the citizens, whose sense of solidarity was in any case growing, felt the need to build fortifications of their own, as happened at Liège at the end of the tenth century at most of the Meuse and Scheldt towns in the eleventh century and at the Brabantine ones in the twelfth. At first a ditch and a rampart of earth with a palisade on top would be constructed around the place, but by the twelfth century stone walls began to appear, although in some places they did not replace the primitive ramparts until the fourteenth century. Quite often these fortifications would include the original heart of the town, a sure sign that the centre of gravity had now shifted to the mercantile suburb. The walls took in a large area – thirty-two hectares at Antwerp, sixty at Louvain, seventy at Bruges, eighty at Ghent and Brussels – but still the later growth of the towns caused the population to overflow. In some cases, the walls were extended to include the new quarters as circumstances required, for instance at Ghent on eight occasions between 1213 and 1384, but elsewhere, as with most of the Flemish towns in the thirteenth century and the Brabantine ones in the fourteenth, new walls were all put up at once. The few town gates that still survive, at Brussels, Malines and Bruges, for instance, belonged to these. The major towns thus enlarged became quite sizeable: Ghent spread over 644 hectares, Brussels over 449, Bruges over 430 and Louvain over 410.

3 URBAN SOCIETY

We do not know much about the origins of urban society. Our earliest witness is a monk from the diocese of Utrecht, and perhaps also from the Tiel region, though he was called Alpert of Metz. Early in the eleventh century he wrote a diatribe against the scandalous behaviour of the merchants of Tiel, whom he described as a band of shameless rascals. A modern scholar, in describing the precautions taken by the Anglo-Saxon king Harthacnut to guard his ship when it stopped at Bruges in 1042, tentatively compares them with the pioneers of the Wild West, and much the same might be said of a *negotiator* (merchant) around 1000 who, ruined by shipwreck, went to rest in the chapel of an abbey at Ghent, stole its golden chalice to refloat his affairs and promised the holy patron that he would pay it back, and more, if he succeeded – a vow that he was able to keep. Life in the young towns, as everywhere else, was rough.

There has been much debate about the origins of the merchant class. Some historians believe that it was quite separate from the early agricultural population, and that it started with a group of foreigners who had broken all links with their native lands and spent their time travelling except when all travel was interrupted by hostile weather. But other historians have asserted that the merchant class arose among local villeins when production exceeded demand and a labour surplus became available to market it. Perhaps both theories are too simple. The villeins of St Vaast Abbey at Arras, for instance, enjoyed preferential treatment at its tolls, and so many foreigners applied for admission to this villeinage that at the end of the tenth century entry to it had to be restricted, which shows that villeins had at least a share in trade. It would be absurd to suppose that, whoever the earliest merchants and whatever their origins, the locals ignored their activities.

The people of medieval towns, motivated by strong loyalties, formed fraternities which sometimes had religious, charitable or professional purposes as well as social ones. Many Frisian merchants set up guilds at Scandinavian market-places, sometimes open to the locals. Other guilds thrived in the Low Countries. The people of Tiel whom Alpert so much disliked were united under oath in a guild which organized drinking sessions that perhaps reflected ancient Germanic fellowship. They also did business together. The quite explicit statutes of the guilds of Valenciennes and Saint-Omer which have survived mention religious functions as well as professional ones, and perhaps Alpert's disapproval caused him to pass over the Tielers' religious involvement in silence, for he could not have disapproved of that. Brothers of the Valenciennes guild were supposed to help each other when travelling on business. They, like those of Saint-Omer, probably tried to monopolize retail trade in their own town. Merchant guilds of Arras and Ghent also date back to the eleventh century and more still emerged in the twelfth. The Groningen guild, with four sections representing the chief trading areas, may have been as old; and Dordrecht had one in 1201. They became especially numerous in the thirteenth century, a time when professional and other aims tended to prevail over the religious and charitable ones.

In fact the merchants and their guilds took the lead in emancipating the citizens from feudalism. Many lords had welcomed the growth of a town on their manor and protected it. However, they differed too greatly from the merchants in outlook to respond to mercantile needs, and conflict was sooner or later unavoidable. The townspeople began by claiming recognition of their communities as a specific legal entity distinct from the agrarian and seignorial surroundings. The episcopal towns of Cambrai and Tournai seem to have obtained such recognition in the tenth century, that of Liège around 1000. The process is obscure, but some indication of what it involved appears in a charter of liberties which the bishop of Liège granted in 1066 to the town of Huy, the oldest such charter north of the Alps. To prevent arbitrary or brutal justice, Huy was exempted from trial by combat or ordeal, as was Tiel after the 1020s. They were promised that justice would be speedy, which suited the needs of merchants who were always travelling. Private vengeance was prohibited, for the keeping of the peace was considered essential. The inhabitants were also protected against their former lords, who were required to furnish proof of a man's status as a serf, which must often have been difficult to do.

Gradually personal freedom grew. The activities of merchants presupposed freedom, and all limitations of it were sooner or later abrogated in new charters, or fell into disuse because they could not be maintained in a more mobile and wealthier society. The saying 'town air makes free' became common, as the burghers became one of the determining factors in society, capable of defending their rights. Sometimes forty days' residence was enough to free the burgher from his villeinage, though usually a year and a day were needed, and, where agrarian economic and social traditions persisted, as in Guelders or Overijssel, as long as thirty years. Even if, as often happened up to the end of the *ancien régime*, some lordships persisted within urban communities, their inhabitants soon lost all links with their agrarian past and the lords could only levy taxes on trade and handicrafts. At Ghent, the lords' taxation rights seem to have been bought up from the abbeys which owned the land between 1050 and 1100. The same thing happened at Arras in 1245, at Aardenburg in 1230 and at Bruges in 1127 when the rights were made over to the town by the Count of Flanders as landowner.

Freed from their lords, and equipped with a mercantile law (*jus mercatorum*), the towns got their own administration, mayors and aldermen appointed by the princes or other lords. Some even managed to become virtually independent, without any princely control, as in Italy and Germany. Cambrai, the first known commune in western Europe, was established in 1077 after a long battle with its lord the bishop. It survived, except for a short break, until 1227 and sparked off a similar movement in many episcopal towns in northern France. The communal movement had its first successes in such episcopal towns, for the bishops appear to have been quite unable to defeat the burghers' revolutionary aspirations. At Liège, a commune was recognized in 1161, and the other towns of the prince-bishopric got elected councils

by 1200. The possessions of the bishop of Utrecht were undergoing similar changes at the same time. Tournai shook off the
bishop's temporal authority by 1200 and only nominally recognized the king of France as its lord until Charles v took over the
town in 1521. In the lay principalities, elected councils acquired
administrative powers. In Flanders it happened after the dynastic
crisis of 1127-8 which weakened the sovereign's authority, but the
count stopped this by 1200 and handed over administration and
justice to magistrates whom he himself appointed. In most of the
Brabantine towns this process was repeated a century later, but in
Holland and Zeeland, where towns were backward, the elected
magistrates usually had to make do with a subordinate role.

Whether elected or appointed, the magistrates were now
chosen from among the notables of the town. Historians have
described them as patricians. Their fortunes were not identical in
origin: there was much variation in the Flemish towns. If some of
the patricians in what is now northern France may have been
descendants of seignorial families, in Ghent after the twelfth
century only landowners in the town were eligible. Elsewhere the
only criterion we can safely suggest is participation in long-
distance trade or finance. The patrician families sooner or later
gave up direct economic activity and, as wealthy landed proprietors, adopted the ways of the country nobility and, of course,
even if they were still part of urban society, they rose far above the
masses. Their clothes were rich and they lived in stone houses, the
steenen, some of which can still be seen, especially at Ghent, whereas
the poor lived in ramshackle huts, usually of wattle, of which
there is no trace.

Of the poor, certainly the great majority of the population, we
know almost nothing. Our sources for this period deal only with
the notables, and the poor appear only in their relations with these.
Trade had given decisive impetus to urban life, but could not
guarantee by itself an indefinite growth of the urban population,
for the towns could grow only if there were some industrialization
capable of attracting migrants looking for a livelihood. The food,
building and clothing trades, for example, would then be able to
develop enough for the original single market to be divided into
separate markets. Those for fish and meat were usually the first to
appear. Industries are mentioned after 1075 at Arras and Saint-
Omer, and in many cases they developed an extensive export trade.

Trade was the primary basis of the patricians' wealth. They would buy raw materials abroad, and would sell their artefacts all over the European market. The isolated artisan's output was too small for him to travel far for the necessary materials or to sell his goods at long distance and in any case, following a universal custom, the patricians used their administrative powers to forbid strangers from retailing in their town. They acted as entrepreneurs and were thus certain of a role in the export trades. To guarantee quality, production had to be controlled, a job undertaken by the town magistrates in Flanders from the twelfth century and in Brabant and Liège from the thirteenth. They appointed super-visors chosen wholly or partly from among the artisans, even sometimes from among those without any prior connection with the trade involved, and grouped the workers in proto-guilds which, like the charitable fraternities that had also issued from a single trade, gave the artisans a natural centre in which to discuss their interests.

From the thirteenth century on these associations vigorously combated the patricians, who used their administrative powers to dictate wages and rules that were as profitable to employers as they were disadvantageous to the workers, or to ensure their own impunity. The artisans' opposition was put down by policing, and there were continuous strikes and disorders in the second half of the thirteenth century. The patrician regime finally lost; but it did enrich the artistic patrimony of western civilization with the halls and belfreys of Ypres, Bruges and other towns, which survive as monuments to the economic power of these capitals of trade and industry in the thirteenth century.

3 The Apogee of Trade and Commerce in the Middle Ages

I TEXTILES

Until the Industrial Revolution it was not heavy industry and the output of fixed capital that predominated in European manufacture, but rather textiles, which met the most essential need, after food, in temperate climates. Throughout the West there were countless spinners and weavers of wool and linen who made cloth for themselves and their families. Textile corvées had fallen out of use with other manorial burdens, but the peasants still made their coarse clothes for themselves, with rudimentary tools and techniques. These domestic activities were not subject to regulation, and so do not appear in our chief source for industrial history. For many centuries autarchy kept its grip on agrarian society, perpetuating primitive industrial methods in which eventually the urban authorities sometimes took an interest.

Early on the towns became textile centres, for their trading activity attracted men seeking a livelihood by selling handicrafts outside their own locality. The Low Countries soon came to share with Italy the first place among European nations producing for long-distance trade. The wealthy classes shied away from manual labour, and many artisans were prevented from catering for their own requirements by the division of labour in urban industry, incomplete as it was. There thus arose outlets, for which workers could produce goods.

At first textiles mainly used native raw materials. The chalk pastures of Artois, French Flanders and Hainault, the salty meadows reclaimed from the sea, the Campine and Ardennes moors were all suitable for sheep-rearing, and many soils in this region of temperate, humid climate suited the culture of flax. The chalk lands were first to produce material for other regions. As early as 1013 a merchant from Tournai was bringing such goods to Ghent, and clearances in Flemish Zeeland were at least partly meant to meet the needs of Ghent's textile industry, which they stimulated. In 1120 a Ghent patrician raised sheep on the large salty marsh he rented from an abbey. Around 1250 wool came from the Campine moors to Brussels and Louvain via Antwerp, and in the Ardennes sheep were raised for the burghers of Huy.

However, although these local wools never quite disappeared, others were soon imported. Perhaps the local ones no longer satisfied growing demand, or perhaps stock-raisers shifted to cattle once a demand for meat, and perhaps also for leather, arose in the towns; perhaps price and quality were the decisive factors. The first recorded export of English wool, certainly destined for Flanders, goes back to 1113, and it became common in Flanders by the end of the twelfth century. The exports came in mainly via the Zwin, which was connected by waterway with the chief industrial centres of the country, Bruges, Ypres and Ghent. Consequently Artois lost its lead. The Brabantine towns also called on English wool in the 1200s. After an Anglo-Flemish conflict had caused the English to embargo wool exports to Flanders, the licences issued in 1273 reveal the shares of other parts of the Low Countries in this trade. Of a total of 32,743 sacks (each of 165 kilograms), 2.5 per cent went to Liège merchants, and some 11 per cent to merchants of Malines, Louvain, Brussels and other towns in Brabant. If we leave the share of English exporters out of account, the proportion of Brabantine importers was even as high as one sixth. Year in, year out after the shearing, many merchants would go round the Cistercian and Premonstratensian abbeys and other great Engish sheep rearers to buy wool for shipping to the Low Countries.

Apart from wool, clothing needed dyes. Woad, for blue, was cultivated on the alluvial soils of northern France, Hesbaye and the Namur area, and it spread rapidly in the thirteenth century, to such an extent that some villages there had as many as five woad mills. Red came from madder, which was grown on the clay soil of northern France and Flanders, or, more rarely, from brazil wood from the East or from the kermes, an insect that lived in certain

Mediterranean oaks. Yellow was obtained by use of weld, which was frequently found in the Low Countries. The colours were fixed with alum, from Asia Minor, Italy, Algeria or Castile.

The wool was transformed into cloth by a complicated process. The new urban industry differed from its manorial predecessor in the nature, and probably also the division, of labour which was more advanced. From the little we know of the old manorial cloth industry, it seems that women were mainly involved, whereas the new urban one was an essentially masculine affair, women being employed only in some preparatory work such as sorting and spinning. But if there had not, apparently, been much division of labour in the countryside, in the towns combing, carding, dyeing, weaving, fulling, stretching, shearing and finishing could all involve thirty different operations, about half of which were indispensable. There was therefore some specialization early on. The mention of fulling vats at Douai before 1100 does not necessarily imply specialization, but in 1135 there were weavers at Maastricht, Tongeren and Saint-Truiden, in 1150 there seems to have been a shearers' guild at Arras, while by 1200 Douai and Ghent had their Fullers' Street.

The technical equipment was not complicated. The only important innovation of the Middle Ages, the fulling mill, was rare until 1200 because it was considered too risky in an era of regulation aimed at marketing quality products. Many towns were famed for specialities, though these were quickly imitated. From the thirteenth century on there were *estamforts* in the Low Countries, copied from those of Stamford in England, and they were themselves copied in the Mediterranean area. In Bruges, at least, the breeches of which became famous through the songs of the German Minnesingers, the drapers turned to tailoring.

Advanced division of labour needed management, and this was undertaken by master drapers. Jehan Boinebroke of Douai, who died about 1286, was a typical figure. He probably raised sheep himself, but he also bought wool in Flanders and from the Cistercian abbeys of Lincolnshire and Cumberland, either himself or through an agent in England. One of his farmers cultivated madder, which he also imported, together with woad and alum. These raw materials were used partly in his own dyeing plant and workshops for, modest as it was, the equipment was too expensive for some workers. However, the work was mainly carried out in the houses of the artisans, some of whom had assistants, who got the materials as they were needed from Boinebroke and brought him their finished work. Even if they were masters of their own craft, they were really only wage-earners, paid by the piece and entirely dependent on him. In fact they could consider themselves lucky if they got the agreed wage, for the complaints about him in this connection are highly revealing. The artisans had no part in selling their goods; this too was Boinebroke's affair. Some workers were all the more dependent on their employer because they owed him money as tenants or debtors, and could pay him only through their work. 2008710

The production of linen, like that of cloth, became widespread. It flourished at Liège and Huy in the twelfth century. These towns met only regional demand, but the linen industry of the chief towns of Flanders and Hainault, Louvain and Nivelles in Brabant, Tournai and Cambrai developed rapidly. As with the manufacture of cloth there was specialization, under patrician entrepreneurs, in quality products such as tick or table linen. It was, however, never as important as the Champagne manufactures, and was far behind the cloth industry of the Low Countries which accounted for most of their exports, with a market in the twelfth century all over Christendom and even beyond. Until the nineteenth century textile was the main basis of the Low Countries' trade, and it was in fact one of the pillars of European commerce until the seventeenth century, when their lead passed to foreign competitors.

The first stages of this expansion remain obscure, but it was well launched by about 1100. Around 1150 Flemings had stands at the Winchester fairs, and up to the 1300s Flanders cloth was popular with the wealthy classes in England, where it figured especially in royal wardrobes. The early development of a cloth industry in England itself, where high-quality wools were produced, hindered the competitiveness of Flemish products. The promised lands for cloth exports from the Low Countries were elsewhere, and merchants came to England especially for wool.

Germany and her zone of commercial influence were an important market. By 1103 merchants of Liège and Huy were granted a favourable toll tariff and permission to retail linen and cloth at the Cologne fairs, and they were still selling it in 1253. When Cologne tried to forbid Flemings (especially from the cloth towns of Ghent and Ypres) to sail up-river on the Rhine, Emperor

Frederick Barbarossa set up fairs at Aachen and Duisburg in 1173 where Flemish cloth could be marketed as hitherto at Cologne. The Flemings whose cloth was pillaged around Saint-Truiden in 1190 were probably bound for the Rhineland. In 1248 cloth from Louvain, Flanders and Huy was sold at Trier. New markets emerged in the Baltic as it was opened to western civilization by Germanic colonization. By the twelfth century, Ypres cloth was a normal phenomenon at Novgorod, the ancient Russian trading centre on the shores of Lake Ilmen; a few years after the Teutonic Order had occupied Prussia in 1231, its tolls included cloth 'from overseas', i.e. Flemish in the main. Ghent, Bruges and Ypres, even the little Flemish towns of Dixmude and Poperinge, Tournai or Maastricht and perhaps Utrecht, were renowned as centres for cloth at Visby, on the island of Gotland, which was at the time a great sea-trading market. The cloth also figured in the tolls and other German sources in the basins of the Weser, Elbe, Oder and Vistula, as far as Brandenburg, Upper Saxony, Silesia and Volhynia.

If Flemish products dominated the north, those of the Meuse towns probably led in southern Germany where they entered the Danube basin via the Rhine. There were merchants of Maastricht at the fairs of Enns in Upper Austria around 1150. Low Countries cloth was so famous that the dyers of Vienna were called Flemings in 1208. From Austria the cloth went on to Hungary and further east. A thirteenth-century toll applied on the Austro–Hungarian border mentions cloth from Ypres, Ghent and Tournai, and a contemporary Viennese toll also cites cloth from Arras, Valenciennes and Huy. Bruges breeches were known in the Austrian capital around 1280. The Danube region also got cloth from the Low Countries from the fairs of Champagne.

The export of cloth spread to the south as well: Arras merchants were at Provins by 1137, i.e. at the earliest fairs, and we can assume that they were there as vendors, because they had an important role in the European cloth trade from the beginning. The admirable cartularies of Genoese notaries first mention cloth from beyond the mountains at this time. It is described as French, but quite possibly it also came from the Low Countries, for such cloth was being sold by the later twelfth century not only at Genoa but also at Milan and elsewhere in Lombardy, Venetia, Tuscany and the Appenines. Rome and even Sicily. It reached the

Mediterranean coast of Spain perhaps through Marseilles, and certainly Aigues-Mortes, once it had been opened by St Louis in 1246; and the great urban republics of Italy formed, with Marseilles, routes towards Byzantium and the Arab world, and the Crusader principalities in Palestine. Linen and cloth from the Low Countries were often sent via these routes to Constantinople, Antioch or the Mediterranean ports of Africa, from Egypt to Morocco. Arras cloth led the field here to start with, but gradually lost to Ypres. The other Flemish cloth towns followed: Saint-Omer, Lille, Douai and Ghent. Among the Brabantine towns, Brussels cloth was first to be mentioned in Venice in 1265. Linen was sent from Liège to Italy and even to Constantinople by 1200, and from Lille to Genoa by 1263.

The Atlantic coast of France and the Iberian peninsula also took cloth from the Low Countries. If we take a somewhat dubious reference in a toll for Jaca and Pamplona (at the foot of two important Pyrenean passes) to indicate Bruges, then the oldest mention of a local speciality in cloth dates back to the eleventh century. Flemish cloth was certainly being sold at Poitiers in 1180. Spaniards bought it at Arras in 1222, and it was imported about 1250 into both Portugal and Castile, as far as Jerez de la Frontera which had just been seized from the Moors. It was mentioned at the end of the thirteenth century in a tariff for the Asturian ports.

The random nature of our evidence leaves gaps in the overall picture, but clearly cloth from the Belgian provinces had conquered the European markets and even the fringes of other civilizations, from where it could spread. If the description is correct, Malines cloth was part of the stock of a Venetian merchant who died in 1264 at Tabriz in Azerbaijan. Low Countries cloth was among the weapons by which Europe won economic supremacy from the East in these decisive centuries.

2 METAL INDUSTRIES

Although textiles were well represented in the Walloon areas, the characteristic foundations of trade and industry there were mines and metallurgy. Many deposits of iron ore had been exploited south of the Sambre-Meuse trench since Roman times and even before. We know almost nothing of the industry at this time, however: its output seems not to have gone beyond local markets, and since we have no commercial sources we know only of dona-

tions or conflicts relating to abbeys. Presumably iron was used in
the making of agricultural implements and other objects in common use. Until the eighteenth century the ore had to be converted
by charcoal from the dense local forests, for the noxious elements
in coal, detrimental to its quality, could have been alloyed in the
smelting. There was, though, no difficulty in using coal in forge
furnaces, and it was being mined quite early on, even before 1200,
at Liège, around Mons a few years later and around Charleroi in
1297. A coal mine may have existed at Rolduc near Aachen in 1113,
although our source is dubious, but coal mining in Dutch Limburg certainly dates back to the mid-thirteenth century. The
Walloon region's coal mines are the oldest on the Continent, and
only the mines of northern England are of earlier date.

The fame of the Walloon metal industry in these centuries was
due more to its brass than to iron. The fact that brass developed in
a country lacking all the essential raw materials is a mystery –
perhaps explicable only in terms of technical skill. Copper ore had
to be brought from the Harz mountains in Germany, purchased
either in Cologne or directly in Goslar, which merchants of the
Meuse towns were visiting by the twelfth century. It was alloyed
with tin and zinc mineral, the first bought in Cornwall and in the
Rhineland, especially at Cologne. Zinc was mined around Namur
and Huy, and abundant deposits of calamine (a carbonate of zinc)
at Altenberg, or the Old Mountain, which has given its name
both to the site of the mine, La Calamine, just west of Aachen, and
to the present-day worldwide trust, *La Vieille Montagne*, which
took over the mining in 1837. The calamine was burnt with charcoal from the near-by Hertogenwald, and was shipped along the
Meuse to the manufacturing towns where it gave the brass its
characteristic yellow colouring. A clay from the Condroz was
particularly suitable for crucibles and moulds and may have contributed to the manufacturing of brass in the near-by towns.

In 1104 Dinant, Namur, Huy and Liège were supposed to pay
their tolls to Coblentz in brass objects. Among these towns
Dinant gradually drew so far into the lead that its name passed into
contemporary and modern usage with the term *dinanderies*. At Huy
cloth appears to have taken over from brass as the leading
industry by the thirteenth century, and although the town had
produced various household goods – pots, pans, cauldrons and so
on – not many of them have survived. Decorative objects, some of

which are masterpieces of romanesque metal sculpture, provide us with more information: the baptismal fonts of St Bartholomew's at Liège (circa 1113), for instance, and the chandeliers, reliquaries and similar works of art. Nothing is recorded before the fifteenth century of the social conditions in, or the organization of, this industry, and we can only guess at them from what we know of later conditions, assuming them to have been essentially the same. The picture that emerges is similar to that of the cloth industry – entrepreneurs imported raw materials, gave them to artisans to work and sold what these artisans produced. At the height of the medieval economy the brass industry, like the cloth trade, had a capitalist organization, dominated by the merchants.

3 THE MERCHANTS

In the Low Countries trade was conducted in two ways – either foreigners could visit the country, or the merchants could sell abroad. Both methods were employed at different times and in different places. It is in this context that the Netherlands of today come into their own in this chapter. Their industry had not developed much, but they had agriculture and fisheries and were able to act as carriers for other regions.

Frisian traders had lost their European significance but still exported the produce of stock-farming, horses and salt to Denmark, Sweden and the rest of the Baltic. They were able to share in the herring trade, for herring fisheries had developed in the Sound since the thirteenth century, as had cod fisheries in northern Norwegian waters. Exports of fish were the more important because of the medieval church's imposition of frequent and lengthy abstinences. The Frisians of Stavoren and other places on the Zuiderzee sold it, together with the output of their own fisheries, in England, Flanders and Germany as far as Cologne. Since Friesland did not produce enough grain, it was imported from England, especially through Boston and Lynn, from Lower Saxony through Hamburg and even from the Baltic ports. They also supplied Norway with it and returned with various cargoes from the Baltic to the North Sea. When in the thirteenth century Lübeck tried to monopolize Baltic trade by causing difficulties for merchants of the North Sea crossing the isthmus of Holstein, the Frisians were among the first to attempt the dangerous rounding of the Skaw.

For some time, Utrecht was the main centre for Netherlands

commerce. Merchants from the surrounding countries came there and its own citizens traded fish and salt for wine and other goods in the Rhineland as far as Speyer, visited Hamburg and England, and by 1250 probably also had their own establishments for curing herring in Scania, the southern part of Sweden. Groningen, linked by land routes to the Weser and the lower Elbe, and the towns of the IJssel – Kampen, Zwolle and Deventer – which were connected with western Germany via the Rhine, also took a large share of the Frisian inheritance. There were merchants of Deventer, whom we have already met in the Coblentz toll of 1104, living at Cologne in the twelfth century. Their merchant guild is mentioned by 1249, and they joined the Frisians in reconnoitring the new maritime routes towards the Baltic: we find one Bernard of Deventer at Riga in 1224.

Deventer belonged to the bishop of Utrecht. The counts of Guelders, clearly in competition, helped the trade of Zutphen, their own port on the IJssel. Its merchants and those of other Guelders towns, especially Nymegen and Doesburg (both mentioned in a tax register at Worms in the later eleventh century) exported Rhenish wine. Nymegen's trade with England was large enough for the town to be the only one, other than Lübeck, mentioned in a privilege granted in 1258 by the emperor, Richard of Cornwall, to the London merchants. Harderwijk, Guelders' main port on the Zuiderzee, took part in maritime commerce with the Weser and the Elbe in the thirteenth century, and when there was famine, bought grain in places as far off as Stendal in the Old Mark of Brandenburg.

Ruremonde and Venlo, the Guelders towns on the Meuse, distributed Rhine wine, like the up-river towns of Liège, throughout the whole basin of the Meuse. In the twelfth and thirteenth centuries, Maastricht seems to have played the most important part on the middle Meuse in the export of cloth and brass. Maastricht merchants attended the fairs of Enns around 1150 and in the thirteenth century they were travelling to Hungary and perhaps even further east. At the same time, if not earlier, a Maastricht merchant guild trading with Scania had no equal as far inland, and merchants of the Meuse towns travelled to Cologne and beyond to get raw materials for *dinanderies*. Merchants and brokers from Huy had acquired citizenship at Cologne and Vienna in the thirteenth century. Huy sent its cloth to the fairs of Champagne, and by 1214 had depots for this at Metz on the road to Champagne, and in the market-town of Troyes. By 1242 its merchants were requesting safe conducts in England and were given licences to export wool during the embargo against Flanders of 1270. During the first half of the twelfth century a new toll in London shows merchants of Lotharingia (most of them certainly subjects of the prince-bishop of Liège) importing wine, armour and other metal objects from Mainz, as well as precious stones, silver and tapestries from Regensburg or Byzantium, the oriental merchandise clearly reflecting their travels to the Danube basin. As we have seen, Liège merchants were selling their cloth at Genoa by the first decades of the thirteenth century. They also had a share in Mediterranean trade.

Brabantine commerce had made great strides in the twelfth century. Antwerpers travelled through Cologne after 1104, apparently heading for the vineyards of the upper Rhine. They figure a little later in the London tariff mentioned above, and by the thirteenth century they occur with increasing frequency in the English sources, together with citizens of the cloth towns of Malines, Louvain and Brussels. All sold wine in particular there, as well as silver ore, probably from Central Europe, and herring. It was probably wool that they mainly imported, and perhaps they also dealt in lead and tin ores from Cornwall and Devon. In 1273, during the embargo against Flanders, men of Louvain and Malines contributed almost three-quarters of the wool exported by merchants from the Low Countries. Brabantine merchants also had an intermediary part to play between Germany and England. Communications with the Rhineland were for many years the chief preoccupation of the dukes of Brabant. In 1204 they managed to share in the bishop of Liège's authority over Maastricht, where highly important commercial routes crossed the river, and in 1288 they conquered the duchy of Limburg between the Meuse and Aachen. In 1203 they even used force to guarantee on behalf of their subjects fair treatment in the tolls of Guelders.

The merchants of Malines had a cloth hall at Lagny, in France, one of the towns of the Champagne fairs, after 1202. It was Flemings, however, who took the greatest share in south-bound trade. They had traditionally bought wine in the south, and as trade developed sufficiently, religious institutions tended to dispose of their vineyards and get their supplies from merchants.

Early on the Flemings were buying the wines of Laon and Soissons, and were not slow to appreciate the best growths of the Loire and Gascony: by the early 1200s they were sailing towards La Rochelle, while sailors of Oléron and Bayonne transported wine to the North Sea. The Flemings then exported some of it to England and it was probably through them that Loire wines were introduced to Liège in 1198, for hitherto the town had depended entirely on local or German vineyards.

In return the Flemings mainly exported their cloth. Their chief outlet was Champagne, where there were fairs all year round at Lagny, Bar-sur-Aube, Provins and Troyes successively, which made up the busiest market of the twelfth and thirteenth centuries. Arras merchants were at Provins by 1137, and just before 1200 they were joined by merchants from Saint-Omer, Lille, Douai and Valenciennes, whilst after 1250 Ypres took the lead. Douai, Arras and Ypres each had their hall in the towns where fairs were held. Shortly before a fair began, a caravan of merchants from each of the great cloth towns would start off for Champagne, led by a 'mayor' or 'count of the merchants', accompanied by clerks acting as notaries or accountants, and perhaps armed guards to guarantee safety on the way. Other merchants travelled alone. The great towns of Flanders kept teams of messengers at the fairs to supply the merchants with useful information and particularly to warn them of dangers they might encounter on the way.

The meetings of Flemish and other merchants in Champagne brought about the Hansa of the XVII towns as a common framework for their trade at the fairs. The name Hansa originally meant a sum that merchants abroad paid to guarantee their safety and generally protect their interests. The merchant guild of Valenciennes levied it from the third quarter of the eleventh century. The Hansa of the XVII towns can only be shown with certainty to have existed from 1230, but it may have been considerably older. The number seventeen is a puzzle. When it first appears the Hansa already contained merchants of twenty-three towns, i.e. the textile centres of Flanders, then Tournai, Cambrai, Valenciennes and Huy, as well as six towns in Picardy and three in Champagne itself. There may have been seventeen towns to start with, or perhaps seventeen merely meant 'many'. The equally problematical title 'Seventeen Provinces', which we shall encounter later on, has been explained in this way. Whatever the case, the Hansa decided if its members were to participate in a fair, dealt with the authorities in Champagne and helped its members in legal matters. Its members being industrial entrepreneurs, on the defensive against their workers, the Hansa could also expel trouble-makers from all the affiliated towns.

However important the Champagne fairs were for Flemish commerce, Italy, the great centre of medieval civilization, attracted Flemish trade also, although Italian merchants appeared in Flanders before the Flemings became accustomed to visiting Italy. Contacts between the two countries developed with the rise of the Champagne fairs, which were assiduously attended from the twelfth century onward by Piedmontese and Lombard merchants, particularly those from Asti. By 1200 Flemings were visiting Genoa, Milan and Venice. Apart from textile workers, there were merchants buying cloth at the Champagne fairs or arranging for it to be sent to them from there. However the local citizens, or those of the rapidly growing Tuscan cities of Florence, Siena, Pisa or Lucca gradually took over and after 1250 the Flemings hardly went beyond the Champagne fairs, where they could be sure of finding enough Italian buyers.

While Flemish merchants sold wines from Poitou or Gascony in England, their trade with the British Isles was particularly in textiles. A story of about 1130 has some merchants crossing the Channel with a considerable sum of money, to purchase wool for storing at Dover. The English Cistercians were concerned at the news of a serious defeat suffered in 1253 by the Flemings, and feared that they would not come and buy the newly sheared wool. These Flemings sold their cloth in England, but after about 1200 relations were frequently perturbed by political differences. Whether Flanders, which certainly was an important factor in the balance of power on the North Sea coast, was directly involved in Franco–English conflicts or not, her trade frequently suffered from piracy. Originally the Flemish clearly had the upper hand in trade with the English. Saint-Omer at first took the lead, but lost it after Artois was attached to the Capetian domain in 1212, for the province thus became exposed to English hostility. Around 1240 first place passed to merchants of Douai and Ypres. But English trade grew rapidly in the thirteenth century when increasing numbers of English merchants visited Flanders, and their hold was firmly established there by 1270. During the mutual embargo between England and Flanders, both sides seized enemy property and when peace was restored in 1274 it was noted that English losses in Flanders were twice as great as Flemish losses in England. In this case, the men of Douai had lost most heavily, for about half of the seized Flemish goods belonged to them.

As trade with the Champagne fairs had done, Anglo–Flemish commerce called into existence an inter-urban organization, the Flemish Hansa of London. It had been preceded by many local Hansas. That of Saint-Omer, whose statutes of 1244 refer to an earlier document, remained independent. Those of the other towns seem to have become confederated after 1241. The late inclusion of the Bruges Hansa, after the losses that the conflict of 1270–74 had inflicted on Douai and Ypres, brought the number of confederated towns to seventeen (hence some confusion, at one time, between the London Hansa and the Hansa of the xvII towns). Bruges henceforth exercised control. Like the earlier Hansa of Saint-Omer, it chiefly aimed to limit the number of merchants participating in overseas trade. Artisans were admitted only after abandoning their trade for a whole year and paying considerable membership dues. As to its activity on the English market there is little information, and all trace of it vanishes in the later thirteenth century.

It appears surprising that an important textile centre such as Ghent had no share in the two great Hansas so far mentioned. This was because Ghent had its own, documented from 1127 on, and aimed to control trade in Germany, another domain of Flemish influence. In the Rhineland Flemish cloth was once again traded for wine and if the share of Flemings and Rhinelanders had originally been equal, the institution of a staple at Cologne after about 1150 put a stop to foreign navigation beyond this town and reduced Flemish traffic towards the upper Rhine. The shift of traffic, however, from the Scheldt and Rhine routes to the land routes through Maastricht and Brabant opened new possibilities for trade between western Germany and England through the Low Countries. In all probability sales of wine from the Rhine in Flanders also diminished because of the increasing preference shown by the Flemings for the wines of Atlantic France.

Flemish traders were also active in Lower Germany. From the start of the thirteenth century Flemings exported grain from Lower Saxony and the Old Mark of Brandenburg through

Hamburg. They reached Lübeck through the Holstein isthmus, and bought tar, ash, furs and other goods in the Baltic. The Flemings even visited Novgorod: an agreement between German merchants and the Russian authorities declared any association of Flemings and Russians illegal. In fact, Lübeck attempted to keep this promising outlet for itself and its satellites, the future Hanseatic towns, and the Germans themselves came in growing numbers to the Low Countries in the first half of the thirteenth century to sell Baltic products and to buy the cloth the Flemings had introduced to northern markets. These goods sometimes went by land, though usually by water. But seafarers were not bold, and preferred to avoid the high seas, using the rivers and canals linking the Zeeland archipelago with the Zuiderzee. They navigated the channels through the archipelago between the Zwin and Dordrecht, then the Lek to Vreeswijk south of Utrecht, where a canal had been dug to attract such trade. The canals that to this day mark the centre of Utrecht, with a street on one side and depots and cellars on the other, date back to before 1200. Beyond Utrecht boats continued via the Vecht and the Zuiderzee to reach the mouth of the Elbe.

Whether this network of navigable waterways deteriorated or whether the growing volume of ships ruined them, the route through Utrecht was gradually abandoned in the course of the thirteenth century in favour of others between Dordrecht and the Zuiderzee, either by Gouda, Leyden, Haarlem and Amsterdam or up the Lek and down the IJssel to Kampen. The merchants of Dordrecht, which was admirably situated at the mouth of the Meuse and the chief branches of the Rhine, sailed up the rivers with salt from the Zeeland salines and cloth from Flanders and Brabant, and returned with Rhine wines and metal goods. But the Hollanders were not only heirs to Utrecht's trade, they also took over Flemish trade, for as foreigners came increasingly to Flanders a passive market developed there, and the lively Flemish trade abroad contracted and disappeared.

4   THE MARKETS OF THE LOW COUNTRIES

When trade revived demand and supply were still low, and the best way to revive them was to bring them together at a fixed time and place. Fairs, generally held on a religious festival, attracted many people and played initially an important role in commerce for they provided the necessary infrastructure. The oldest ones in the Low Countries, those of Visé, are mentioned in 983, whilst Ghent, Douai and Saint-Omer had fairs by 1000. The bishop of Utrecht set one up at Deventer in 1049. Those of Maastricht, Huy, the abbey town of Gembloux and Namur go back to the twelfth century at least, like those of Utrecht, where four were held annually by 1178. In Guelders, Doesburg's fair was transferred in 1230 to Doetinchem, up-river on the Old IJssel; another was established at Harderwijk in 1231, and Arnhem had three annually by 1240. The *nundinae hollandenses* mentioned in 1213 probably consisted of three fairs held successively at Vlaardingen near Rotterdam, and at Valkenburg and Voorschoten, both near Leyden. Another was set up at Schiedam in 1270. Fairs, to which Carolingian origins were attributed, were even held at the abbey borough of Saint-Hubert in the barely populated Ardennes. Usually the fairs' privileges protected visitors against violence particularly, even on the journeys there and back, and gave tax reductions for the duration.

The amount of business done at most of these gatherings should not be exaggerated. That a fair was set up does not prove that it was a success, merely that a prince had expected it. In fact, most fairs had only small, essentially regional, trade. This was not, however, the case with the Flanders fairs. None of the above-mentioned ones was of major importance: the Ghent fair is not referred to after 1200 and the fact that Douai and Saint-Omer tried to establish new ones at the end of the thirteenth century proves that the earlier ones had fallen by the wayside. Fairs had been instituted at some of the new towns founded by Count Baldwin v. The abbey boroughs of Messines and Torhout, which set up fairs in 1071 and 1084 respectively, did not grow as towns, whereas Lille and Ypres did and their fairs are mentioned from 1127 onward. The Flanders fairs were born at the period of the country's industrial and commercial expansion. They therefore served as collection-points from which the cloth went off to export markets. Like others – the Champagne and English fairs, for instance – they avoided the disadvantages of discontinuity by establishing a cycle that went from March to October spanning the whole business season. They helped the growth of Flemish trade to such a degree that Bruges in its turn requested a fair to give further stimulus to its trade. One was authorized in 1200.

It is not certain what this contributed towards Bruges's development into a market of European importance. More and more foreign merchants undertook the journey to the Low Countries instead of waiting for merchants from there to arrive. No other region could attract them as Flanders did, for the cloth industry, supplying a marketable product universally favoured by fashion, was unrivalled in Europe. Since the formation of the Zwin, Bruges had become more accessible. Damme, founded in 1180 at the point where the Zwin ended, became a convenient port of entry to Bruges.

The dominant position of the English in the trade between their country and Flanders was now established. In 1252 German trade in Flanders had become sufficiently important to require legal standing. Lübeck and Hamburg sought a grant of extra-territorial status, comparable with that enjoyed by the Steelyard in London or St Peter's Yard in Novgorod, but the count's power was too strong in Flanders for foreign residents to acquire such *de facto* independence. Meanwhile the Italians had opened new trade routes. The first Genoese galleys reached the North Sea through the Straits of Gibraltar in 1277 followed soon after by Venetian ones. This caused a relative decline in land traffic with Italy, at a time when the annexation of Champagne to the Capetian domain in 1284 deprived its fairs of the advantage of virtual neutrality and imposed the increasing burden of royal taxes. The presence at Bruges of Germans and Italians, the peoples who gave most to trade in the later Middle Ages, allowed Bruges' market to attain greater importance, for more than a century, than any other business centre in Europe north of the Alps.

4 *Money and Credit*

The Carolingian economy has sometimes been regarded as a natural one, which functioned without recourse to the circulation of currency. Many payments were indeed made in kind, beginning with the dues which the villeins owed their lords. Monasteries also avoided monetary expenditure by acquiring vineyards abroad, and perhaps procured their salt in the same way. Commercial links were weak and precious metals rare.

This does not mean that money played no role at all in social life and attitudes. In the examples cited above, common requirements were involved, but sometimes the abbeys had needs which went beyond the ordinary. They had to buy lead in England to roof their churches, and they certainly paid money for this in the ninth century. Some manorial dues were also stipulated in cash or, if in kind, a certain portion in cash was added, for instance in the great majority of tolls, the rates of some of which must have gone back to Merovingian times. There is no reason to suppose that the fixed sums were merely a standard of value and that the payment was made in a certain quantity of goods. Even if payment in kind was occasionally accepted, the rule was unquestionably payment in cash. Around 1000 the villeins of a manor belonging to an abbey at Trier had to deposit the money for their rents in the hollow at the top of a stele which was emptied from the top, and the monks of St Truiden, if we can believe their chronicle, grew tired from carrying the pennies offered to their church. Men of quality could amass considerable sums in ready money. The bishop

48

of Liège, dismayed by his subjects' distress in a famine around 1050, distributed not only grain but also two pennies weekly in cash. On the other hand, fifty years later, peasants coming to market at Cambrai who were unable to pay the penny they owed at the town gates could leave a pledge that could be redeemed from the proceeds of their selling. The same interaction of common custom and relative scarcity appears in a decree of the count of Flanders during the famine of 1125–6. The price of bread had risen to one penny, and the bakers were ordered to bake loaves of half the normal weight to supply people who could pay only a half-penny.

Thus, although money was rare in some circles, other situations demanded payment in cash. The fact that debts were stipulated in cash is enough to prove that it was always the real standard for many people, despite the legends about a natural economy. The fact is the more remarkable as the money in circulation was desperately inadequate. To cope with the scarcity of gold in the West, the Carolingians had limited the minting of gold coins to a few places close to the borders of the empire, Friesland in particular, for example, to meet the needs of external trade. The Frisian colony of Duisburg owed the abbey of Prüm, in the Eifel, a rent of one pound's weight of gold in 895. But at the same time the minting of gold coins ceased in Friesland because of the insecurity and uncertainty of gold supplies. If gold coins did not wholly disappear, the rare ones which now circulated in the West came from abroad, particularly *besants*, Byzantine shillings, or coins of the Moslem caliphates. Perhaps these coins came from the sale of slaves from the West to these countries, which had retained a gold standard. The oriental designs were imitated in the West if by chance it was possible to get gold, so great was the superiority of the Byzantine or Moslem monetary system over that of the West in the commercial relations of the three civilizations. These coins, which could hardly be used in daily life, were probably hoarded by the rich to preserve their wealth. In 1071 St Hubert's Abbey lent the countess of Hainault five hundred *besants*, which had come to it as a gift.

The only existing coins were the *denier* (penny) weighing about two grams to start with, during the Carolingian monetary reforms, and the *obol* (half-penny). The *sou* (*solidus* or shilling) of twelve pennies and the pound of twenty shillings were only units of account, used to express large sums more easily but never coined. From generation to generation men were forced to deal in *deniers* and *obols*, unless they could barter. The right to mint coins, originally a royal prerogative, soon passed either by grant or, more frequently, seizure, into the feudal princes' hands. Gradually each town of major importance got a mint, though as trade developed the circulating coins were not enough to meet needs. As silver stocks did not increase proportionately, the easiest way of resolving the problem was to devalue, either by decreasing the weight of the coins or by reducing their silver content. In Flanders, for instance, the net weight of pennies, which was still about 1.2 grams around 1000, had fallen by 1200 to 0.45 grams, and was kept at this level in the thirteenth century – a stability that may have fostered the growth of the Flemish economy.

However England, which had an adequate supply of silver ore, managed to keep her 'sterling' pennies roughly stable from Carolingian times. The grant by William the Conqueror to the counts of Flanders of a rent fief, i.e. an annual payment, paid almost without interruption for two centuries, as well as a balance of payments manifestly favourable to Flanders, had brought to that country a great quantity of sterling. This at least partly made up for the imperfections of the local coinage. However, when the balance of trade went the other way, after Flemish cloth exports to England declined, and when payment of the rent fief stopped, supply of this superior and stable type of money came to an end. In 1250 this stimulated Flanders to counterfeit sterling, which was then worth four pennies of Flemish money, in imitation of French practices. Brabant followed in 1273, and then most of the other principalities. In 1275 the first 'double sterlings' of eight pennies were issued in Flanders, and again Brabant rapidly followed suit. Finally, around 1300, most princes undertook to mint a 'groat' (*gros*) of twelve pennies or one shilling, once again following a French practice, itself borrowed from Italy.

Before gold returned to circulation, it was difficult to make large payments, however rare. More than once the problem was met by the use of precious stones or valuable objects, which the wealthy were accustomed to keeping as part of their property. When Godfrey of Bouillon sold possessions to the bishop of Liège to get funds for his part in the First Crusade in 1096, the bishop not only took the gold-leaf cover from the shrine of the patron saint of his diocese, he also seized all the chalices, crosses of silver and gold and precious stones he could lay hands on, from other churches. At the same time the abbot of Gembloux sold many liturgical objects stored up in his treasury to buy, at low cost, the lands of neighbours stricken by famine. Objects were accepted for the value of their metal, as is nowadays done with ingots. In other cases part-payment would be made in cash, part in precious metals and part in other goods – horses were particularly appreciated.

However imperfect their monetary system, the Low Countries were in advance of other countries, some of which did not yet have money at all. Thus Frisian coins since the ninth century, and coins of the Flemish and Meuse towns since the tenth, circulated extensively in central and eastern Europe and Scandinavia as far as Iceland and Russia, where they are seldom missing from treasure hoards. Around 1100, in these medieval developing countries, the coins played the same role as, latterly, Austrian *thalers* or British sovereigns. When they began to mint money, those countries often began by imitating Low Countries pennies with which they were familiar, and the originals virtually lost their significance in international payments.

Minting was, in every principality, entirely a matter for the government, and traders therefore had to change money into the local coinage. To this end the authorities gave licences to money-changers. They existed at Arras from 1180, and in all other important towns in the thirteenth century. No less than twenty-eight money-changers' booths were opened during the Torhout fairs. At Bruges three *changes* were held in fief of the count of Flanders shortly after 1200, a fourth was set up in 1224 and a fifth, a kind of itinerant caravan, a century later. This was still not enough, and other 'unlicensed' ones were tolerated in return for payment of an annual recognition-due to the licensed chargers. There were twelve of these by 1300. The money-changers, experts in matters of coinage, were, as it were, destined to become masters of coin. Moreover, as they had iron chests to protect their stock from theft, the burghers gave them, for safe keeping, objects of value and cash of which they, for the time being, had no need. This practice occurred after 1246 and soon conferred on the changers the role of bankers.

2 CREDIT

Certain deficiencies in the money supply could be corrected by use of credit. The first instances of loans occur in connection with religious institutions. Their treasuries could also be used to extend credit, often with the ultimate intention of rounding off their property. For this purpose, they made use of the *mort-gage* (*mortuum vadium*) by which money was lent against a pledge of land, the income of which the creditor would take for the length of the contract without the debt being amortized by it. In the oldest instance we know, the bishop of Liège lent money in 1002 to the abbot of St Riquier's, near Abbeville, who pledged twelve *mansi* situated in Liège territory, to be redeemed whenever he wanted after twenty years. These dealings seem to have been frequent in the eleventh century in the Meuse region, where the church had great wealth. They spread to Flanders, where they remained common until around 1300 as a way of investing ecclesiastical resources. It is true that in 1163 the Council of Tours declared the *mort-gage* usurious and demanded restoration of the pledge as soon as the income had covered the capital of the loan. It exempted only former ecclesiastical estates so that a church could recover its property. This exemption was soon extended to all former church property, and presumably the clerks hardly bothered with canon law, using the *mort-gage* every time it was in their interest to do so.

From the eleventh century on many princes, lords and occasionally even abbeys borrowed money in return for landed property, tithes or other sources of income. On the eve of the Third Crusade, in 1189, the abbot of Ardres near Boulogne is said to have advanced some thousand pounds to various knights and barons who needed ready cash for their venture to the Holy Land against the tithes they possessed; the income of these loans varied between 11.25 and 24 per cent of the capital sum advanced. It is not surprising, therefore, that creditors generally prevented their debtors by contract from redeeming the property before three, six, nine – even forty or forty-nine – years had gone by. Besides, the debtor was quite often unable to repay the loan on term, and the creditor was usually ready to acquire the property by paying a supplement, often not large. The relationship between the estimated value of the pledge and the capital lent varied between 37.33 and 40 per cent but it could rise to 80 per cent and overall the loans we know had an average of 58.5 per cent. The freezing of the funds lent meant only minor inconvenience for the creditor, for the money would have lain idle in coffers, whereas now it returned, increased by the income it had earned, or, at a small cost, it brought in at the term valuable property.

Important as were the church's mortgage dealings, it never had a monopoly of credit. From the eleventh century, the chronicles and lives of the saints accuse laymen of profiting like leeches from the distress of the people struck by famine or other woes. Clerks and merchants of Liège around 1084 advanced two hundred marks, i.e. a hundred pounds' weight of silver, against an unknown security to the abbot of St Truiden to enable him to buy a manor from the countess of Hainault. These clerks had probably taken minor orders only to enable them to escape civil justice, which on occasion could be severe on usury. When around 1096 the abbot of Gembloux tried to take over the lands of neighbours who were in financial difficulties, he had to face competition from other lenders. Count Baldwin of Constantinople suspended the payment of all interest on current debts around 1200, during a famine in Flanders. The role of petty money-lender may have been assumed to some extent by Jews, who were therefore all the more hated by the populace in times of crisis: princes could win easy popularity by banishing their Jewish subjects. Henry III, Duke of Brabant, gave this instruction in his will of 1261, though the clause was probably not executed. When his widow consulted Thomas Aquinas as to the treatment that Jews deserved, since their wealth came from usury, he replied that the fairest procedure would be to force them to earn their living by working like others.

But there was no question of Jewish dominance in the field of credit in the Low Countries. Liège seems for many years to have been the most active centre for this. One Jean of Liège was lending money at Genoa shortly before 1200, particularly to the bishop of Liège who had returned from the Third Crusade. Again around 1250 the abbot of St Truiden borrowed from a citizen of Liège at an interest rate equivalent to 48.57 per cent annually. But Liège lost its primacy as a financial centre to Arras. Having been at the forefront in the twelfth century because of its active trade, Arras turned increasingly to finance in the following century, perhaps because of the attachment of the province of Artois to the French king's domain, which seriously harmed cloth exports to England. Thereafter, Arras capital probably had to be invested more in landed property, and from the income of this loans were made. Low Countries financiers had been active before this, if not at home then abroad. William Cade of Saint-Omer was a famous London usurer in the 1160s and on the eve of Bouvines in 1214 Simon Saffir of Ghent acted as banker to King John. But although the patricians of Ghent, for instance, still lent money, it was the merchants of Arras who played the greatest part among financiers from the Low Countries until the end of the thirteenth century.

As early as 1208, Pope Innocent III lamented to the bishop of Arras that if the interdict on usury were strictly observed, no church in his diocese would remain open. But religious censure did not deter the lenders: the poet Guillaume le Breton declared shortly after that the town was founded on usury. The Crespins and Louchards, who were the main financiers, had kings and princes as clients, particularly the counts of Flanders, who were highly involved in Western politics and had to borrow a great deal. In 1278 Countess Margaret of Constantinople owed the financiers of Arras £18,600 and her son Guy de Dampierre £65,100 by 1295. King Philip the Fair had borrowed £6,200 by 1286. The debts of towns were greater still, for the princes often used them as intermediaries: if a debtor defaulted, his creditor could more easily lean on a town's inhabitants, who were considered collectively responsible, than on a sovereign. Little is known of urban finance in the thirteenth century, but it is clear that in 1275 almost all of Ghent's debt, some £38,500, consisted of loans made by Arras financiers, while in 1299 Bruges owed the Crespins alone the enormous sum of £110,000, equal to nearly four-fifths of the income of the duchy of Normandy in the same year. Lay seigneurs and abbeys, hard hit by the decline in the real value of their rents, and anxious to keep up their standard of living, also borrowed heavily.

Acting alone or in temporary association, the lenders used only their own capital unless they increased the funds by mortgaging their lands. The loans were generally not guaranteed by real securities, but rather by a notable's personal promise. Although usury had been condemned by the Third Lateran Council in 1179 and that of Lyons in 1274, interest was sometimes openly stipulated. More often it was camouflaged by a demand for the repayment of a higher sum than the actual capital lent. The rate varied from 10 to 17 per cent p.a. during the second half of the thirteenth century. The debtor paid the interest when he repaid the capital, or separately during the term of the loan. If he defaulted on either capital or interest, further credit was advanced for capital augmented, if necessary, by the interest which was owed.

A new form of loan, *rentes* or annuities, became popular after about 1250, in the great Flemish towns. They could be extended for life or for an indefinite period, and were payable so long as the debtor did not refund the original sum. To judge by Ghent's example, life annuities may have produced a return of 12.5 per cent, and others 10 per cent. They were a favourite investment of rich patricians.

Italian merchant bankers were as important as native patricians in the thirteenth century. At this time they still conducted their business in France, especially in Paris or at the fairs of Champagne. It was there, after 1220, that the counts of Flanders, followed soon afterwards by other princes of the area and some towns as well, took on new debts from merchants of Siena like the Buonsignori or the Salimbeni, the Scoti of Piacenza, or the Pucci, Bardi, Peruzzi or Frescobaldi of Florence. Such debts were usually repayable at the next fair, and were granted against personal guarantees. The Siena firms dominated this type of business at the time. On occasion the counts of Flanders and Hainault used a further financial force, the Paris house of the Knights Templar.

A distinction has to be made between Italian high finance and the Lombards, who were also used by those eager for credit. Despite their name, or the even more deceptive one of Cahorsins, all the Lombards known to us after 1244 came from Asti or Chieri in Piedmont. To begin with the Lombards lent money, usually small sums, against securities. This made them as unpopular as the Jews and, like them, they were banished under the terms of the will of Henry III of Brabant in 1261. If their business suffered from the strictures of the Council of Lyons it was only for a short time. Perhaps it was then that money-lending was subject to a special licence, in exchange for which the princes could usually obtain a loan. In Brabant a general licence appears to have been given for the whole duchy, and in Flanders between fifteen and twenty are known to have been issued between 1275 and 1300, valid each

E.H.—3

time for a single locality, but there may have been one in each town and even in small villages.

As far as we know, the Lombards were the only money-lenders operating in the area of the present-day Netherlands, where there are no traces of patrician or Italian high finance. They appeared at Utrecht in 1260. The Council of Lyons gave the Count of Holland a convenient excuse to expel them but they had reopened their shops by 1283 at the latest. We do not know what interest they charged, but regulations issued in the fourteenth century which limited the rates to a level that still appears exorbitant to the modern observer, suggest that they had been even higher hitherto.

Quite soon credit was used not only for consumption beyond or in advance of income, but also for trade. The bill of exchange, an Italian invention, was commonly used by Italian merchants at the fairs of Champagne and possibly also in the Low Countries. It relieved men of the need to carry cash, which was clumsy and dangerous; it could also be used as a security. It was usually made out to the bearer, and so could be a general method of payment. It was clearly in imitation of this practice that *lettres de foire*, bills falling due during fairs, became a standard means of payment among Flemish merchants in the thirteenth century. Unlike the bills of exchange, they were payable not only in cash but also in an agreed amount of goods or even in the execution of some task. They were payable at one of the fairs in Flanders or Champagne or, more rarely, at fairs abroad. The decline of active Flemish trade abroad, which gave way to foreign trading in Flanders itself, and the simultaneous decline of fairs as forums for exchange, caused this method of finance to disappear in favour of bills of exchange.

PART TWO

The Medieval Economy and Society in Crisis
1300–1500

1 Population

Historians concur in regarding the end of the Middle Ages as a period of economic and social crisis. This is certainly borne out by evidence of a contracting population. We have no statistics but population growth appears to have been the main impulse to economic progress from Carolingian times to the thirteenth century. Given that there had been no considerable technological advances, a growing population, producing and consuming more, must have been the main factor. Had this perhaps eventually led to over-population? Clearances, fully worked by the surplus rural population, must by now have affected all land that was exploitable by contemporary agrarian techniques, and the cultivation of marginal lands to feed a growing population may have disrupted the economic balance. Another element of the population surplus had found an outlet in handicrafts in the expanding towns: but to what extent could the towns absorb them, as competition expanded and ate into export markets? There was bound to be a crisis sooner or later. The Black Death has often been considered the turning-point, but the crisis seems really to have arisen earlier than that in the Low Countries. Having been among the first to develop, they were first to experience the effects of the crisis, by the latter part of the thirteenth century.

There had of course been famines before. A bad harvest or the ravages of war, together with the problems of importing food from elsewhere, had been enough to cause them. However the impression that they had been less frequent and less serious than they were later does not seem merely to reflect the silence or scarcity of our sources. A bad harvest almost throughout Europe in 1315 inaugurated an era of high death rate in 1316. The famine was a prelude to dysentery, which created havoc in a population already badly underfed. Between mid-May and late September of that year the municipality of Ypres had to bury, at public expense, almost 2,800 bodies, probably a tenth of the population. At Bruges, where the population was greater, the public authorities had to bury only a little over 1,800: imports by sea may have been easier there, and the authorities had also bought grain which they sold at a loss, a common practice on such occasions. At Louvain and Brussels new cemeteries were opened, and every day cartloads of dead were buried in mass graves.

Bubonic plague struck Europe in the mid-fourteenth century. The famous Black Death came from the East through Italy and France, striking Tournai in 1349 (where it killed much of the agricultural labour force of the region), and Ypres as well, where again paupers had to be buried by the authorities. In 1350 it arrived from the Rhineland in the north-eastern areas of the Low Countries. In a parish of Deventer, the register of deaths reveals that fifty-four benefactors died between 11 May and 29 September, as against 841 for the whole of the preceding century. In some families there were several deaths on a single day, a clear indication of the plague. Half of the monks and 120 of the 200 lay brothers in the Cistercian abbey of Aduard in Friesland also succumbed. Even so, vast regions were unscathed and the silence of many chronicles of these areas is in striking contrast to the horrified tales we hear from elsewhere. The Florentine Matteo Villani stated, with astonishment, that the plague spared Brabant. Of course he was a distant observer, but his account is borne out by the stability of excise revenues on foodstuffs in many towns of this duchy and Flanders as well, both before and after the plague: had there been a great decline in the number of consumers, it would have been shown in these figures. Moreover the tax-collectors of the Apostolic Camera in Avignon ascribed the decline in the income of St Truiden's Abbey not to the epidemic but to wars that had devastated its properties.

This is not to minimize the effects of the Black Death in the Low Countries. Even if the most active areas were less affected than elsewhere in Europe, the terrible ravages suffered by their

customers unquestionably did great harm to the export trade. All
Europe was now plunged into crisis, and the epidemic recurred
several times over the next century and a half, not sparing the
Low Countries, which indeed appear to have suffered greater loss
than at the time of the Black Death itself. The population seems
temporarily to have fallen, followed by production and consumption. There is some statistical evidence for this.

Some of these statistics are like snapshots, taken on the occasion
of the raising of the militia in the two chief towns of Flanders. At
Bruges 7,234 men took the field between July 1338 and July 1340.
These figures suggest a population of between thirty and thirty-
five thousand, which makes Bruges one of the dozen largest towns
in Europe at that time. Similar sources for Ghent suggest a figure
of fifty-six thousand in 1360, making Ghent (with Paris, Milan,
Venice, Florence and Naples) one of half a dozen European towns
with over fifty thousand inhabitants. It is even possible that the
town had been larger in earlier times, for by then the cloth trade of
the great Flemish towns had passed its peak. Ypres was probably
not much smaller than Bruges early in the fourteenth century.
Census figures of the fifteenth century illustrate the utter ruin of a
city where the decline of textiles was not offset by the development of other trades. By 1412 Ypres had only 10,700 people,
twenty per cent of them bachelors (which accentuates the picture
of local poverty). Twenty-five years later, eleven per cent of the
population consisted of bachelors, which suggests both that
immigration to the declining town had fallen, and emigration
from it had risen. By 1491 the population was down to 7,600.

Peasants in the Low Countries had often emigrated in search of
new lands. In so far as this movement persisted, it became quite
different in character. Because of the agrarian depression all over
Europe, there were no great outlets abroad, and the men who now
emigrated were artisans, expelled from home by the decline of
their trades. Edward III of England (1327–77) brought Flemish
and Brabantine weavers to England, especially to London, where
about a hundred were apparently established, and to York. It
would be erroneous, however, to ascribe the rise of the English
wool industry to this, as historians used to. Others went to
Florence, and there was even emigration from Bruges to the
newly discovered Azores after about 1450, though not on a
considerable scale.

As for the regions, there were Brabantine fiscal censuses between 1374 and 1526 which, though lacking the rigour of today's censuses, reveal the movement of population in the duchy quite well. The first census was incomplete and is of little use, but the *fouage* (hearth census) of 1437 shows 92,758 households, and if we assume that there were 4.5 persons per household on average, the population will have been about 417,000. The approximately eleven thousand square kilometres covered by this census nowadays support five million people, but of course this includes many large towns. The later censuses recorded 91,957 households in 1464, 85,527 in 1472, 86,483 in 1480 and 75,343 in 1496. The population of Brabant thus appears to have been some 340,000 in the later fifteenth century, a decline of some 20 per cent in sixty years.

There were differences between town and country and between regions and towns. Among the chief towns only Antwerp grew as its commerce expanded. It doubled in size in two generations, from about 15,500 to 30,000, rapidly overtaking Louvain which, though larger to begin with, was hard-hit by the decline of the Brabantine cloth trade. In Brussels the same decline was made good by the position the town enjoyed as capital of the Low Countries under Duke Philip the Good of Burgundy (1419–67).

NUMBER OF HOUSEHOLDS IN THE CHIEF TOWNS OF BRABANT

	1437	*1464*	*1496*
Antwerp	3,440	4,559	6,586
Bois-le-Duc	2,583	2,335	3,456
Brussels	6,376	7,165	5,750
Louvain	3,579	3,296	3,069

In the following generation this advantage passed to Malines. In 1482 there began ten years of civil war in the Low Countries, with its sequels of famine and epidemic. Antwerp now took from Brussels the place of most populous town in the duchy. Its prosperity affected the towns in its own commercial network, such as Bois-le-Duc, the numbers of which rose from about 11,600 to 15,500 between 1437 and 1496 despite a fire that devastated the place in 1463 (a common happening in medieval towns, which were composed of thatched huts). Bergen-op-Zoom, with fairs which complemented the Antwerp ones, also rose from 5,000 to nearly 7,700 in population.

Their development was quite unlike that of other secondary towns. In those sixty years, their total population seems to have declined by a third, from about 58,000 to 40,000: the ruin of their export trades relegated them to supply centres for the surrounding countryside which was just as hard-hit by the crisis. Between 1437 and 1464 the number of rural households underwent only a slight decline, from 63,130 to 62,539, and this was due solely to the Louvain administrative district, for the surroundings of Antwerp and Brussels had even slightly increased their population, a reflection of these towns' prosperity. But the decline between 1464 and 1496 was general for the whole of Brabant, which fell to 45,442 households by the latter date, a decline of 37.5 per cent since 1437. Agrarian crisis and political chaos had won. A chief consequence was the increasing degree of urbanization in the duchy. Its towns, large and small, held 32 per cent of the population in 1464 as in 1437, but their share amounted to 40 per cent in 1496. Distress and insecurity led many peasants to leave the land and find refuge and a living within the town walls.

The figures for paupers, however, who were excluded from hearth taxes, are unsatisfactory. The figures are complete only for the 1437 census, and there are no later figures for comparison for the administrative region of Bois-le-Duc. Antwerp had the highest proportion of paupers among the large towns in 1437, probably because many people had been attracted there by the town's growth, whereas the growth had not gone far enough to absorb them right away. Later on Antwerp was exceptional because although everywhere else poverty worsened, it was not as severe in Antwerp itself, in the countryside round about, or in the little towns of the Antwerp area, although such little towns everywhere else had a catastrophic level of poverty.

There are also fiscal censuses, though less complete than the Brabantine ones, for the countryside of Hainault. The figures for 1365 are plausible and show some 30,750 hearths, i.e. a population of about 138,000 in the countryside. Subsequent censuses deserve less credence until that of 1440, which indicated 27,281 hearths. The higher figure for 1458, 29,212, fell substantially later on. So far as we can compare it with the figures for 1481, which are fragmentary, there appears to have been a fall of 44 per cent. In 1469

Charles the Bold planned to levy a uniform hearth tax in the whole administrative district of the Lille Chamber of Accounts, but he achieved this only for the countryside. A census then gave 51,873 hearths in the Flanders countryside, 27,933 in rural Artois, 12,828 in rural Picardy and 1,688 in the county of Namur. The figure of 29,212 for Hainault was obviously lifted from the census of 1458, which makes the other figures suspect, and the same reservation must apply to the 25,000 households counted in a hurried census

NUMBER OF PAUPER HOUSEHOLDS IN BRABANT
PER DISTRICT, PERCENTAGES OF TOTAL HOUSEHOLDS

	1437	1480	1496
Antwerp			
chief town	13.5	10.5	—
small towns	9.3	17.3	—
countryside	20.7	26.0	—
Bois-le-Duc			
chief town	10.4	—	—
small towns	24.8	—	—
countryside	35.8	—	—
Brussels			
chief town	10.5	—	17.1
small towns	9.5	—	29.6
countryside	31.5	—	36.3
Louvain			
chief town	7.6	18.3	—
small towns	8.6	36.0	—
countryside	37.8	38.6	—

of 1470 in Liège. The population of Overijssel has been estimated at 52,660 in 1475. For Holland, the only data are from 1494, and will be discussed below.

In the case of town populations, the registers of admission to citizenship give some details as to the force and range of their attraction. The grant of citizenship involved costs that not all new townsmen could or would meet, but it was generally essential for qualification as master in a guild. Naturally the towns' attraction rose in force and range with their economic potential. In the borough of Hulst in Flemish Zeeland, the newly admitted burghers of the first half of the fifteenth century (the figures are not complete) came from surrounding villages. But in Middelburg, growing trade was reflected in the increasing numbers of registrations of new citizens: the yearly average rose from 32.8 between 1360 and 1399, to 41.1 between 1400 and 1449 and to 66.3 between 1450 and 1499. At the same time the recruitment area progressively widened: for the periods concerned, the town's immediate surroundings in the island of Walcheren accounted for 62, 32 and 21 per cent of the new citizens, in so far as we can tell their origins. The number from other towns rose from 26.5 to 45.7 and 49 per cent. Leyden, with its industrial troubles, went the other way. The annual average intake declined from 47.2 between 1365 and 1400 to 44.2 between 1401 and 1450 and 37.5 between 1451 and 1500, and those coming from Holland itself supplied 14, 38 and 40.4 per cent of the new intake. A town of European status, such as Bruges, took in 197 new citizens annually between 1418 and 1450, 142.2 between 1456 and 1478, and 84.6 between 1479 and 1486. However, the really foreign element, judged by modern standards, remained quite low, accounting for 406 registrations out of 11,171 in the whole period. Foreigners could pursue their trade without registering as citizens, and registered only very rarely. But the overall decline in registrations does have some correlation with the general economic movement.

2 *Agriculture*

1 AGRICULTURE AND STOCK-RAISING

Cereals were traditionally the main crop in Western agriculture, and in the Low Countries population density had originally promoted this. Priority was given to winter corn, the risks of which were less because it could always be replaced by summer corn if bad weather destroyed the grain, and particularly to rye and spelt, which were most resistant to bad weather. Rye also provided abundant fodder. It predominated until recent time not only on sandy soils, but even on the clay ones that nowadays constitute the great wheat region of Belgium. Spelt was commonest on the poor soils of the Veluwe and south of the Sambre-Meuse trench, but it could also be found on the more fertile ground north of this line. Despite its vulnerability to hard winters, wheat was also grown on the best soils. Around 1325–30 a peasant on the polders north of Bruges even sowed the greater part of his fields with it. Buckwheat, which presumably came to thirteenth-century Europe with the Mongol invasions, appears in the poorest sandy areas of the Low Countries after about 1400. It was eaten either as a mash or a pancake. As it was sown late, in view of its vulnerability to night frosts, it was often substituted for winter wheat if that crop had to be replaced. It grew easily, even unmanured, and killed weeds, so it was particularly suited to the poorest and recently cleared soils.

But these basic food crops seem to have declined in importance in the later Middle Ages. In any case local resources no longer sufficed to feed Flanders or Holland. The rich grain regions of

66

Artois and Picardy were the first to export their surplus. Significantly Ghent, the town to which the Scheldt and the Lys carried
most of these exports, set up a grain staple for down-river traffic
in the mid-fourteenth century to make sure of its own supply of
grain: the grain had to be offered to the local population for a
fixed period. It is also revealing that by the later fourteenth
century Baltic grain, which had earlier been used only in time of
famine or high prices, was regularly imported. With this demand,
the nobility of Poland and other countries of the Baltic littoral
extended their grain areas, though it is not within the scope of this
work to consider the disastrous consequences this had for their
peasantry. Baltic rye, cheaply produced and transported, caused
what may be called the first agricultural invasion: to a large extent
it deflected Flanders and the neighbouring countries from cereal
production.

Indeed, the price of cereals, vital human nourishment, did in
fact decline, as everywhere in the West. Supplies from the Baltic
rose, while the decline of population reduced demand in the West,
and the abandonment of marginal lands resulting from the high
death rate made agricultural production cheaper. Temporary
famines could of course cause abrupt price rises, but the overall
pattern of selective averages gives a clear picture of the long-term
tendencies at work. Between 1330 (the date of our first satisfactory
sources) and the 1470s, the nominal price of wheat trebled at
Douai. The income of an abbey of that town between 1325 and
1375, a period of wars and epidemics, did not rise much above a
quarter of its former average. At Bruges, wheat prices had risen by
a third between this later period and the mid-1460s. But if these
prices are converted into silver (the monetary standard and index
of purchasing power, the Flemish silver groat having been reduced by 1470 to 30.9 per cent of its 1360 value, and to 15.6 per
cent of its value in 1330), then clearly the real value of wheat had
fallen by rather under half at Douai and to two-fifths at Bruges
between the dates quoted. Much the same calculations can be made
for Antwerp and Utrecht. Wheat was, of course, generally consumed only by the rich, but as it is frequently encountered in the
accounts of religious institutions, it provides the best figures. The
price of rye, the commonest consumption cereal, remained low for
years in the fifteenth century, at a constant rate of sixty per cent of
the price of wheat. When wheat prices rose some consumers

would shift to rye, and its price would rise to over eighty per cent of the price of wheat.

Peasants tried to make up for the fluctuating price of cereals by growing crops less subject to crisis. This included industrial crops. As the Plague generally struck the towns harder than the countryside, the number of artisans seems to have declined quite markedly in Europe as a whole. The relative scarcity of industrial goods gave their prices a stability greater than that enjoyed by agricultural goods, and the cheapness of food, which allowed part of real income to be diverted to other ends, helped to stimulate industry, even in the countryside. Peasants generally founded their industries on their own output of raw materials. The linen industry, which had been widespread for many years, underwent rapid development in the Low Countries in the later Middle Ages, and flax growing is mentioned more frequently from then on, though it has been suggested that this might be merely a matter of sources rather than a growth of consumption. At all events it is in the fourteenth century that we first hear of large-scale cultivation of madder in the Zeeland islands and the neighbouring parts of northern Brabant. Around 1350, the cultivation of oleaginous plants for both food and lighting as well as manufacturing in Holland and around Utrecht had gone so far that Antwerp sought the staple for them. Rape and mustard were being harvested in south-eastern Flanders by the fifteenth century, if not before, and the new brewing process also stimulated hop growing, at the latest by 1360 or 1370 in Holland and northern Brabant, and early in the next century west of Brussels as well.

Although the taste of beer had improved with hops, local viti-culture reached its peak in the later Middle Ages both at Louvain and Huy, where vines were planted on plots used for cloth frames in the later decades of the fourteenth century. Market gardens also developed outside and inside the town walls: the end of population growth meant that the extensive areas within the vast fourteenth-century walls were never quite built up before the nineteenth century or even our own. A great variety of vegetables, perhaps of Arab origin, brought to Flanders via Italy and from Flanders to other parts of the Low Countries, became common to the markets and the hawking trade of the larger towns. Only red cabbage is said to have originated in Flanders. Apples, pears, plums, cherries, chestnuts and strawberries became more usual.

The cheapness of grain also allowed considerable consumption of meat and dairy produce. At Louvain, which had less than fifteen thousand inhabitants, 2,419 cows or oxen, 11,084 calves or sheep, 4,682 lambs, 4,029 pigs and 1,494 goats were slaughtered over ten months in 1473 although, of course, the animals had less meat than nowadays. Just north of Bruges a peasant trebled the number of his cows between 1325 and 1334, and in the fifteenth century an avarage of 1,019 cows or oxen and 4,302 sheep were raised in the forty-five farms of Tongerlo Abbey, most of them on the Campine heath. Certainly the cows gave relatively little milk, which was a popular drink in the towns. Butter consumption was probably confined to the rich, but cheese was more popular. Both were a speciality of the coastal polders, which exported them. In this respect Holland did better than Flanders towards the end of the fifteenth century, perhaps because of the conversion from pasture to flax, stimulated by Flemish industrial progress.

Horse breeding seems also to have developed, at least on the heavy soils. The number of horses seems, however, to have declined quite substantially throughout the fifteenth century in the Campine properties of Tongerlo Abbey, probably because on such poor soil they were not indispensable as draught animals when oxen due for slaughter could be substituted. On the other hand, the ploughing of clay soils needed the strength of horses, and our peasant north of Bruges more than doubled his stock between 1325 and 1334. On the wet soils of the lower Meuse an abbey had one horse for every three hectares of land. Remounts were also raised in Flanders: Rhenish noblemen who were arming in the 1420s and 1430s had them bought at the fairs of Flanders and Brabant. Stock-raising stimulated the cultivation of oats and barley, for which there was also a demand from the brewers, and in general brought about an increase in the amount of land given over to pasture. Moreover, since the demand for meat and dairy produce went on all year round, it was necessary to winter cattle in better conditions. To this end, fodder crops had a regular place in agriculture, and the change was the point of departure for a European, or even a worldwide, revolution in agricultural technique.

2 AGRICULTURAL METHODS AND IMPLEMENTS

Flanders and Brabant found many ways of increasing the quantity of fodder their animals needed. The first was to alternate sowing and pasture on the same soil. There is one instance of this in 1323, south of Ghent. Grass was sown after the fallow period, and after a few years (normally three or six) the artificial meadow was converted back to arable land and another meadow sown elsewhere. Another method was to let the fallow period fall every sixth rather than every third year, and there could be a harvest of vegetables or feed crops, as happened in 1328 near the coast of French Flanders. The peasant could also sow feed crops as a second growth maturing after the main one. Turnips were used like this north-east of Louvain in 1404, and near Ghent and in the Campine in the mid-fifteenth century. The sowings were often so dense that only the leaves could grow normally and were cropped where they were. Spurrey served the same purpose in the poorer Campine soils. Finally, the fallow period could be dropped altogether and replaced by alternate harvests of feed crops – vetch around Louvain and St Truiden in the later fifteenth century. It is said to have happened around Tournai even in 1278 but perhaps not as a substitute for the fallow period. In 1480 broom cultivation is said to have taken the place of fallow, again near St Truiden. These improved crop rotations may, of course, have been exceptional and not quick to spread, but they do indicate the Low Countries' pioneering role in European agriculture.

In breaking the vicious circle of the three-field system, hitherto the most advanced system of rotation, the peasants were not only likely to increase their incomes by producing meat and dairy goods as well as cereals; the increase in their animal stocks also gave them more manure for their sowing overall and guaranteed better yields without their having to leave the land temporarily inactive. The need for manure may also have encouraged new methods of animal breeding. Perhaps the habit of stalling the stock so that none of the manure would be lost – which is still common today in the Campine – goes back to the later Middle Ages. At all events, in the Campine as in other sandy regions such as the Veluwe, where there was no straw, the peasants would cut heather and clumps of grass from the commons to use as bedding. Such cutting became so widespread that it had to be limited. The many commons regulations point clearly to the tendency to reduce the scope of extensive agriculture in favour of more rational exploitation of natural resources. There are 127 of such *wijsdommen* for the area of the modern Netherlands, dating back to the fourteenth century, and another 122 from the fifteenth, as against 37 from earlier times. A great number of pigeons were bred at least on large farms (they could have harmed the sowing on small ones). They could be eaten and their droppings used as manure; indeed, like street refuse and the contents of nearby town cesspools, they were even traded in the most advanced agricultural regions in the fifteenth century.

Miniatures in the calendars of Books of Hours in Flanders offer remarkable illustrations of the agricultural techniques used. Many of the tools had been perfected no doubt to economize on labour so as to give more time for handicrafts or to avoid the wage rises characteristic of the epoch. The single-handed plough, our oldest example of which dates from about 1430, could easily be managed by one man, without the need for a second to drive the team. This plough was particularly suited to forming the strips of a field, which now included from six to ten furrows or even more to give proper drainage and to protect winter sowings from bad weather. As they were shifted from year to year every inch of ground was used in the long run. The Flemish peasant worked much more with the spade than other European peasants did, and thus bit more deeply into the earth. The oldest mention of a windmill to supply power for the pumps in the polders dates from 1408. Instead of the sickle, which cut only the ears, a short scythe – called in English the 'Hainault scythe', for unknown reasons – was used, and a hook with which the straw was grappled. The peasants thus had more straw for bedding, which was all the more valuable since deforestation and the restrictions of use of the commons limited the quantity of leaves and similar material available. The short scythe was known after 1326 at the latest in Artois and the polders north of Bruges. The first reference to it concerns vetch harvesting, for which it was especially suited because of the tangled growth and short stem of the plant, but it was soon used for other plants. The invention of a churn equipped with a log which moved up and down within a covered barrel not only economized on labour but also gave a better result than the beating of butter by hand in an open vat.

Too little is known of yields in the Low Countries for exact figures to be supplied for agricultural progress in any one region over a sufficiently lengthy period. The differences may simply depend on climatic conditions from year to year. The mean yield of wheat was 8.7 times the weight sown near Saint-Omer in the 1320s, 12.8 near Béthune in the Pas-de-Calais in the 1330s, and eight around Douai between 1329 and 1380; the yield of oats was respectively 3.7, 6.8 and 6.0. In the polders near Bruges, in the years 1359–68, the harvest was 4.3 times the sown weight of wheat, and on sandy soils the rate rose to 6.64 for rye. Around 1400 the yield was 8 to 1 for wheat around Brussels, and in the polders of the lower IJssel 9.7 to 1 for rye and 8.4 to 1 for oats in the 1410s. In a manor near Apeldoorn on the edge of the Veluwe there was an increase in the rent in rye from 6.4 to 1 in 1334 to 7.4 to 1 in 1496 – though it may have been caused by more extensive farming. These yields were much in advance of other countries', particularly England's, about which we know incomparably more.

3   THE CULTIVATED SURFACE

The Low Countries' progress in agricultural technique, as an answer to the crisis, was not enough to restore the prosperity of the countryside. There is a sign of this in the losses suffered from natural disaster. The coastal plains reclaimed from the sea were constantly threatened by it. At the peak of the medieval economy, when the dykes burst, the sea would quickly be pushed back and quite often reconstructed dykes would take in even more land than before. The changes have been ascribed to the climatic conditions; but, as agricultural prices fell, the peasants were not inclined to devote their resources and energy to reclamation of land, and were even reluctant to spend either on keeping up the dykes or repairing them when they had burst. Political troubles helped weaken defences against the sea, and in some cases the extraction of peat also caused the land to subside and made recovery of flooded lands still more difficult.

In 1287 a tidal wave ravaged the whole Dutch coast and inflicted lasting damage in the Zeeland islands and the surroundings of Amsterdam. New breaches were opened in 1322, 1334 and 1336 between Haarlem and Alkmaar, while Zeeland, especially Flemish Zeeland, turned out once again to be extremely vulnerable. The flood of 1362 ravaged them further, and also began the formation of Dollart bay on the present-day Dutch–German border. The last quarter of the fourteenth century began an era of worse calamities: the tidal wave of St Valentine's Day (14 February 1373), south of Rotterdam, was followed by others, in the western part of Flemish Zeeland, probably in the winter of 1375–6, south of Dordrecht in 1393, around Leyden in 1403. On 19 November 1404 the first tidal wave of St Elizabeth's Day flooded much of the Flemish polders, and a second, seventeen years later, caused terrible damage in Holland and Zeeland. Thirty-four parishes were submerged around Dordrecht, which, even a century later, appeared as an islet in the middle of a vast flood. To this day the Biesbosch to the south-east of Dordrecht has a hybrid appearance because of this cataclysm. It was men that destroyed the dykes in Flanders during the English invasion of 1436, the revolt of Ghent in 1452–3 and the troubled regency of Maximilian of Austria from 1482 to 1494. The river dykes were just as badly maintained as the sea dykes, and the tidal waves ravaged far inland. They also often gave way at high water. Sometimes, if peasants failed to repair the damage, merchants and officials of the princes would buy the flooded land for almost nothing and drain them for speculative purposes.

Drifts, as well as floods, reduced the cultivable area. In 1440 Philip the Good allowed the planting of trees around Bois-le-Duc and Tilburg to retain the sands that threatened the vegetation of the commons. The silting-up of the fens in the Drenthe interrupted the formation of peat deposits. Pollen analysis has shown that moorland then pushed back the beech trees.

The Low Countries, which had suffered less than other areas of Europe from the Black Death, probably had fewer deserted villages, though the subject still needs research. Fields, earlier reclaimed from the forest near Antwerp, were covered in the fourteenth century by heath; others in the county of Namur, as well as around Louvain and Bois-le-Duc, were left fallow or planted with trees. In the north-east, place-names suggest abandoned fields, but their age is not clear. Of 271 properties owned by the bishop of Utrecht in the Twente, 112 were abandoned at some date before 1385; 99 were taken back into cultivation by 1475. Compared with the losses, actual gains of land were extremely rare. The increase of 22 per cent in the number of taxpayers between 1397 and 1475 in the Salland near Twente may perhaps be explained by clearances. The appearance of tithes and quitrents shows that clearances went on in the Veluwe until the mid-fourteenth century. However, if an administration was set up in 1370 for the newly-drained polders along the lower IJssel, the yield of rents levied there went down and there were more and more abandoned farms. In the bishopric of Utrecht half of the taxable lands were said to be empty in 1484, though this was partly a reflection of ferocious civil war.

4 LORD AND PEASANT

The decline of the manorial system and the diminishing purchasing power of quitrent incomes had hit many nobles hard. Incomes paid in kind often gave a pittance, and as the lessors, the nobles would suffer from any fall in agricultural prices. It cannot have been rare for lords of modest rank, who had almost fallen back into the peasantry, themselves to farm part of the old demesne, using what remained of the corvées. Whereas elsewhere in Europe the new seignorial system was designed to make up for the decline of manorial farming by developing taxes and judicial revenues, the advance of the princes' power held this up almost throughout the Low Countries. Moreover, a huge transfer of property seems to have been occurring from old nobles as they died out or became impoverished, particularly by inheritance, to nouveaux riches who emerged from the bureaucracy or the urban bourgeoisie and who wanted the prestige that was still attached to seignorial status. In fact, the economic fate of the nobility in the later Middle Ages is not well known and needs research.

Religious property suffered not only from economic conditions but also from the demands of voracious ecclesiastical taxes, as well as the communities' own aspirations to a comfortable, luxurious existence, for they were increasingly losing their ideals in this phase of the Church's decline. Despite the parsimony of abbots who sometimes tried to avert ruin, many monasteries were forced sooner or later to borrow or mortgage their property, could not pay off the debts and had to sell something. Now they could hardly expect much generosity from benefactors. In any case, rational exploitation of their property by direct farming was unthinkable, because the priesthood could hardly be combined with manual labour, lay brothers had become scarce and agricultural labour was too expensive.

The impoverishment of the peasants was such that at this time they could hardly go on extending their virtual ownership of the lands they tilled. Only classes privileged enough to have income from public service or industrial and commercial undertakings could buy land on any scale, with or without seignorial title, and even if no such title were attached to the land, the purchase could still be to the disadvantage of peasant farmers. The burdens laid upon them varied from place to place and from one method of tenure to another. They could still be heavy where the manorial system had not quite disappeared. Seven manors in the Veluwe which belonged to Prüm Abbey in the Eifel owed the abbey annually, as late as 1405, a sum of money, tithes and quitrents in kind that absorbed a quarter of their rye harvest and a fifth of their barley.

The Low Countries show no sign of the seignorial reaction experienced by large parts of Europe after the Black Death – perhaps because of the weakness of the epidemic, perhaps because the exceptional development of the towns gave a good refuge to peasants if their burdens were increased. Unlike elsewhere, their emancipation went ahead. In 1358 the abbot of Paderborn had to agree to his villeins at Putten in the Veluwe limiting his right to take any object he liked (usually the best head of cattle) in a dead man's inheritance, and much the same happened with the villeins of Soest in the fifteenth century who were able to exchange their condition for vassalage to a monastery in Utrecht. In Brabant, around Nivelles, the last payment of mortmain taxes occurred in 1430, and in Hainault the annual average of such payments fell from thirteen around 1350 to seven around 1400 and four fifty years later. Serfdom was dying and marriages of serfs with women of 'free' birth gave it a death-blow.

In infertile regions agrarian burdens meant that small farms could not feed their occupants. Little farms in the Veluwe extended in 1405 over four or five hectares of sandy soil, of which, under the three-field system, a third was annually left unused. Once grain had been kept back for sowing, the remaining rye sufficed to keep two persons only, whereas a peasant household had an average of nine. The flight from the land there makes it unlikely that this could have been made good by other sorts of crops. At the same time we find in the Namur region farms no greater than one, or at most three hectares. Out of almost three thousand rebel Flemish peasants whose property was confiscated after their defeat at Cassel in 1328, 1,632 had less than 4.4 hectares and among these 1,183 not even half of that. After a new rebellion in 1382, out of 1,564 countrymen of the Courtrai area, whose property was also confiscated, 365 had no land at all under cultivation, 686 had less than 1.4 hectares and 935 less than 4.2. Around Ghent, two or three hectares was the normal size for farms.

Peasant revolts against the princes can partly be explained by the princes' demands. Establishment of an effective administration imposed heavier and heavier taxes on the impoverished countryside. In many areas, excessive density of population had caused increases in the number of small, even tiny, farms. The rural proletariat thus created in Flanders was the very soul of the peasant revolt of 1323–8 and others later on, and of the revolt of 1491–2 in Holland. They could no longer live from agriculture alone. Large parts of the Low Countries had thus started on a course of industrialization that developed in the fourteenth and fifteenth centuries.

3 Industry

I THE CORPORATIVE SYSTEM

The growing conflict between patrician employers and workers in the industrial areas of the Low Countries in the thirteenth century came to a head in the early fourteenth century in Flanders with the fall of the patrician regime. The patriciate had been weakened by the concentration of foreign trade on Flanders, which broke their near monopoly and reduced their margins of profit. Political events hastened their ruin. They had tried, with the help of Philip the Fair of France, who was delighted to attack his virtually independent and powerful vassal, the Count of Flanders, and to remove the magistracies of the large towns from his control. The count opposed the patricians, and the artisans of the export trades, oppressed by the patriciate, took the prince's side. The Flemings' struggle for independence thus took on a social aspect, and their victory at Courtrai in 1302, which was won chiefly by the artisans, brought about a profound change in the urban hierarchy. Patrician magistrates were replaced by the chiefs of the popular party, the seats being divided among various artisan groups. Each large trade had at least one, and representatives of numerically less powerful trades, grouped in 'nations', took the others in rotation.

The example of Flanders stimulated a popular movement in other principalities. Artisans of Liège and Brabant were admitted to the magistracy in 1303. But the patricians, who remained more powerful there than in Flanders, reacted to this and were not finally eliminated from the administration of Liège until 1384 or

77

from that of St Truiden until 1393, after a lengthy struggle. They finally had to share power with the 'commons' in the other towns of Liège (Huy in 1342, Dinant in 1348) and Brabant (Louvain in 1378, Brussels in 1421 and Antwerp in 1435). The popular party seized power at Utrecht in 1304 and took a share in the administration of Dordrecht in 1367. In the other Dutch towns the industrial element was too weak to promote itself in this way or even to get political recognition.

As they assumed power the trades of the Flemish towns changed from organs of economic control, set up by the administration, into autonomous corporations, which elected their own heads and were invested with powers to regulate and mediate in professional issues. It was the same elsewhere in the Low Countries, sometimes even before what is called the Democratic Revolution had succeeded. The extent of the professional domain largely depended on the degree to which labour was divided among the guilds. Ghent had about sixty of them in the mid-fourteenth century, Bruges fifty-two in 1308, Ypres fifty-three in 1436, Louvain forty in 1360. The less important Flemish towns naturally had fewer: Dixmude had only fourteen in 1380, for instance. They were also generally less numerous in the other principalities, either because industry was less developed or because the patricians managed to maintain their control for longer. Nonetheless, wherever the guild system was created in industry, the bakers, butchers, smiths etc., and also the textile artisans, were commonly organized in guilds.

The professional groups tended to multiply. The number rose from twelve in 1298 to thirty-two around 1380 in Liège, from nineteen in 1386 to at least thirty-three in Antwerp a century later. Moreover the growing strength of written law caused many more trades to request a statute from the authorities. Sometimes they would remain dependent to some degree, as at Brussels where the chiefs of the first four guilds, instituted in 1365, were nominated as before by the magistrates. The oldest bye-laws were usually quite succinct but later on they were more ample, intended to tighten up the monopoly of the guild for the benefit of its members. No foreigner – which meant anyone not of the town – could practise a trade that had a guild in the town, and the artisans sought to extend the sphere reserved for their guild to the surrounding countryside. This was certainly the greatest stimulus to the establishment of guilds. The anxiety of groups thus advantaged to enjoy their privileges to the full caused some limitation of political rights, or at least limited the institution of new guilds. Moreover, the floating and sometimes quite large mass of regular unskilled labourers was always excluded from the system. They are estimated to have been six or seven thousand strong in Ghent's population of 56,000 in 1360.

The guilds of the Low Countries had the same structure and aims as elsewhere in the medieval West. Professional training was one of their chief functions. Apprenticeship usually began at the age of fourteen, sometimes as early as eight. Its duration varied from place to place, according to trade – the average was three or four years. Apprentices were probably taken on gratis to begin with but later often had to pay an increasingly high registration fee, the first sign of a tendency to restrict access to the trade. The restriction of the number of apprentices for any one master was another sign, though it may also have been a symptom of a petty-bourgeois mentality quite common in the guilds, which wanted to maintain equality of production and income among the various artisans as far as possible. Once a man's apprenticeship had ended, he became a companion, in some trades after a display of his skill. The number of companions working with a single master was in turn limited and some went elsewhere to perfect their skills, though this happened less often perhaps in the Low Countries than in France or Germany.

The skilled companion could get his mastership after the statutory period and for a fee that also tended to rise, frequently to a level that in practice barred his promotion. Moreover, at this stage in a man's career he was quite often required to execute a costly and extremely testing 'masterpiece'. Many workers were thus virtually excluded from mastership and were obliged to remain wage-earners for their whole lives. The sons of masters, however, usually exempt from all of this, were admitted gratis and with full rights. Besides, more and more guilds adopted the principle of heredity. In some trades, butchers and fishmongers for instance, the number of masters corresponded originally with the number of booths in the hall where they had to sell. The Ghent shipwrights also managed to 'close' their guild quite early on.

The masters were normally alone in having the right to elect the heads of their guild. The violent opposition of masters and wage-earners found in many guilds contradicts the picture of perfect harmony between employers and employees that romantic historians imagined. Many guilds fixed the level of wages payable to companions and this, of course, caused much strife. The companions often had their own religious brotherhoods and charitable organizations, which developed into bases for the defence of their professional interests, as had similar centres for artisans in pre-guild days. Only Flanders had guilds (chiefly for the textile trade) in which companions could share in the election of the heads, or even become heads themselves.

As part of the town administration, guilds also constituted particular units in the urban militia until the growth of the princes' power made the possible opposition of the militia intolerable, and recruitment of mercenaries deprived it of a role in the princes' own forces. Moreover, the guilds and brotherhoods were a framework for religious and charitable activity, helping poor or sick members and their widows or orphans. Artisans who because of age or infirmity could no longer gain a living received shelter in their alms houses, some of which survive in Bruges and elsewhere.

The guilds, like the town authorities themselves, were particularly concerned with the quality of industrial products. Raw materials and work were closely regulated. The prohibition on night work and the limitation of daily production met this concern. The artisan had to mark all that he produced, and the guild would add its own guarantee. Supervision was made easier by the fact that tradesmen were often required to sell in a hall or some other specified place.

The masters in a guild did not necessarily have full economic independence. If such independence was normally the rule in trades working on direct orders for local markets, the workers in export trades, masters though they might be, were usually wage-earners. The relations between masters and their employers could be quite strained, especially in the cloth trade, the difficulties of which were at the root of many trade disputes in the later Middle Ages, from strikes to urban revolt.

2 THE WOOL INDUSTRY

Europe's economic exhaustion and the competition of new industries, particularly in England and Tuscany, which reduced the market for Flemish cloth, ended the golden era of the Flemish cloth towns. The social problems of the later thirteenth century and the weakening of the patriciate were reflected in commercial crisis. The decline became clear from the fourteenth century. In Ypres, which had 1,200 to 1,500 looms, we can tell from the number of lead seals used as warranties for the cloth that production fell from 59,000 cloths or half-cloths a year on average between 1310 and 1320 to 32,200 forty years later, and 19,600 in the 1360s. The Brabantine towns at first profited from the crisis in Flanders, but were rapidly affected as well. The excise revenues show that the Malines cloth trade rose in the 1320s to a peak of 720,000 ells, i.e. some 24,000 cloths, in 1333, but fell within a few years to a third of this. Around 1345 Louvain produced nearly 750,000 ells, but only just over half as much around 1380 and hardly 30,000 around 1470. The gravity of the crisis for the great cloth towns can be seen in the position that wool workers occupied in these towns. In Bruges weavers, fullers, croppers and dyers made up thirty per cent of the population in 1340, and rather over fifty per cent in Ghent in 1357 and in Ypres, which lived almost wholly from the cloth trade even in 1431, when the trade was in deep depression.

One reason for the decline was English competition in traditional markets. Average English cloth exports rose from five thousand per annum around 1350 to eighty thousand in 1500. Each temporary crisis in the English market prompted the restoration of the Flemish and Brabantine cloth trade, and each new advance hastened its decline. The Low Countries were not sheltered from this invasion. Although Philip the Good several times forbade imports of English cloth after 1428, Charles the Bold's (1467–77) desire for English goodwill virtually put an end to the prohibition.

The growth of the English cloth trade also made rarer and more expensive the English wool that had been used for the best cloth in the Low Countries. Wool exports went through the staple which had been set by Edward I in 1294 to give him funds near his theatre of war, but which soon turned out to be a good way of putting pressure on continental princes and became permanent. It was shifted around at first, but remained at Calais from 1360 until the French took the town in 1558. We do not know how much wool cloth traders from the Low Countries bought there, but direct English exports generally went down from an average of thirty-five thousand sacks in the early fourteenth century to less than eight thousand during the second half of the fifteenth.

Still, English competition does not explain everything. The cloth trade of Holland began to work English wool only at the end of the fourteenth century and quickly won a place in the European market. Its chief centre, Leyden, produced nearly ten thousand cloths yearly around 1400, and almost 25,000 a century later. It would also be wrong to blame the Low Countries for technological backwardness. The rise of the English cloth trade has been largely attributed to an 'industrial revolution of the fourteenth century' – widespread use of the fulling mill. But this mill was not unknown in the Low Countries; it was, in fact, abandoned there in the fourteenth century, except for a few places in Artois, the cloth trade of which was not apparently very successful. Blame has been laid on the cloth's poor quality, and the example of Leyden, where the industry developed without the fulling mill, shows that there was still a market for fine cloth, although the new fashion stimulated trade in luxuries such as silk, cloth-of-gold or silver, and furs. It is doubtful if these caprices really sufficed to kill off the great cloth trade of Flanders and Brabant.

A little-noted factor, but one that must have been largely responsible for the decline, was production costs. Although there is no comparative study of this, it would seem that the political role of the Flemish and Brabantine towns, as well as the growing calls the princes made on their resources, had gradually imposed such a burden that they were obliged to tax their people very highly. This was done at the time by excise duties levied on consumption, which raised a cost of living already high enough in these populous towns which had to import supplies at great expense. Subsistence wages inevitably rose too. This explanation applies to the towns of Brabant later than those of Flanders, because of their later development and less dynamic politics. The towns of Holland had still not reached the stage at which they would suffer the consequences of this crisis.

The large towns of Flanders attributed their woes in the fourteenth century to the emergence of a cloth trade in lesser towns and in the countryside. But these did not produce the luxury cloths of the large towns. As far as medium-quality cloth was concerned, their lower tax burden and wages gave the 'new draperies' of lesser towns and many villages an unquestionable advantage over the large towns. Of course, agriculture was no longer able to meet the needs of the population of the sandy plains of Flanders, and the peasants had therefore to produce a cloth for the market as well as what they made for their own use. The chief areas of the new cloth trade were the Lys valley from Courtrai to Aire, with important centres at Menin and Comines, and the surroundings of Ypres, including Poperinge. Further north the boroughs of Hondschoote (Nord) and Ghistelles were famous for their serge.

Apart from wage levels, technical differences contributed to the lowering of the production costs of the new cloth trade and to the opening of new markets that were all the larger since crisis conditions favoured the cheaper product. Spinning and weaving were simplified perhaps, and finishing certainly was. English wool did not entirely disappear: Courtrai produced 3,289 fine English woollen cloths in fifteen months in 1468-9. But as trade expanded the coarser and cheaper local wools could be used, or those from Scotland, Germany (especially the Lower Saxon moors) and particularly Castile, where Flemish imports stimulated sheep-raising. Moreover, even if sooner or later the new cloth trade became subject to regulation, it was never like the detailed interference usual in the old industry. The new centres could thus easily adapt to changes in fashion.

Whilst the new industry depended for its markets essentially on the commercial system of the large manufacturing towns, the cloth artisans of the towns were resolutely hostile. As early as 1297 Ghent secured a ban on the measuring or selling of cloth in the countryside less than two miles away, and on framing and dyeing it less than three miles away – five miles in 1327. Several times in the fourteenth century the artisans of the great Flemish towns raided the villages nearby to destroy their equipment. However, the counts' increased power was used to protect the new cloth trade after 1350, for obviously it had more of a future than its rivals, and the large towns were once more reduced to soliciting bans, which were often granted but were seldom effective.

Like that of Flanders, Brabant's rural industry developed towards commercial production, and Louvain and Antwerp took measures against this in 1327-8. It grew especially on the Campine heath, where sheep-raising spread. After 1425 the little town of Weert on the eastern edges of the heath became the chief centre of cheap cloth production. Indeed, around 1400 Brussels allowed such cloth to be produced because of the poor sales of dearer stuffs, and public charitable institutions often bought and distributed it to the needy, although such efforts to adapt were still rare in the old centres. The magistrates and artisans usually persisted in their belief that keeping up the old techniques and varieties of cloth that had made them prosperous before would always be their best resort, and that they would defeat competition by quality. Some artisans sought a future in emigration to England or Tuscany, though not many of them. The strength of the old textile trade certainly declined. In Bruges, 1,016 weavers of military age had gone on campaign in 1339–40, but by 1381 their guild had probably only 343 members. The decline would have been quicker if the gradual devaluation of Flemish and Brabantine money had not kept up the sale of cloth from there – probably not a conscious calculation on the part of the authorities.

The Flemish patricians had ceased to play the role of industrial entrepreneurs since the decline of active trade and the ruin of their supremacy in administration. Manufacturing was managed by men from the ranks of the workers, chiefly master weavers who took their raw materials from foreign importers. They squeezed the wages of fullers, weavers and other workers to produce and sell at lower cost. Violent tension often resulted. Jacques van Artevelde, who set up a dictatorship in Flanders with the help of weavers from the large towns, took the country into the Hundred Years War in alliance with England so as to continue his wool imports, and was overthrown by a revolt of the Ghent fullers in 1345.

The new Flemish drapers did not have the importance of their patrician predecessors. Those of Courtrai only marketed on average between forty-four and forty-eight cloths per annum in the fifteenth century. They were clearly dependent on foreign merchants who could export their output. The Hansa at Bruges prescribed conditions of manufacture for Poperinge cloth as early as 1347, and fifty years later agreement was made with the borough to take all its output at a fixed price. Since the stated quantities were not produced, the Hansa tried to come to a similar arrangement with Oudenaarde. At the end of the fourteenth century Italian merchants in Bruges supplied to the drapers of the Lys boroughs dyes and wool, which was worked for export on their account. The function of masters in the Flemish cloth trade had passed from urban merchant patricians to foreigners. By contrast, in the Brabantine towns the local burghers still fulfilled that role, though on the more modest level that the trade's decline had necessitated. In Leyden and other places in Holland the cloth trade also developed under the hands of employers belonging to the town community.

3 OTHER INDUSTRIES

While the wool industry of the Flemish and Brabantine country-side developed, the linen industry did so too. Linen was woven in the towns for the locals and even for export, as with table linen or the coifs of Nivelles, Cambrai and Tournai, for which England seems to have been the main market. The old declining cloth trade may have shed some of its work force to linen, as certainly happened in Louvain in the fifteenth century; and the appearance of a guild of linen weavers in many towns at the end of the fourteenth century, or in the first half of the fifteenth, suggests that the industry had grown enough to make regulation of it desirable for artisans, clients and authorities.

The towns largely manufactured luxury goods for a clientele that was wealthy and able to support high production costs. But the rural linen industry produced coarse goods, comparable with those of the wool industry and cheaper. Low Countries linen was assisted by external factors in its conquest of the market. France, earlier the main producer, was severely affected by the Black Death and the Hundred Year's War, which caused widespread insecurity; and German linens of the Rhineland, Westphalia and Silesia were often – and sometimes for long periods – excluded from the English market by the fifteenth-century conflicts between England and the Hanseatic League.

At this time the chief centre of the rural linen industry was the Dendre valley, which early on benefited from effective commercial organization. Besides the Mons market, which had operated since 1265, others opened probably a century later at Ath, Lessines, Braine-le-Comte and Enghien. As usual they brought with them some standardization, for the authorities admitted only merchandise that met their regulations and matched the buyers' needs. These rules were imposed on the whole of Hainault in 1418. After much competition, Ath was named as central staple for linen in 1458 and the other markets declined, although this restriction may have benefited Flanders. In any event the hostility of the great

Flemish towns towards the rival cloth trade stimulated the manufacture of linen there. Since they did not believe themselves
threatened to the same extent by linen the drapers did not oppose
its development in the countryside. To begin with the Flemish
area between the Dendre and the Scheldt sent its output to the
markets of Hainault. Ghent, Courtrai and Lille opened new
markets in the fifteenth century, and Ghent tried in vain to get the
staple in 1430, like Lille in 1462. Many peasant weavers maintained
their independence, selling their produce freely in the markets or
to merchants buying from door to door, or even to dyers who
treated the linen before exporting it. Instances of piece-work,
the thread being supplied by merchants, are found from then
on.

The renown of textiles has overshadowed other industries,
among them leather. Skins served many more purposes than nowadays: pails and winebags, for instance, were made of leather; the
walls of many rich houses were covered in worked leather, and
parchment was popular. The vogue for furs was also important.
There were tanners, curriers, shoe makers and purse makers in any
moderately sized town. In Bruges, towards 1340, they constituted
a good ten per cent of the artisans. Lille, Brussels, Malines and
Bois-le-Duc seem to have worked leather and furs imported chiefly
from the Baltic. In many regions the countryside probably played
its part in this trade which was based on stock-raising and the
tannin of the forests.

A division of labour clearly occurred between the towns,
especially the large ones, and the countryside. With their high production costs, the towns had to specialize in luxuries or semi-
luxuries produced by highly skilled artisans, the prices of which
were of less importance than their quality. In the villages not-so-
skilled labour produced everyday items on the whole. One of the
urban industries, of concern to the art historian as much as to the
economic historian, was tapestry. It was used, like leather, to
decorate walls, seats and benches, or even to split long halls into
smaller rooms to live in. In the thirteenth century Arras began to
imitate Parisian tapestries with geometric motifs, flowers and
animals or scenes of daily life from legend or history. The name
arrazzi by which tapestry is still known in Italian is a testimony
to its success. Arras lost its position in the mid-fifteenth century
when Bruges, Ghent, Tournai, Brussels and Louvain took the

lead, perhaps because the famous painters of these towns supplied cartoons of high quality to the makers of tapestry.

The princes, nobles and rich townsmen who bought these goods also built the town houses, monumental churches and other public edifices that are still the glory of several towns in the Low Countries. Some workshops remained on such work for more than a century. Though less imposing, the construction of houses was no less important economically, and the number of admissions to the masons' guild in Brussels rose considerably under Philip the Good (1419–67). Their wages also rose. The Duke made Brussels his capital, which attracted high society and a wealthy middle class. There was also a great deal of building at Antwerp. Quarries were worked exhaustively, in the Tournai region for instance, from where the stone was transported along the Scheldt for extensive use in Flanders. The Dutch regions took stone from the upper Meuse and the Rhineland. In areas where no stone was to be found, however, brick increasingly became the usual building material, even for public monuments. The right clay could be found in the coastal polders and in many river valleys, and the fuel, peat or wood, was not difficult to find. Many towns had their own brickworks, particularly where they were building ramparts or churches. Premiums were often given to citizens if they agreed to build in hard materials which reduced the danger of fire, and gradually the authorities demanded that new buildings should be built of stone, brick and tiles. In the area of today's Netherlands the custom of ballasting ships with bricks helped both maritime trade and the brick industry.

The rise of building industries stimulated lead mining. Many mines were exploited, especially around Namur, though often without lasting success. Dinant kept its lead in the brass industry but began to decline after the mid-fifteenth century, possibly because brass was overtaken by tin or iron. Charles the Bold's sack of the town in 1466 hastened its decline and caused the entrepreneurs losses which proved irreparable. Even before then brass workers had emigrated to Aachen and many now set up at Malines, where there was a clay suitable for moulds and good markets because of the presence of the central administration and the proximity of Antwerp.

Meanwhile the iron industry had progressed and gradually assumed first place among the metal industries. The water-mill, which was important to the wool industry, also caused a revolution in iron working, for hydraulic power could move heavy hammers and powerful bellows for the furnaces. These latter could also take such quantities of wood that higher temperatures could be obtained, which in turn made fusion all the easier especially since the ore had already been broken up. The contact of the ore with the fuel hitherto had made cast iron too fragile. By 1400 this technique was improved through the 'indirect method', by which the iron was refined by being heated to white heat and then beaten for a long time. The term 'Walloon process' which is applied to this technique all over the world suggests that it was invented or propagated by Walloons. High-quality iron was now much easier to get, and man had truly entered the Iron Age, in the sense that iron now passed into common use.

The exhaustion of the minerals and forests supplying the fuel had caused the abandonment of the middle-Meuse furnaces downriver from Namur by the mid-fourteenth century, but many others were built in upper Belgium where there were both veins of ore and forests, and where the rivers and rapidly flowing watercourses made water-mills possible. The higher-temperature furnaces required heavy investment, and often princes, landed nobility or abbeys built them and leased them to concessionaires who exploited them with wage-labour. Even by the late fifteenth century many furnaces would be used only for a few weeks in the year when their workers were not busy farming. Whereas earlier metal working, from smelting to manufacturing, had been done in the same place, now the processes were separated. The furnaces were limited to the treatment of the mineral and the cast iron was sold to artisans who would forge it into household goods and similar products.

The more extensive use of forges created a greater need for fuel. Coal mining extended to the Charleroi basin where it had started by 1297. At first open-cast mining was tried, but later shafts were sunk. The miners had difficulty with subterranean water which had to be drained, often by hand, unless the mine were sited on a hillside so that a conduit could be built for the water to flow into the valley. Such drains became too expensive for the local peasants to manage, although they had usually been the first to mine the coal with the agreement of the land-owning lord. The merchants to whom they usually sold the coal supplied capital to work the mine and reduced them to wage-earners. This was a new field for commercial capitalism.

The gradual rise in the cost of fire wood and peat soon stimulated the use of coal in homes and breweries. But the most remarkable change in brewing was the replacement, in the fourteenth century, of *grute*, a mixture of wild herbs, by the hop, which improved the taste and durability of the beer. Hop-beer was brewed by adding hops to a must of oats mixed with wheat. It began in northern Germany and came via Hamburg and Bremen to the maritime provinces of the Low Countries. After vain resistance by nobles who held the monopoly on *grute*, it was brewed in many parts of Holland from about 1325. It was made in Bruges in 1351, and in Louvain in 1378, where its output equalled that of *grute* beer by 1415 and completely replaced it by 1435. Holland still led in this field, and its beer was soon well known throughout the Low Countries and even Germany. Each town of any significance had its brewing industry, but Haarlem, with over a hundred master brewers in the fifteenth century, was in the forefront. Another beer, *koyte* (probably invented in Holland), in which barley rather than hops was added to the malt, was cheaper and popular at the time.

Salt production was also widespread along the coast of Flanders, Zeeland and Friesland. Salt was derived from either sea-water or the burning of salt peat. Zeeland was particularly well known for this, and the little town of Biervliet in Flemish Zeeland produced about seven million litres of salt in 1407–8. Many neighbouring salt areas had already been flooded and Biervliet was soon to suffer irreparable damage. It also had to face competition from 'bay salt', from Bourgneuf south of the Loire estuary, which had become the chief supplier of Atlantic Europe. In the mid-fifteenth century Biervliet produced only 1,600,000 litres of salt.

Much of the salt was used to preserve fish. The Zuiderzee supplied flat fish and the North Sea haddock and cod. Since the Baltic was dominated by the Hanseatic League, only the Dutch towns belonging to it had access to the Scanian herring banks. But in the fifteenth century the herring went north along the Swedish coast, probably because of changes in the current, to waters the Hansa could not so easily control. From then on Hollanders, Zeelanders and Flemings, who earlier had fished herring on the coasts of

England and Scotland, also fished in Scandinavian waters and took the lead from the Hansa.

Herring was, to begin with, unsuited for lengthy preservation. According to an ancient tradition, Willem Beukels, a pilot of Biervliet in the early fourteenth century, invented pickling, which involved removing the gills and other perishable organs immediately after the catch. The truth seems to be that the Flemings adopted this process from the Hansa only about 1390, for until then the Hansa alone had practised it; a naval war at that time had interrupted transport of Hanseatic herrings to Flanders. The Hollanders and Zeelanders were quick to take it up, partly because the port of Yarmouth, where they usually sold the herring they caught off the English coast, silted up, and if the herring could not be pickled at once it would rot before reaching the coasts and markets of the Low Countries. Among these markets Brill developed best. As the fish could now be carried for longer, many ports maintained large fishing fleets which increasingly went out to the open sea, particularly to the Dogger Bank.

This caused changes in the structure of business. As men could stay longer at sea, larger boats were built, capable of storing larger amounts of fish. Social distinctions arose between the masters and other shipowners, who sometimes no longer went to sea, and the crews. The produce brought back from fishing was too valuable to be bought up in every case by the same retailer. The intervention of wholesale merchants, the 'hosts', opened up a way for commercial capitalism in this field as well. They began to finance fishing expeditions and in time came to control them.

But fish was not the only field of maritime enterprise. Commercial navigation offered new possibilities for the people of the coastal areas. The moment had come for Holland and Zeeland to join the north-eastern provinces and lay the foundation of their future dominance of European and even world trade.

4 Trade

I THE NORTH-EASTERN REGIONS OF THE LOW COUNTRIES

In the later Middle Ages the towns of the north-eastern Low Countries maintained their trading links with northern and north-eastern Europe. Their sea-going trade developed especially well, partly because of the quality of their ships. The cog may have been a Dutch invention, but if not, it was rapidly successful there, and Dutch shipyards may have introduced improvements that allowed this angular type of boat, with its stern-post rudder, to sail in heavy seas against the wind and with a heavy cargo. By the mid-thirteenth century the cogs sometimes displaced as much as two hundred tons and were thus ideal for the *ommelandvaert* north of Jutland. These Danish straits became one of the chief avenues of European trade, free of the obstacle of double transshipments in the estuary of the Elbe and at Lübeck, and the tolls of the Holstein roads. The merchants of Groningen, Friesland, the IJssel, the Zuiderzee coast and even Guelders took advantage of this.

The close links of this region with the German hinterland encouraged many of these towns to join with the great cities of northern and western Germany to defend common trading interests. In the later 1290s Kampen and Zwolle tried, with Lübeck, to close the Baltic to Flemish and Frisian sailors, and the North Sea to sailors from Gotland. Solidarity between the north-eastern Dutch towns and German traders gave the former the advantage of the latters' privileges, though it also sometimes involved them in wars, such as that against Valdemar iv of Denmark, when the Confederation of Cologne (1367) supplied the

91

German Hansa with a sort of constitutional charter. Many other towns subsequently joined the League. At its height it included some twenty Dutch towns of Friesland, Overijssel and Guelders, as well as Groningen. Groningen and the Frisian towns did not have a sovereign, while the power of the bishops of Utrecht over their IJssel towns had become largely nominal, and that of the counts and later the dukes of Guelders was slow to develop. Affiliation with the Hansa was therefore a matter for the towns alone. It also did not stop them from pursuing their own ends when it was in their interest. Kampen did not take part in the blockade of Flanders decreed by the Hansa in 1360, and took advantage of it to develop its own commerce with Flanders; and when Hanseatic solidarity and the authority of Lübeck were challenged, as happened increasingly in the fifteenth century, the Dutch towns remained impervious to Lübeck's injunctions.

Friesland's commercial role continued to decline. In Germany the ports tried to monopolize trade with the hinterland; the towns of the IJssel had developed their trade with the Rhineland and Flanders, while Holland had extended its own, especially with the British Isles. Friesland, faced with this competition, and with no industries of any importance, lacked resources for trade. The expansion of stock-raising, the products of which were, together with Scanian herring, the characteristic offering of the Frisian merchant, may have been a consequence of this, because of the Frisians' need for new openings. The country was also devastated by political quarrels in the fifteenth century. However, although the Middelzee silted up and many of the old commercial centres were cut off from the sea, the sea ports, especially Hindeloopen and Stavoren, remained open and still sheltered sailors who shuttled between the North Sea and the Baltic for English and German merchants. Of the six hundred ships leaving the port of Hamburg in 1369, two-thirds had captains with Frisian names, and between 1350 and 1400 Stavoren was one of the main ports for imports of hop-beer from Hamburg. Yet Holland's and Zeeland's maritime commerce gradually assumed the lead, and this new threat turned many Frisian sailors into pirates – the *Vitalienbruder*, based chiefly in Friesland, ravaged the North Sea and the Atlantic in the first quarter of the fifteenth century.

Groningen, by far the most important town of the northern Netherlands, had come to dominate the surrounding countryside in the fourteenth century, and became the major market for its stock, even diverting rivers to this purpose. Herds of cattle left Groningen in great numbers, now and for centuries to come, bound for the great cattle markets of Brabant, Westphalia and the Rhineland, and even overseas, although the town's sea-going trade was in decline. Utrecht had only the memory of its former commercial greatness, especially as the guilds used their political influence to limit foreigners' liberty to trade; but its episcopal court and monasteries, with their considerable purchasing power, ensured that Utrecht remained an important market.

The IJssel towns were the main heirs of the sea trade of Friesland, Groningen and Utrecht. The IJssel carried timber, stone, coal, iron-ware and wine (much sought-after in northern countries where viticulture was impossible or disappointing). In return, they took Prussian wheat to the West (where they probably introduced it) and sold Scanian herring and Norwegian cod all round the North Sea and even the Baltic. In 1335 Kampen, the most active port, had 270 of her citizens and, in 1409, 120 of her ships, simultaneously at sea. The town had the passages of the Zuiderzee marked with buoys and had a lighthouse constructed and maintained on Terschelling island at its entrance. Kampen's sailors were the only ones of the area to travel to the French Atlantic coast, and its merchants were also alone in trading the wines of Poitou and Gascony around the Baltic or in supplying Bay salt from Bourgneuf for the herring fisheries in the Baltic. Other towns of the area had only a small share of distant trade.

Among these Deventer, thanks to its fairs, was one of the chief meeting-points in north-western Europe. By 1340 there were four fairs, from June to November, and a fifth, at mid-Lent, was set up in 1386 to cover the entire business season. Holland sent fish, beer, butter and cloth, and also imported English cloth and French wines as her sea trade developed. When, in 1349, Kampen levied a toll to compensate its traders and those of Deventer for losses inflicted by privateers from Holland and Zeeland in a war with the Hansa, the imports of these two provinces amounted to some 425,000 twelve-groat florins for the two years. The Deventer fairs also retained their links with the German hinterland, as far as Brunswick, Magdeburg and even Breslau. Some villeins from Lower Saxony had, as a sort of corvée, to attend the fairs, sell their lord's grain and buy what he needed. Deventer's role as a great centre helped to spread the religious reforms of Modern Devotion that was fostered there in the late fourteenth century.

The fairs declined in the fifteenth century: the IJssel became less navigable, which may have affected the river valley as a whole. But it was particularly the development of the trade of Holland and Zeeland that brought about their emancipation from Deventer as mediator in the trade with Germany, and attracted to them the former commerce of the fairs.

2   HOLLAND

The counts of Holland had steadily fostered the trade of Dordrecht since the thirteenth century. After 1273 they took measures (which would by turns be moderated as they encountered opposition from other Dutch towns, and reinforced in the interest of the counts' treasury) to grant Dordrecht an extensive staple, formally instituted in 1298. By 1344, after much fluctuation, it applied to all goods shipped along the Meuse, the Waal and the Rhine, though not if they had been bought or were due to be sold in the up-river staples of Venlo on the Meuse or Cologne on the Rhine, or if they were bound straight for Flanders. These exceptions apart, every ship arriving at Dordrecht had to unload there. But the other Holland towns resented Dordrecht's monopoly, and the vicissitudes of the country's political history, from the mid-fourteenth century to the accession of the Burgundians in 1428, gave rise to various contradictory measures. The problem was resolved not by the vagaries of politics, but by nature. Earlier the increasing tonnage of ships had reinforced the staple, because both goods that came down-river for export by sea, and, especially, those going up-river, had to be unloaded and transferred to other ships. But the tidal wave of 1428 affected the navigability of the rivers on which the staple was based, and diverted shipping.

To begin with, Dordrecht's trade involved essentially a bartering of Holland and Zeeland produce against goods from up-river on the Meuse and the Rhine. Rotterdam, a simple fishing village before 1340, had a canal dug at this time towards the Schie and was thus able, like Schiedam, to take over a modest share in the transporting of cargoes going from continental Holland towards Dordrecht. Zeeland salt would be taken up the Meuse as far as Mézières in the French Ardennes, the terminus of river navigation. As return freight the upper Meuse supplied lime, stone and coal, and the Rhineland a great variety of goods, especially wine (from Cologne and other ports of the German Rhine) at an annual average rate of 32,000 hectolitres from 1380 to 1385. Dordrecht's attempts to stop the wine trade of Nymegen and other towns of Guelders caused a bitter conflict in 1442–5, and their allies in Holland also resented the staple. Until about 1380 Dordrecht enjoyed a clear lead in up-river traffic. Thereafter many towns tried to protect their own trade, especially by gaining a franchise for tolls on the rivers. As a result the rivers were divided into separate sections, each dominated by a town with special rights.

Meanwhile Dordrecht and, to a lesser extent, other towns of Holland had extended their trade beyond the old inter-regional framework. This expansion was stimulated by a need for new out-lets for the growing economy of Holland, and England was its first target. Dordrecht's merchants went there before 1300. There-after the fishing fleet of the Dutch delta ports gradually supple-mented their activities, carrying freight to England and back, outside the fishing season at first. As the trade of the Low Countries and the Rhine increased, and the economy of Holland grew, these ships began to play a permanent part in the English trade. As had happened with fisheries, the growing size of ships induced the masters of merchant ships to leave large-scale com-merce and created a clearer separation between commercial activity, the ownership of sea-going ships and the task of their captains.

Since the mid-fourteenth century merchants from Dordrecht had seemingly been content with the profits they got from their staple. They left trade with the British Isles to other towns in Holland, which increasingly attracted English merchants bound for the continent. In 1294 Dordrecht had been chosen, essentially for political reasons, as the principal seat of the English wool staple, but had kept it only a year. The cloth trade of Holland developed after this, and by 1450 the Hollanders were taking one thousand sacks annually, about one-seventh of English wool exports; by 1480, they took two thousand, or about a quarter. Despite difficulties from time to time caused by the political relations between the dukes of Burgundy and the Lancastrian dynasty, and the protection given to Flemish cloth, Holland exported English cloth to Germany and the Baltic, and imported, for her own use, English grain as well as Newcastle coal for the breweries. Holland's exports to England consisted mainly of fish, either freshly landed by the fishermen or salted beforehand, salt and hop-beer (the English adopted this way of making beer only in the fifteenth century), bricks and wine from the Rhine or France.

The Hollanders also extended their commerce to the north, along the routes taken by the fishermen, and to the south. Fishermen of Brill, Dordrecht, Schiedam, Amsterdam, Enkhuizen and the island of Wieringen in the Zuiderzee, like those of Stavoren, had their own depots in Scania by 1368 at the latest. At this time ship owners from the *Waterland* (the polders just north of Amsterdam) were already involved in coastal trade with the German North Sea ports, especially Hamburg, where they loaded up with beer. A county toll levied after 1323 in Amsterdam registered the entry of 35,000 barrels of Hamburg beer in eighteen months between 1352 and 1354, imported for the greater part by Hamburg merchants. Some Hollanders, particularly from Amsterdam, were already involved in the trade, and their share gradually rose, while Holland's sea-traders also shipped other goods.

Their first contacts with the Baltic economy may have occurred at Hamburg. The Baltic had developed to such a degree that Prussian and Livonian ships no longer sufficed for exports of bulky goods such as wheat, timber, tar, pitch, potash and the like, and higher-priced articles such as amber, wax, honey and some furs. By the mid-fourteenth century ships from Holland came to load up with these goods in the eastern Baltic. Merchants followed, appearing in Prussia in the early 1370s and in Livonia early in the next century, to set up trade between these countries and Holland, England and Flanders. In exchange they established markets for Flemish, Dutch and English cloth, their own fish (which helped their fisheries) and Western wines and salt, for which merchants and sailors of Holland went as far as the Loire estuary.

The chief maritime towns of the Hansa, especially Lübeck and its neighbours, were disturbed at the competition. By the late fourteenth century, they were prohibiting Hollanders from sailing in the winter, which, for reasons both of control and security, was also forbidden to their own citizens, and they forbade the Hanseatic League to build ships for foreigners or to sell them. The Dutch were also ordered not to stay in Livonia to learn Russian. Though the other Hanseatic towns conformed with these measures, the Hollanders evaded them by anchoring in lonely creeks where they traded directly with the natives, much to the detriment of staple-towns. Relations between the Hansa and Holland worsened and in 1438 there was a real war at sea, particularly between Lübeck and Amsterdam. The truce agreed in Copenhagen in 1441 proclaimed freedom of trade, and it now grew so rapidly that in a short time the Baltic links were the most important in Holland's trade overall. In 1443 Holland won another victory over the Hansa, including its Low Country members, in Norway, when it acquired privileges that made it easier to import grain in exchange for dried cod and timber.

All of this turned to Amsterdam's profit and allowed the town to gain the lead in Holland's trade. Its merchants and captains (we know of a hundred between 1467 and 1477) came with increasing frequency to Flanders and Brabant with Baltic and other produce. Its citizens invested in ships registered outside the town, especially in the *Waterland*. In 1477 the loading-up of foreign ships was prohibited unless they had come to unload at Amsterdam, as ships stationed in the town were forced to do. Maritime enterprise therefore developed elsewhere in the county. In 1477 Enkhuizen was the home port for thirty-two ships, and Hoorn for forty, with a good hundred barges as well.

Earlier, Dordrecht had been the main commercial centre of Holland. By 1276 the counts of Holland were vainly trying to get the Hanseatic towns to trade there rather than in Flanders, and in 1313 they exempted from tolls all goods coming directly to Dordrecht. A new opportunity to undermine the hegemony of Bruges arose when the Hansa, having declared an embargo on Flanders, shifted their 'factory' to Dordrecht in 1358. But Holland's hopes were dashed because the blockade (which was not fully observed in any case) was lifted in 1360 and the Hansa returned to Bruges. These events were repeated when a new Hanseatic embargo was levelled against Bruges in 1388–92, and the privileges earlier granted to the Hansa were then extended to the Italians, Spaniards and Portuguese. The geographical advantages that had made Dordrecht a magnificent crossroads for commerce were partly lost in the flood of 1421, and shortly thereafter Holland's annexation to Burgundy forfeited for the town its position as alternative when the Hansa quarrelled with Bruges or its princes. During a new embargo of 1451–7 the Hansa 'factory' was officially shifted to Deventer and then Utrecht, but in fact the Hanseatic merchants chose Amsterdam as their main centre. In so far as Dordrecht's heritage did not pass in its entirety to this fortunate rival, the ports and markets of the Zwin and the Scheldt were ready to take over what remained.

3 THE BRUGES MARKET

The fall of the Flemish patriciate and the rise of Bruges's local trade as a consequence of the concentration of foreign merchants in the town did not altogether ruin Flemish foreign trade. It kept up best, despite the rise of piracy in the Hundred Years War (1338–1453), in the Atlantic areas of France and Spain. Bruges took grain from Normandy, wines from Poitou, wools from Castile, which Flemish merchants bought as far inland as Toledo and Cordoba, as well as rice and sugar. The volume, however, was far from equal to the trade of foreign merchants importing to Bruges. This had unique importance in north-western Europe up to the end of the Middle Ages. Merchandise from everywhere arrived in great quantities on the Zwin. The gradual silting up of this water-way had made Damme inaccessible to sea-going trade, so Sluis ('lock') was founded in 1290 at the entry of the gulf, to replace Damme as the port of entry. There cargoes were unloaded on to lighters to be taken to Bruges.

The Brugeois were from the start fearful that the ports of entry could take over the business themselves. This threat worsened in 1322 when Sluis was given in fief to the Count of Namur, a younger son of the Flemish dynasty, who seemed anxious to develop this town at the expense of Bruges. The Brugeois resorted to violence, devastated Sluis, and forced the Count of Flanders to grant them a staple in 1323, under the terms of which Bruges became henceforth nearly the only market where all goods entering the Zwin could be sold. The merchants of Bruges exercised jealous supervision of Sluis and punished any infraction of their staple. The chief exemption concerned wine, which could be sold at Damme: at least 96,000 hectolitres of Poitou wines annually changed hands around 1380, but the revolt of the Flemish towns of 1379 caused a transfer of the trade to Middelburg, and it did not return to the Zwin.

Apart from such exemptions, Bruges was the normal centre of

business in the fourteenth century. The presence of foreigners stimulated the local artisans, a crowd of transport workers served them, town citizens boarded and lodged some of them, and innkeepers the rest. These latter, the 'hosts', had an intermediary role in business and would act as guarantors of foreigners' purchases. They were helped by brokers who were usually attached to an inn and whose mediation was mandatory. Finally the communal authorities allotted the merchants the measurers, gaugers, etc., they required.

England continued to enrich the Bruges market by her exports, especially of lead, tin, skins and wool. The Wool Staple, frequently shifted according to political and economic conditions, was set up at Bruges in 1325-6, 1340-8 and 1349-52, before it was finally moved to Calais. But wherever it was, the wool was taken to Bruges and sent on from there to the various Flemish cloth towns. English wool exports eventually declined as local manufacture began to need the wool, as the Flemish cloth trade now increasingly produced cheaper varieties made of Spanish wool, and as Holland took Flanders's place as chief outlet for English wool. Bruges's trade in wool must have fallen and the fall was not compensated by a larger volume of English textile imports which, as they competed with Flemish products, were prohibited by the mid-fourteenth century, if not before. Even wool in transit, which was permitted, was often disturbed, for Flanders was too great a power not to be involved from time to time in Anglo–French quarrels, and each time confiscation and piracy brought reprisals that disrupted the ordinary course of trade. English cloth found a warmer welcome on the Continent via Dordrecht and the Scheldt towns, and in any case its success on the home market affected Flemish cloth exports to England.

Scotland was a commercial power of much less importance. She exported to Flanders chiefly wool and cloth, though of coarser quality, which was one reason why her competition was not considered as dangerous by the Flemings, and the cloth was not prohibited until 1470. By that time the crisis of the Flemish cloth trade had affected even rural manufacture.

By far the most numerous of the foreign groups, and probably also the main one in terms of volume of business (though we have no data), was the Hanseatic group. It was as diverse in its imports as in its origins – Rhine wines, iron goods, silks and haberdashery from Cologne, linens from Westphalia, beers from Bremen, Hamburg and other nearby towns, salt from Lüneburg and woad from Thuringia, and Baltic goods in particular – cereals grown in the vast plain between Mecklenburg, Prussia and Poland; minerals from the Carpathians via the Oder and Vistula; timber and its by-products, potash, pitch and tar, skins, furs, wax and honey from the immense Russian forests, brought by merchants from Reval, Riga, Danzig, Stettin, Rostock and many other towns, but above all from Lübeck. Lübeck was also the chief centre for trade in Swedish copper and iron, Scanian herring and Norwegian dried cod. The need for salt to preserve fish and the consumption of wine in northern Europe had shown the Hansa the way to the French salt centres, and later to Portugal and Andalusia, as well as to the ports from which French wine was shipped.

The Hanseatic trading system thus went from the Gulf of Finland to the Guadalquivir. It was based essentially on four 'counters' or 'factories' set up at Novgorod, Bergen in Norway, London and Bruges, which had close links among themselves as well as with the Hanseatic towns. The Bruges 'factory' had its origin in the Low Countries' trade in cloth, which never ceased to be the main commodity. If the Germans had failed in 1252 to gain extra-territorial status for their merchant colony in Flanders, they were able, with the support of the Hanseatic towns, to exert strong pressure on Flanders, and Bruges in particular, whenever the honouring of the extension of their privileges was involved. The most effective weapon was a Hanseatic embargo, the first of which, in 1307–9, led to a temporary shift of the 'factory' to Aardenburg. It was followed by others, at Dordrecht in 1358–60 and in 1388–92, and then successively at Deventer and Utrecht from 1451–7. When Utrecht fell under Burgundian influence there was no commercial centre in the Low Countries independent of Burgundy where the 'factory' could retire, and the weapon became ineffectual.

The Italians were also important in Bruges. They brought fruits of the south – cane-sugar, silks, velvets and other luxury artefacts – and they were above all the main intermediaries between Christendom and Islam, Byzantium, and the Venetian and Genoese Levantine and Black Sea colonies, where the long trade routes from Asia ended. These goods came to Flanders by sea, sometimes on the state galleys of Venice and Genoa, as well as by land. The

Hundred Years' War caused such insecurity both at sea and on the French land routes that traffic shifted from the French to the Austrian or Swiss Alpine passes. The rapid growth of Venice rather than Genoa as trading partner of the Low Countries must have been either a cause or a consequence of this. The political divisions of Italy were reflected in the merchant colony of Bruges, where Italian merchants were split up into half a dozen 'nations', under consuls, each with its individual privileges.

The commercial role of the Catalans was similar to that of the Italians, but on a more modest scale. Portugal sent to Flanders olives, figs, sugar, cork and other agricultural goods. She included pepper from Guinea, ivory and other tropical goods once she had begun to explore the African coast in the fifteenth century. Castilian wool increasingly replaced English wool in Flemish industry, and the Cantabrian mountains were a fine source of iron ore. Like that of Italy, the political geography of the Iberian peninsula had created many Iberian 'nations' in Bruges. The foreign trade of France, a great exporter of wine and grain, was largely in the hands of the Hansa, which was also very active in Castile and Portugal, and the Italians. Hollanders were also taking an increasingly large share. Gascony, an English possesion until 1453, was also until this time a favourite market for English merchants. The French presence at Bruges was particularly characterized by Parisians who sought markets for their artisans' luxuries.

It has been assumed that the simultaneous presence of so many merchants from so many places gave Bruges the status of a 'world market', the nodal point for various parts of Europe and even the whole of the Old World, since Africa and Asia communicated with Europe through the Mediterranean. There was certainly no legal obstacle to this, for most of the non-Flemish merchants could, by virtue of their privileges, trade among themselves, although this does not seem to have happened much, and sources for the history of the market at Bruges suggest that such trade was only of minor importance. The different countries of Europe had, of course, enough direct links to do without the intermediary role of Bruges on the whole; only the countries of the Baltic littoral could perhaps find it a distinct advantage to link up there rather than use the long land route across the redoubtable Alps. The Bruges market seems to have been essentially 'national' in character, in the sense that its imports were intended mainly for

Flanders and her hinterland, and the Low Countries with their high population density and their numerous and wealthy upper class which was paralleled nowhere except in Italy. It was also the Low Countries that provided Bruges with its principal return freight of various industrial goods, among them cloth which was still popular. This 'national' trade was quite sufficient to raise Bruges to the level of a leading market in the fourteenth century.

In the cloth export trade, products from Brabant took the lead over those of the Flemish towns in the first half of the fourteenth century, but after 1350 they lost it again to the small towns and countryside of Flanders, which probably exceeded in quantity the sales of the more costly cloth from the great towns hitherto. The 10,246 pieces of cloth and serge imported from Bruges by the Teutonic Order between 1393 (immediately after an embargo had been lifted) and 1399 were mostly stuffs of quite modest price, and so was the assortment offered to the Cracow market in those years. In 1387 Venetian galleys at Palermo unloaded two thousand cloths from Courtrai, Wervik and other boroughs of the Lys valley, and ten years later another 1,740 from the same towns, belonging to Florentine, Catalan and other merchants, were awaiting shipment at Sluis on the same galleys. Between 1394 and 1410 Francesco Datini of Prato sent 1,618 pieces to his warehouses at Barcelona, Valencia and Majorca for retail.

Tradition ascribed the decline of Bruges to the silting up of the Zwin, a permanent concern for the town. With great difficulty the canal linking the town with Damme and the passage from there to Sluis was kept open. Of course, conditions worsened in time, and in the fifteenth century ships arriving at Sluis and lighters from there to Bruges more than once ran aground, but whether these events were critical is not really certain. The silting up had already happened before the Bruges market developed, and did not prevent that market from expanding. Indeed, it was increasingly usual for ships to anchor in the Walcheren roads in the fifteenth century. Their cargo would be shifted to lighters that took it to Sluis, where it was usually loaded on to carts for Bruges. This system certainly increased costs, but the fact that it was used shows that those costs were not always prohibitive.

Probably the spirit of coercion characteristic of a staple and, more generally, of medieval organization of foreign trade which predominated at Bruges – and the compulsory use of brokers, whether they were needed or not – contributed as much as, or more than, difficulties of navigation in turning the merchants away. The thirst for freedom was not only a matter for the Renaissance writings that proliferated in the fifteenth century; it was also to affect businessmen. The chief cause of the decline of Bruges seems, however, to have been the decline of the Flemish cloth trade, which had provided visitors returning from there with their most common freight. The Teutonic Order, which had exported from Flanders an annual average of 10,246 pieces of cloth between 1393 and 1399, brought in all only 1,230 pieces from 1420 to 1436. Perhaps the decline of its political power allowed Prussian merchants to escape the monopoly it had hitherto exercised; but probably this serious decline reflected above all the victory of English competition. In the Mediterranean Tuscan draperies also invaded the old markets of the Low Countries in the fifteenth century, to such an extent that Italian ships unloading at Sluis often left again under ballast and had to look elsewhere for their return freight. The Hanseatic world had, like Catalonia and the Balearic Islands, and probably also Castile, a passive balance of trade with Flanders for many years, whereas Italy and probably England, too, exported to the Low Countries more than they took from there. Unless the Low Countries could keep up cloth exports to countries which supported the commercial system of Bruges financially, the balance of Bruges trade would be disrupted. This may explain the monetary policy of the dukes of Burgundy, and the growth of rival markets such as those of Amsterdam and the Scheldt.

Of all the foreign 'nations' at Bruges, only the Hanseatic 'factory' had really linked its fate with the town's. Lübeck and other 'Wendish' towns, neighbours on the Baltic, tried to maintain it to defend the Baltic trade from Holland's competition. The Hanseatic assemblies decided in 1447 that cloth imports to the Hanseatic towns must come from Bruges alone. Conversely, a great number of goods for export were to be sent there and if, having been sent on to the fairs of Brabant, they remained unsold, they were to be returned to Bruges. Bruges's staple, a Flemish institution, was thus reinforced by a Hanseatic staple. Moreover, Hanseatic merchants could only use Hanseatic ships. The great majority of them did not observe these injunctions and the staple was a total failure, although the 'Wendish' towns kept it up until 1530. Long before then the departure of almost all other 'nations' to Antwerp left Bruges only a melancholy memory of its former splendour.

4 THE RISE OF THE SCHELDT MARKETS

The fall of the patriciate and the concentration of commerce at Bruges had weakened Ghent's foreign trade. She had adapted to the new conditions by digging a canal towards Damme in the second half of the thirteenth century, and was thus able to play an intermediary role between the Zwin and the Scheldt basin. Moreover, this river and the Lys continued to bring grain from Artois and Picardy. Since the mid-fourteenth century Ghent skippers had enjoyed a monopoly of grain transport through the town, and any foreign ship had to unload for their benefit. Their guild had even gone to war in 1357 with 730 men, but the number of its masters was limited thereafter, even though there were not enough to manage the traffic. If none of these masters was available, then an 'unfranchised' shipper might be used, i.e. one not registered in the guild. Ghent substituted shipping and grain traffic for the cloth industry as the basis of its economy. Not surprisingly, Bruges's project of digging a diversionary canal from the Lys above Ghent to the Zwin to improve the waterway system on the latter put Ghent into such a fright that the town rose in 1379. After six years' civil war, the danger was banished.

In the thirteenth century nothing could have foretold the rising fortunes of Antwerp. A little sea trade, especially with England, and a market essentially limited to foodstuffs for the area between the Scheldt and the Meuse, was all it had. The trade was based on a staple for fish, oats and salt going up the Scheldt, which had to be sold on arrival at Antwerp. Malines was exempted from the obligation in 1238 and in 1358 even got the staple in Antwerp's stead. After much litigation the dispute was resolved in 1414-15 in such a way that the staple ceased to be a reality. If in the outcome the fish trade of Antwerp developed on an inter-regional level whereas that of Malines remained limited to Brabant, the cause was not the constraint of the staple. Malines had not disappeared from large-scale European trade, but figured there especially as an exporter of cloth. Malines had a cloth hall at Paris by 1334 at the latest, and in the next century was still represented at the fairs of Chalon-sur-Saône. After 1340 this was also true for Frankfort, where there was a Malines hall a century later. Merchants from

Malines appeared around 1400 in Danzig and Torún; in 1407 in Bergen in Norway and after 1470 in Breslau.

The trade of Louvain and Brussels remained quite active in the fourteenth century. The Louvain drapers had counters in Boston in 1315 and at the fairs of Provins in 1346, and their counterparts in Brussels took over part of Douai's hall in Paris in 1325. However, their entrepreneurial spirit gradually diminished when their industry followed that of the Flemish towns into decline, and, as in Flanders, their foreign trade gave way to visits by foreign merchants to Brabant. By 1377 these foreigners bought 5,400 pieces of cloth at the Louvain cloth hall, as against 760 sold by men of the town abroad: in 1420 the figures were respectively eight hundred and 390. It was apparently in a desperate attempt to stop the decline that the Louvain drapers acquired a hall at the Frankfort fairs by 1446 at the latest. This produced no great success, for only 89 and a half pieces were sold in 1467–8.

The first signs of Antwerp's brilliant destiny date from 1296. Edward I of England set up the Wool Staple there for political considerations but also with a view to the growing consumption of wool in Brabantine industry. It was shifted elsewhere after only a year, but returned to Antwerp in 1315–18, and 1338–40; and wherever it was, Antwerp had clearly become the port for wool imports for the duchy and further afield, too, perhaps. The market which developed there attracted other goods and other merchants, Brabantine, Rhenish and even Italian. Pegolotti, author of *Pratica della Mercatura,* the most famous manual of foreign trade in the Middle Ages, managed the Antwerp house and bank of the Bardi in 1315. The dukes of Brabant stimulated this trade by concessions of privileges to foreign 'nations', and especially by developing the commercial infrastructure of Antwerp by instituting, probably in 1320, two fairs to be held annually, one at Whitsun and the other in October. The lord of Bergen-op-Zoom, twenty miles down-river on the eastern Scheldt, which was then the river's chief branch, quickly followed this example and instituted two fairs in that town, at Easter and in November.

Meanwhile the movement of trade also favoured Zeeland. In the thirteenth century the modest towns of Zeeland, lost in the midst of polder pasture-land – Middelburg and Veere on the island of Walcheren, Zierikzee on the island of Schouwen – had a meagre trade of regional character and some fisheries. The decline of

Flemish foreign trade may have stimulated some commercial navigation, of which the fishing fleets were, as in Holland, the first instrument. Middelburg and Zierikzee were exempted from the tolls of Holland and the staple of Dordrecht in the fourteenth century, which indicates some progress in commerce, and was also a further stimulant. Ships and merchants from Zeeland could be encountered in increasing numbers from the Baltic to the French Atlantic coast and especially in England. In 1393 a ship from Veere was loaded in England by Italians, with a cargo for Pisa. Moreover, the roads that opened at Middelburg – half-way between the Baltic and the French salt or wine ports – also tempted Hanseatic merchants to winter there. Walcheren tended to replace Sluis as a terminus for sea trade going to Bruges.

It was inevitable that Middelburg, over which the Flemish authorities had no control, would constitute a market independent of Bruges. The wine trade shifted to there, and so did the English Wool Staple, in 1348–9 and from early in 1383 until March 1388, during the troubles in Flanders, 21,500 *sarplers* of wool – perhaps 5,500 tonnes – went through Middelburg. There could hardly be a better place for English cloth than this town so close to Bruges where it was prohibited, and by the 1380s it seems to have become the chief market for English cloth in the Low Countries, perhaps even in the whole continent. Given the attitudes of the age, it was natural for Middelburg to foster this spontaneous growth by enforcing a staple. In 1405 all merchandise entering the western Scheldt was obliged to unload at Middelburg, where it became liable to the taxes of the town, as well as those of the Count of Holland and Zeeland.

By an irony of fate, at the very moment when this privilege was granted, the storms that came one after another from 1400 on – of which the tidal-wave of 1404 was the greatest – considerably deepened the western Scheldt, which gradually became the main branch of the river. It was now possible to navigate with impunity, and without unloading at the Walcheren roads, between England and the fairs of Antwerp and Bergen-op-Zoom. Meanwhile, the Antwerp fairs had prospered. In 1358 Antwerp had acquired the staple for dairy produce and other agricultural goods from Holland. The output of Holland's and Zeeland's fisheries found there one of its most promising markets, and Antwerp was becoming a market for Mediterranean goods in particular, now that Italian traders preferred to use the Swiss or Austrian passes, from where the goods went north to one of the towns on the Rhine. These Rhenish towns, and Cologne in particular, had for a long time had very close links with Brabant, which probably took more Rhine wine than Flanders where there was greater competition from French growths. The Rhenish towns increasingly took their fish from Antwerp. The Mediterranean goods which came along the Rhine needed these towns as intermediaries on the last stage of their journey to the Low Countries. They were, of course, directed to Antwerp. By 1400 Brabant and its neighbouring lands to the east bought their spices at the Scheldt fairs.

More and more merchants came there, and this offered the English greater opportunities than anywhere else in the Zeeland archipelago, which was more difficult for their cloth trade's continental clients to reach. By 1415 merchants from Cologne were selling English cloth in central and southern Germany, and it was commonly known by then that a toll levied on ships bound for Antwerp or Bergen profited heavily from the four fairs, and especially from their English visitors who had shifted the bulk of their trade there. Since neither Antwerp nor Bergen had a serious cloth trade to protect these English traders were all the more welcome. Even the measures to protect Flemish draperies, which were extended in 1428 to Holland and Zeeland once Philip the Good took over their government, had hardly any effect, for Middelburg evaded them by getting a safe conduct for the English. When it was renewed in 1434 the prohibition was also applied to Brabant, to which Philip succeeded in 1430. This time it seems to have been more strictly enforced, which probably explains both the revolt of Middelburg in 1434 and the astonishing fall of English broadcloth exports from nearly 14,000 to just over 2,000 between 1433–4 and 1434–5: the Low Countries were clearly already the main market for them. But the zeal of ducal officials was usually short-lived and this was probably the case with the prohibition edicts of 1447 and 1464 too. English exports again fell from 31,000 pieces in 1463–4 to 11,800 in 1464–5, but with the accession of Charles the Bold in 1467 the alliance between York and Burgundy enabled English exports to grow. Since the mid-fifteenth century the finishing of English cloth had become common in Antwerp, and the imports were all the more welcome.

The merchant colonies in Bruges had to adapt to the success of the fairs. Around 1400 almost all foreigners resident there, and locals involved in business, attended the Antwerp and Bergen fairs. Gradually the fairs assumed a role in the commercial life of the Bruges market that was virtually equal to that of Bruges itself, and Brugeois traders did a brisk business there that was second only to that of the English.

But a new force in central Europe was also contributing to the rise of the Brabantine fairs. The Alpine traffic had enriched the citizens of the German towns at the mouths of the passes, and they had invested capital both in the production of linen in the nearby areas and in the prospecting and mining of mineral resources in the mountains that stretched in a giant arc from Tyrol through Bohemia and the Carpathian Mountains into Transylvania. The output of these enterprises had at first gone through Cologne and other Rhenish towns, for which upper Germany had always been a sphere of influence, but the merchants of Swabia and Franconia soon crowded to the Frankfort fairs, the Rhenish centres and eventually to the Low Countries themselves. They appeared at Antwerp in the first years of the fifteenth century and gradually wrested a growing part of the trade between the Brabantine fairs and central Germany from the Rhenish merchants, with whom they had often originally been associated. The fact that after 1465 Burgundian monetary policy overvalued silver, which they produced, gave a stimulant to this trade. Whereas they had played only a modest part at Bruges, they became one of the pillars of the commerce of the Brabantine fairs.

Other differences soon emerged between the new trading system and the earlier one. There was never any question of Bergen's or Antwerp's submitting this trade to a staple, imposing on it the presence of unnecessary brokers, etc. Middelburg had tried at first in 1435 to extend its staple to the eastern Scheldt, but at the same time had allowed merchants to buy their freedom for a tax of 5 per cent. In 1447 the town displayed a sense, rare for the period, of the real needs of trade in spontaneously renouncing the staple and, shortly afterwards, the tax that was the alternative to it as well; and some other medieval vestiges of its commercial organization, such as the prohibition on direct trade with foreigners or the compulsory use of 'hosts' and brokers, also fell into disuse. The supremacy of the Brabantine fairs in the Scheldt's commercial system became so obvious that Middelburg found it profitable to act as an outer harbour – indeed, she had one herself at Arnemuiden – as it had already done in the case of Bruges. Many ship's masters of their own accord preferred to unload rather than go up a Scheldt still encumbered with shallows. The river trade became a major livelihood for the sailors of Walcheren, without affecting their maritime trade, which went on so long as the Walcheren roads were one of the important stages for the trade of other countries. The end of the Hundred Years War gave a surprising fillip to their coastal trade, and in 1478–9 more than a hundred Breton ships brought salt and wine in exchange for herring. The borough of Veere had particularly close links with Scotland, from which it bought wool, skins and cloth. This was because one of its lords, a member of the most powerful family in Zeeland, had married a daughter of James I of Scotland. Louis XI of France, who thus became his brother-in-law, also gave privileges to traders from Veere in his kingdom.

From the outset Antwerp was more favoured as a principal market than Bergen as it had a larger population and was more frequented, as well as being nearer the most populous areas of the Low Countries, the Rhenish hinterland, and hence the lands beyond. Moreover, as the direct possession of powerful sovereigns, it could count on greater support from them than Bergen could get from its lords, however exalted in lineage. Finally changes that occurred in the bed of the Scheldt were to the detriment of Bergen, since ships from the high seas or Holland no longer had to pass it before coming to Antwerp. Bergen's survival can be explained by the conditions of trading at the fairs. As those of Bergen preceded or immediately followed those of Antwerp, they lengthened the time available for business which had been limited originally to the duration of the fairs. Moreover Bergen several times acted as a refuge when merchants had grievances against Antwerp and put pressure on the town by boycotting its fairs. However, Antwerp rapidly outgrew these limitations and became a permanent centre of trade. In 1465, when Louis XI organized the Lyons fairs that he had recently established on the model of Antwerp's fairs, and in 1470 when he dreamed of diverting Antwerp's trade to France so as to deprive his Burgundian rival of this source of wealth, the name of Bergen was not even mentioned. The Bergen fairs did remain in existence, in the end, only to mark the term of payment for dealings that had been concluded in the great commercial metropolis of Antwerp.

5 Money and Credit

I MONEY

The needs of trade had provoked the minting of silver groats and by 1300 gold coinage was reintroduced as well in Flanders and Brabant, on the model of the Florentine florin and its French imitations. The revival was premature, probably because there was not enough gold: it depended on the balance of trade and had to come from the African fringe of the Mediterranean. Gold coins were minted again only after 1325 in Flanders, 1330 in Brabant, 1340 in Hainault, 1350 in Liège and 1388 in Holland, where gold coining was clearly a reflection of attempts to involve Dordrecht in large-scale European trade. Thereafter the mints produced gold coinage virtually without interruption. Silver coins continued to predominate, however, and were adapted for purposes of circulation. After 1373 Flanders struck double groats, which were rapidly taken up elsewhere, and in 1466 quadruple groats were minted in all the Burgundian Low Countries.

The end of the Middle Ages was a period of great monetary instability. The most obvious cause was the coexistence of a gold with a silver standard, between which no lasting relationship could be achieved. The value of both foreign and local coins was officially fixed, but the rate on the free market fluctuated independently of the official one. Differences of weight or alloy led men who knew about coins to hoard the best. To prevent the trouble this caused, the import of base coins or the export of native coins was often prohibited, but sooner or later the authorities had to adapt their rates to the market. Flanders, Brabant and England agreed to adopt a common monetary system in 1339 for the sake of trade, but it did not outlive the political agreement that had brought it about, even though formally re-established from 1384 to 1396. Still, the transactions of trade did, to some degree and without formal agreement, make a particular coinage supreme outside its original principality. Brabant and Holland usually adopted the Flemish coinage, Liège, Guelders, Utrecht and the north-east, the Rhenish florin, though there was often some inconsistency.

Monetary problems worsened when gold and silver temporarily ran out. The gold stock of the European economy depended on Europe's balance of trade with Moslem Africa, and on the Moslems' own balance with black Africa beyond the Sahara; both of these were subject to short-term fluctuation. The exhaustion of the European silver mines was also a constant, which added its deflationary effect to the long-term crisis of the age. It is significant that mints were set up as far as possible to the east of a prince's lands, the more easily to capture silver from central Europe, which was then its chief source. Philip the Bold, for instance, established a mint at Malines in 1388, and even one at Valkenburg, east of Maastricht, in 1389. The princes also tried to attract for their coins the particular metal they lacked by overvaluing it. They applied this policy to silver in the fourteenth century, to gold until 1465, and then to silver again.

These measures inevitably affected economic and social affairs. The revaluing of silver probably had only minor consequences for large-scale trade, which was paid for in gold; and in any case its agents, used to dealing at free-market rates, hardly concerned themselves with official ones. On the other hand, for a country largely dependent for its food on foreign countries, the overvaluing of silver amounted to a reduction in the wage-earner's purchasing power in silver prices. It both stimulated the export industries, particularly the old cloth trade of Flanders and Brabant in the fourteenth century, and fomented social discord among the workmen who were victims of the policy. The overvaluation of gold would raise a product's cost and aggravate the industrial problems until wages had again been lowered: hence the nadir of the depression in the first sixty years of the fifteenth century.

If supplies of precious metals had a profound effect on long-term movements in the economy, the condition of the coinage had short-term effects that contemporaries understood better – and not just in the Low Countries. It was not only that many pieces, struck by hand, were irregular in shape and invited clipping, which made the coins still less equal. It was also a matter of the handling of the mints and the chicanery of the princes. They leased their mints, until about 1420 generally to Italians who had a high reputation as experts in finance. The alloy and weight, as well as the seigniorage (the tax levied by the prince on the metal used) were usually prescribed, and sometimes the maximum price, too, at which the metal could be bought. Of course the coiner bought it as cheaply as he could and took his profit from the difference between his purchase price, his own costs in striking and seigniorage on the one hand, and the value of the coins on the other. As the lease did not prescribe which coins were to be made, the coiners struck coins of types that gave the greatest profit, reducing or even halting their output of others, without regard to the economy's requirements.

The princes were mainly concerned with the income from seigniorage and did not hesitate to raise it by frequent use of their undisputed prerogative of decreasing the weight or alloy. Louis de Male, Count of Flanders from 1346 to 1384, changed the silver groat no less than fourteen times in his reign, during which a total of 65,000 kilograms of gold and 240,000 of silver were minted in his workshops. It was mainly the same monetary stock that was involved. The current coinage would be demonetized and melted down, to reenter circulation in another form. But the seigniorage he got came to about half a million *livres parisis*, or between a fifth and a sixth of all treasury income in the period. Given the lack of silver, the deterioration of the coinage that this involved led inevitably to a return of the devaluation that the relative stability of the thirteenth century had halted. Between 1318 and 1346 the fine weight of the Flemish silver groat fell from 4.55 to 2.15 grams. On Louis de Male's death in 1384 it was only 0.97 grams and, when Charles the Bold died in 1477, only 0.61.

Both the instability of coins and their great variety soon led men to express value in a fixed coinage. Some coins had ceased to be minted and were therefore unalterable – the old silver groat of St Louis (1226–70), for example, or the imperial *écus* of Philip VI of France (1328–50) or Louis of Bavaria (1314–47), which were all gold. Their universally recognized value permitted conversion into current coinage according to its fine weight. Other standard coins were related to pieces still in circulation and their value was subject to variation. In Brabant several gold pieces played this role in the fourteenth century. They were, of course, more stable than the silver coins in which the bulk of payments was made in everyday life. In Flanders the silver groat was the most popular standard coin from the fourteenth century on. Brabant adopted it as such before 1400, probably because Flemish coins were much used in the duchy, which had close links with the Flemish economy.

Business men in a wider context tried nonetheless to escape the uncertainties of the local monetary circulation by expressing their sums in their own bills of exchange in a coinage of international reputation, always a gold coinage, a practice which became widespread in the later Middle Ages.

2 CREDIT

As use of the fair-bill declined, there was scope in Flanders for the financial techniques the Italians had developed for trade, which were thus the first stage in the extension of Mediterranean practices to the Low Countries. One of the first of such practices was the use of legal deeds by which one party promised to repay a sum, that he acknowledged having borrowed, at a later date, in a different place and in different coinage. Frequently the sum repayable was higher than that originally received, for it included the interest prohibited by canon law. In the case of *cambium nauticum*, the repayment was conditional on the safe arrival of a certain ship or cargo. These deeds were widely used in commerce between Italy and Flanders from the later thirteenth century until around 1320, especially in Genoa, where many have survived.

The formal, prolix style of these bills was not suited to business life. As the merchants' sophistication increased, they made use of clerks in their affairs who conducted business by letter. Gradually the letter which accompanied the deed came to replace it as a 'letter' or 'bill' of exchange, in which four parties were involved: the deliverer, the taker, the drawee banker, and the payee. Such payments would be made, not in cash but by credit transfer. A bill could thus be used to settle a debt by assigning it to a creditor. As yet there was no discounting, but a bill could be sold before its term at a price determined by the going exchange rates.

In the fourteenth century Bruges became perhaps the most active exchange and money market outside Italy. The scene of such transactions was the public square, called the *Beurze* or *Bourse* after an inn of the same name run by the van der Beurze family and situated near the consular offices of Genoa, Venice and Florence, where most of the Italian merchants usually met at certain times of day to discuss affairs. Through the intermediaries of Antwerp and Amsterdam, Bruges's successors, the Bourse in Bruges gave its name to all exchange or money markets on the European continent. It was subject to seasonal fluctuations. Money was rare before the Bruges fair and the departure of the galleys for Italy; in the meantime, the purchases of foreign merchants put considerable sums into circulation. Those familiar with the Bourse also knew, for instance, that it was more profitable to send money to Italy via Barcelona than directly because Catalonia's favourable balance of trade with Flanders had built up accounts there. There were frequent manipulations of the money market, leading to temporary restrictions. The Bruges money market had influence far beyond the Low Countries. The London market was closely linked with it; and Germany, Poland and the Scandinavian kingdoms, whose financial organization was backward, carried on their international transactions at Bruges. The return of taxes levied by the Holy See on the holders of benefices in these countries was handled by Hanseatic merchants who converted the taxes into products which they sent to Bruges. The money earned there was deposited with the papal bankers in Bruges to be credited to their correspondents in Avignon.

One common form of speculation was the swapping of bills of exchange for the same amount between a banker in Bruges and another in Italy, in the expectation that a profit could be made out of the difference between the exchange rates in the two places. This led many bankers to draw bills of exchange purely with a view to the profits of arbitrage. Also merchants who would not or could not sell in market conditions were able to get money to finance their purchases by drawing bills of exchange. But many of the bills did not spring from trade at all. A secretary at the papal court at Avignon drew the income from his prebend in Antwerp by bill of exchange on Rome; a student at the university of Pavia collected his pocket money by bill on Milan; while in 1440 Philip the Good sent the large ransom for his brother-in-law, Charles of Orleans, who had been captured at Agincourt in 1415, by bill on London.

The Italian bankers were much in demand in public finance. Trade with Italy, in which most of them took part, built up large balances in Flanders, which could be lent out. To get such loans, the princes often offered the bankers lucrative public appointments for which they were supposed to be particularly skilled, such as the management of mints or the receiving of certain taxes or tolls. The first loans were subscribed at Bruges in the later thirteenth century, but until around 1330 their repayment was still made in Paris or at the Champagne fairs. But these fairs soon lost their financial role, as had happened with the Arras patricians and the Templars whose order had been dissolved at Philip the Fair's request in 1312. Thereafter the Italians dominated the capital market, with a few Catalan firms in their wake. Among the Italians, the Sienese held first place until about 1325–30, and then the Florentine bankers took over, especially the famous Bardi and Perruzzi. Balducci Pegolotti managed the Bardi agency in Flanders in 1315, and Giovanni Villani, the famous chronicler and friend of Dante, the *Perruches* bank in Bruges from 1306 to 1308. The discomfiture of the two houses in 1343, a result of dealings with the king of England, weakened Florentine finance so seriously that for almost a century the lead passed to Luccans. One of these, Dino Rapondi, advanced the 200,000 florins needed to ransom John the Fearless, who had been captured by Sultan Bayezid after the disaster of Nicopolis in 1396; another, Giovanni Arnolfini, lent large sums to Philip the Good and the town of Bruges, and is familiar from the Van Eyck portraits.

In the fifteenth century the Florentines again won the lead. In 1439 Cosimo de' Medici, who had just taken over the government of Florence, established an agency at Bruges where his bank had earlier made use of correspondents. In 1465 the branch was entrusted to Tommaso Portinari, a descendant of the brother of Dante's Beatrice. He largely financed the wars of Charles the Bold, and on the duke's death in 1477 his loans amounted to 13,000, perhaps even 16,000 pounds of groats. Justly dismayed at this, Lorenzo the Magnificent wound up the Bruges agency in 1480. In Antwerp in this period there were only the beginnings of a money market but, significantly, merchants from upper Germany played a modest role in the market by 1409, together with the town and the Lombards.

Ecclesiastical strictures against payment of interest were fully maintained, but they could always be side-stepped. The rates of bank loans varied according to supply and demand, and also according to the character of the borrower. The main impression is that they were generally higher in the fourteenth century than in the thirteenth – perhaps because of the dearth of currency. The credit of princes was singularly low. In 1275 the Countess of Flanders had to pay interest of 45 to 50 per cent per annum; the Count of Guelders 50 to 54 per cent in 1347. In 1360 Duchess Joan of Brabant, who paid only 25.33 per cent, was more fortunate, and so was Mary of Burgundy in 1477 when she borrowed at 16 to 20 per cent against her gold and silver plate. The large towns of Flanders and Brabant were, of course, safer debtors, and never had to pay over 33.3 per cent; on occasion it was as little as 10 per cent.

The towns sometimes borrowed in the short-term on bills of exchange and sometimes used the expedient of buying goods on credit and selling them for cash: Ghent and Bruges did this from 1350 to about 1425. In 1425, too, Duke John IV of Brabant financed a military expedition by buying a quantity of spices and English wool in Bruges on credit, and re-selling them for cash, in some cases to the same people from whom he had bought the goods. According to the cases we know of, the losses in such dealings were tantamount to interest payments of between 15 and 26 per cent. The issue of annuities, to which the towns and other institutions increasingly had recourse, was a less heavy burden for debtors than financiers' loans. They were therefore preferred. Perpetual annuities, a favourite investment nowadays among religious institutions, were least expensive of all. Some were available at 10 per cent in the later thirteenth century, and at 6 or 5.5 per cent in the fifteenth. Life annuities remained at 12.5 per cent in Ghent around 1350, as in the later thirteenth century, and they were being sold at 9 or 10 per cent fifty years later in Antwerp and Louvain. Those for two or three lives were even cheaper. They had the inestimable advantage of liquidating themselves at their term.

The middle classes happily put their money into annuities, which, supported by mortgages, could also be used to borrow money. By the later Middle Ages there were few houses and lands that did not have such annuities attached to them. But credit could also be obtained from pawnbrokers on the security of goods or, more rarely, of personal promises. This sector of credit was still dominated by Lombards, most of them, as before, from Asti or Chieri, who were often grouped into companies that ran a number of shops simultaneously, especially after 1400. By 1309 there were shops in seventy-seven places between the Meuse and the Scheldt. After the promulgation of the canons of the Council of Vienna in 1317, which revived the denunciation of usury of 1311, the Lombards were pursued by the law in many areas, and the pawnshop in St Truiden was even sacked by the mob, but Pope John xxii (1316–24) moderated the zeal of the persecutors and the trade of the Lombards became rather less dangerous. In Brabant the towns allowed licensed usurers to include interest quite openly, and fixed a maximum. Until the early fourteenth century Flanders generally prohibited usurers, but lessened the effects of this apparent severity by imposing fines only from time to time, so that the Lombards were really operating quite freely in exchange for a tax. The permitted rate of interest was usually two pennies per pound per week, or 43.33 per cent per annum, but in 1303 the Antwerp Lombards were allowed to charge foreigners three pennies, and in 1462 this was regarded as the normal rate for all debtors. In 1477 Mary of Burgundy fixed it at one penny in her lands, but the effectiveness of this measure is open to doubt. In Bruges usurers came not only from Lombardy but also from the northern fringes of the French-speaking world, especially Valenciennes, Tournai, Lille and Saint-Omer. Since the fifteenth century only non-licensed usurers had been persecuted, but Charles the Bold closed the pawnshops of his states in 1473 with the sole aim of extracting a large sum in exchange for a new ten-year permit.

The profession of money-changer was generally reserved to citizens of the towns. They were indispensable auxiliaries in business because of the great variety of coinages in circulation, including those brought to the great commercial centres by foreign merchants, and they helped the authorities every time they demonetized certain coins and withdrew them. As depositors for the ready cash of individuals, the changers could also regulate payments by transfers of accounts in their books. In fact payment by transfer or cash was used only in small purchases or if there was reason to mistrust the debtor. Normally commercial debts were settled at a term, by signature of a note of hand or bill of exchange, but the use of these latter was really restricted to merchants of Mediterranean origin, who could call on their colleagues in banking. Other people used promissory notes and often supplemented them with one or more guarantees. These promises could be transferred to third parties, and were soon being made out to the bearer. They were probably settled sooner or later by transfers in the money-changers' books. Two sets of these for Bruges have survived. Those of Colard de Marke contain 1,100 current accounts for the period Christmas 1368 to 20 May 1369, for citizens of Bruges and foreign merchants during their stay. As he was not the only changer, obviously such services were in great demand. Most current accounts bore no interest, but others, opened in the name of orphans or those without legal standing, had a fixed term and drew 10 per cent per annum. Some changers at least, knowing how improbable it was that all their accounts should be withdrawn simultaneously, incurred the risk of investing part of the money, either to farm a communal excise or, probably more often, to advance money to clients. We do not know how far they could profit from such dealings, but, as there was no system of discounting, there was a danger that clients in a crisis might withdraw their deposits while debtors would not be able to pay. Between 1366 and spring 1368 Colard de Marke's loans amounted to between 25 and 29 per cent of his deposits; by Christmas 1368 they amounted to 58 per cent, and in May 1369, when he seems to have gone bankrupt, 46 per cent. When his colleague Guillaume Ruyelle went bankrupt in 1370 his advances were twice his deposits.

The changers had an interest in devaluation of the coinage, which reduced their obligations towards depositors and brought a large quantity of demonetized coins into their coffers. Understandably, it was in the fourteenth century that these activities reached their peak. When the dukes of Burgundy tried to effect a policy of stabilization of the coinage, they ascribed its problems to changers whom they suspected of exporting the valuable coins of their mints in exchange for inferior ones. They tried to reduce the changers' activity to manual exchange, forbidding them in 1433, 1469 and 1489 to act as depositories or bankers. Indeed, the deposit banks gradually declined and had altogether disappeared by the later fifteenth century. This may have been a result of ducal decrees, but the doubtful efficacy of legal measures in the economy of that period should not be forgotten. Possibly it was the rise of Italian high finance that eliminated minor finance: the problem remains to be solved. In any event, once Antwerp became the chief market of the Low Countries, the mechanism of payments remained considerably clumsier than at Bruges in the fourteenth century, at the height of its commercial and financial activity.

PART THREE

The Dawn of the Modern Economy: The Golden Age of Antwerp and Amsterdam *1400–1670*

1 *Population*

The death of Charles the Bold in 1477, and still more, that of Mary of Burgundy in 1482, opened an epoch of disorder and revolt against the monarchy, represented by the rule of the duchess's widower, Maximilian of Habsburg. Elsewhere in Europe a recovery from the economic crisis had set in, but the crisis seemed to oppress the highly populous areas of the Low Countries even more harshly than before. Flanders, Brabant and Holland were ravaged by armed bands of both sides, and the endemic insecurity made the country people seek refuge behind the town walls. It was only after Maximilian's suppression of the various revolts and the return of peace in the 1490s that economic recovery went ahead, encouraging expansion of the population which also stimulated the economy.

A Brabantine census of 1526 enables us to measure the extent of the progress within one generation. Since 1496 the number of households had risen from 75,343 to 97,013 – nearly one-third. Brabant's population was estimated in 1526 at about 450,000, more than in any previous census. The rural areas, where the number of households increased from 45,922 to 63,464, experienced the largest growth (38.2 per cent), partly because people returned to the now peaceful villages and partly because economic conditions improved. Good agricultural prices and markets for rural handicrafts encouraged the establishment of new families and the birth-rate rose. There was still much local variation but, overall, the population of the Brabantine countryside recovered to its level of 1437.

123

The small towns remained far behind the countryside, with a growth of only 13 per cent. Their export trade had not recovered, and some towns did not even return to 1496 levels of population. Only those whose situation on the roads to Antwerp – Helmond, Eindhoven, Breda, Bergen-op-Zoom, Steenbergen and Lier – placed them within reach of the metropolis saw a 25.4 per cent increase in the number of households from 1496 to 1526. The four large towns of Brabant were also varied in pattern. The return of refugees to the countryside deprived them of their temporary

NUMBER OF HOUSEHOLDS IN MAJOR TOWNS IN BRABANT

	Antwerp	Bois-le-Duc	Brussels	Louvain
1496	6,586	3,456	5,750	3,069
1526	8,479	4,211	5,953	3,299

recruits. Louvain, relying only on its citizens for growth, increased by a mere 7.5 per cent although it had a famous university where Erasmus taught from 1517 to 1521; Brussels, where the governor general's court returned (from Malines) only after 1530, rose by 3.5 per cent. By contrast, the population of Bois-le-Duc, a satellite of Antwerp, rose by 21.8 per cent, despite the proximity of Guelders, and Antwerp itself rose by 28.9 per cent to 38,000. Perhaps the usual factor for conversion, 4.5 persons per household, should be increased in the case of an exceptionally flourishing town like Antwerp, which must have had a large number of bachelors in lodging houses. Calculations based on a factor of 5 or 5.5 suggest that Antwerp's population would have been between 42,000 and 46,000 people, i.e. a growth rate of 40 or 53 per cent, even higher than the rural rates. Around 1560 the town undertook a new census which gave a population of 90,000. With a population of this size, Antwerp was among the largest towns in Europe.

In the countryside of Hainault the number of households rose from 29,212 in 1458 to 34,286 in 1540, or 18.7 per cent, but the lowest point of the graph was probably reached in the later fifteenth century here as well. The number of town households was estimated at 14,000 for 1540, giving the whole province a total population of some 216,000. An incomplete census of 1560 suggested a slight decline, probably because this frontier area had been devastated several times during the wars with France. Several censuses were also held in the countryside of Luxembourg. Apart from the capital, there were only a few over-sized hamlets in this vast but highly wooded and thinly populated province, although they were defined legally as towns and had a corresponding fiscal status different from that of the countryside that provided the census figures. If we assume the 'towns' to have made up a fifth of the rural population, the total number of inhabitants must have risen from about 68,000 in 1501 to about 95,000 in 1554.

Of the northern provinces, only the county of Holland was subjected to two fiscal censuses, but there were gaps, different in the two cases. It has been suggested that the number of 27,350 households reviewed in 1496 for two-thirds of the county should be increased by half, which would give 185,000 people; including some 15,000 for clergy, nobles, and Jews, who were not reviewed in the census, the figure amounts to about 200,000. The census of 1514 left out only one-seventh of Holland, and if we increase the resulting figure of 45,857 households in the same proportion, there must have been some 260,000 inhabitants, i.e. an increase of thirty per cent in eighteen years.

According to the enquiry of 1514, the most populous towns in Holland were Leyden and Gouda, with about 14,300 and 14,200 inhabitants respectively, but because of their industrial troubles, the population of neither had risen since 1496. However, Amsterdam, with 13,500, had gained 31 per cent and caught up Haarlem, the centre, like Delft, of an important brewing industry, which had 11,700. Dordrecht, formerly the chief town of Holland, had fallen victim to the decline of its staple and had only 11,200. Among the lesser towns the satellites of Amsterdam, which lived from the shipping of its merchants and ship owners, made the most spectacular advance. Rotterdam, though still small, with a population of only 5,200, rose by 17 per cent. By 1550 Amsterdam had become by far the largest town in Holland, with 30,000 inhabitants, while Dordrecht had fallen to ten thousand.

There is not much information for the rest of the Low Countries. Extrapolating from the results of a census in 1511–14 that has survived for half of Friesland, the whole area must have had about 75,000 inhabitants. The Veluwe had about 36,000 in 1526. For Flanders we know only that the population of Ypres had risen from 7,600 in 1491 to 9,500 in 1506 and that in 1557 the castellany of Oudenaarde contained 4,372 households, or about 19,400 people, at forty-seven per square kilometre. This density was slightly above the forty-four of Brabant in 1526 and of Hainault in 1540, or the forty of Holland in 1514 but was greater than the twenty-two people per square kilometre in Friesland and seventeen in the Veluwe; Luxembourg in 1554 did not even have a density of 5.5 people per square kilometre. In 1544 Malines contained 3,860 taxable households, so that, including paupers, clergy and monasteries, it must have had about 25,000 inhabitants. The population of other Dutch towns has been estimated from the density of buildings around 1560, as shown in the remarkably detailed sketches of Jacobus van Deventer, but the conjectured figures are an obvious exaggeration.

In 1566 a courtier close to the governess, Margaret of Parma, put the population of the Spanish Netherlands (i.e. excluding Liège) at ten million. The Venetian ambassador, Francesco Badoero, estimated it at three million in 1557, which once again displayed the Venetian capacity to arrive at reasonably accurate figures from quite fragmentary data, for the estimates of modern historians, though based for much of the area on mere impressions, tend to bear him out. Nowadays, the same region contains eight times as many people, but there is nothing exceptional in a rise of this kind in western Europe: England, for one, had a similar increase.

Contemporaries were particularly struck by the importance of the towns in the economic and social structure of the more active regions of the Low Countries. If the repopulation of the countryside reduced the number of people living in towns in Brabant from 40 per cent in 1496 to 34.5 per cent in 1526, the corresponding figures for Holland, where cattle were raised, and fewer agricultural labourers were required, indicate that urbanization increased to 52 per cent as early as 1514. The registers of admission to citizenship confirm the attraction of the towns. Antwerp was easily in the lead with 15,609 registrations between 1533 and 1600, most of them in the first half of the period. Middelburg had 6,888 between 1477 and 1567; Bruges 1,438 from 1479 to 1496 and 1,063 from 1530 to 1588; Leyden 1,645 from 1480 to 1574. A larger proportion of people than before came from other towns since the countryside now offered better prospects for subsistence. A new attitude also emerged which encouraged mobility. The

Low Countries with their striking prosperity quickly won the reputation all over Europe of a promised land, and were a magnet for all fortune-seekers.

Poverty had not, of course, completely disappeared. It was always there in the past, especially in a period of rapid growth, because the creation of new employment was often slower than the rise of available labour, the abundance of which also tended to keep wages low in an inflationary period, much to the profit of entrepreneurs and merchants. The prosperity was thus a class phenomenon, although it appears that, even for the common people, circumstances must have been better in the Low Countries than elsewhere. Censuses for Brabant and Hainault early in the sixteenth century show, still, a high number of pauper households, but comparison with the earlier situation (see pages 63–4) does reveal encouraging features.

In Hainault in 1540 26.9 per cent of rural households were exempted from taxes for reasons of poverty, but we are not able to compare these figures with earlier ones, and the same is true, still more regrettably, of Antwerp and its administrative district. Their methods of comparison differ in turn from those of other Brabantine administrative districts. In those of Brussels and Bois-le-Duc, pauper households had declined by 36.3 per cent and 29.7 per cent respectively between 1496 and 1526, and by 35.8 per cent and 16.5 per cent as against 1437. Only in the district of Louvain had pauper households risen, from 38.6 per cent in 1480 to 41.5 per cent, but since 1496, it should be stressed, there had been an astonishing rise of 80.4 per cent in the population. By contrast, the towns in general showed an increase of poverty, at Brussels from 17.1 per cent in 1496 to 21 per cent in 1526, at Louvain from 18.3 per cent in 1480 to 21.7 per cent, at Bois-le-Duc from 29.6 per cent in 1496 to 34.4 per cent. Unlike their chief town, the little places in the district of Bois-le-Duc, Eindhoven and Helmond, profited from the rise of Antwerp and poverty declined, from 24.8 per cent of the households in 1437 to 19.4 per cent, and those of the Louvain area, though for reasons that are less clear, fell from 36 per cent in 1480 to 28.1 per cent in 1526.

Of course, the different economic development of the various towns must be taken into account, and the fact that they were subject to a constant influx of paupers. Not only was the accumulation of wealth in individual hands greater, but the charitable institutions were more numerous and better endowed than in the countryside, so that begging was more lucrative. The professional beggar was a social phenomenon as well known in the towns of the Low Countries as elsewhere in Europe, and in the long run this was a great problem for public charity, again by no means unique to these countries. The resources available to public charity, dispensed in the parishes and monastic communities, were often inadequate in the long term to meet the needs of the poor. There was hardly any agreement among the various charitable institutions, and skilful professional beggars could get a pittance from several of them at once, to the detriment of other paupers whose fate was particularly appalling. Some towns offered charity to paupers in their own homes, but were anxious to give their alms to their own citizens and not to those from elsewhere.

After 1461 Philip the Good forbade begging by those able to work. In the sixteenth century edicts against vagabonds and beggars came one after the other, particularly after the laws around 1525 took on a more repressive character, in harmony with the action against Protestantism. Beggars were condemned to the galleys, and even, in 1542, to hanging, though it is doubtful whether the sentences were ever actually carried out. Besides, the town of Bruges opened a training school in 1514 for poor children, so as to teach them a trade and keep them off the streets. The example was followed elsewhere.

Pauperism was not, of course, unique to the Low Countries. In 1501 Johann Geiler von Kaisersberg preached in Strasbourg that the towns must control public charity. The Lutheran doctrine of salvation by faith alone, without the help of good works, supported this theory, and Wittenberg, Luther's own town, was the first to apply it in 1522. It forbade all begging and merged the resources of charitable institutions in a common fund administered by the magistrates. In 1524 or 1525 the Spanish humanist, Juan Luís Vives, who lived in Bruges, supported this with a tract entitled *De subventione pauperum* and in 1525 the towns of Mons and Ypres carried out a census of paupers to whom help should be given. Money was gathered first by house-to-house collection and through the church poor-box, and then municipal subsidies were added. They also united the charitable institutions into a single fund. Bruges followed this model in 1526, and Oudenaarde in 1529. The example of Ypres was imitated by Lille in 1527 and perhaps even Paris in 1533. The towns of Holland almost followed in 1529 but could not overcome their reluctance.

Reorganization of charity did not meet with a universally favourable response. It was not the growing secularization of the alms that offended some; since the Middle Ages the town magistrates had exerted some control of the parish, and in any case the parish clergy were consulted as to the distribution of alms by the new 'Community Funds'. They also collaborated to prevent abuse and exhorted the faithful to give generously. The opposition came from the mendicant orders, which were forbidden to solicit alms and would therefore lose their main source of income. They accused those who supported the reform of being Protestant sympathizers, and stressed that the reforms were being applied in many notoriously Protestant towns of Germany. But the Sorbonne, when consulted in 1530 by Ypres as to whether the reforms were consistent with orthodoxy or not, pronounced favourably on them and in 1531 the government told all towns in the Low Countries to apply the new system of charity: though not to much effect.

The failure of the reform sprang from different causes, however, for destitution and charity were engaged in a race against time. If poverty grew more rapidly than the assistance that was supposed to mitigate it, there would be no hope of success in the battle against pauperism. The battle was lost: the population rose faster than the means of subsistence. In many areas the prohibition on begging had to be lifted on behalf of the towns' paupers, and in 1556 Philip II revoked the sanctions, in recognition of the fact that the reforms had not succeeded.

2   THE GREAT MIGRATION

Emigration is a universal feature of economic crisis. In the Reformation religious persecution gave it a further stimulus, one related to the economic incentive, since the vacillations of the economic cycle themselves affected the spread of Protestantism and its repression. The naval war between Holland and Lübeck in 1533–4 coincided with the rise of Anabaptism and the large-scale persecution of its adherents, and caused the first noteworthy emigration of the sixteenth century. But too great a weight has been given to the religious motives behind this emigration; Catholics, who were concerned at the decline of business and hoped to find better conditions abroad, also emigrated. Often they accepted the Reformation in their adopted countries only for reasons of social conformity or compulsion. Moreover, many merchants and traders with no religious motives at all set up in Spain or Portugal and their overseas possessions to which they had been attracted by the highly profitable colonial trade; and the same was true of Italy.

The Reformation progressed more rapidly in the Low Countries after 1540 as Calvinist preachers began preaching, and particularly as many high nobles reacted against the absolutism of Philip II (1558–98), thus restricting his capacity for repression. The devastation and looting of Catholic churches in the iconoclastic revolt of 1566 decided the king to entrust the defence of his authority and of Catholicism to the energetic Duke of Alva. A sudden panic gave decisive impetus to emigration, and the economic crisis that followed the Baltic War of the Three Crowns (1563–70) also played its part for insecurity in the Sound made grain costly and caused widespread unemployment. Thus 229 out of 412 Hollanders who established themselves in London during the course of ten weeks in 1568 were in fact Catholics. That same year there was an uprising of the political as well as the religious opposition to Spain and the Low Countries experienced the horrors of war, although by 1574 Holland and Zeeland were definitively liberated except for Amsterdam, which took the king's side until 1578. Twenty years later all territories north of the lower Meuse had also been liberated.

The Belgian provinces, at the cost of terrible destruction, were regained by Spain. From about 1590 the war was limited to the north of the Spanish-controlled territories. After the interruption of the Twelve Years Truce of 1609–21, the resumption of the Eighty Years War not only gave the United Provinces independence, as recognized in the Peace of Westphalia, but also annexed to them Northern Brabant, the greater part of Dutch Limburg and Flemish Zeeland. These events explain why only modern Belgium suffered the blood-letting of a long and widespread emigration. The loss of so many merchants and artisans was a severe blow to Belgium, but it gave their new homes considerable economic potential. It was the germ of an economic revolution.

The émigrés turned towards neighbouring countries, but

France attracted relatively few of them. Her economy was backward and religious war raged, so she was unsuitable as a refuge. Flemish tapestry weavers did go there at Francis I's invitation in 1539 and at Henry IV's in 1601; and in 1570 there were four hundred people from the Low Countries residing in Paris. Walloon linen weavers and tapestry makers also settled in France, where they had a common language, and some Antwerp merchants went to the French Atlantic ports.

Henry VIII's effort to strengthen the English economy by calling in skilled artisans was of greater consequence. Moreover, after his breach with Rome his country willingly (except during the Catholic revival under Mary Tudor from 1553 to 1558) took in Protestants who were victims of persecution. After 1550 the Walloon Reformed Church in London had between six hundred and seven hundred members, and the Dutch-speaking church almost as many. Soon this became the chief emigrant community for, though weakened by the Catholic revival, its membership rose from 350 in 1558 to 1,900 by 1596, despite the presence of several other churches elsewhere. By mid-century there were refugees at Canterbury and weavers from Hainault at Glastonbury. The emigrants in Sandwich, four hundred of them in 1561, were a quarter of the population three years later. Some left in 1565 for Colchester, and probably Norwich, where some thirty families of Flemish weavers are recorded. Norwich seems to have become overpopulated in turn, for 176 emigrants left it in 1568 for King's Lynn. There were sixty families in Maidstone in 1567, and a group of fishermen from Zeeland who probably arrived in 1568 counted 104 families at Great Yarmouth in 1571. By then, Dover had almost three hundred emigrants and Flemish religious communities are known to have existed at Stamford (Lincs), Ipswich, Thetford (Norfolk) and Coventry. Most of the emigrants were textile workers, and a popular ditty attributed to them the introduction in England of the 'new draperies' made of combed wool. These merchants excited the envy of their English colleagues, and the Brussels government suspected them of financing the Sea Beggars who, based at English ports, preyed on trade with the provinces still under Spain.

In Germany, eastern Friesland – an early citadel of Calvinism – took in the first refugees from Holland, Flanders and Hainault in 1544. By 1560 there were nearly five hundred at Emden, most of them merchants who forced a European role on this hitherto insignificant town which attracted the English Merchant Adventurers in 1564–5. After 1567 Hamburg, an old trading city, took in emigrants whose colony is said to have numbered a thousand by 1600. They introduced new business techniques and raised the town, through the widening of its commercial horizons, to a leading place in European trade. When the *Girobank* was founded there in 1619 thirty-two of the largest accounts were held by men with Flemish names. Inland there were refugees as far as Brandenburg, Electoral Saxony, Franconia and Swabia, but most of them were, of course, in western Germany, near their own country and linked for centuries with its economy. In 1534 the faithful of the Low Countries had rushed to Münster to share in the establishment of the Anabaptist New Jerusalem. Aachen, where Catholicism reigned almost without interruption, could hardly welcome Protestants, but Wesel took them in after 1544 and by 1545 sixty-six subscribed to the Augsburg Confession there. Unharmed by the Catholics, their church, characteristically nicknamed 'Little Antwerp', had six hundred members in 1577. The first emigrants were recorded in Duisburg, where Mercator worked, in 1554, in Emmerich in 1560 and in Goch in 1566. Everywhere the local textile industry was stimulated by their expert skills, and at Crefeld Antwerpers set up a silk industry.

No town attracted so many refugees from the Low Countries as Cologne did after 1544 and especially after 1566. By 1568 there were 150 families there, among them Rubens's parents. In 1570 the measures taken by the magistrates to safeguard Catholic orthodoxy compelled between one thousand and two thousand emigrants to leave the town, which was thenceforth hospitable only to Catholics, but they had given new life to the silk industry and had introduced new commercial methods. A Bourse was opened in 1566 and in the 1580s a large number of new businesses, from fifteen to twenty-five Portuguese, about forty Italian and sixty 'Flemish,' established at Cologne restored it to a place among the great European trade centres.

For many Protestants Cologne was merely the first stage of exile. Some set up at Siegen or Dietz, at the invitation of John of Nassau, brother of William the Silent, Prince of Orange, and leader of the Dutch Revolt, but many more went to Frankfort, the fairs of which were connected with the commercial system of

Antwerp. The first forty emigrants arrived there in 1554 and there were over two thousand by 1561. Outbursts of Lutheran intolerance caused several hundred Calvinists to leave in 1562, and they took refuge in the Palatinate at Frankenthal. It happened again in 1600, when some of them filled the new town of Mannheim, founded in 1606, and others set up at Hanau, residence of a son-in-law of William the Silent, in a new quarter where two thousand emigrants were involved in textiles, diamond cutting or jewellery. In the meantime, Frankfort took in new emigrants. We know the names of 140 merchants from Antwerp who set up there, eighty-six of them between 1585 and 1600. At the beginning of the seventeenth century at least half of the richest taxpayers of the town had come from the Low Countries. Further up the Rhine, at Strasbourg and Basel, for example, where distances became too great and where there were not so many attractions, the exodus was more sporadic.

But emigration to these countries was not on anything like the same scale as the movement that contemporaries regarded as internal migration in the Low Countries. As the Spanish conquest advanced, particularly after 1578 under Governor-General Alexander Farnese, Duke of Parma, a wave of refugees made for the areas which were still unconquered. Thus no less than 175 weavers and silk merchants, most of them from Flanders or Tournai, were registered as citizens of Antwerp between 1579 and 1582, after which the encirclement of the town grew tighter, and the number dropped to a nominal few annually. When Antwerp surrendered to Farnese in 1585 those inhabitants who refused to embrace Catholicism were allowed to move out with their property within a certain period, a concession that was usually granted when towns surrendered. In 1582 Antwerp had had 83,700 inhabitants, half of them Protestant. This number had fallen to 55,000 by 1586, and to 42,000 by 1589, when the period of grace expired.

Since the Spanish conquest had begun Holland and Zeeland, the most prosperous provinces and bulwarks of the resistance, had been the main refuges for the emigrants. Since their final liberation, many of their own emigrants had returned. In 1574 William the Silent ordered those resident at Emden, whose commerce perturbed the Hollanders, to return, and 3,300 are said to have done so within two months. The Zeeland refugees at Great

Yarmouth went home in 1576. After the fall of Antwerp, Holland and Zeeland took in still more refugees; Middelburg admitted 1,174 to citizenship between 1580 and 1591, and by 1600 around 1,600 of the eight thousand inhabitants of Rotterdam were emigrants.

But the towns that attracted them most were Leyden and Haarlem, the leading textile centres, and Amsterdam, the chief commercial town. At Leyden forty-six of the 608 new citizens registered between 1570 and 1574 came from the southern provinces, but the figures rapidly changed, both absolutely and relatively, with sixty-nine registrations (51.5 per cent) in 1575–9; 232 (74.4) in 1580–4; 299 (82.6) in 1585–9; a peak of 440 (78.3) in 1590–4 and, despite the calm in the war, 240 (70.2) in 1595–9, 194 (63.6) in 1600–4 and 228 (54) in 1605–9. Amsterdam had received only fifty-five new citizens from the Belgian provinces between 1531 and 1579. There were as many in 1580–4, then 315 in 1585–9, 285 in 1590–4, 250 in 1595–9 and 308 in 1600–4. Their quota, only 10.9 per cent in 1570–9, rose to 44.2 per cent in the next decade, after which it fell again, for the fame of Amsterdam was already drawing migrants from many places. Among the town inhabitants who married between 1578 and 1601, 1,565 husbands (13.1 per cent) were of Belgian origin, nearly half of them from Antwerp, though probably many of the others had taken refuge there temporarily before coming to Holland. Between six hundred and seven hundred Belgian families set themselves up in Haarlem between 1587 and 1596.

We have only sparse details on this emigration, relating to no more than a few places, and the registers of citizenship give an incomplete picture of the movements of refugees. Contemporaries and historians of older generations unduly exaggerated the number of emigrants. Early in 1566 there were said to be 30,000 in England, whereas in fact two thousand at most would be a more credible figure for this period, before the great wave that followed the iconoclasts' revolt. Historians used to estimate the loss suffered by the Belgian provinces at half a million. A modern observer gives England, at the peak of her appeal, around 1570, only 25,000 refugees, and half of that number to Germany.

Although this historian's conjectures cannot be verified, let us suppose that France took in 2,500, but that half of the total of 40,000 for England, France and Germany migrated to or returned to the provinces freed from Spain. This leaves some 20,000. If we then allow that citizens coming from the southern provinces who registered in the Dutch towns – there were 4,730 in the figures quoted above – each had a family (we will calculate 4.5 members to a family) and if we add 650 families at Haarlem and the 1,600 inhabitants of Rotterdam, the figure we come to is 26,000. This may then be multiplied by four to take into account the countless places of refuge that were less popular and on which we have no information, and the many emigrants who did not feel a need to acquire citizenship in their new homes, and the overall result of these calculations – utterly hypothetical as they are – comes to about 180,000, at most 10 per cent of the population of the southern provinces, assuming that they were the only places from which emigration was final. The losses were, of course, more serious in quality than in quantity, for they deprived the south of valuable potential for trade and industry and gave the north a strong stimulus to economic growth. The refugees played a decisive part in the shift of economic supremacy from Belgium to the United Provinces in the seventeenth century.

3 THE SEVENTEENTH CENTURY

The economic rise of the United Provinces and the influx of emigrants from the south caused a great increase in population. Holland held a census in 1622 which left out only foreigners in temporary residence, sailors and soldiers in the Indies, homeless beggars and some categories of prisoners. The result – 672,000 inhabitants – might be increased to 700,000, or almost three times the figure for 1514. The growth had especially benefited the towns, which now accounted for 56 per cent of the population as against 52 per cent in 1514. There are still visible traces of this expansion. Amsterdam increased its territory in 1585, 1593 and 1612, when the belt of canals was built which, flanked by the houses of the wealthy burghers, give a majestic quality to her old quarters. Rotterdam extended its area in 1572, 1597 and 1609, and Haarlem in 1595 and 1610.

Amsterdam was thenceforth unquestionably the largest town of the Netherlands, with at least 105,000 people, followed by Leyden, Haarlem and Delft, the most important industrial centres, with 45,000, 39,500 and 22,800 respectively, and then by the maritime ports Enkhuizen (21,000), Rotterdam (19,800) and Dordrecht

(18,300). The Hague, which had become the administrative centre of the Confederation of the United Provinces, is said to have had 15,800, Gouda 14,600, and the port of Hoorn 14,100. Unfortunately there are no more complete statistics before the later eighteenth century. The population of Holland is thought to have reached a peak around 1680 at about 880,000; Leyden also had a peak then, with at least 60,000, and Rotterdam, judging from the number of batptisms and allowing for some gaps in the figures, must have experienced a slight decline by 1690. By 1680 the population of Amsterdam is thought to have reached 217,000, which was not exceeded until the mid-nineteenth century, for the last noteworthy increase in its area before then dates from 1660. The rural area west of the Zuiderzee ceased to grow around 1650, and that to the south of the IJ twenty years later. At some stage after the mid-seventeenth century, progress gave way to stagnation and decline.

The same is generally true of other parts of the United Provinces. A census of 1689 gave Friesland a population of 129,000, but examination of baptismal and death registers shows that around 1650 there must have been 150,000, almost double the figure for 1511–14. Rural Veluwe had risen by only 11 per cent since 1526, with 27,600 inhabitants around 1650, when the towns there had 13,100. Overijssel was one of the few parts of the United Provinces to have been badly hit by the religious war: thus the districts of Salland and the Twente, with about 20,000 inhabitants in 1601, had fewer people than in 1474–5, but they had doubled by 1675. Its three main towns, Kampen, Zwolle and Deventer, damaged by the shift of trade to Holland and Zeeland, had hardly increased over two centuries, with between six thousand and seven thousand each. Northern Brabant, conquered by the United Provinces in 1625 after many years' wartime damage, had also been badly affected by the commercial decline of Antwerp. By 1665 Bois-le-Duc had probably only some nine thousand inhabitants, half the figure for 1526, and the countryside was able to recover only after the battles had ended, shortly before the Treaty of Westphalia; it too fell victim to decline after 1700.

The Spanish Netherlands had experienced the war at its most devastating, during Farnese's reconquest. Even when it was over, the enemy garrisons of Ostend and Sluis kept up their harrassment far into the interior of Flanders: in the Bruges district, near their hide-outs, whole villages had been abandoned by 1577-8, and the excises on beer and wine brought in only 84 pounds instead of the 25,000 in 1575-6; even in 1655 the figure was still only 5,000. Taxes in the Ypres district brought in only 5 per cent in 1577-8, and in 1607-8 rather under a quarter of their returns for 1576-7; similarly around Courtrai they produced only 8.3 per cent of their 1575-6 returns in 1587-8 and 17.6 per cent in 1599-1600. There was, of course, no extermination of the villagers, many of whom had simply gone to the safety of the nearby towns, but general poverty completed the work of the violence, leaving the way open to epidemics that ravaged the place. Although they suffered less, the Brabantine villages which were exposed to enemy raids were also victims.

Once the dangers were past, the population could recover. It seems, according to the evidence of one test case, that the devastated areas were largely repopulated by immigration. Of the 499 peasants working at Langemark near Ypres in 1610, only 130 were of local origin and most of the others came from nearby villages, with 69 from Artois or Picardy. In both parts of the Low Countries the first half of the seventeenth century appears to have been a period of great increase in population; the social crisis of the later seventeenth century (which was both cause and effect of a serious economic crisis) appears to have arrived late in the two cases, in the Spanish Netherlands because of the terrible gaps that had to be filled after the wars, and in the United Provinces because of the exceptional prosperity and the openings that provided. At Theux-lez-Spa the population rose by 40 per cent between 1600 and 1650, and then fell again to below its level in 1600. Unlike this village far from the war zone, recovery in Flanders went on until the end of the century, when the Nine Years War marked the turn of the cycle.

It was much the same in other Belgian towns. Antwerp, still the most populous, soon recovered, rising from 42,000 to a peak of 67,000 in 1699. There are hardly any census figures for other important centres, but decennial population graphs have been calculated for many of these on the basis of changes in the number of baptisms: these can be translated into population figures by the application of a birth rate obtained by correlation of later census figures with the contemporary number of baptisms, assuming a constant rate. At Ghent, after an increase from 31,000 around 1610 to 50,000 by 1670, the population was stable until 1690 and then fell; Bruges rose from 27,300 around 1620 to a peak of 37,900 by 1700. The two Flemish cities had thus recovered nearly to their fourteenth-century levels. Malines rose from 11,000 around 1590 to 24,100 by 1680 and Louvain from 7,500 to 14,600, not counting students. Finally Ypres recovered, with 13,250 persons in 1689, a rise of 76 per cent over 1491. Smaller places varied in accordance with the condition of their chief economic enterprise. The borough of Saint-Nicolas expanded as the linen industry of the Waasland grew, and the population of Ath decreased as the same industry declined in Hainault.

Parish registers, from which some of these data have been taken, indicate certain basic social changes. Each disaster is reflected in a decline of marriages, but as soon as it was over the number of marriages rose rapidly because there was land and employment for young couples, and because widowers and widows remarried. The death rate was naturally affected by the almost continuous warring in the Spanish Netherlands: the Dutch Revolt and the wars of Louis xiv occupied sixty-seven years of the seventeenth century, and occupation or campaigns were regularly followed by epidemic and famine.

If it was true that the Plague disappeared from the Low Countries after 1670 – with a final eruption that caused an increase of 5 per cent in the death rate in Flanders between 1665 and 1670 – and that the last case of leprosy occurred at Malines in 1677, dysentery took their place. The first outbreak was noted at the end of the sixteenth century, and a particularly savage epidemic in 1676–80 carried off perhaps a tenth of the population in Flanders and the neighbouring provinces. The severity of the disease depended to a large extent on the degree of resistance people derived from their food. It seems that the maritime provinces of the United Provinces, which were well supplied with protein and vitamins from the abundant dairy products, fish and fresh vegetables, escaped disaster. The rise in the average age at death in some monasteries in Belgium, from forty-five years and nine months in the first half of the sixteenth century to fifty-three and a half years in the second half of the seventeenth, may also have been brought about by improvements in the diet. The poorer classes were always threatened by famine, which raised the death rate, lowered the marriage rate and forced couples to minimize their family burdens either by limiting sexual intercourse, by abortion, or even by deliberate contraception. It is also possible that the lack of essential vitamins normally contained in bran prevented conception or that the consumption of grain blighted by ergot caused miscarriages. Agricultural production was, therefore, the first concern of the population from day to day.

2 *Agriculture and Fisheries*

I LAND

The recovery of Europe, which would ensure high agricultural prices, had been delayed as far as the Low Countries were concerned by the troubles of the late fifteenth century. It was only when peace came that long-term land-reclamation projects could be resumed. In Flemish Zeeland new polders were created almost annually, and by the eve of the religious war the country had assumed approximately its present shape. Draining was easier because the western Scheldt formed shallows on the southern banks. But this process pushed the water towards the Zeeland islands, and they had to endure several tidal waves. The worst of them made the port of Bergen-op-Zoom almost unusable and did much to end its trading role, and it almost completely engulfed the islands of Noord- and Zuid-Beveland. Other islands suffered as badly from floods in the first half of the sixteenth century, and some losses were only slowly made good. The Frisian islands were also ravaged by storms, but in 1505–8 in continental Friesland dykes were put up on the Middelzee, north-west of Leeuwarden. In 1545 Groningen began to drain the bay of Dollart, and part of the Zuidhollandse Waard, near Dordrecht, was drained again, for it had been flooded since 1404. Between 1540 and 1565 Holland appears to have reclaimed some 37,000 hectares of polder.

Meanwhile the increasing need for fuel in the rapidly expanding towns of Holland had prompted intensive peat cutting around them, and the pools left after the cutting now spread. The lake of Haarlemmermeer was formed by the junction of several of these between Amsterdam, Haarlem and Leyden, and its surface increased from 5,600 hectares in 1531 to 14,500 in 1647. The religious war contributed to this process. While soldiery wandered over the country, maintenance work was neglected. Besides floods were a way of defending besieged towns, as in the case of Haarlem, which made use of flood to repel the Spaniards in 1573. The opening of the locks of Rotterdam also enabled the Sea Beggars to sail in 1574 to the help of Leyden, forcing the Spaniards to raise their siege. Moreover, the tidal wave of All Saints' Day in 1570 ravaged Holland and Zeeland. Almost the whole of the region north of the IJ disappeared under the waves. In 1576 two-thirds of the province of Holland was still flooded.

After Amsterdam had joined the rebellion in 1578 and fighting in Holland ended, and when the rise of the towns had created a demand for foodstuffs, there was feverish reclamation of the land that had been lost and of the new land as well. In the present-day Netherlands only 8,000 hectares of polder had been drained from 1565 to 1589, but 36,200 were gained from 1590 to 1614 and 75,300 from 1615 to 1689. Here and there the waters were even successfully raised to two levels with the help of windmills. North Holland was reconverted, within some thirty years, from a swampy tract into solid land with a continuity never before achieved. In Zeeland, too, the breaches were made good and north-east of the Zuiderzee the draining of the Middelzee and the Dollart went ahead.

The large towns of Holland soon needed peat to such a degree that local resources were not enough. The provinces of the north-east had large reserves of peat, which hitherto had served only local needs. By 1551 people began to exploit these reserves in Friesland, around Groningen, and from about 1614 in the upland fens of the Drenthe, the least developed region in the Netherlands. After the peat had been removed the soil could be converted into arable land or pasture, and could be peopled. Many colonies which were established there at that time bear traces of their origin in their names (in the term *veen*), as well as in their shape, a ring of farms built on either side of a canal, dug to carry the peat. Most of the colonists, both in the north-eastern provinces and in Holland's polders, who temporarily enjoyed the tax exemptions accorded to clearances, came from the nearby villages, but some came from Germany, then ravaged by the Thirty Years War (1618–48).

The initiative in these clearances was sometimes taken by the authorities. The dykes of the Middelzee were constructed by the Estates of Friesland, and in 1629 the town of Amsterdam drained the Diemermeer at its gates. Groningen was especially active in this respect, undertaking the creation of polders and the large-scale exploitation of the peat bogs in its own area on the former ecclesiastical properties that had been confiscated after its conversion to Protestantism. The extensive network of canals that still characterizes the landscape of the province was dug. But the greater part of the new lands were reclaimed by individuals. The high demand for agricultural products and the rise in their prices made investment in land attractive, the more so since commercial ventures, however successful, were thought risky. Some of the best-known names were behind the clearances. From the 1560s a company of Antwerp merchants, and many others who had come to Holland, took over from a canon of Utrecht who had failed in draining the Zijpe, south of the Helder, and were able to reclaim the polder by 1597, although it had been flooded again in the troubles. Other noteworthy refugees from Antwerp, Dirk van Oss and Willem Usselinx, invested money in draining the Beemster, south-east of Hoorn (1607–12), and the Oldenbarnevelts also took part. Moreover, exploitation of the peat in the north-east, which involved notables of that area and of Utrecht, was essentially undertaken by capitalists of Holland.

In the Spanish Netherlands the continuing war made long-term projects difficult to sustain. The only large-scale enterprise there was the draining of the Moëres, west of Furnes, which was begun in 1620 during the Twelve Years Truce by Wenceslas Coberger, financial adviser to the government, whose name is also connected with the foundation of official pawnshops. In other regions primitive agricultural techniques made extension of the clearances difficult, as in the sandy areas of Overijssel, where the infield–outfield system was followed as before.

2 LANDOWNERS AND FARMERS

In these two centuries there was a further large shift of landed property. As in most European countries, the princely domain was affected increasingly by rising administrative and military costs. Since the time of Charles the Bold domain property had been alienated and pledged, and as the state of the treasury seldom allowed redemption of the pledge, there was usually a sale in the end. Domain income fell from 244,000 pounds in 1531 to 173,000 in 1559, following wars with France. The Dutch Revolt made the situation desperate, although attempts were made to redress the situation in the Twelve Years Truce. In the United Provinces, the old crown domains passed to the provincial authorities or, in the case of northern Brabant and the other conquered areas, to the Estates-General. The ecclesiastical properties were secularized at the Reformation. But the Great-Power policy of the Netherlands, and the bourgeoisie's objections to paying taxes for it, caused the public domain to suffer still further losses.

The property of nobles, judging by the example of Hainault, was considerable and grew even more between 1475 and 1500 at the expense of peasant land, owing to the greater reserves that extensive possessions gave the nobles. It seriously declined, however, in the sixteenth century. The court life of many nobles was very costly, and the loans contracted for this would sooner or later have to be repaid by mortgages or sales. As they no longer lived on their lands, they had no interest in rents in kind, and the quitrents due to them rapidly lost value with the price revolution, especially after about 1550; the government also increasingly deprived them of income from justice. Men throughout the nobility who found a new source of income from a court, military or administrative office were lucky. Others, particularly the lesser nobility, the hardest hit, fell prey to social discontent that left them vulnerable to the Reformation and revolt against the monarchy. Their poverty earned them the nickname 'Beggars' in 1566 and it was extended to all supporters of the Revolt, in which many of them played an important role.

Absentee landlords, who were common in Flanders, Brabant, Zeeland and Holland, as well as Hainault, where many castles were occupied only for brief sojourns in summer or for hunting, hastened the end of the manorial system. The erosion of serfdom went on; in the princely domain of Hainault, between 1500 and 1564, the death registers record only twenty serfs, and the last serf bought his freedom in 1567. In Flanders and Holland, where corvées were maintained, they involved only insignificant obligations of cartage. However, after the United Provinces became independent, the judicial powers of the lords were no longer curtailed by the state and were often kept up. Amsterdam, Haarlem, Leyden and Rotterdam bought up some local lordships to combat the competition of village industries with their own.

In less advanced regions, such as Namur and the Ardennes or the sandy plains of the East, many manor houses remained in the possession of country squires, when war did not call them to the army, and the seignorial system was maintained. Often they were distinguished from the larger farmers only by having a wall around their dwelling, barns and stables, a more or less imposing porch, with a coat of arms, and a private chapel. The lords lived a life often very like that of their villeins, and even worked on what remained of their demesne. On the other hand they continued to exact their rents and their taxes, and as before used corvées to mow or store their grain; sometimes they made their villeins work in the iron works which certain of them possessed. A lord of the sixteenth century, who lived south of Charleroi, hired out corvées to another iron manufacturer, and there were instances when villeins who wanted a drink could have it only at the lord's tavern.

Seignorial status did not necessarily coincide with landed property in the modern sense. A lord might be proprietor of only a small part of his lordship, but might have properties elsewhere without seignorial rights. Moreover there was great regional variation in the shares of landed property owned by the different social classes. The shares of nobility and clergy in lands cleared between the eleventh and thirteenth centuries were usually insignificant: from 11 per cent in the duchy of Limburg (to-day's Pays de Herve), noble land rose to occupy 20 per cent of the area east of Dinant and almost fifty north of Namur, where nobles had retained large forests. In Overijssel, the Salland and the Twente, nobles owned nearly 30 per cent of the land in 1601–2, perhaps slightly less than in 1520, at least in the Salland. Ecclesiastical property hardly made up 3 per cent of the Pays de Herve, and between 2.5 and 10 per cent on the eve of the Reformation in the polders created in the Middle Ages in Holland; but at Heilo, a village on sandy soil south of Alkmaar, the Abbey of Egmond owned 88 per cent of the land before secularization. The share of religious institutions reached 10 per cent north of Namur and remained sizeable in Flanders and still more in Brabant. The parishes and charitable institutions attached to them often had considerable land – up to one-third of the soil of Zeeland, for example.

The urban bourgeoisie continued to buy land. Once country-men seeking their fortune in the towns became established there, they would still, even as townsmen, keep their share of their patrimony. In the sixteenth century townspeople's property predominated on the polders of Holland and made up a third on the frontier between Holland and Guelders as well as north of Namur. Inland Flanders also included many peasant proprietors, mainly on small farms, but large farms (the *censes* of the Walloon region and the numerous farms in the polders of Flanders, Brabant and Hainault) generally belonged to religious institutions or noble families. The troubles of the later sixteenth century seem, in regions particularly exposed to insecurity and large-scale flight from the land, to have caused a considerable shift of property from the peasants to country squires or townsmen, especially rentiers and magistrates. At Meigem, twenty kilometres west of Ghent, peasant property fell from 18.6 per cent in 1571 to 6.7 per cent in 1673, and in the Salland from 10 to 7.2 per cent between 1520 and 1601–2. By contrast, in the newly created polders of Holland, townsmen often sold their land after draining had been completed. By 1660 21 per cent of the land in the Zijpe polders had passed to the peasantry.

Share-cropping could also still be found both around Ghent and in the Walloon region. Payments in kind were becoming rare, but they still existed in backward regions. The proximity of the towns, with their great variety of possible livelihoods, offered many peasants good openings to escape from the demands of rapacious lords, and so their lot improved. Since the sixteenth century the Flemish farmers had been receiving compensation, when their leases ran out, for any improvements they had made to the land and any manure they had left on it. Most rural leases still required a fixed rotation of crops, fallow periods and the use of various techniques. The large landowners or farmers tended to evict the poorer users from the still extensive commons. The commons at Hilversum were split up in the sixteenth century among the local landowners, and this was repeated in many places in the Pays de Herve in the following century. One wonders whether there was an enclosure movement comparable with the English one, with its profound social consequences.

Restrictions on the use of commons made small-scale farming very difficult. Fiscal investigations ordered by the Duke of Alva after 1570 and other sources show that many peasants – one-third of them in the thinly populated polders of Zeeland, and up to two-thirds in the surroundings of Tilburg – had farms that were barely sufficient to feed them and their families. The number of such farms probably rose even higher in Overijssel in the sixteenth and seventeenth centuries. Generalizing from the case of Meigem, it seems that the number of small farms fell slightly in Flanders during the wars of religion, when great landowners could buy up abandoned lands at low cost so as to increase their own farms, but it rose again in the seventeenth century. Unless they went to the towns or found a supplement to their incomes by working at least part of the year for larger farmers, the peasants had either to work in domestic industry or to make more of their land.

3 AGRICULTURAL PRODUCE

The major preoccupation was still, most often, food for the family or, if the harvest left a surplus, for the market. In 1557 in the villages south-west of Ghent consumption of cereals was estimated at from 650 to 715 grams of rye or from 700 to 765 grams of wheat per head per day, and in 1693 at Lichtervelde, south of Bruges, at 800 grams of rye or 850 of wheat. But it is unlikely that much wheat bread was eaten in the countryside. (Around 1570 the Frisian peasant Rienck Hemmema sold the wheat he harvested and bought rye for his servants.) This was why wheat growing was relatively rare, except on farms that belonged to abbeys and had to deliver food for the monks, and in Flanders, Zeeland, Holland and Friesland. The risk of bad weather was partly avoided west of Brussels and in southern Flanders by the cultivation of maslin, a mixture of wheat and rye. Despite some progress with wheat, rye thus remained the chief bread grain except in upper Belgium where spelt was still grown, at least on the farms of the abbey for which we have evidence.

The high consumption of wheat bread in large towns is none-theless surprising; charitable institutions even distributed it as alms, and the number of rich people who ate wheat seems to have risen. At Bruges in 1525 the bakers mainly made wheat bread. This may not be particularly representative, for many ordinary people bought grain and baked the bread themselves, or bought rye bread from local peasants at the market; however, in times of famine at Ghent, the stored cereals contained in 1594 equal proportions of rye and wheat (27.5 per cent each with 36.1 per cent barley); in 1698 wheat accounted for 25.2 per cent, rye only 13.1 and barley 9.2, but buckwheat as much as 47.3. This last had become popular in the sixteenth century in the Campine and Waasland, and even, in the following century, in the clay soils of Brabant. The high prices of cereals caused a shift in consumption of bread cereals, from wheat to rye, and rye to barley or, in the seventeenth century, buckwheat, which was replacing leguminous plants in the diet of the poor in hard times. Price rises were thus proportionately greater for the coarser cereals and buckwheat than for wheat. Attempts were often made to moderate them by prohibiting the use of grain for anything other than bread – beer or gin, for example.

Since foreign growths of good quality were now imported in large quantity, local wines had no satisfactory market and the vine virtually disappeared from the Belgian countryside in the sixteenth century, especially because the beer tasted better and had replaced wine in popular consumption. The needs of brewing may have increased the cultivation of barley and hops. Hemmema grew more barley than any other cereal, presumably for brewers of Groningen or Holland. Hops were also grown west of Breda and along the Dendre. Industrial crops were especially cultivated in the maritime provinces, where Baltic grain was easy to get, but flax, which was grown almost universally in Flanders, the great centre of linen, also spread to the Campine and, in the seventeenth century, to the Twente when it began to develop a linen industry. Of the plants grown for their dye, woad fell to competition from tropical indigo, but madder became a key product of Zeeland's agriculture. Among the oil crops, coleseed spread from Holland to Friesland, Groningen, Flanders and Brabant in the sixteenth century: its rich oil and the cakes which could be made from it as cattle fodder made it more useful than rape. Oil was also produced from linseed. When the taste for tobacco was no longer limited to sailors, cultivation of it began about 1625 in the surroundings of Amersfoort, and it was also recorded in Belgium, near Ath, after 1650.

Horticulture was stimulated by the taste of the rich for more varied cookery. While the ordinary vegetables kept their place on ordinary tables, finer types that became known as other lands were discovered – salsify late in the fifteenth century, chicory, cucumber, green beans and sorrel in the sixteenth – began to be used in *haute cuisine*. The high degree of urbanization in Holland caused much of the arable land to be devoted to horticulture. The sandy strip at the edge of the dunes in particular specialized in the production of luxury vegetables of low nutritive value, such as lettuce, spinach, cauliflower. Strawberries, at first a curiosity, became a commercial product in Holland, and so did grapes, apricots, redcurrants and greengages. Apples, pears, plums and cherries were cheap, and were eaten by the masses. Many of today's fruit regions, like the Betuwe and the island of Zuid-Beveland, date from this time. The Fleming Busbecq brought back tulips and hyacinths from Asia Minor in 1562, and fifty years later commercial growing of flowers had developed on the sandy soils of the coast of Holland. The taste for gardens spread, and they were planted around country houses, and even behind the town houses of the notables. Holland's tree growing, which first appeared in the sixteenth century around Gouda, also originated in this new vogue. It developed in the seventeenth century at Aalsmar, near Amsterdam, where it found its best customers.

Peat was the main fuel in the Dutch maritime provinces, although elsewhere wood was more common. Ill-considered long-term exploitation seriously reduced the forests which provided pasturage especially for pigs (acorns and beech-mast), as well as the timber needed for building and for utensils. The rise of various industries using technology dependent on heat threatened the forests with exhaustion. The first attempts at rational exploitation occurred in the 1500s: Count Henry of Nassau called in experts from Nuremberg to plant a pine wood in his lands near Breda. Perhaps the experiment had something to do with clearance of moorland, for the rapidly growing conifers not only matured quickly, their needles also provided useful humus for cultivation.

As to existing forests, many measures were decreed (in itself a sign that they were not observed) from Charles v's time onwards to reduce rights of usage. Sometimes the rights were confined to villagers cultivating a certain area of land, smallholders being excluded; sometimes the forest would be divided between the owner and the communal users, which partly protected it. There were frequent attempts to limit the number of animals that could be allowed into the woods, and to exclude those that would damage them most, such as sheep and goats, and the government also tried to limit felling, by dividing forests into cantons, only one of which could be used in any one year. In the forest of Soignes, south-east of Brussels, the massive groves of oaks and beeches were divided into eighty cantons, and the bush into nine or ten.

The small peasants' rights on commons being limited, stock-raising had to be undertaken on large farms. Unlike elsewhere in Europe, the horse had become the commonest draught animal except on the light soils of the Campine and northern Brabant. There were unusually high numbers of them, up to one per hectare of arable land on the poor soils of Overijssel in 1601–2, and they were also needed for carrying the heavy clods used as fertilizer. They must have been a great burden for the peasants. Even the four horses that Hemmema had for his 8.5 hectares of fields in Friesland were a large number, and were probably kept for carrying manure. Sheep-rearing declined as the commons diminished or foreign wools increased. Pig-raising was not undertaken on a large scale. Hemmema, like the peasants of Overijssel, kept one or two for his own consumption. It is difficult to estimate the number of cattle. Around 1570 there were 220 on forty farms, the size of which is unknown, in the sandy surroundings of Kampen; Hemmema had at least twenty on seventeen hectares of pasture. About 1600 the inhabitants of small towns quite often kept a milch-cow.

Pasturage and fodder crops tended to spread to the detriment of cereals. The uncultivated lands confiscated from the commons were converted into pasturage, as was the arable land of the Pays de Herve area, at least on peasants' and townsmen's properties. The religious institutions and nobles were more conservative in the leases they granted. Cultivation of clover became popular, starting perhaps with the Waasland, as was claimed, although the first mention of it, with reference to this part of Flanders, was made only in Sir Richard Weston's *Discourse of Husbandrie used in Brabant and Flanders* in 1645. An artificial clover meadow was created at Schagen, south of the Helder, as early as 1599, and fifty years later peasants of Holland had also adopted the custom of manuring their meadows and hay fields. Feed crops not only made stock-raising less dependent on natural meadows, but also did much to enhance the progress that agriculture had made since the later Middle Ages.

4 AGRICULTURAL METHODS

The rise of agricultural prices and rents as conditions improved was as important a stimulant to progress as the need to lower costs in the crisis of the later Middle Ages had been. The chief advance was the abandonment of fallow. Substitution of fodder crops for the three-field system ceased to be exceptional in Flanders by the later sixteenth century. Clover was increasingly used, and thereafter the less densely sown turnip was common; this was grown in the Waasland, of which it became the heraldic symbol, and probably also in the Campine. All this seems to have become general in Flanders and to have spread to Zeeland and northern Brabant in the seventeenth century. But outside Flanders, Hemmema left at most an eighth of his land fallow in the 1570s: he probably followed a seven- or eight-year cycle.

There was presumably rather less progress elsewhere, and we do not know enough about it. Progress seems to have been made particularly on directly exploited farms of small or middling size on sandy soils, for the peasants there were best suited to put their fields to intensive use. On the heavy soils the rate of progress was slower. The conservative spirit of proprietors mistrusting change, however, was always a serious hindrance. Many leases still insisted on triennial fallow, at least at the approach of the term of the lease. But the new methods did encourage peasants to give up traditional systems, especially cereal monoculture: Hemmema alternated cereals and legumes. The rotation, without fallow, of flax, turnips, oats and clover, the last sown as a secondary crop and occupying the land for four or five years, was greatly admired by Sir Richard Weston on his journey to Flanders in 1644. By 1577 Barnaby George had recommended to his fellow-countrymen in England turnip fields such as he had seen in Flanders. The *Discourse of Husbandrie used in Brabant and Flanders*, published after Weston's death by the Pole, Samuel Hartlib (a friend of Comenius and propagator of his educational ideas), aroused the interest of many English squires in Flemish agriculture and stimulated experiments which eventually produced a revolution in farming throughout Europe.

The new methods broke the vicious circle of traditional rotation, for which fertilizers had run short. Fodder crops allowed more animals, and hence also manure, especially if the cattle remained more or less constantly in the byre. This method of cattle-raising was initiated in these years. Moreover, the peasants used more of other types of manure than before – the droppings of pigeons kept in the great houses, or the sludge and sewage of the towns. By 1572 Hemmema was buying twelve barges and 113 cartloads of manure in Franeker, usually from citizens who had cows. The town of Groningen, in the first half of the seventeenth century, even compelled peasants of the fenland colonies to buy the contents of cesspools and sludge, which explains why the streets of towns in the Netherlands were cleaner than elsewhere, a striking feature of the Dutch and Flemish paintings of the time. Gin distilleries were a further source of manure from the towns, for the distillers fattened butchers' beasts with the draff. Coleseed was another, for cakes of it were used as cattle fodder and directly as manure. After about 1500 the fields were also spread with mud from the ditches and with lime, and ash from peat burnt in Holland was sold in Flanders. Local resources were often used on poor soils: in the Drenthe the flocks of sheep belonging to the entire community spent the night in one after another of the fields of each villager to fertilize them. In the Campine the right of collecting sheep droppings in the commons was subject to tender, and the heather on which the animals slept in a stable, since it was impregnated with manure, was also spread over the fields at ploughing time. Clumps of grass were put to the same use, and sometimes the area was burnt. Humus was reconstituted in Overijssel by mixing clods and manure.

This was not the limit of agricultural progress in Flanders. Ploughs were again improved, with the replacement of the two heavy wheels by a smaller one, and harrows broke up clods and uprooted weeds. In the Waasland Weston saw an instrument that remained peculiar to Flanders, the *sleep*, which was a bundle of branches that could cover the sowings as well as even out the fields.

Hemmema's average wheat harvest in 1570–3 was ten times the yield of the *béguinage* at Lier, and in 1586–1602 rather more than that. Not far from Hemmema, a Frisian farm achieved a yield of 8.4 for wheat in the years 1604–17, a large abbey farm at the gates of Liège 8.7 in 1610–59, another around Huy only 4.66 in 1651–9. For rye, there were yields of 5 and 8 times the sown quantity in a Salland village in 1601, and those of the farms near Liège and Huy,

E.H.—6

quoted above, were on average 8.4 in 1610–59 and 6.1 in 1651–9 respectively. Hemmema reaped 9 times the quantity of spring barley he had sown, and 7.5 times that of winter barley, and elsewhere in Friesland yields of 7 and 5.8 for barley in 1604 and 1608 were known. Hemmema's oats produced only 3 or 4 times the sown weight, beans 6.6 and peas 12 to 15. Near Liège, spelt yielded 8.8 times in 1610–59, and 4 in 1651–9 near Huy. Comparing these figures with the later medieval ones, there is no great increase, but too many factors, beginning with the identity of the places themselves, are missing for the comparison to be valid, and there is unfortunately no evidence for Flanders, where agriculture had progressed most. Even so, our evidence is better than for any other European country, except in the cases of a few pioneers, such as the Englishman, Robert Loder, whose yields in Berkshire in the years 1612–20 became general in his country only two centuries later.

The spread of fodder crops allowed improvement in cattle breeds because the hazards of cross-breeding on the commons could be avoided. As horses of the Frisian type were in great demand, especially for armies, the Estates of Friesland took steps from 1610 to select stallions. Animals for slaughter in the sandy regions were regularly sent to the polders for fattening. Hemmema's output of dairy produce, about 42 kilograms of butter and 27.5 of cheese per cow annually, was astonishingly high, although most of his milk was probably used for this since it was seldom drunk either on the farms or in the towns. In the polders of Holland the output of dairy products rose in the seventeenth century after horsepower was used for the creamers. The diet had attained a degree of equilibrium for most people that was probably unique in the world.

5   FISHERIES

This balance was also encouraged by the yield of fisheries. Fishing had developed since early modern times in northern Holland, especially because the rural economy was based on stock-raising which needed little labour, and was limited in any case by the stretches of marsh. Fisheries were also developing at the mouth of the Meuse, owing to its favourable position on the North Sea. If Brill, which had eighty fishingboats in 1477, was on the verge of decline, Schiedam and Vlaardingen were expanding and attracted fishermen from everywhere in Holland. Their fleet of herring boats was estimated at two hundred by 1550, and Charles v gave it an escort of warships during his French wars. The Sea Beggars almost managed to paralyze it early in the Dutch Revolt, and the Governor of Holland foresaw that between five and six thousand fishermen might be unemployed. As a herring boat had an average crew of fourteen, he must have been assuming about four hundred vessels. Ten years earlier Zeeland had had about two hundred and Flanders around one hundred, though usually of lower tonnage.

The Sea Beggars' occupation of Brill in 1572, followed by the Spaniards' vain efforts to regain it, turned the mouth of the Meuse into a theatre of war and many fishermen fled to the more peaceful ports of the Zuiderzee, especially Enkhuizen. The rebels consolidated their hold on Holland, however, which made things easier at the mouth of the Meuse, and they also controlled the sea, whereas Flemish fishing was inadequately protected by the Spaniards and declined, particularly after Dunkirk was ceded to France in 1659. During his exile in Bruges, Charles ii of England had permitted the town to send fifty ships to herring fisheries off the British coast, but no use was apparently made of this. Holland's herring boats rose in number to 450 around 1586, and there was a peak of five hundred later on – considerably less than the three thousand imagined in 1620 by the Englishman, John Keymer. In the seventeenth century almost half of them were stationed at Enkhuizen. Many ships belonged to inhabitants of North Holland: those of De Rijp, south-east of Alkmaar, apparently had seventy-five at sea in the 1670s. By 1600 the herring boats of Rotterdam again numbered some hundred, those of Schiedam fifty and Delf-shaven had eighty-five at sea in 1637.

Dutch herring fishers managed to win the lead in the European market. These ships, the tonnage of which was higher than those of the English or Scottish fleets, could go to sea for longer without returning to their home port, and they could also treat the herring as they caught it, much to the product's advantage. The fresh herring, which soon deteriorated after salting, were caught far into the banks off northern Scotland and were then carried by yachts specially sent to unload them as fast as possible. The first Stuarts had, for political reasons, given up restricting or taxing Dutch fisheries in their territorial waters; the greater size of the trading vessels of the United Provinces had also reduced considerably the role of fishingboats in carrying goods out of season. Dutch commercial growth also fostered fisheries, and so did natural conditions, for around 1560 the herring which inexplicably appeared off the Swedish coast of Bohuslän disappeared again just as mysteriously in 1589, and left the Dutch traders of North Sea herring dominating the Baltic outlet. The annual yield of Dutch herring fisheries was estimated around 1630 to be some 240,000 barrels.

Since increasingly large and expensive ships were used for fishing, the habit grew of dividing the property among many shareholders. This was a tempting investment for the middle class of artisans and rentiers, as well as for merchants and fish exporters. Moreover, as the herring shrank after salting at sea, the barrels had to be refilled with herring on land before they could be retailed or exported. Even before the war of independence, kegging had constituted a large industry at Amsterdam and Dordrecht. Gradually it declined at Dordrecht but the chief home ports of herring fisheries, Rotterdam and Enkhuizen, developed the industry, and refused to allow herring that had been unloaded at their ports to be kegged in Amsterdam.

Cod and haddock were caught in the Dogger Bank but mattered less than the herring. The chief ports for these fisheries were Vlaardingen and nearby Maassluis: forty to fifty boats may have been stationed at Maassluis in the first half of the seventeenth century, and it became the chief port for cod from Icelandic waters, an industry which developed after 1650. Hollanders also took part in whaling in the Arctic Ocean, which had been explored in the hope of a new trade route. Following the English example, and using in at least one case an English pilot, some whalers were fitted out in 1612. As the English Muscovy Company tried to cut out competition, those concerned set up the *Noordse Compagnie* ('Northern Company') in 1612 and got the Estates-General to grant it a monopoly on whale-fishing between Novaya Zemlya and the Davis Strait. Like the India Companies, it was composed of various Chambers corresponding to its associates' home towns in Zeeland and Friesland. The oil was usually boiled on the shores of Spitzbergen, where each of the Chambers had its boiler. Each one had a fixed share, and the oil was used for lighting as well as for soap. After 1633 the whale bones were also shared out, for they were used in the manufacture of hoop skirts and corsets. The products were sold at prices established by cartel.

Other whalers had been hunting whale since 1616 in the waters off Jan Mayen's Land where, they claimed, the Company's privileges did not apply, but in 1622 they joined the Company. The monopoly was not renewed in 1642 and the number of whalers, which had not been above twenty before, quickly went up. There were 246 in 1684. A large fleet like this would, of course, have eventually exterminated the whales or pushed the remaining ones to the edges of the pack-ice and exposed fishermen in the ice floes of polar waters to financial risk. Consequently the trade became increasingly concentrated in the hands of Amsterdam capitalists. The workshops at Spitzbergen and Jan Mayen's Land were abandoned, and the oil was boiled for metropolitan uses in places in the Zaan, which became a kind of industrial suburb.

3 *Industry*

1 WOOL

The chaos that the Low Countries experienced in the last quarter of the fifteenth century had hastened the decline of the old urban cloth trade. It had already been affected by the restoration of English exports after the Wars of the Roses and by the growing fashion for silk and velvet. By 1516 Lille had only five or six drapers, and in 1543 Ghent was said to have only twenty-five working looms – certainly an exaggeration, though the fact that it could be made at all shows that there must have been a collapse. In Ypres by 1545 there were only about a hundred left of the three or four hundred looms functioning in 1511. Around 1500, only 60,000 to 90,000 ells were being produced in Malines, barely 10 or 15 per cent of the peak figures, and production stopped altogether in 1585. The thirty master weavers in Louvain in 1477 had become thirteen by 1597–8, and there was only a single master shearer in place of the thirteen of a century before. Leyden produced between 21,000 and 28,000 cloths at the end of the fifteenth century, under ten thousand by 1548 and only about a thousand in 1573, while Hasselt produced 2,500 in 1541 and only 980 in 1575, although the town provided subsidies.

The authorities' support for this industry, which was still regarded as the foundation of urban economy, makes its decline all the more striking. Ghent, Bruges and Ypres had taken advantage of the dynastic crisis in 1477 briefly to restore their monopoly over the surrounding countryside. As late as 1484 Maximilian of Austria upheld the prohibition on dyeing. In 1501, 1512 and 1545 Ypres obtained confirmation of the old prohibition on handicrafts in its suburbs, and in 1539 Ghent did the same, but the effort was fruitless. After vain attempts in 1515 and 1525, the towns of Holland, led by Leyden, obtained an interdict on the establishment of new industries within a mile of their walls in 1531. This *Order op de buitennering* was undermined by lords of the area who had strongly opposed it. Finally Leyden had to negotiate with several of them to get them to limit the industry on their lands, and even bought up some of the lordships. It was for this reason that 150 villagers suddenly became citizens in 1542, the usual number being about ten, but many others set up their works beyond the range of the town magistrates. In the end a judicial decree of 1554 forced the lords to observe the prohibition. After independence the increased political influence of the towns of Holland enabled them to suppress rural industry more effectively. The Friesland towns vainly sought a similar interdiction in 1532. In the long run the government's growing financial needs, both in the United Provinces and the Spanish Netherlands, helped towards a solution. By enforcing their tax collection in the countryside, they evened out production costs there and in the towns and weakened the competition.

Besides measures against the rural cloth trade the towns of Flanders won a virtually complete ban on silk and velvet in 1497. Embargoes against English cloth, usually decreed during political quarrels, were more effective, although towns whose trade and industry depended on such imports protested: the standard of dyeing and finishing of English cloth, Antwerp's speciality, was higher than in England. Around 1564 1,600 workers were apparently involved in this trade in Antwerp and it carried on to some extent into the seventeenth century. Finishing went on to a lesser degree in the sixteenth century in Malines and Bruges, and was transferred to Amsterdam during the great migration. Yet when the great cloth towns of the Belgian provinces were consulted in 1611 about how the economy should recover, they were unanimously in favour of protection and when in 1635 Bruges sought the staple for English cloth, the town was of the opinion that the trade would be better abolished altogether.

Some towns took measures of their own, such as banning the wearing of foreign cloth, to save their cloth trade. Wool buying was subsidized at Ypres in 1523, and at Courtrai in 1529, and the export of cloth to the Frankfort fairs by Louvain in 1530. Gradually, however, enlightened magistrates became convinced of the wrong-headedness of this narrow conservatism. Their efforts may have been supported by the numerical and political decline of the guilds, which had lost much of their power under the dukes of Burgundy. The building of fulling mills at Hasselt (1512), Malines (1524), Ath (1525), Ypres (1543) and Louvain (1560) shows that the towns were abandoning their prejudices against cloth treated in this way. Elsewhere, for instance at Leyden, the mistrust persisted and men feared that the mills might make trouble for fullers who lost their employment, as had happened at Malines. Some guild regulations were amended to allow use of Spanish wool. In the first half of the sixteenth century artisans were several times brought to Bruges from places that produced fashionable cloth, so that it could be imitated, and the same happened at Louvain in 1518. These activities were subsidized and either their output was bought at an agreed price or town retailers were obliged to take a certain quantity of it. These efforts failed as long as there was a gap between the production costs of town and country.

In the meantime the 'new draperies' of the countryside went into decline. In the Ypres region they were dying by the eve of the Revolt. The competition of the 'light' cloth of bays, says and serges harmed them as much as English cloth. The general adoption of underclothing, and the settlement of Europeans in the tropics, created great possibilities for these light fabrics, which were entirely or partly made of combed wool. Hondschoote specialized in such cloth from the later fourteenth century; output there rose from 28,600 pieces in 1527–8 (our first figure) to 97,700 forty years later. The troubles caused a decline, at first slow, to 82,900 pieces in 1578–9, but the Spanish reconquest hastened it. The town was burnt in 1582, and commerce collapsed, even though production rose from 12,800 pieces in 1585–6 to 60,700 in 1629–30. Finally, the Franco–Spanish war of 1635 affected this frontier area very badly, and even before its annexation to France in 1659 Hondschoote had lost its importance as an industrial centre. Its remarkable rise had been due to the liberty the industry had enjoyed: emerging in the countryside, it was never corporatively organized. Regulation and control were carried out by the magistrates alone, who were usually the largest entrepreneurs. They were closely linked with merchants in Antwerp and, like their patrician predecessors in the days of the growth of the urban cloth trade, imposed conditions on their workshops that served their trading interests.

By the fifteenth century the success of this industry had inspired Lille, Douai, Tournai, Valenciennes and Mons to start it up. Some of Hondschoote's closest neighbours followed, as did Bruges which, after unfortunate starts in 1512 and in 1514, invited artisans from Hondschoote to set up in the town in 1549. Ypres and Malines had followed by 1560. Courtrai and other towns hit by the 'new draperies' also started up their own, but none competed seriously with Hondschoote in its great days. After this disaster say-weaving was one of the bases of Lille's prosperity so long as the town was part of the Spanish Netherlands, that is until 1668. Bruges annually produced eight thousand pieces of serge around 1620, and probably more later on, as its commerce with Spain, the chief market, rose. In 1664 Hondschoote vainly sought protection from the imitation of her says in Bruges, but perhaps by then the imitation had already passed its peak. By 1680 it was thought to have declined to barely 580 pieces. Liège, with its political neutrality that helped industrial growth, produced about 20,000 pieces around 1660, and the industry was also carried on in the surroundings of the town.

But it was chiefly Leyden that took up where Hondschoote left off. Light cloth had been made there by 1497 at the latest, but Leyden recovered from the crisis only after the great sixteenth-century migration. Between 1580 and 1609, 129 textile workers from Hondschoote became citizens, followed soon after by other Flemings, the vast majority of whom worked in the manufacture of light cloth, and the migration continued in the seventeenth century. During the first decades of the industry, Flemings also held a dominant place among textile entrepreneurs. Soon both artisans and entrepreneurs were coming from Liège and Limburg as well. In all 1,188 migrants from the Belgian wool industry, 37 per cent of the overall figure, came to Leyden as citizens between 1580 and 1665, the apogee of the industry. The cloth sold all over Europe.

The influx of expert labour greatly stimulated the manufacture of light cloth. By 1584 Leyden was producing 26,000 pieces, by 1600 49,100, by 1624 66,300 and then, after a decline to 50,900 in 1644, 67,600 by 1664. The output was very varied, so that a decline in one sector could easily be offset by progress in others. Meanwhile the fashion for austere Spanish costumes had unexpectedly revived the drapery trade. Imitation of English cloth rose from an annual output of 1,500 pieces around 1600 to 20,000 in mid-century. Leyden, like Hondschoote, had no guild system. The town magistrates were alone in laying down regulations and even this infringement of total liberty annoyed entrepreneurs who wanted to take immediate advantage of changing fashions. One of them, de la Court, was such a vehement advocate of this in his tract *Welvaren der stad Leiden* ('The prosperity of the town of Leyden') of 1659, that Dutch liberals two centuries later regarded him as a pioneer.

The Leyden entrepreneurs were often concerned at lack of labour. The first fulling mill was set up there in 1585, and the mills were generally worked by windmill or horsepower. Around 1600 a haberdashery loom, worked by a crank, was invented, which could weave a dozen ribbons and galloons at the same time. It was soon in use throughout Europe. The time was not ripe, however, for great labour-saving machines. One of the most flagrant social abuses in Leyden's industry was the excessive employment of children, sometimes only six years old, in uncomplicated work such as spinning and spooling, where their low wages squeezed those of the women who were also employed to a pittance. 1,542 orphans of the town were employed between 1608 and 1643. Supplementary child labour also came from the orphanages of other towns in Holland, from working class families in Leyden itself and even from abroad, from the Rhineland, Westphalia and the principality of Liège. 7,500 of these 'apprentices' were registered at Leyden between 1638 and 1664. Moreover, a large part of the manufacturing process was frequently turned over to artisans outside the town. In 1648 the millers objected to fulling being carried on at Zaandam, but the dyers could not check the supremacy of Amsterdam over their trade, which rapidly declined after the middle of the century.

This decentralization worked particularly well for specialized preliminary work. Wool was spun mainly by women in the surrounding villages, and sometimes as far off as Brunswick and Prussia. After the conquest of northern Brabant in 1632, the drapers of Holland laid heavy dues on the output of rural industry but after 1637 the Leyden entrepreneurs put out wool to be worked on – including the fulling – although they kept the dyeing and finishing for themselves. Once the Treaty of Westphalia had confirmed Dutch possession of the conquered lands, these half-finished products were allowed in free after 1650. A large number of the six or seven thousand looms at Tilburg in 1663 worked for these Leyden drapers at wages 45 per cent lower than those in Leyden. The drapers also made use of the labour that became available in the Pays de Herve, as it changed from agriculture to stock-raising, to work the coarse local wool. By 1638, however, at Aachen, Eupen, Verviers and other places, small entrepreneurs emerged who bought Spanish wool in Amsterdam on their own account and sent the products to Leyden for finishing only. The drapers there tried to have wool exports taxed, but Amsterdam's trading interest prevailed. By contrast, the bishops of Liège taxed cloth imports so that Verviers and nearby places developed from modest villages into manufacturing boroughs. The auxiliaries of the past had gradually become competitors by 1670, and they were a considerable threat to Leyden's future.

Until about 1630 small enterprise dominated Leyden. On average the drapers had four looms each, and never more than twenty, which were worked by their own families as far as possible, or otherwise by domestic weavers who sometimes had to rent their tools from the drapers. The other stages of production would be completed in the same way, and they sold the finished product in the cloth hall. From the later sixteenth century on finishers usually bought the half-finished cloth and then sold it after finishing it. After 1630 merchants, who were better informed about market conditions and well endowed with capital, managed the production, placing orders with the artisans and even grouping the workers together on occasion to supervise them. One of these merchants had thirty weavers working at his workshop in 1640, as well as many others in their homes. This was still exceptional, but it heralded the factory system.

Mixed cloth was fashionable in the sixteenth century – that is, fustians, made of linen or cotton and combed wool, which was Italian in origin but had been imitated in Upper Germany and spread from there. Bruges, in 1513, and Antwerp, in 1536, tried to produce the cloth by employing Italian weavers, but the attempts were not very successful. Flemish weavers introduced it to Leyden, where output rapidly rose to 34,000 pieces in 1624. Changes in fashion – the revival of drapery – caused production to fall a decade later, and in 1664 not even 5,000 pieces were made. Another mixture of linen and wool, *warpen*, had a short-lived success after the mid-seventeenth century, with a peak of 19,350 pieces in 1664. The contemporary success of *greinen*, made of angora wool, a mixture of goat's hair or camel's hair and silk, was very marked: at its height in 1669 67,300 pieces were produced. Adding together all the woollens produced at Leyden, production rose from 26,600 pieces in 1584 to 64,300 in 1604 and 101,800 in 1624, then declined temporarily to 83,900 in 1644 before reaching its peak in 1664 with 144,700 pieces. At this time Leyden was the outstanding manufacturing centre for wool in Europe and perhaps in the world, as Lyons was for silk and as Ghent had been with her wool industry three or four hundred years previously.

2 OTHER TEXTILES

If Flanders had lost her lead in the wool industry, she had acquired one in linen production. Markets for this widened considerably after Spain and Portugal, having conquered their colonial empires, fell into economic dependence and allowed their textile industries, earlier the great wealth of the Moorish kingdoms, to stagnate. From now on Flanders took the lead from Hainault, which persisted in maintaining the regulations that had guaranteed the quality of its produce since 1418, without adapting to the growing demand for cheap textiles. Moreover, even after the manufacturing centres far from Ath had managed to have its staple abolished in 1553, they lacked a trading system capable of developing their own produce. Hainault exported to Spain only between 10,000 and 15,000 pieces of cloth in 1553, as against Flanders's 90,000. Nivelles also failed to keep up. In Brussels and its surroundings about 25,000 people were said to be working on linen, particularly tick, which also became the speciality of the fast-growing borough of Turnhout.

In Flanders, the growing population on tiny farms was more than ever forced to seek income from handicrafts, and the creation of new linen markets for the output of nearby villages, chiefly in the Lys valley, such as Courtrai (1569) and Menin (1570), show how industry was growing in volume and range. Most of these markets offered great economic opportunities, unless they happened to fail in competition with other nearby ones. The revenues from excise on sales of linen are revealing in certain cases. Sales in Eeklo rose from 6,000 pieces in 1508–9 to 63,900 in 1564–5. The iconoclasts' revolt of 1566 began a decade of uncertainty, after which sales again rose to 54,200 pieces in 1575 and 126,500 in 1581, just before the collapse that was caused by the Spanish reconquest. In the next three years sales fell to 5,000 pieces, then 100, and finally none at all. The pattern was repeated at Oudenaarde, the excise returns of which we know from 1544–5 on, when sales reached 24,700 pieces. They almost doubled within twenty years, then fluctuated for a decade, grew again to 48,200 pieces in 1574–5 and 77,000 in 1579–80, and fell again to 12,800 by 1588–90.

The war drove many weavers from their homes. Usually they went to Haarlem. Industrial growth had led to a shortage of bleacheries in Flanders, and though some of the linen was sent to Brabant for bleaching, most went to Holland and especially to Haarlem. The sandy soils at the edge of the dunes supplied an abundance of very pure water, and stock-raising supplied buttermilk needed for the process. The linen would then be finished, and from the sixteenth century many linens woven in Flanders were actually marketed as Haarlem linens. The arrival of the Flemings helped Haarlem's linen industry still more. Its hitherto relatively insignificant weaving industry produced some 44,000 pieces in 1610, and these also were much more varied than before, including luxuries such as damask.

By mid-century the figure declined, as had wool at Leyden, because production costs were too high in a relatively populous town. From 1641 the magistrates tried to apply the edict of 1531 which prohibited rural industry, but the merchants whose orders dominated production wanted only to profit from the low wages of the countryside, and they did so in Spanish and northern Brabant, at Turnhout, Eindhoven and Helmond, and even in Germany, at Bielefeld and Elberfeld (now part of the town of Wuppertal). The linen industry gradually escaped from their influence because small entrepreneurs managed it for themselves, much as had been the case with wool in northern Brabant and the Pays de Herve. By contrast, Haarlem's bleaching and finishing trades grew more important. Its bleachers produced from 80,000 to 100,000 pieces in 1628, as against 18,000 to 20,000 in 1586. These firms favoured centralization. Instead of forty-two firms, with an average of five workers each in 1586, there were only between twenty and twenty-four around 1600, but with from forty to sixty workers each. They were a good instance of what was at the time called a *traffic*, i.e. a finishing industry for foreign products designed for re-export.

Brabantine weavers had shifted their tick production to Utrecht, Rotterdam and Schiedam. In 1617 Utrecht permitted them to employ a maximum of five looms instead of three. The persistent obstacle of the guilds explain why this trade failed. The two Meuse towns gave the industry greater liberty, but it was abandoned in favour of trade in ticks sent from Turnhout where the industry recovered (with six thousand pieces in 1617). Besides, the recovery was general in the Spanish Low Countries once the fury of the war had declined, and particularly after 1598 when the Peace of Vervins made trade with France and Spain easier. By 1600–1 the Oudenaarde market had again reached its level of 1560, with 34,200 pieces, and the figure rose to 103,900 in 1647–8, its peak. Other markets opened or re-opened, and as the gap between urban and rural production costs closed, linen ceased to be an almost exclusively rural trade. Ghent, especially, became involved in linen production. The recovery was stimulated by government requirements regarding quality which were applied to all Flanders in 1619: and this may have had something to do with the stagnation of weaving in Haarlem and other towns of Holland. The recovery of linen prompted some opposition to the export of flax or thread to Holland and France, especially from the Cambrai and Valenciennes region where there was a lively twisted-thread industry.

Lace provided a new use for linen thread. Earlier it had been a ladies' hobby, but it became fashionable in the sixteenth century and was commercialized. By 1560 burghers of Ghent were complaining that they could not find maids, because girls from the neighbouring villages were earning a living from lace making. In the seventeenth and eighteenth centuries, Flanders, Brabant and Hainault became the main lace centres in Europe, although the great migration had taken women to foreign countries, for instance Honiton in England. Once lace was widely used in coifs and other clothing, many women and girls of the countryside produced quite coarse lace, while fine lace was produced in the towns, especially in Bruges, Ghent, Lille, Antwerp, Malines, Brussels, Binche and Valenciennes, many of which have lent their names to patterns that are still known. Nuns, lay sisters and other women kept schools where they taught the refinements of lace making.

The Renaissance involved more than the spread of Italy's admiration for classical civilization to all Europe. The ostentation of rich Italians was also imitated, and their fashions for silks, velvets and satins. In 1497 the wearing of these materials was forbidden to the common people, at the insistence of the cloth towns. Whereas the Low Countries had hardly any silk industry before, it developed far enough in Bruges for a guild to be established there in 1496. It was, however, the great metropolis of Antwerp, where the raw silk arrived, that became the chief centre; from there it was brought to Holland during the troubles, especially to Amsterdam, where 431 of the 490 silk workers who married between 1585 and 1606 had actually come from the south. The industry grew in the seventeenth century, when it no longer depended on limited deliveries from the Mediterranean: some Portuguese ships captured in the Far East gave Amsterdam its first supply of China silk in 1604, at a time when there was a shortage of Italian and Levantine silk. Some Marraños (ostensibly converted Portuguese Jews) were encouraged by the magistrates and installed spinning shops. Regulations were made to govern quality.

As Asian trade grew Amsterdam was regularly supplied with China silk and became particularly famous for dyeing, so that the half-finished silks were often sent to Amsterdam from elsewhere, especially Hamburg. In the first half of the seventeenth century about 120,000 pounds of raw silk were worked annually. Children were often used for the preliminary work. The labourers worked for the most part at home, although some manufacturers did have workshops, as had happened in the wool industry. The high cost of a raw material from so far away and of the tools required, as well as the extreme sensibility of manufacture to general economic conditions gave commercial capital a considerable advantage over artisans. In comparison with that of Amsterdam, the silk industry of Leyden, Haarlem and Utrecht or Antwerp, which continued to exist, played only a subsidiary part.

The sumptuous tastes of the Renaissance also influenced tapestry and provoked the use of silk as well as wool. In the first half of the sixteenth century Brussels held first place in the industry: in 1515 Pope Leo x had the series 'The Acts of the Apostles' woven there, and it survives in the Vatican to this day. It was copied from Raphael cartoons which also survive in

London. The workshops of Antwerp grew after 1525, stimulated by the merchants' wealth, and took over the lead from Brussels mid-century. The town authorities opened a hall there in 1537, where tapestries produced elsewhere could also be sold; and they were still often produced to the designs of painters in Brussels. Thereafter the prosperity of the chief towns of the United Provinces encouraged the art to develop there as well. In 1554 Charles v instituted regulations concerning quality for the entire Low Countries.

The gradual popularization of the taste for luxury led to the production of tapestries that were artistic but inferior in quality. They were made cheaply in Flanders, especially around Oudenaarde, by peasants who wanted the supplementary income they could earn from this, as had happened with cloth and linen. The edict of 1554 subjected them to the control of the neighbouring town's guild, which was perturbed by the competition, but this did not have the hoped-for results, and by 1560 many tapestry weavers had even left Oudenaarde for the surrounding villages so as to practise their trade in complete liberty. Political and religious troubles caused many to leave their homes, generally, again, for Holland. The magistrates of Gouda converted six disused monasteries into workshops for dyeing or weaving. Other Flemish tapestry weavers established themselves in Paris, where their workshop developed, by 1667, into the celebrated Gobelins factory. Yet the industry rapidly recovered in the Spanish Netherlands. In the seventeenth century it was usually organized in capitalist fashion: between 1636 and 1645, for example, a merchant in Oudenaarde employed about a hundred weavers and annually gave them about six thousand pounds of wool to work. This system, which first appears in the textile trades, gradually spread throughout industry.

3 HEAVY INDUSTRY

A capitalist system was already common in the metal industry. Since the sack of Dinant in 1466, Malines had become the centre for copper, with about forty workshops around 1500 and some sixty in the sixteenth century. Not only were its kitchen utensils and church furnishings famous, but also its bell casting, a consequence of the fashion for carillons. The Malines architects were often called upon in this period to construct public monuments, and this may also have given work to the bell casters. Around 1480 the town also became the main cannon foundry in the Low Countries. Bronze was preferred to iron for the manufacture of cannon, especially the smaller ones, and Malines supplied them to England, Spain, Portugal, Italy and even Persia, probably because of Charles v's alliance against Turkey. Malines suffered increasingly from German competition. The Dutch Revolt was a death-blow, for it ruined the entire copper industry of the Low Countries until the present century.

The indirect method had set off a large-scale revolution in the Walloon iron industry. Seen through modern eyes, this industry was still quite small: around 1500 a well-equipped blast furnace could produce six or seven hundred pounds of cast iron in a week, but work was never continuous. Labour still came from local peasants who were supplementing their farming incomes, and in the summer power was often lacking because the river was not high enough to sustain the water-mills unless expensive dams were built. Fuel was also frequently scarce. The seven or eight labourers working a blast-furnace depended on ten times their number of wood cutters and charcoal burners, and the transport of charcoal along the appalling roads often came to a halt in wet weather. Some furnaces in the Spa area could only work for six weeks of the year in 1509, others for only four months of the years between 1619 and 1631. But contemporaries were struck by the development of the industry, which was unique in Europe at that time. Although it produced only 842.5 tonnes of cast iron in 1562, The principality of Liège was lyrically compared with Vulcan's forge, and many men sought concessions for iron ore or for the construction of a water-mill.

The capital required to establish the costly equipment of the blast furnaces was originally supplied by citizens of Liège or other large towns. The forge masters sometimes set up companies of a peculiar type, in which each participant had the right to use the factory for a certain time. They were keen to see technical improvements that could lower production costs. Techniques were invented for laminating, wire drawing or ingot splitting, the last of which was to assist in the production of nails. By 1625 there were even plans to reduce the ore by the use of coal at Liège, although the time was not ripe for this. The forge masters also sold their own output. A merchant of Liège who had contracted to supply 400,000 pounds of cast iron in Antwerp in 1566, passed the order to the forge masters and paid them on delivery. But at this time only twenty-five merchants were buying the cast iron of the whole principality of Liège. Late in the century they began to invest in the industry directly, delivering mineral and fuel to the blast-furnaces after buying them from owners of forests and mines. Later, they bought forests and ore deposits themselves, and thus achieved perfect economic integration.

Nail manufacture was a typical supplementary activity for many Walloon peasants in the sixteenth century. Almost all farms between the Sambre and the Meuse had smithies, and there are still traces of them. All forty-nine peasants of Charnoy, the cradle of today's Charleroi, were making nails in 1602. This industry, too, was subject to a system of commercial capitalism. Merchants bought cast iron from the blast furnace, distributed it to the peasants and sold the nails they made. In 1551 a single merchant sent 21,000 pounds of nails to Antwerp, Ghent, Bruges and Ostend, and in the first half of the seventeenth century another was employing some hundred nail makers.

Quite early on the town of Liège specialized in the production of weaponry, which it sold to belligerents even-handedly because of the ruler's neutrality. Originally it produced cannon-balls in particular: the Brussels government ordered 133,000 in 1551–2 for the campaign in Lorraine. In the Dutch Revolt it produced a great quantity of firearms, especially light ones such as muskets and pistols, the quality of which was guaranteed by a testing-bench set up in 1672. They were forged locally by arms manufacturers working for merchants who contracted to supply the troops; the Liégeois, Jean Curtius, was the great supplier of arms to the Spanish forces in the Netherlands, and when the Twelve Years Truce indicated that needs would fall off, he went to Spain at the invitation of Philip III to develop her arms industry. His compatriot, Louis de Geer, who had emigrated to Dordrecht and Amsterdam, sold arms after 1615 to Sweden and in 1617 entered Gustavus Adolphus's service. In association with another compatriot, Guillaume de Bèche, who had preceded him in 1595, he brought Liège iron workers to Sweden and laid the bases of a modern arms and iron industry, which gave Sweden her power in the Thirty Years War. At its end, men from Liège revived the German iron industry. Others helped the industry's technical progress in England and elsewhere. In 1598 Curtius undertook to supply powder to the Spanish troops in the Netherlands, and was thus a pioneer of the chemical industry. He boiled quantities of saltpeter, mined sulphur, and also manufactured vitriol and alum for the purpose. German workers were often used in the industry, since they had the best technical knowledge.

The growth of techniques based on heat, and the gradual exhaustion of peat and timber reserves, stimulated the use of coal. Coal from Liège was carried down the Meuse to Holland and then up the Rhine as far as Frankfort, or was shifted towards the ports of the North Sea or the Pas-de-Calais in competition with England. The prince-bishop's taxes show that 48,300 tonnes were produced in 1545–6 and 90,000 in 1562–3, although there was a decline by 1566–7 to 37,000, perhaps because of the economic crisis of the Baltic war and the insecurity caused by the iconoclasts' revolt. Mining made rapid progress. Many new shafts were sunk with the aid of an empirical knowledge of geology, not to be bettered until the advent of the scientific age. Open-cast mining still went on in the older mines, which could be up to a hundred metres in depth.

Drainage of subterranean water made for increasing problems, and the conduits had to be extended again and again. At Liège some were constructed up to fifteen kilometres in length, which led to the Meuse and served several mines. They were also used to supply the fountains and public pumps of Liège. If the water could not be drained into a valley, it could be lifted by buckets on a windlass, but human muscle had increasingly to be replaced by wind- or watermills, horsepower, or by a treadmill. However the pumping was conducted, new shafts had to be dug so as to make it possible for the coal to be lifted, for it was impossible to have galleries that ran more than 300 or 350 metres from the ventilation shaft, and new ones had to be sunk. Quite often flooded mines had to be abandoned, much to the authorities' regret, if only because it lost them a source of income. Not surprisingly, inventors were greatly concerned with the problem of pumping, and in 1530 a pumping machine was invented at Liège, though we do not know how it worked, if at all.

In any event, coal mining needed more and more capital. The old type of peasant mine disappeared in the sixteenth century. The merchants who contracted with independent miners supplied them with capital for mining and were given shares in the existing or new company in exchange, which gave them the right to have a man work for them on their own account. New shafts were generally exploited from the start by wage-earning workers, and such capitalist enterprise soon became widespread; mining became a permanent occupation. An edict at Liège in 1487 forbade coal miners to leave their trade except in wartime or for the harvest, as the industry still had clear links with the peasantry; but by 1607 a further edict omitted the harvest, and the miners were treated as a purely industrial labour force. Thereafter increased division of labour was reflected in greater mining output: the average number of miners per shaft rose from ten to fifteen early in the sixteenth century, and to about one hundred during the seventeenth. Heavy industry was in the process of becoming large-scale enterprise.

4   OTHER INDUSTRIES

Louvain was beginning to emerge as the great brewing town. Brewing became subject to industrial centralization. Whereas the number of brewers fell from seventy-two in 1477 to twenty-seven fifty years later, their output, 77,000 hectolitres in 1520, rose by more than inverse proportion, and this was also true at Haarlem. A populous town like Amsterdam ought to have had a large brewing industry, but that was not the case. Perhaps the low quality of the water provides an explanation of why this happened in the context of brewing, but there is another, more general, explanation: the Zaan region, just north of the town, became an industrial suburb in the seventeenth century, owing, particularly, to its windmills, for it was a bare plain and an ideal industrial site. Wages were also lower there than in Amsterdam, and among the notable food industries which the Zaan took over from Amsterdam were milling, oil pressing and mustard-making.

By contrast, Amsterdam was the main centre for sugar refining which needed not power but heat from the cauldrons of the refineries. This industry had been preceded by that of Antwerp in the 1500s, where Italian artisans, who had been experts in the matter since the Middle Ages, were employed. Later some Antwerpers bought plantations in the Canaries and in Brazil. Refugees brought the industry to Rotterdam and Amsterdam, where it prospered, with sixty refineries at its height in 1661 as against barely three in 1605. They imported raw sugar from

Bengal, Siam and Formosa after 1616, from Java, where the first plantations started up in 1637, from the West Indies and from Brazil. In Brazil, which was mainly occupied by the Dutch between 1630 and 1654, many of the planters were Portuguese Jews, whose relations with their sephardic co-religionists probably explain why these had such an important share in the refining industry in Amsterdam. Its fame was such that artisans from the town were used to start up the industry elsewhere, particularly in many of the French ports and in Hamburg. Gin, familiar from the sixteenth century on, was the product of repeated distillation of barley malt and rye flour with juniper berries and became a speciality of Schiedam after 1630, which it has remained. It soon became a favourite drink of sailors.

Tobacco processing was probably brought to Holland during the occupation of Brazil. After the loss of that colony, Virginia tobacco was imported from England, and as Rotterdam held first place in trade with the British Isles, it also had the first place in this industry. When tobacco growing was started in the United Provinces, it was also processed at Utrecht, Amersfoort and the Zaan. In the early 1620s some Englishmen had begun to manufacture clay pipes at Rotterdam and this was later developed at Gouda in particular, although the indispensable kaolin had to come from Maastricht or Cologne.

Like all European countries, the Low Countries had always had a scattered ceramics industry. Under the stimulus of Renaissance Italianism, Antwerp established the first majolica factory, set up by an Italian from the area of the Urbino early in the 1500s. Antwerp artisans of the new style dispersed during the troubles and they introduced the techniques to Rotterdam, Gouda and Delft where the local clay was suitable for baking. Delft soon emerged as leader, probably because of personal factors so important in artistic creation. Delft pottery, blue or multi-coloured, was an imitation of the colours and motifs of Chinese porcelain, which had become fashionable through Eastern trade. When the Manchu succession disrupted the trade in 1644 the market was still more eager for Delft imitations. The number of faience workshops rose from about ten in 1650 to some thirty in 1670. Delft tiles, sometimes assembled to make up whole pictures, became desirable decorations for the walls of private houses, not only in the Low Countries but also in monasteries in the Iberian

world, while Delft vases and crockery looked attractive among the
furniture of wealthy houses.

Population expansion and the continued transformation of the
towns as existing buildings were rebuilt gave sufficient stimulus
to the manufacture of bricks and tiles. Seizing on the opportunities
offered by the rise of Antwerp, Gilbert van Schoonbeke had
undertaken a vast building programme in the middle of the sixteenth century, for which he bought up gardens, vaulted watercourses and planned new streets. He built twenty-four breweries
after 1552 in a new industrial quarter north of the old town. In
1542 he had undertaken the construction of new fortifications, for
which he used some thirty brick ovens in the town's surroundings,
fuelled by peat lifted from his own peat bogs around Breda. The
arrival of Brabantine and Flemish refugees had the effect of
improving the quality of brick in the United Provinces, which are
said to have produced a good 200,000,000 bricks annually in the
seventeenth century. In South Holland and the provinces of
Utrecht, Friesland and Groningen, a suitable clay was available, as
well as peat, to heat the ovens. The Leyden brick-makers set up a
cartel in 1633 to guarantee high prices by supervising the output
and the level of wages. More than ever bricks were used as ballast
for ships leaving for the Baltic, where they were sold, and the
silting up of the German, Polish and other harbours by sand
carried as ballast and dumped overboard in the port came to an
end. The import of bricks from Holland naturally led the coastal
countries to employ Dutch architects for their buildings, and these
men built the palaces and castles of Denmark and Sweden, and the
rich houses of the burghers of Danzig, where whole streets,
faithfully reconstructed after their destruction in the second
world war, strongly recall the urban landscape of Holland.

Italianism was no less influential in glass making than it was in
pottery, despite the survival since Frankish times of a native product in popular use. 'Crystalline' glass making, after the famous
fashion of Venice and Murano, was brought to Antwerp in 1537;
in 1541 a Venetian founded a mirror factory there and in 1552 an
artisan from Brescia produced fine goblets and window-panes. A
glass blower from Cremona set up in nearby Lier in 1549 and
when Queen Elizabeth established a glass factory in London, she
sought expert labour from Antwerp, probably the chief centre of
the industry north of the Alps.

Refugees and other Italians, who continued to emigrate, introduced the process to the great towns of the United Provinces.
Amsterdam glassware was compared in the seventeenth century
with Venetian glass. In Belgium Antwerp lost its primacy to
Liège, where Italian glass makers had also set themselves up. In
the mid-seventeenth century the Liège family of Bonhomme
managed to control a great many glass works, not only in the
principality, but also in the Spanish Netherlands, Maastricht and
Bois-le-Duc. This trust, which marketed goods that were of fine
quality because of the high temperatures of its coal-fired ovens,
soon collapsed in internal dissension. After Spa had become a
famous thermal resort in the sixteenth century, trade in its mineral
water gave rise to a bottle-glass industry. The custom of bottling
wine grew as well. Gradually window-panes came into common use
in houses, since clear glass could be obtained in the new high-
temperature ovens.

The first diamond cutters were also established at Antwerp in
1478, and flourished in the sixteenth century because of the
patronage of wealthy courtiers and merchants of Antwerp. The
stones probably came from the Portuguese Indies. Emigrants
from Antwerp are said to have brought the art to Amsterdam in
1588, and Brazil, under Dutch domination, supplied the uncut
stones – as was the case with sugar, the relationship was stimulated by the presence of Jews in both places. Presumably it was
religious solidarity that led to the employment of German Jews
as cutters; some of them had set up as master cutters by 1680. The
industry survived at Antwerp as well, but guilds obsessed with
economic Malthusianism, and the cutters' dependence on supplies of uncut stones from Amsterdam, limited its prosperity there.
The number of masters declined from 164 to about a hundred
between 1618 and 1648.

The taste for luxury was still illustrated by the fashion for
Cordoba leather in rich houses. Perhaps it was Philip the Fair's
brief rule in Castile (1504–6), during which time many courtiers
from the Netherlands travelled there, that introduced them to this
art in which the old Moorish city had excelled for so long. Its first
mention in the Low Countries occurs at Malines, then the seat of
the court, in 1511. It survived there throughout the sixteenth and
seventeenth centuries, and like so many other industries passed to
Holland during the great migration. In 1627 a currier contracted

with an Amsterdam manufacturer for annual deliveries of 16,000 French calf skins.

Leather was also needed for book binding. Printing started in all of the large towns of the Low Countries in the fifteenth century, and the trade was so successful that it became famous throughout Europe. The press founded by Christophe Plantin at Antwerp in 1555 and carried on after his death by his son-in-law, Jan Moretus, acquired a monopoly, in association with the Escorial monastery, for missals and breviaries in Spain and her colonies. With many other presses at Antwerp, it specialized in the printing of devotional works in Dutch and French, as well as Castilian, in the seventeenth century. The spirit of tolerance, which gained ground in the United Provinces once religious controversy had declined around 1625, stimulated the printing in the Republic of a great many works by free-thinkers who could not have published them at home. Atlases also became a Dutch speciality, for they were based on the most recent information of navigators and explorers.

Ships were built at all Dutch ports. The wonderful prosperity of Dutch commerce in the sixteenth century naturally stimulated shipbuilding, and its quality greatly helped sea trade and the economy in general. The flutes, first built at Hoorn in 1595, were long, broad-bellied ships that were fast and able to carry large cargoes with quite a small crew. Soon they had superseded most of the earlier merchant ships and they dominated the sea for a century to come. At the same time the exploitation of the windmill to saw wood facilitated the work, and not only that of the shipyards. The ferocious opposition of Amsterdam sawyers to the installation of windmills meant that the Zaan, the region where windmills were most widespread, became the chief centre for ship building. Oak from the Black Forest in particular was used there. In the Zaan wind-power was also used to make rigging, ropes, and canvas sails. Around 1650 it was estimated that the Dutch merchant marine made 250 or 350 sea-going ships annually, to replace those that had been lost through wear and tear, wreck and war. In the course of time the Zaan's reputation for high-quality ships brought orders from France, England, Italy, Spain, Denmark and Sweden, for both trading vessels and warships.

4 The Golden Century of Antwerp

In the fifteenth century the fairs of Antwerp and Bergen-op-Zoom had become direct competitors of Bruges. In the last quarter of the century the great Flemish cities had led the opposition to the regent, Maximilian of Austria, and in 1484 and 1488 he instructed foreign merchants to leave Bruges, which was in open revolt against his monarchical policy.

It was on the second of these occasions that the foreigners departed for Antwerp, where they had been invited. The Zwin also remained closed to traffic from the summer of 1487 until Christmas 1492, when Sluis surrendered to Maximilian's armies, and in 1491 Antwerp was granted the alum staple. But as soon as Bruges had made peace with the Archduke, the town at once tried to get the merchants to return, and most of the 'nations' did so, as could be expected from such traditionally-minded institutions. Antwerp, however, traded increasingly outside the season of the fairs; by 1498 Philip the Fair had forbidden their prolongation, but the prohibition, though repeated several times, remained ineffectual and in the first years of the next century the foreign consulates almost all followed their merchants to Antwerp. The town had meanwhile received a further stimulus when, by 1498 at the latest, the king of Portugal's factor set up there to conduct in the north sales of the products of the crown's colonial monopoly. The natives of Africa traded these goods for copper articles. When Vasco da Gama reached India in 1498, he discovered that silver there was considered more valuable than gold, so that silver

175

exports to Asia were very profitable. Antwerp acquired increasing quantities of copper and silver from upper Germany, and so the Portuguese could link their trade with that of Antwerp.

The arrival of the first spice cargo from the Indies in 1501 began a regular trade, and Antwerp became the centre from which Portuguese cargoes from Africa or the Indies were distributed throughout almost the whole of Europe as far as the fairs of Lyons and Marseilles. They arrived in such quantity that prices at first tended to fall and spices ceased to count as luxuries. The traditional spice trade through the Levant and the Mediterranean temporarily lost out to such competition. But the royal factor's monopoly of supplies rapidly created a monopoly of distribution from 1506, for Italian houses contracted with him to take, within a fixed period, all spices disembarked at Antwerp. Soon the powerful German firms of Fugger, Welser, Höchstetter and others, who supplied the metals, replaced the Italians and most of the time took the spices. To these the Germans owed an appalling reputation as leeches and a huge increase in their profits.

However the supremacy of Antwerp in the spice trade was rapidly challenged. The rivalry of Charles v and the Valois, and the Franco-Turkish alliance that resulted, took the French market for spices away from Antwerp and back to the Levant, where the trading system had recovered and adapted under Venetian domination. Elsewhere in Europe, too, Mediterranean trade again competed with the Portuguese monopolies and those of distribution. Presumably this was why the Germans became less interested in the monopoly after 1525 and abandoned it to the Marrańos and others. Finally, the opening of the silver mines at Potosí in 1545 and Zacatécas in 1549 flooded Castile, Portugal's neighbour, with so much silver that the Portuguese crown no longer had to get it from the Low Countries. Lisbon itself replaced Antwerp as centre for the distribution of spices, and the *feitoria de Flandres* was abolished as a permanent centre in 1548.

In the meantime the Portuguese colony had grown considerably, in particular because of the many Marrańos who had been chased from their homes by religious persecution and had been given a safe conduct by Charles v. In 1526 there had been only twelve Portuguese merchants in Antwerp but by 1570 there were ninety-seven. Besides spices, they brought oil, sugar, fruits from the south, and above all salt from the Setubal plants that had profited from the gradual decline of Bourgneuf. Of the 1,293 Portuguese ships noted in the accounts of anchorage dues at Arnemuiden, which survived except for gaps covering twenty years between 1518 and 1571, 750 ships, perhaps even 782, were wholly, and fifty-five partly, loaded with salt. The commodity also arrived in the holds of ships of other nations. By 1524–9 an average of 80,800 hectolitres was imported annually; in 381 working days in 1551–3 224,000 of them were unloaded. In exchange the Portuguese exported woollens or linen, at least 200,000 ells of the latter in the reign of Manuel the Great (1495–1521), and a vast quantity of consumer goods.

The Portuguese spice market had been set up at Antwerp with an eye to deliveries made there of goods from upper Germany. Between 1495 and 1521 the Portuguese factor sent on to Lisbon over 14,000 marks (2,426.5 kilograms) of silver and over eleven million pounds of copper, as well as 47,500 pounds and 14,000 single basins of the same metal. About half of the copper extracted from the Fugger Hungarian mines was sent to Antwerp between 1507 and 1539. In 1527 they had in stock 200,000, and in 1546 as many as 500,000 florins' worth. Apart from Portuguese spices, the great merchant houses of Augsburg, Nuremberg and Ulm imported English cloth, and the brilliant period of urban civilization at the time of the *Meistersinger* made Swabia and Franconia an eager market for many other products obtained through Antwerp. After 1525 these houses turned increasingly towards finance. Their share of trade in goods was probably partly taken up by lesser German firms, about whose activities we lack evidence, and their withdrawal also stimulated trade from the Low Countries at the Frankfort fairs. The transporting was generally undertaken by carters from the Spessart in Hesse, and their memory survives in the name of the *Hessenhuis*, the ware-house they used at Antwerp, and the *Hessenwegen*, the wide earth roads in the eastern provinces of the Netherlands, which they are alleged to have used.

The attraction which German metals held for the Portuguese spice trade thus made Antwerp temporarily a world market for tropical products. Before that it was the chief market for English cloth, which was much sought-after throughout Europe, and this role was strengthened when the promise of free trade in the Baltic, contained in the Treaty of Utrecht which ended an Anglo-

Hanseatic conflict in 1474, was not fulfilled, and when the *Inter-cursus Magnus* of 1496 between the English and Burgundian govern-ments gave the English freedom of trade in the Low Countries. Soundly organized into the Fellowship of Merchant Adventurers, under London's leadership, the English cloth merchants made as much as they could of the competition from Bergen-op-Zoom and Middelburg to put pressure on Antwerp and get the most favour-able terms for their commerce. But Bergen-op-Zoom lost its trading role after 1530, and Middelburg was no better as a choice since the vast majority of merchants resided in Antwerp.

By 1530 the Antwerp market had finally risen above the sea-sonal trading characteristic of fairs (despite their prolongation over the past generation) and merchants from other towns either resided there or were permanently represented in the town. By contrast, the Adventurers continued to cross the channel at the period of the fairs and only for as long as they lasted. They were probably the largest group of merchants at Antwerp: by 1550 around six hundred would cross annually for at least one of the fairs, and for its duration only. An annual average of 83.5 English ships paid for anchorage at Arnemuiden in 1538–41, and the figure was 129 in the years 1564–8. Others sailed straight into Antwerp from fifty English and even Irish ports, but the great majority were from Hull, Ipswich and especially London.

English cloth was usually exported undyed and was finished in the Low Countries, principally at Antwerp. Not until 1555 did England try to prevent the export of half-finished cloth. Around 1500 London, whose export made up about two-thirds of the total, sent around 50,000 pieces of cloth on average per annum, intended probably for the Scheldt markets. Exports rose by half up to 1525, before the devaluations that brought the pound sterling from thirty-two *sous* of Flemish groats in 1526 to thirteen *sous* and four groats in 1551, and by 1554 the figure had risen to just under 135,000. The accounts of an import duty levied in the Low Countries show that Antwerp received 122,000 cloths in 1549–50, 41 per cent of them being broadcloths, and as many kerseys, which were of coarser quality. Export to Germany was estimated in 1565 at 50,000 cloths and 25,000 kerseys, while Italy took as many of the latter.

The Low Countries also took English coal, lead and tin, skins, cheese and beer; in return they exported fine cloth, light woollens and linen, estimated at 100,000 Flemish pounds both in 1530 and 1576. England remained an important market for these, as it did for tapestry, silks and other manufactured goods characteristic of a way of life more refined than that of Tudor England. A whole range of goods of diverse origins was also sent to England, as to other countries, which apparently accounted for between 25 and 40 per cent of all trade. Compared with this Scotland's share, based as before on exports of wool and skins, remained modest. Despite Middelburg's attempts to take over the trade, the Scottish 'nation' remained loyal to Veere on the whole from 1508 until the end of the eighteenth century. 329 Scottish ships anchored there between 1561 and 1571, as against ninety-eight in the other Walcheren ports. They rarely went beyond these outer harbours where they had some share in the transporting of French salt.

The salt from the Bay of Bourgneuf, and that from Brouage which gradually supplanted it, were still strong competitors for Iberian salt, and were the most important element in French trade with the Low Countries. The shipping was done by Scots and Englishmen, Basques, Hollanders, Hansards and especially Bretons who won their reputation as great sailors in this trade. They also took an active part in the exploitation of Andalusian and Portuguese salt-mines. During the seventeen years of the period 1518–50 for which we have records, Bretons carried 3,675,000 hectolitres of salt to Arnemuiden, but French salt was only 12.5 per cent of the total of 105,000 hectolitres unloaded there in 1551–2. French grain also had a small part to play in the trade, but it appeared only at times of famine because Baltic grain dominated the market.

French wine, however, had remarkable success in the Low Countries, although Rhine wines were still favoured in much of the country, and although wine had tended to become a luxury replaced by beer at the level of the people. Wines from Burgundy, Champagne and the Paris basin were brought in quantities along the land and sea routes, and the frontier posts of Artois, Hainault and Namur registered 84,000 hectolitres in 1550. Brabant took its supplies from the Namur market in particular. Breton shippers prospered from the carriage of Poitevin and Gascony wines, which were unloaded at the mouth of the Scheldt near the great centres for consumption of Flanders and Brabant. Middelburg, which had obtained the privilege of gauging in 1508, acquired an almost total monopoly of the unloading and distribution. In the two years 1518–20 the Bretons alone accounted for 226,000 hecto-litres of the wine brought to Arnemuiden. However, Middel-burg's privileges were restricted in 1546 to the advantage of Zierikzee, Antwerp and Bergen-op-Zoom. Middelburg protested but in practice kept much of its lead, for of the 313,000 hectolitres of wine imported into the Low Countries in 1550, 113,000 were unloaded at the Walcheren ports, as against 45,000 in Flanders itself and 26,500 in Antwerp, while 75,500 hectolitres came in via Holland and Utrecht, almost all of it from the Rhine.

Imports of Languedoc woad were greater in bulk than wine and in value than salt, and supplied the textile industry with an essen-tial dye which was even re-exported to manufacturing centres in Germany despite the competition of Thuringian woad. Around 1560 there were thought to be some 40,000 bales of such imports; in 1543, although there was a war, Giovanni Battista Guicciardini imported 12,000. France, despite the rise in the Low Countries of a native linen industry, still exported quantities of linen, haber-dashery and fashion articles, and imported from there quantities of herring and other fish, skins and leather and, despite their southern origin, spices, fruits and alum from the Papal States, and luxuries as well. The printing of French books at Antwerp, for one, was a sign of the French market's overall importance to this trade.

The Castilians remained to some extent loyal to Bruges, where by the sixteenth century they were the only merchant colony of any significance, numbering some fifty. They brought wool, which they sold direct to the nearby centres of the Flemish cloth trade so as to reduce transport costs. Lighters brought them from Arne-muiden to Sluis, the average annual quantity being 2,500 tonnes in the years 1503–9 and 2,700 in 1550–68. Consulates of the Biscay area, instituted for merchants and sailors from the Basque lands, and of Navarre, the latter probably established by Castile after the conquest of southern Navarre in 1512, were set up at Bruges in 1455 and in 1530 respectively, but they were not very important and were given up during the troubles around 1575. The consulate for 'Spain' – i.e. for Castile – lasted until 1705.

Merchants from Spain, even when established at Bruges, did not neglect the Scheldt markets. In 1552 some two hundred of them took a share in Antwerp's exports to the south, and in 1560 about a hundred Spanish firms were established there. The Andalusians, who had been subjects of Castile since the fall of Granada in 1492, had their consulate at Middelburg between 1505 and 1564, and the consulates of Aragon and Catalonia were transferred from Bruges to Antwerp in 1527. All of them imported wines, oil, southern fruit and sugar to the Scheldt markets. After about 1550 they were able to recover an intermediary role in the spice trade, though the spices were now probably Portuguese, and their trade in Andalusian salt was highly prosperous, since it accounted for twice as much imported salt in 1551–3 as the Portuguese salt trade. From the Low Countries textiles were their main export.

However, although the Low Countries exported throughout Europe goods of a quality that testified to the brilliance of their civilization, it was still Italy that led in this respect. There had been many attempts to imitate Italian luxuries, but cloth-of-gold and -silver, fine woollens, silks, velvets, furs, tapestries, jewels, earthenware and much else were still brought in great quantities from Italy, mainly to Antwerp. In 1551 there were twenty-three firms in the Lombard 'nation' in Antwerp, thirty-eight Genoese, twenty Luccan and thirteen Florentine. Apart from these merchants organized into consulates, there were other Italians to represent the rest of the peninsula, from Venice to Sicily. They shared in the spice trade, and were almost as constantly involved in marketing alum from Tolfa in the Papal States or Mazarrón in Spain. To guarantee its markets, the Holy See would not hesitate to use its spiritual authority. Agostino Chigi of Siena, to whom the Pope had rented his mine, strengthened his monopoly in 1508 by taking a lease on imports of alum to the Low Countries. In 1544 Gaspar Ducci of Pistoia took over the latter monopoly in association with Alexis Grimel, formerly Antwerp factor of the Welsers, and Sebastian Neidhart of Augsburg. In 1559 the Genoese Negron de Negro and Giovanni Battista Spinola, in association with Balthasar Schetz, a citizen of Antwerp, and his son Conrad, contracted to import sixteen hundredweight of Mazarrón alum annually, for nine years.

Sea trade between the Low Countries and Italy remained relatively limited, restricted chiefly to cheap, bulky goods that were ill-suited to long and expensive cartage. Up to 96 per cent of the transport (judging from the accounts of an export tax in 1543–5) was carried out by a few specialized firms of Genoa or Milan, in little staging-posts on the German side of the Alpine passes, such as Füssen or Reutte, or in Fontenoy in Lorraine. These firms relieved the merchants of their worries regarding delivery, offered fixed rates, which made the calculation of transport costs easier, and maintained relays on the great roads. The two main routes ran through Switzerland to Milan, and over the Austrian passes to Venice and their hinterlands. For the two years covered by our source, 1,095 convoys left Antwerp with loads worth 587,000 groat-pounds; 185 of the three hundred merchants involved were Italian, accounting for 63.2 per cent of the value of the merchandise. As far as we can tell the chief destinations were Ancona (34.9 per cent) and Venice (29.3 per cent), which suggests large-scale transport to the Balkans and the Levant, important purchasers of English cloth. The cloth of the Low Countries went essentially to the Italian market. Such convoys occurred most frequently between March and July, because of the intermediary role of Italy. The August convoys were too late in the year to reach the Adriatic before winter interrupted sailing. Exports to Italy have been reckoned at about a sixth of Antwerp's business.

The Hansa had shared commercial supremacy with Italy in the later Middle Ages. The rise of upper-German trade had removed the central German market from the Hansa, while Dutch and English competition weakened its hold on the Baltic. However, when upper Germany gradually gave up traffic in goods, and when the abundance of American silver enabled Spain to increase her purchases in the Baltic, there was a revival of the Hansa. Concerned at Dutch competition, the Hanseatic towns again tried to divert trade from Amsterdam by concluding an agreement with its only possible rival, Antwerp. A new 'factory', a compulsory residence for Hansards, was set up there in 1553, to replace the one at Bruges which had been in decay since the later fifteenth century. These efforts were futile, and Amsterdam's lead in this trade only grew. If Antwerp's exports of Flemish and Brabantine manufactures did rise a little, the great Scheldt market nevertheless remained essentially dependent on Holland for supplies of Baltic grain and other goods.

2 THE ACTIVE TRADE OF THE LOW COUNTRIES

The presence of numerous merchants 'of all nations and tongues' (as the proud inscription on the new Bourse of 1531 ran) had made

Antwerp the outstanding cosmopolitan town of the century, where, as early as 1516, Thomas More had sited his meeting with the man who revealed to him the mysteries of Utopia. If it outshone Bruges in this respect, it also seems to have maintained, in its Golden Century, a greater foreign trade. Perhaps it was the departure of the foreign colonies that decided the merchants of Bruges to set up a company for trade with Portugal in the last quarter of the fifteenth century. The drapers of many Brabantine towns exported what was left of their output to the Frankfort fairs; and the closeness of their relationship was illustrated in 1511 when eighty-seven men from Antwerp and Malines bound for the fairs were held to ransom by soldiers from Guelders. Nicolas van Rechtergem, who had come from Aachen to Antwerp, sent the first Portuguese spices to upper Germany in 1503. His son-in-law from Maastricht, Erasmus Schetz, was the lessee of the calamine mines in the Vieille Montagne and held an honourable position among the traders who bartered metal for colonial goods. He also set up a sugar refinery in Brazil that still had links with Antwerp in 1579. Another Antwerper of German origin, Jacon van Groenenborg, planted sugar-cane in the Canaries from 1515 onwards and described himself as their lord. The business was still alive in 1562.

The van der Molens of Antwerp exported cloth to Italy, chiefly on commission from Italian houses. Other merchants from the Low Countries were established in Italy herself – Martin de Hane of Brussels, for instance, lived at Venice from the early sixteenth century on, where he imported English and Low Countries cloth and exported silk through factors at Verona, Antwerp and London. He was one of the richest merchants in Venice and a patron, with his sons, of art and literature. Jan della Faille the Elder, the son of a Flemish peasant who had come to Antwerp to seek his fortune, entered business as de Hane's factor before setting up on his own in trade with Spain and the Baltic. From the late fifteenth century there was in Lisbon a numerous 'Flemish' colony, and another such colony had a considerable share of Seville's trade in the mid-sixteenth century and later. Sailors from Middelburg and Antwerp not only played a large part in the coastal traffic between the mouth of the Scheldt and the British Isles; as the trade increased merchants of Antwerp, much to the Adventurers' distaste, also took over some of the English exports to the Low Countries.

E.H.—7

In the Baltic they may have profited from the war of 1509–12 between Denmark and the Wendish towns, which temporarily weakened the latter. But the Antwerpers were much helped here after the mid-sixteenth century by the rapprochement between their town and the Hansa. The town's receiver-general, Gérard Gramaye, founded several companies between 1562 and 1565 for trade with Italy, Portugal and the Baltic. They exported Swedish iron, linen, skins and leather, especially through Narva, which was then the main port to Russia, in exchange for salt and luxuries for which the Swedish court was eager. King Eric xiv himself was not only a client, but also a shareholder in one of Gramaye's companies. Another Antwerp company loaded ships with cod and furs on the coasts of the Kola Peninsula, on the track of English Arctic explorers and the Muscovy Company.

Antwerp's enterprise in the Baltic could never take the lead from the Hollanders, the supremacy of whom was shown by comparison not only with other provinces of the Low Countries, but even with the other commercial powers of Europe. The first accounts of Sound tolls show that Holland's share was 70 per cent of the annual average of 711 passages. The western coasts of the Zuiderzee accounted for nine-tenths of the trade. These ships came from various ports, but the vast majority were loaded by merchants of Amsterdam, who sometimes even chartered ships from Friesland. Lübeck still attempted to cut its great rival down to size, either by arms, as in 1510–12, 1533–4 and 1542–4, or by having the king of Denmark close the Straits more or less completely to Dutch shipping. Dutch passages did in fact rise by only 77 per cent between the beginning and middle of the century, whereas Hanseatic passages trebled, owing, of course, to the almost total shift from the crossing of the Holstein isthmus to the sea-voyage around Denmark.

Even with only half of the passages, Dutch sailors nonetheless held the chief place, with 1,262 yearly crossings of the Sound on average between 1557 and 1570. The toll accounts also show what the cargoes were. Between 1562 and 1569 the Dutch ships imported to the Baltic 66 per cent of the salt (162,300 lasts), 74 per cent of the Rhine wine and 64 per cent of other wines, as well as 76 per cent of the herring (23,000 lasts), and exported from it 81.5 per cent of the rye (310,000 lasts) and 70 per cent of the wheat (23,000 lasts). In the 1530s the town of Amsterdam had tried to get ships' masters to reside within its walls, and as a result the proportion of Low Countries ships stationed at Amsterdam and crossing the Sound had risen from 12 per cent around 1540 to 17 per cent around 1565, while the proportion for the town's immediate sur-roundings declined more obviously, from 44 to 17 per cent. Many ship owners, fearing the high cost of an expanding town for their families, as well as the less liberal regulation of trade, seem to have preferred to reside at little towns and villages further off in north Holland, where the share of traffic rose from 23 to 33.5 per cent. The ports of the right-hand shore of the Zuiderzee underwent an astonishing revival, from 16.5 to 27 per cent. The rest of the passages was accounted for by ships from Zeeland. The number of crossings did, of course, rise constantly and the Dutch marine rose in consequence. In 1512 it was estimated at four hundred large ships.

The Hollanders' crushing superiority in the Baltic trade made certain that Antwerp's attempts to take over the market there would fail. The principle that trade follows the flag was in this case borne out: Amsterdam's merchant capital had been almost exclusively placed there, whereas for Antwerp merchants it was only one investment among many. Amsterdam clearly had a great deal of capital, the largest amount in Holland and Zeeland except perhaps for that of Dordrecht, about which there is no informa-tion. Amsterdam paid 194,000 florins in 1543 as a tax on merchant capital in the two provinces, and Middelburg came next, a long way behind, with 33,000 florins. Amsterdam was also the main grain staple for the Baltic trade with the West, which was stimu-lated by the absence of any tax on such commerce, a privilege the Scheldt merchants never obtained. At Amsterdam were stocked not only rye and wheat needed to feed the Low Countries them-selves, but also grain re-exported to England and, through the intermediary of Antwerp and its fore-ports in Zeeland, to France, Spain, Portugal and Italy.

The growth of the Baltic grain trade also meant progress for the commonest return-freight, salt from France or Iberia. Dutch trade with the Baltic diversified, however, and because of this it drew many secondary industrial centres and markets into its orbit. The fairs of Deventer were maintained because of their role in collection and distribution for the Baltic trade; Dordrecht, and the neighbouring ports that had eventually succeeded in reducing

Dordrecht's staple to a small due, increased their returns by transit of goods from the Meuse and the Rhine basins. The rise of Amsterdam was clearer day by day. Its trading function in a sense complemented that of Antwerp; while Antwerp in general received and distributed the general goods from England and the south, Amsterdam dealt with the bulky merchandise from the Baltic and the Atlantic coasts. The two centres were in constant communication, acting as distribution centres for each other, with Bois-le-Duc as a frequent intermediary. There was, however, a profound difference in the traders involved. Despite its progress in trade abroad, foreigners still predominated in Antwerp, whereas in Amsterdam the local merchant class was absolutely supreme.

The nature of trade in Antwerp gave its market an incontestable primacy over others in the country in terms of value. War against France caused a tax to be raised on imports to the Low Countries in 1543-5, and it was levied mainly according to the taxpayers' own declarations. It brought in, on average, 7,500,000 florins per annum, even though trade with France had ceased because of the war, and despite the exemption from the tax that the English enjoyed. 77 per cent of the value of exports was accounted for by Antwerp, and if the receipts of the tax-offices at Bergen-op-Zoom and the Walcheren ports are added to this (for they belonged essentially to the same trading system), the percentage rose to 82 per cent. Amsterdam, on the other hand, accounted for only 4.5 per cent of the value of exports, other offices in North Holland barely 0.2 per cent and those of the mouths of the Meuse and the Rhine only 1 per cent.

An attempt has recently been made to extrapolate from the value of the transactions declared in 1543-5 figures for normal peacetime conditions around 1560, and a figure for annual exports (mainly textiles) in this period of 16,000,000 florins has been suggested, whereas the value of imports has been put at 20,000,000 or more, of which colonial goods (in the wider sense) appear to have accounted for between one-fifth and one-seventh. The deficit was made up by imports of silver sent by the Spanish government to maintain its troops, by income from loans placed at Antwerp and finally by what are now called 'services', particularly freight charges paid by foreigners to the Dutch merchant marine.

Any calculation of this type must be treated with reservation because of the lack of information and the subjectivity that is necessarily involved. If it is accepted, it shows the high degree of commercialization in the Low Countries' economy at this time. Accepting the population figure for the Spanish Netherlands that was quoted earlier, imports must have been just under seven florins per head, whereas the comparable figures for France and England were hardly 1.5 florins. It is clear, even without statistical estimates, that trade had grown considerably in the sixteenth century as compared with the later Middle Ages, and that at Antwerp and Amsterdam it no longer had the 'national' character it had had at Bruges. In its Golden Century Antwerp unquestionably deserved its status as a world market, for it distributed goods from abroad to all countries in Christendom.

3 THE DECLINE AND FALL OF ANTWERP

The departure of the Portuguese factory in 1548 had ended the outstanding role played by Antwerp in tropical trade in the past generation. It still had enough advantages not to be too deeply damaged by this, for the industrial growth of the Low Countries was sufficient guarantee of foreign custom. The turning-point in the cycle came only after 1560, first of all in relations with England. The revaluation of sterling put cloth exports into depression, and the Merchant Adventurers attempted to redress the situation by having measures taken in England against foreign merchants trading there, especially those of the Low Countries. The situation rapidly worsened and led to reciprocal embargo. Conscious of the importance of German outlets, and of Germany as a road to Italy, the English 'nation' shifted in 1564 from Antwerp to Emden, which seemed to have a fine future since it had taken in many Protestant refugees. This town proved disappointing, however, because of its still faulty commercial system and the Adventurers had to return to Antwerp early in 1565, without any real settlement of the dispute. Indeed the lack of English cloth there had stimulated sales of Flemish cloth and encouraged the protectionist current that had hitherto been contained, to the Low Countries' profit.

The war between Denmark, Sweden and Poland of 1563–70 disrupted trade in the Baltic, especially as regards grain, at a time when the rough winter of 1564 caused a bad harvest in the Low Countries. Probably the famine and general poverty did much to cause the ferment leading eventually to the iconoclastic riots in August 1566, which in turn produced a hardening of the repression of heresy and an attempted restoration of the king's power. The Reformation had for some time been gaining adherents among the foreign merchants in Antwerp: the great majority of English and Hanseatic merchants were converted, and many Marraños and Frenchmen, too. The town magistrates had hitherto prevented the religious edicts from being applied there, but whether this would still be the case under the military dictatorship heralded by the approach of Spanish troops under the redoubtable Duke of Alva was far from certain, and the uncertainty caused many merchants to emigrate, fearing for their safety.

This was the situation when the English seized Spanish ships which had been laden with silver to pay the troops in the Low Countries, and which had taken refuge at Plymouth to escape French pirates in December 1568. This brought about a further conflict between Spain and England. Once more trade between England and the Low Countries was almost completely paralyzed. During the painful negotiations that had dragged on since 1565, the Adventurers had been concerned to find a staple that would be more convenient than Emden, for they believed they would have to leave Antwerp again. They came to an agreement with Hamburg, and went there in 1569. At the same time Alva tried to make royal authority less dependent on the vote of taxes of popular representatives (the Estates-General or the provincial Estates) by introducing permanent new taxes. Although these plans were only partially realized, the new element of insecurity affected trade.

There was, however, a more serious threat. Since 1568 the Sea Beggars, religious refugees and sailors and fishermen who had been affected by the continuing economic crisis, had been giving trouble to the Low Countries' sea-trade because of their piracy. They seized the ports of Brill and Flushing by surprise in April 1572, and thus gained control of the river approaches to Antwerp. Within three months almost all of Holland and Zeeland had gone over to the rebels, either because of their Protestantism or because trade could only be restored by collaboration with the Beggars. A rebel government was set up in the two provinces. Once established in the conquered ports, the Beggars subjected trade with the enemy to licence, which Zeeland adopted in October 1572 and Holland in spring 1573. Philip II also forbade trade with the rebels, although this was ineffective for they were indispensable middle-men for the supplies and general commerce of the loyal provinces.

It seems curious, in these circumstances, that the Adventurers decided to take their staple back to Antwerp in 1573. Hamburg had turned out to be a good choice for the marketing of kerseys in Germany, and shipment of them to Italy, but it was clear that the Low Countries were still an irreplaceable outlet for their finer cloth. Even after their return to Antwerp, they did not give up consignments to the Elbe, and their trade with Antwerp also became difficult because of Zeeland's political situation – she was in revolt, whereas Brabant remained loyal to Spain – and such problems obviously damaged trade. Other dangers came from the presence of soldiery whose pay was always in arrears and who were therefore inclined to mutiny. Antwerp had escaped being sacked in 1574 only by paying a large contribution to the troops, and did not escape it at all in 1576, when the Spanish Fury subjected it to a twelve-day sack, during which there were many thousands of victims, among them merchants, and five million florins' worth of damage, an enormous sum for the age. A further wave of merchants fled the horrors.

When the shock had passed Antwerp joined the rebels, which removed the political barrier that had severed it from the sea. But this did not bring the expected advantages, for the Zeeland foreports had managed to direct to themselves a large part of the trade that had gone on at Antwerp before the troubles; and they were not inclined to give it up again. Zeeland maintained the system of licences to which Antwerp had been victim. Besides, the Revolt became daily more identified with Calvinism, and many Catholics were impelled to emigrate. The Portuguese 'nation' officially shifted to Cologne in 1578, although only a minority of the Portuguese actually went there. Perhaps it was the departure of so many foreigners that led to new efforts by the local citizenry and others. A 'nation' of 'African' merchants, apparently Jews from the Barbary Coast, appears at Antwerp in 1580 and a Turkish 'nation' for trade with Constantinople in 1582. In 1580 the merchants of the Low Countries engaged in trade with England were allowed to organize themselves on the Adventurers' model, to strengthen their position in England, and in 1583 a similar corporation was established for trade with Spain and

Portugal, which was frequently damaged by prohibitions on both sides, but was usually tolerated. The following year Antwerpers tried to take advantage of dissension between Venice and the 'Levant Company' to take over English commerce between the Mediterranean and the North Sea.

But the end of Antwerp's drama was approaching. Since 1577 the governor-general, Alexander Farnese, had been attempting to reconquer the rebellious provinces. As this proceeded, Antwerp's hinterland, which supplied industrial goods for its markets, shrank and continental communications were cut. The Merchant Adventurers transferred to Middelburg in 1582. In 1584 Farnese laid siege to Antwerp. The town surrendered on 17 August 1585, and the curtain fell on its Golden Age.

5 The Golden Age of Amsterdam

I THE TRIUMPH OF AMSTERDAM

The exodus of merchants from Antwerp benefited the United Provinces most, for the merchants were attracted there by the freedom of communications guaranteed by the Beggars' domination of the sea, as well as by the long-standing economic symbiosis of the northern and southern provinces. The Flemings and Brabantines were also able to use their own language, while Calvinists found their creed raised to the status of the established religion. Some went to Middelburg after this town joined the revolt in 1574, or Dordrecht, or Rotterdam, but Amsterdam, the chief commercial centre of the maritime provinces even before the troubles, easily reigned supreme when it abandoned the royal cause in 1578. Amsterdam became Antwerp's main successor and, often at the instigation of refugees or with their participation, its commercial horizons were widened to include countries in which Antwerp had shown the way. Amsterdam also took over business methods and techniques used in Antwerp.

The Baltic trade, the basis of Amsterdam's growth hitherto, continued to be the *moedernegotie*, the 'mother-trade' or 'soul of all trade, on which other trades and businesses depend'. Every year, in the first days of spring, a large fleet that had wintered in the Vlie or Texel roads set sail for the Sound. Grain was, as in the past, the chief Baltic cargo. While Amsterdam had been loyal to Spain the Sea Beggars, who had also occupied Enkhuizen in 1572, had hindered the movement of its ships and Dutch transports of rye had been damaged. They rose again, from 38,500 tonnes per annum, on average, between 1580 and 1589, to 87,000 from 1610 to 1619, and fell, owing to the ravages of the Thirty Years War, to 80,000 in 1640-9. These figures represented 61.5, 83 and 70 per cent respectively of the total weight of rye brought out of the Sound. Dutch transport of wheat grew from an average yearly figure of 4,300 tonnes in the 1580s to 28,400 in the 1640s, 58 per cent and 88 per cent of the total respectively. As the grain was usually loaded at Danzig, the Polish-Swedish war of 1655-60 deeply disturbed the trade which was slow to recover. Many old warehouses still reveal the importance of the grain trade to Amsterdam: it was stored there in bulk before being re-exported to the rest of Europe, although Dutch ships did carry a certain amount directly to the south.

Apart from grain, the volume of which depended on the harvest of the consuming countries, the Baltic supplied Dutch ship builders with timber, hemp and flax, pitch, and tar. As before, other products of forest industries came via this route, while the Swedish metallurgy, growing largely because of industrialists from Liège, gave considerable quantities of copper and iron for the Dutch arms industry, which was essential to the Republic's position as a great power. Transport was usually in Dutch ships until Gustavus Adolphus (1611-32) gave Sweden a merchant marine.

Until about 1620 many ships still sailed towards the Baltic under ballast – hence the export of such quantities of Dutch brick and tile. As Amsterdam developed its European and colonial trade the ships could be loaded in Holland with a vast assortment of available goods, and such cargoes were in a majority between 1625 and 1650, after which the balance between ships leaving with cargoes and those under ballast was restored. Among the imported merchandise, salt came first in volume, and the share of Dutch shipping in transporting it rose almost without interruption from 24,400 tonnes (58 per cent) on average in the 1580s to 44,300 (80 per cent) in the 1640s. In contrast with their return voyages, the ships usually went straight from the producing countries to the Baltic: sometimes the number of Dutch ships that travelled directly amounted to a quarter of all Dutch ships passing the Sound. The salt usually came from France in the first half of the seventeenth century, because of the Dutch war with Spain.

The development of relations with France was probably responsible for the spreading of the taste for French wines in the

Baltic. Dutch merchants took a large part of this trade, with 11,400 pipes in 1580 (50 per cent) and 33,900 on average in the 1640s (59 per cent), and Dutch sailors also carried a great deal of the wine, with 12,500 pipes (58 per cent) and 31,700 (55 per cent) respectively over the same period. The popularity of French wines in the Baltic affected the demand for Rhine wine, imports of which had come to the Baltic almost wholly from the Republic. They declined considerably, to 5,300 *aunes* per annum in the 1580s and 3,360 in the 1640s, although the share of Dutch shipping in this trade rose from 70 to 77 per cent. Among items exported from Holland herself herring held an important place. In the 1580s Holland fisheries still felt the effects of the troubles and exported to the Baltic only 1,700 tunes per annum, but sixty years later the figure was 16,200 and the share of Dutch ships in the Sound trade in herring was 81.5 per cent instead of the previous 30.8 per cent. The miraculous rise of industry in the United Provinces was reflected in the increase of cloth exports to the Baltic. The 720 pieces exported annually, on average, in the 1580s had represented only 3.7 per cent of all trade; the comparable figure was 35,460 for the 1640s, or 58.5 per cent of all such trade. Despite the rise of English sales in the interval, Dutch cloth had taken the lead since the 1630s. As for transport, the Dutch easily accounted for most of such cargoes – 52.5 per cent of them in the 1640s as against barely 4 per cent in the 1580s. Dutch shipping through the Sound increased, as the following table shows:

PASSAGES OF SHIPS THROUGH THE SOUND

	ANNUAL AVERAGE NOS.		PERCENTAGES		
	ALL SHIPS	DUTCH SHIPS	DUTCH SHIPS	HOLLAND (AS %AGE OF DUTCH SHIPPING)	FRIESLAND
1580–9	4,921	2,587	52.5	79.5	17.6
1590–9	5,623	3,275	58.2	80.4	15.8
1600–09	4,525	2,691	59.4	77.1	20.1
1610–19	4,779	3,290	68.8	74.7	23.3
1620–9	3,726	2,405	64.5	73.4	24.2
1630–9	3,383	1,990	58.8	70.3	27.8
1640–9	3,499	2,010	57.4	68.1	29.3
1650–9	3,015	1,991	64.5	68.2	28.0

The apparent decline of Dutch shipping after 1600 is illusory, for between 1600 and 1650 the average tonnage of Dutch ships rose in such proportion that their overall capacity stayed at least equal and perhaps even grew. In the 1580s 126 ships based on the Belgian provinces had passed the Sound, but there were in all only eighteen from 1593 to 1639, and there was only a temporary revival to seventy-four from 1652 to 1654, which is explained by the use of neutral flags for shipping in these years of Anglo-Dutch war. Among the Dutch ships Holland had a constant lead, although, as had been true in the sixteenth century, ships from Amsterdam were fewer than those from surrounding villages even though measures were taken from time to time to force ships' captains to reside in town. There were actually fewer ships registered in Amsterdam than in the secondary towns of north Holland, such as Hoorn and Enkhuizen, or even the islands of Terschelling and Vlieland, considered separately. The Frisian merchant fleet also grew. All the hamlets around the Zuiderzee could supply sailors more cheaply than Amsterdam, but if the town had only a subsidiary role to play as far as ships were concerned, it was more than ever the great freight market and its trade depended on sailors from all over Holland and the eastern provinces.

The Sound dues show the commercial relations of the Netherlands with the Baltic with an exactitude that is exceptional for the times. Only rarely were they seriously inaccurate, as in 1645 when the alliance of the United Provinces and Sweden caused Denmark to close the Sound to Dutch shipping, and in that year only fifty-nine passages were registered. In fact a Dutch fleet had forced the Sound on 26 June and let through the three hundred ships it escorted; the straits were kept open until 14 November for 645 other ships entering and 688 leaving the Baltic.

The Dutch took timber for ship building from the ports of southern Norway. The volume of this trade was estimated in the first half of the seventeenth century at about 250,000 tonnes per annum. Dried cod was also taken on at Bergen. Quite soon the Dutch went beyond these familiar shores. Antwerpers had been first to trade with Lapland around 1565. Ten years later Russian fur traders visited Dordrecht. Giles Hooftman, an emigrant from Antwerp, sent a ship in 1578 to the mouth of the Dvina, where Archangel was to be founded a little later, and soon there was a regular trading link between the Dutch and Muscovy. The

English Muscovy Company lost its privileges when the Tsar withdrew his favour in 1649 and the Dutch profited from the death of Charles I in that year. Their trade increased: in exchange for arms, munitions and a great variety of luxuries and semi-luxuries delivered to Archangel, the United Provinces got timber and its by-products, skins and furs, flax and hemp, salmon, caviar and even, when grain from the Baltic was scarce, grain as well. Around 1650 about fifty Dutch ships sailed annually towards the White Sea and the Dutch constituted from time to time the largest foreign colony in Moscow.

Trade with northern Europe was chiefly supplied by goods from France and the south. These supplies were often disrupted by the privateers of Dunkirk, who raided Dutch trade until the Treaty of Westphalia. The United Provinces not only imported salt, but also spirits, barley for brewing, and a great deal of French wine which the merchants would go to collect at the grape harvest, and which was stored by Dutch coopers. In all parts of the French Atlantic coast, from Dieppe to Bayonne, Dutch merchant colonies dominated business life and were resented by the local bourgeoisie, whose demands for protection were increasingly loud, demands echoed by the drapers who were harmed by imports of Dutch cloth.

Relations with Spain and Portugal, united under a single crown between 1580 and 1640, depended on political conditions. During the Dutch war of independence, from 1568 to 1648, Spain forbade all trade with the rebels, but as she could not manage without imports of Baltic grain and many other goods, she generally tolerated it. From time to time bellicose outbreaks would prompt an embargo, or the pressing needs of the fleet provoke the seizure of Dutch ships anchored in Iberian ports, or an explosion of zeal by the Inquisition encourage the pursuit of the heretic, but matters settled down soon enough.

There was a similar situation on the part of the Dutch, when fanatical Calvinists or the military sometimes demanded cessation of trade with the enemy. After a brief time they would have to give way to the merchants who wanted to keep up their exports and feared that, if they did not deliver the goods, Madrid would get supplies from their Hanseatic competitors. Besides, the income from permits for trade with the enemy was important to the recovery of the Republic's war expenses. Even at times when trade was officially broken off it would be continued under cover, using the name of a Spaniard or a subject of the Spanish Nether-lands, usually from Antwerp, or a foreign (usually Hanseatic) flag – a stratagem that was also used at ordinary times to conceal deals that could hardly be openly admitted, such as the supply of arms to Spain despite her war with the Republic.

In exchange for Dutch imports Spain's increasingly parasitical economy could hardly offer more than salt, oil, southern fruit and the rare products of her American possessions. American silver flooded into the Republic even before the middle of the seventeenth century, thanks to Spain's balance-of-trade deficit. The silver was delivered during the war by detours, through Hamburg, from where it was exported to the Republic. But even before the Treaty of Westphalia was signed there was an agree-ment with Spain in 1647 over American silver to be sold in the Republic. Zeeland fought Amsterdam bitterly for this trade, but Amsterdam won by offering better prices. It was therefore able to take over Antwerp's heritage here as well.

This was also the case with Mediterranean trade, where Antwerpers had led the way. Martin della Faille, for one, sent several ships from England to Venice from 1582 onwards. His brother Jacob, who had emigrated to Holland, also took part in trade with Italy after 1684. Favoured by famine conditions there, the Dutch took Baltic grain to Italy and instituted regular trade relations. Whereas hitherto only rare ships from the Low Countries, loaded by Italian merchants, had entered the Mediter-ranean, now the initiative in this trade passed to Holland, whose trading horizons were greatly widened in consequence. The first recorded journey straight from the Baltic to Venice, by a captain from Hoorn, dates from 1597. Gradually these links were extended to Venice, Genoa and especially to the recently opened free port of Leghorn. The Dutch exported grain, herring, dried cod and manufactured goods in exchange for wines, southern fruit, oil and alum. The sea route, first used essentially for bulky goods, was increasingly used for general cargo also when the Thirty Years War made the German land route dangerous. Soon, too, Dutch ships were freighted with goods for transport around the Mediter-ranean, for instance to carry grain from Naples and Sicily to Spain, or from Turkey to Italy.

From its foundation Leghorn was an important link between

the West and the Turkish Empire, and for traders from the North Sea bound for the Levant. The first Dutch ships that took this route after 1598 seem to have done so under the French flag, since Henry IV was their own, as well as the Turks', ally. French jealousy prevailed, but in 1612 the Dutch concluded a trade treaty with Turkey and thereafter could use their own flag. Their chief port of call was at first Alexandretta (Iskanderun), at the port of Aleppo which was the busiest terminus for the eastern caravan trade. Its prosperity did not survive the Turkish–Persian war of 1623–39, and Dutch trade then concentrated on Smyrna where it could take Angora wool, cotton, silk and oriental carpets in exchange for grain, salt fish, spices, Leyden cloth and munitions. Links with the Ottoman Empire were at their height when English competition was weakened by the Civil War of 1640–9.

Trade with Turkey had to contend with the corrupt and arbitrary ways of Turkish officials, and Mediterranean shipping generally had to face the Barbary Coast pirates. From the sixteenth to the nineteenth century North Africa was the last pirate paradise, and men went there from all parts of the world, including the Low Countries. In 1625 Amsterdam created a college of directors for the Levant trade and Mediterranean shipping, who were responsible for the safety of shipping, as some two hundred voyages were made every year about 1630. They had power to enforce the convoying and arming of ships, and on occasion negotiated with the pirates, usually to no effect.

Holland now exported spices to the Levant, which had previously been a supplier of them, for Amsterdam had become a world spice market by the early seventeenth century. The English and French began to infringe on the Spanish and Portuguese monopoly, and Holland and Zeeland sailors had similar ambitions. They attempted, between 1593 and 1596, to find a north-eastern passage to the Indies around northern Europe and Asia, where they would not have to encounter the Portuguese defences of the route around Africa. Among the promoters of these expeditions there was a refugee from Antwerp (originally from Tournai), Balthasar de Moucheron, who had also been among the first traders with Russia via the White Sea. The expeditions were abandoned after the disastrous winter William Barentsz spent in Novaya Zemlya. By 1594, however, another expedition went off via the usual African route, with the advantage of experienced sailors such as Jan Huygen van Linschoten and Dirk Gerritsz Pomp, both from Enkhuizen, who had earlier made the voyage to the Indies on Portuguese ships. Although it was a commercial failure, because of incompetent management, its return in 1597 created half a dozen *Compagnieën van Verre* ('Companies for Distant Trade') again with the participation of Moucheron and of another emigrant from Tournai, Isaac le Maire.

These companies were set up, in the usual way of Dutch trade, for a single expedition, for which capital was collected and after which losses and gains would be shared out according to the stake, with a premium for partners who had taken an active part. But the large number of companies would have provoked excessive competition thus raising the prices of spices in the Indies and reducing profits on sale. The authorities therefore urged them to merge, and in 1602 the *Verenigde Oostindische Compagnie* ('Joint East India Company') was successfully launched. To satisfy the particularism of towns interested in trade with the Indies it was organized into six Chambers, allied with Amsterdam, Middelburg, Rotterdam, Delft, Hoorn, and Enkhuizen, which had fixed shares in the Company's expenses – Amsterdam half, Middelburg a quarter and the rest one-sixteenth each. Their influence on the Board of Directors, the *Heren XVII* ('The Seventeen Gentlemen') roughly corresponded to this division. Amsterdam supplied 57.2 per cent of the capital, Enkhuizen 8.4 and Delft 7.3, whereas Middelburg (20.3), Hoorn (4.13) and Rotterdam (2.67) contributed less than the proportion expected of them.

The capital, collected in a month by public subscription, amounted to 6,425,000 florins, a colossal sum for the time. Every subject of the Republic had the right to a share, and some certainly lent their names to foreigners. Although the shareholders were very widely recruited – they even included domestic servants – it was merchants who, from the start, supplied by far the most capital. Refugees from the south were eager subscribers. In the area of the Amsterdam Chamber, they were 301 of the 1,143 shareholders, and provided 38 per cent of that Chamber's capital. Of the eighty-four largest subscriptions (of ten thousand florins and more), thirty-nine were put up by emigrants, who accounted for 21.5 per cent of the sum. Although shareholders were named on the certificates, these could be transferred to the Company's register, and the trading in them which resulted was an important innovation on the Bourse. It also differed from the *Compagnieën van Verre* in its permanence. A decree of the Estates-General gave it an initial monopoly of trade in the Indian Ocean and the Pacific for ten years, and this was always renewed up to the end of the *ancien régime*.

In the Orient the Company encountered hostile Portuguese, English and French traders who often had native allies. To attain its commercial ends its influence spread either by conquest pure and simple – Amboina's conquest in 1605 was the first act in the foundation of a territorial empire – or by assisting one of the sides in a civil war. Within thirty years a costly naval and military effort had resulted in their unchallenged dominance over the whole Indonesian archipelago, from which all competition was soon cleared. Moreover, the Company ruled Formosa between 1624 and 1662, and its factory at Decima, in Nagasaki Bay, was the only door opened by Japan to the outside world from 1638 to 1854. Other factories were dotted along the coasts of Indo-China and the Malacca peninsula, Ceylon, India and the Persian Gulf. To supply Company ships during the long voyage to the Indies St Helena was occupied from 1633 to 1673, Mauritius after 1638 and the Cape of Good Hope after 1651. The Company was at the height of its power. It had only been able to pay its first dividend in 1610 and for the next quarter-century dividends had followed intermittently, and after much pressure from disappointed shareholders. Many dividends were paid in kind, in spices, for example, estimated at more than their real worth. It was only after 1634 that dividends could be distributed almost every year, and in cash. Profits certainly would have been higher but for the corruption that was widespread among the Company's agents at every level.

According to the concept of colonial trade of the time, monopolies were vital and artificial scarcities would be created to raise profits. Nutmeg and mace were produced only in the Banda Islands, in the Moluccas. The natives, having failed to keep their promise to sell to the Company alone, were mercilessly massacred in 1621. Former agents of the Company were established in the Islands and used slave labour to work the spice plantations (*perken*). Their produce was sold to the Company at a rate fixed by it. The quantity of cloves was reduced simply through the destruction of clove trees in some islands, and the planting of clove trees was limited in other islands with the collaboration of native chiefs. The Company did not manage to eliminate European competition in pepper and cinnamon, silk and cotton. Despite all the precautions, the market in Europe was still sometimes over-supplied. In that event the Company stocked the goods until prices rose, or destroyed them to raise the prices. As had happened earlier at Antwerp, they were often handed over to monopolists' consortia, citizens of Amsterdam, sometimes with an undertaking that other goods would not be put on the market for a given period. Quite often the Company directors had a hand in these practices. In view of the indignation caused by rising prices, the Company decided in 1642 to sell the cargoes at the headquarters of the six Chambers, except for those for which it held the monopoly; these it continued to sell at a fixed rate.

As the Orient had hardly any interest in European goods, the Company's purchases had to be paid for by exports of silver, originally Spanish coins (above all *reales de ocho*, to which these countries were accustomed) obtained through trade with Spain. After 1617 Dutch coins were used, and gradually predominated although they were sometimes of inferior quality. The Company also took a growing profit from Asiatic trade. It exported coarse Gujrati cotton goods and the fine batiks of the Coromandel coast to Indonesia. These batiks also found outlets in Guinea and in Europe herself, and eventually the Company organized production in workshops which it opened in India. The Japanese sold copper and silver at Decima, with which the Company paid for its purchases of silks and sugar in China. Once it had taken the place of the Portuguese in Ceylon, it retained its monopoly in elephant hunting so as to export elephants to India. It also supplied silks and spices to all Asian lands. Despite the variety of these activities and the large sums involved, there were still only a few ships equipped in the Republic for the voyage to the Indies. Although the volume of the Dutch merchant fleet in 1634 was estimated at 2,660,000 tonnes, only thirteen ships, of five hundred tonnes on average (larger than normal), were engaged on this route annually, i.e. hardly 0.02 per cent of the total, although the number rose to some thirty by 1675.

The East India Company was nonetheless an essential factor in the extraordinary prosperity of the Dutch. In the second half of the sixteenth century Dutch sailors had taken part in Portuguese colonial trade. With such experience, expeditions could be mounted by the United Provinces in the late 1500s to get salt from the Caribbean and Venezuela and dye-woods from Guiana, whilst others (among them, once again, the indefatigable Moucheron) went to load up with gold, spices, ivory and slaves in Guinea, and slaves were taken illicitly to Spanish or Portuguese America. Finally, once Henry Hudson had reconnoitred the coasts of North America in a vain attempt to find a north-western passage to Asia for the East India Company in 1609, the *Compagnie van Nieuw-Nederland* ('Company of the New Netherlands') began to trade in furs and was granted a four-year monopoly by the Estates-General in 1614.

Meanwhile, the Antwerp refugee William Usselincx had been promoting, since 1619, a great company to colonize the New World. The emigration of peasants from the Republic, which he thought over-populated, was to help in converting the natives to Calvinism. Moreover, its aim would be decisively to weaken Spain by cutting off her supplies of gold and silver, so that it is understandable that the *West-Indische Compagnie* ('West India Company') should have been constituted on the eve of the resumption of war with Spain in 1621. The charter on the colony's foundation, however, did not provide for the settlement of which Usselincx had dreamed and, out of disappointment, he offered his services to Gustavus Adolphus of Sweden. It was thought of as a commercial enterprise like the older company, and its organization was shaped accordingly. But the 7,100,000 florins of capital took three years to assemble, because the public was dubious about the prospects of an enterprise overtly designed to threaten the Great Power that Spain still was. The Estates-General did subscribe 500,000 florins, and the rest was supplied by the five Company Chambers (which elected the Heren XIX): Amsterdam (40 per cent), Zeeland (19.7 per cent), the Meuse (14.6 per cent) – to which the shareholders of Rotterdam, Dordrecht and Delft belonged – North Holland (7.1 per cent), Friesland and Groningen (11.8 per cent). Amsterdam had an interest of four-ninths, Zeeland of two-ninths and the others of one-ninth each.

The misgivings of the general public were soon borne out. In its first years the Company had to confine itself to raiding Spanish convoys from America, with no great success until 1628, when Piet Heyn seized a fleet carrying silver in Matanzas Bay, in Cuba.

This act, immortalized to this day by a popular song, resulted in a booty of 11,500,000 florins, out of which a first dividend of 75 per cent was distributed, and the squadron equipped which conquered the Brazilian coast between the Maranhão and the Rio São Francisco after 1630. The Portuguese gave up their sugar plantations for the most part, although the Marrraños did stay because they appreciated the policy of tolerance practised by the governor, John Maurice of Nassau. Some hundred Dutchmen, especially the Sephardic Jews of Amsterdam who had always been interested in the sugar industry, set up in the new colony.

The exploitation of plantations was impossible without black slaves and factories on the African coast to supply them. To this end the Company occupied all Portuguese possessions on the Atlantic coast of Africa, which were badly defended by Spain, between 1637 and 1642. Up till 1645 it sent to Brazil more than 23,000 blacks from factories at Elmina and from Angola. Then the Portuguese in America revolted, encouraged by the independence regained by their mother-country in 1640. The loss of Recife in 1654 meant the end of the Dutch colony in Brazil. In the meantime the Portuguese had also reconquered Angola and São Tomé in 1648. These events did not, however, terminate the Dutch slave trade, which was in any case not solely concerned with Brazil. Plantations of sugar and tobacco were created under Company auspices on the coast of Guiana and in the islands of Aruba, Bonaire and Curaçao, and Spanish America was a tempting goal for unauthorized traders. Moreover, the Dutch ships transported the greater part of the produce from the French and British West Indies to Europe, as well as the exports of the English colonies in North America, especially during the Civil War, which had weakened English commerce.

North America had her first Dutch colonists in 1624. The 'New Netherlands' on the banks of the Hudson contained some ten thousand colonists forty years later, 2,500 at Nieuw-Amsterdam, as New York was then known, where their memory survives in place-names such as Brooklyn (from the village of Breukelen in Holland), Hoboken (the name of an Antwerp suburb), Staten Island ('The States Island') and Wall Street. Up-river, lands were granted under a system similar to the feudal one: a 'patron' agreed to provide for at least fifty colonists. The fur trade, however, remained the main economic activity of the territory. Faced with the hostility of the Indians on whose lands the 'patrons' encroached, and too thinly populated by comparison with the nearby English colonies, the New Netherlands were conquered by the English in 1664.

The Company, bent under the weight of its military expenditure, was unable directly to exploit its own possessions and handed them over to the patrons in North America, and to shareholders in the tropics. The colonists paid a rent and undertook to use Company ships. The Company retained only the trade in slaves, ivory, dye-woods and munitions. Overwhelmed by debt even by 1665, its prospects looked very poor. Soon it was unable to equip ships, and in 1657 had to lease out its slave trade, offering licences to individuals. Its agony was prolonged until 1674 only by various expedients, and the stubborn support of Zeeland, whose participation in the Company's trade was the essential element of her colonial commerce.

In trade with the colonies, and in Europe, the United Provinces' most threatening competitor was England, whose economic growth had been as great as theirs. But the Dutch had an advantage in the Baltic because of their cheap sea transport and their merchants' ability to export bullion, which the English government would not permit. Trade between the two countries was constant. England took from the Dutch the vast array of goods they could offer, and herself sent cloth, Newcastle and Scottish coal, which was used by breweries, and tobacco from Virginia or the British West Indies. The Merchant Adventurers, who had kept their 'Court' at Middelburg from 1582 to 1587, went back there in 1598 after a period at Emden, and then shifted to Delft in 1621 and to Rotterdam – their main port – in 1635.

Originally cloth was usually exported half-finished, to be dyed and finished in Holland. But England increasingly tended towards protection: in 1614 James I, at William Cockayne's suggestion, forbade the export of half-finished cloth. The Estates-General retaliated by forbidding the import of dyed cloth. This attempt at mercantilism was an utter failure, because the English cloth could not keep its markets without Dutch middlemen, and the prohibition was lifted within two years. The United Provinces, however, maintained their prohibition, though without benefiting their own industry much, for the progress of the English industry meant that dyeing and finishing could increasingly be done at home. Moreover, the English government forbade imports by foreigners of products from the Baltic. In answer to Grotius, who had defended the principle of the freedom of the seas in 1619, John Selden claimed English sovereignty over her own waters in 1635. English mercantilism culminated in 1651 in the celebrated Navigation Acts, which reserved to English ships, with their largely English crews, the transport of colonial goods, and to English ships, or ships of the country of origin, goods coming from Europe, a trade in which the Dutch had traditionally played an intermediary role. At least the Peace of Breda in 1667 brought some relief from the principle of the Acts as regards the basins of the Rhine, Meuse and Scheldt, but the Dutch lead over England was weakening, and by the mid-seventeenth century the English merchant fleet had won the lead from the Dutch as far as trade between the two countries was concerned.

2 THE SPANISH NETHERLANDS AND LIÈGE

The basins of the Scheldt and the Meuse, as well as the Rhineland, provided a fine backdrop for Dutch trade. The neutrality that Liège, which ruled a great part of the Meuse, strove to maintain in European wars helped her exports of timber, stone, minerals, and iron goods along the Meuse towards Holland. Moreover, the Scheldt remained the chief export route for the Spanish Netherlands, and Antwerp their main centre of trade, a fact which was reflected in the constant activity of Antwerp merchants abroad. They were everywhere, in the French Atlantic ports, Portugal, Spain, Italy and as far away as the West and East Indies. By 1600 twenty-one firms managed by subjects of the Spanish Netherlands were flourishing in Venice, and some sixty Antwerpers trading in Cologne laid the foundation, with the help of as many Portuguese and Spaniards, of Cologne's rising importance in European commerce.

From 1572 the Scheldt had been kept closed by Zeeland and its *de facto* closure was legally confirmed by the Treaties of Westphalia in 1648. This did not condemn Antwerp to inactivity, for the closure affected only direct communication with the sea. Any ship entering the rivers of the Dutch delta or arriving at their mouths from Antwerp had to unload on to boats registered in the United Provinces, which thus retained for themselves a general and highly lucrative share of the foreign trade of the Spanish

Netherlands. A large flotilla was used for shuttling between the ports of Holland and Zeeland and Antwerp, paying the licences required by the two governments that henceforth shared the sovereignty of the Low Countries. These licences, which had been instituted in the days when trade was in general forbidden with the enemy, soon changed into simple customs dues, levied on a trade that the war did not interrupt. As long as it lasted ships in the Scheldt were not admitted to enemy territory and had to discharge their cargo once again on the line of demarcation, under the guns of forts built on the river banks by both sides. During the Twelve Years Truce (1609–21), and after the Treaty of Westphalia, Antwerp and the sea-ports agreed to admit each other's lighters without restriction.

The government of the Spanish Netherlands had hoped to remove foreign trade from the supervision of the Dutch. The digging of canals from Ghent to Bruges and from there to Ostend, Nieuport and Dunkirk after 1613 was meant to drain trade from the Scheldt basin, which extended over almost all of Flanders, Brabant and Hainault, towards the Flemish coast. The Dutch had recognized this as a threat to their commercial control and required Spain in the Treaty of Westphalia to levy taxes in the Flemish ports that would be equal to those due from shipping in the Scheldt. The fears proved vain, although Spain evaded the stipulation. The shippers' guilds at Ghent and Bruges forced Flemish canal shipping to unload at their respective towns, causing expense and delay, so that it was still cheaper to pay the licences for the Scheldt. The Spanish Netherlands had hoped that these licences would be abolished after Westphalia, and the Brussels government, in response to Antwerp's wishes, had even set an example. The Republic did not follow, for it could not do without the income. The licences returned in the South in 1654

The government had also tried to facilitate Antwerp's links with the continental hinterland. The land routes leading there continued to carry a substantial trade, and were even used for the transport of goods for the United Provinces to avoid the countless Rhine tolls. There were schemes for a direct water-way between Antwerp and the Meuse or the Rhine, avoiding the enemy-controlled lower course of the rivers, to carry bulky commodities. For this purpose a 'Eugenian Canal' was planned, to link the Scheldt with the middle Meuse near Venlo, and beyond that to the

Rhine above Wesel. Work began in 1624, was soon stopped when money ran short, and was finally abandoned in 1632, when the Dutch occupied the banks of the Meuse in the area where the canal had been planned. Despite this setback Antwerp remained an important commercial town, the economic centre of the country and a *disposionsplatz* where much business was transacted in goods that were sufficiently standardized to be dealt with unseen. It could not claim the unique place it had had before the troubles, which Amsterdam had now taken over, but its prosperity made it attractive as a residence for opulent princes of European painting, such as Rubens and van Dyck. It was not the Flemish ports, but rather the French Channel ports, or Dover, that acted as alternatives to the Dutch ones in the export trade, especially where Flemish cloth was concerned which the merchants sent directly to the Channel ports, without passing through Antwerp. Lille, under the control of the Spanish Netherlands until 1667, was the main stage on the road which led from Flanders to the French coast, and made large profits from the traffic.

3 BUSINESS TECHNIQUES IN ANTWERP AND AMSTERDAM

When Antwerp finally took over the heritage of Bruges at the end of the Middle Ages, only Mediterranean merchants were familiar with advanced business methods. These spread at Antwerp in the sixteenth century and were then adopted, with the arrival of the refugees, in Amsterdam and elsewhere in the seventeenth century. They were gradually taken up by other merchants, both foreign and local. The assimilation of practices that were Italian in origin prompted the use of many Italian terms which have remained in the business parlance of many European countries. Naturally the process was not swift. Both Antwerp and Amsterdam had traditions that resisted change. The magistrates of Antwerp were claiming even in 1565 – though unsuccessfully – that only they were competent to draw up a contract, whereas the Italian habit of having notaries do this had been customary among Antwerp merchants for decades. Although business was now conducted throughout the year, and the fairs, where trade had first developed, merely marked a particularly busy period, their franchise could still be used to protect debtors in default. Despite a greater freedom of exchange than at Bruges, many controls were maintained and the merchants of Antwerp were forced to use the public scales for certain transactions, as well as sworn measurers and assayers.

Antwerp called its business centre the Bourse, a term borrowed from Bruges, but differed from Bruges in that, from the fifteenth century onwards, the Bourse consisted of a covered gallery. In 1531 the town built the famous New Bourse which became the prototype for those of London in 1566 and Amsterdam in 1613, and many other places of trade in modern times. It was primarily the forum for financial dealings, as the one at Bruges had been. Exchange of goods went on elsewhere, at the 'English Bourse', a name which reveals the origin of Antwerp's prosperity. The merchants of Amsterdam were also accustomed to meeting in the open air, but once their Bourse had been built, they dealt there with all matters except grain, for which a Corn Exchange continued to function independently. Wholesale prices were decided there, and soon dominated the entire trade, for they were usually followed by merchants in their individual dealings. Early in the 1600s printed lists of current prices were published for the use of merchants. These could easily be distributed and so increased the authority that the Amsterdam quotations had far beyond the United Provinces.

The transfer of the business world to double-entry bookkeeping is also considered a sign that modern business methods had arrived. Shortly after the Venetian Franciscan, Luca Pacioli, had written his famous treatise in 1494, a schoolmaster of Antwerp, Jan Ympyn, wrote a manual for his Flemish compatriots that was almost a literal translation of it. His widow published it in 1543. Although an English translation came out that same year at London, young Englishmen and Frenchmen came to Antwerp to learn double-entry bookkeeping for many years. It would be wrong to suppose, however, that its use was very widespread there. If the della Failles did keep their books 'in the Venetian manner' (their founder had started up trade at Venice), Christophe Plantin gave up the new techniques after a brief trial, and his successors did not return to them until well into the eighteenth century. If large firms in Amsterdam did adopt the method, many lesser ones did not, and despite its use the balance sheets of the della Failles and the East India Company are very confused and do not provide information about their situation in any detail because there are no profit and loss accounts.

The structure of local firms in Antwerp at first took its form from medieval models. When they involved more than one man, they were usually family firms, run by the head of the family and supported by family money which could only be augmented by deposits from third parties, to whom a fixed interest was paid. Associations among unrelated businessmen, concluded for particular dealings, had generally only an occasional and therefore ephemeral character. The della Failles had begun as a family firm, but on John the Elder's death in 1582 an unrelated associate entered the company, the profits and losses of which were to be divided up at the term of a ten-year contract, in accordance with the partners' interests.

This went on in Amsterdam after the fall of Antwerp. The first colonial companies had only a temporary character, but the commercial associations concluded for lengthy periods between unrelated partners gradually spread. The establishment of large colonial companies involved a change of great importance in business practice. Instead of a small number of partners in companies as hitherto, these companies had their capital subscribed by thousands of shareholders of the most diverse social origins. For the first time a wide public in the United Provinces had the chance to share in the profits and risks of a great commercial enterprise. Moreover, whereas partners in companies of the ordinary type were responsible, with their entire property, for its obligations, the charters of colonial companies discharged their managers from this responsibility, beyond their share in the capital, and the limitation was tacitly extended to all shareholders. Finally, the capital of the companies became fixed, in effect: the grant to the East India Company gave shareholders the chance to withdraw after ten years. The capital had been entirely invested by 1612, however, and since the shareholders could not be reimbursed, the Company was exempted from any obligation to do so, and there was no question of it when the monopoly was renewed. In all these features the colonial companies can be regarded as precursors of today's limited companies.

Intinerant merchants were a survival from the past, but were still active in Antwerp, where there were numerous Frenchmen and hundreds of Merchant Adventurers accompanying their own goods. In the seventeenth century hosts of pedlars came and went, but increasingly merchants would use a factor to represent them permanently on a certain market. Sometimes his only function would be to settle what remained to be done when the 'principal' had left, but others took up residence permanently in the Low Countries on behalf of foreigners, or the foreign countries for Dutch merchants. They lived in a style suited to their firm's reputation, with fixed wages and a commission on transactions concluded through them. Trade by commission was furthered as commercial horizons grew: in a place where a merchant had no permanent agent, he would buy or sell through another merchant who would act according to instructions received for an agreed percentage. This enabled even relatively small firms to extend their business. Commercial houses involved in international transactions increased considerably in number.

Whatever methods were used, links with the factors or commissioners of a trading house required a regular and rapid post. A message might be attached to commodities to be delivered, given to transport companies or sent by the special postal service provided by the Taxis, who had an Imperial monopoly (though it was often infringed). An express letter could go from Antwerp to Paris in thirty-six hours in 1516, and to Innsbruck in five days. By normal courier the length of time would be almost twice as much. Rotterdam had a daily messenger service to Amsterdam by 1612 at the latest. It was also the headquarters for post to England, and managed to retain this function until 1664, although Amsterdam tried to take over the Dutch postal network.

There was no general insurance for despatches of goods in the sixteenth century. As far as transport by sea was concerned, there was an ancient precaution which was widely adopted, of distributing goods over several ships, but insurance for cargo did spread in Antwerp in this century, although there was a lack of precision about the policies that encouraged all kinds of trickery and speculation, from which many Marraños profited. Insurance was subjected to government control in 1559 and the Spanish consulate codified its usage for its subjects in 1569. The innovatory role of Antwerp is clear from the requests for advice over legal questions received by its magistrates from Hamburg and Cologne in the sixteenth century. However, the della Failles did not always insure their goods bound for the Mediterranean, or did so only partially. Premiums could often amount to 10 per cent or more. Despite its growing popularity, insurance was not general in

Amsterdam in the seventeenth century, and many plans to make it compulsory, at reduced premiums, failed through the opposition of merchants who issued the policies: at that time groups of merchants usually assumed the role of insurers, each for a specific sum for they had remained active in the credit market.

6 *Money and Credit*

I MONEY AND PRICES

In the course of the modern period, the Flemish groat was gradually replaced as a unit of account and the foundation of all circulation in the Low Countries by the Brabantine *patard* or *stuiver*. This was an expression in monetary terms of Antwerp's victory over Bruges as a trading centre. This currency maintained a constant rate (except for the years 1525–7) of double the Flemish groat, which served as a standard for the many and irregular coins, of varying origins, which were in circulation.

On Charles the Bold's death in 1477, the Flemish groat had an intrinsic value of 0.64 grams of fine silver. The troubles thereafter soon led to a reduction of this content. During the troubles coiners often neglected small coins, which were relatively expensive to strike, and the masses were therefore forced to use foreign coins of inferior alloy which, in their ignorance of monetary mechanisms, they accepted at face vlaue. They also picked out the better Burgundian coinage which affected the official rates. Merchants were clearer-sighted and took their good coins out of circulation, sometimes with the complicity of foreign mints, such as those of France and of several German princes. The Low Countries' government was periodically forced to change the rates and content of its coins. In 1489 the groat weighed only 0.24 grams fine. At the end of the year Maximilian of Habsburg undertook a draconian revaluation, and trebled its value, perhaps in the hope that he would get a higher return in 'heavy' coinage for the large fines he had just imposed on the rebel towns after

211

their surrender to him. By 1495, however, the fine weight of the groat was only 0.49 grams.

During the wars with France French troops would bring in their own poor coinage and this encouraged the hoarding of native ones, which were again decreased to 0.42 grams fine in 1520. It was then decided to attack the problem at its root, and a new monetary standard, the golden Carolus florin, equivalent to twenty *patards*, was introduced. Perhaps the increase in gold supplies, a consequence of pillaging in the New World, had some influence on this attempt to substitute a gold standard for the shaky bimetallism of the past. For it to succeed, all the silver coins ought to have been reduced to the level of base coinage, but no one dared do this. The coins remained subject to foreign competition, to which they succumbed eventually, the more easily since the maintenance of a strong coinage, while France and England devalued theirs, had a bad effect on exports and hastened the ruin of many cloth towns.

The failure of the monetary reform of 1526 led to the Carolus florin's being made a silver coin in 1542, and shortly afterwards a mere money of account, based on silver. Gradually, however, a new difficulty emerged. The over-abundant silver mines in Spanish America caused an influx of silver into Europe, which profoundly changed the relationship of the two standard metals. The Low Countries were, after Spain, the first in Europe to feel this, because of Spain's despatches of coins for the armies fighting France. By 1548 the rate of gold money had to be raised as against silver. Even so, the quality of the groat diminished once more after 1551. The Dutch Revolt accelerated this process, for the money needed to pay the Spanish troops did not always arrive on time in Brussels, and to forestall mutiny, the face value or the fine weight of coins was reduced, to provide more coinage. The weight of the silver groat fell from 0.40 grams in 1568 to 0.25 just before the Peace of Westphalia. It was held at this level until the end of the eighteenth century.

The war also clearly affected the money in circulation in the United Provinces. Holland and Zeeland, as soon as they became effectively independent, devalued their silver coinage considerably, and an era of confusion followed. Apart from the war, their favourable balance of payments with the Spanish Netherlands and France flooded them with foreign coins, which constantly forced the Republic to new rates of exchange. Moreover, each of the seven provinces, considering itself sovereign after the liberation, claimed the right to mint. Holland had two mints, and if the provincial mints of Friesland and Groningen worked only intermittently, the others did so more or less continuously. But the town of Groningen, and five others in Overijssel and Guelders, had received imperial coining privileges in the Middle Ages. All of them, provinces and towns, farmed out the right to individuals who often tried to increase their profits at the expense of the weight or value of the smaller coins that they put into circulation. All efforts at supervision and co-ordination of their activities by the Masters-General of the Coinage (who were appointed by the Estates-General) encountered regional and local opposition up to the end of the seventeenth century.

While coins in common use were in indescribable confusion, the larger coins were distinguished by their quality, to such a degree that the *daalders*, the Dutch equivalent of the German *Thaler*, were soon accepted on an equal basis with Spanish *reales* to pay the Republic's trade-balance deficit with Russia, the Baltic, the Levant and the Indies. The need for these coins in commerce with such countries was so pressing that the Estates-General, though in principle they prohibited exports of bullion (as was the case in all other European states), exempted *negotiepenningen* ('trade money') from this rule. When a temporary interruption of trade with Spain created a perturbing lack of *reales de ocho*, counterfeits were struck in 1601 at Dordrecht. Once the *daalders* were accepted as a medium for payments in foreign trade, they were struck exclusively for this, and there was no further need for Spanish coins, only for silver. Spain's decision in 1647 to sell American silver at Amsterdam guaranteed the Dutch a wonderful chance of getting the silver they needed for Asian trade, which could not have prospered without it. The Dutch silver market was open to the public, but the Estates-General decided that at least one-third should be reserved for minting in the Confederation. Dutch trade in Guinea also supplied the required gold. Between 1586 and 1659 the provincial mints other than those in Friesland and Groningen struck an annual average of 2,500,000 florins' worth of coins, over 1,000,000 in gold and a little over 1,300,000 in silver, which took $856\frac{5}{8}$ kilograms of gold and $12,237\frac{1}{2}$ kilograms of silver. It has been estimated that, including coins struck for trade abroad, the Dutch money supply rose annually by between 500,000 and 1,000,000 florins.

It is also assumed that the silver output of central Europe, which had been rapidly recovering since the fifteenth century, quintupled from 1460 to 1530. Prices rose in the Low Countries between 1466 and 1490, stimulated by a run of bad harvests and the political troubles that perhaps caused them. Prices would certainly have been higher had the population not declined. Then followed twenty years of recovery, although it is not clear whether the money supply balanced the progress of the economy. By 1510 population and prosperity were recovering and there was a great rise in prices, expressed in terms of silver, and this despite the rise in the value of silver against gold, which deliveries from the New World had made more readily available. After 1530, and especially after the discovery of Potosí and Zacatécas, more silver poured from America into Europe than gold. The result was a rapid inflation, which continued until the end of the century. Between 1500 and 1600, rye prices rose between 395 per cent and 783 per cent in the various places in the Low Countries for which an index can be calculated. They rose even higher in the southern provinces during the disastrous decade of 1581–90 when the war was at its worst and these provinces, largely cut off from Baltic supply, had to make do with their own very inadequate harvests. The restoration of normal supply and more peaceful conditions caused a fall which went on until about 1620, after which prices rose again until the middle of the century. By then grain prices were 50 per cent above their level in 1600. Prices fluctuated in the same way in the United Provinces, where the trade did not have to face long-term problems, but where the rising population posed problems. Although prices declined after about 1600, by 1660 they had risen to some 75 per cent above their level in 1580.

In the meantime the New World exported less silver to Europe, while the progress of European trade with Asia had removed increasing quantities from circulation. By the mid-seventeenth century, a turning-point in conditions was at hand which inaugurated a new era in the economic history of Europe in general and the Low Countries in particular. The disorder in monetary affairs inevitably continued, and throughout this period they were a prime concern for the government.

It was largely to combat the troubles that Amsterdam, in agreement with the public authorities, instituted a public bank in 1609, the famous *Amsterdamsche Wisselbank* ('Amsterdam Exchange Bank'). As the changers were still suspected of taking good coins out of circulation, the town forbade private money-changing and gave a monopoly of exchange to the new bank, which was to hand over to the mint all the foreign coins it received. Moreover, it had an exclusive right to accept cash on deposit, so that it became a kind of reserve into which the mints could dip if need be. The sanction on dealing in precious metals with anyone other than the mint was soon infringed, and by the second quarter of the century the bank was selling back to the East India Company gold that had been exported from Guinea by the West India Company. After 1647 the authorities merely insisted on maintenance of the obligation imposed on the bullion trade to keep back one-third of its imports for the mints. Banks of the same type were set up at Middelburg in 1616, Delft in 1621 and Rotterdam in 1635, and in each case this happened at the instigation of the local English merchants. None of them, though, had a role comparable with that of the Amsterdam bank. This monopoly did not cure the troubles of the money in circulation, however, for the large silver coins of the Spanish Netherlands, which were of a quality suitable to European usage though not as high in value as the Republic's equivalent coins, had destroyed the demand for Dutch coins so that the *daalders* soon vanished from circulation and were soon struck only for export. But if the bank did not succeed in reforming the coinage, it played an important part in the development of scrip money and commercial credit.

2 CREDIT

Payments at Antwerp were not made by transfers of account such as the changers had earlier been able to make, and their methods disappeared late in the fifteenth century, reappearing only in Amsterdam with the emergence of the term 'cashiers'. As in the past Antwerp used either promissory notes or bills of exchange for the purposes of commercial credit, with a bearer clause to facilitate transfer. But the bearer was helpless against a defaulting debtor unless he could show a formal deed authorized by the initial creditor, and until the seventeenth century promises to pay were given before the magistrates for this reason. A more liberal machinery developed, and in 1507 merchants in Antwerp could

E.H.—8

declare that any holder of a bill payable to the bearer should be able to get his money back without further ado. The principle spread rapidly and was adopted by Charles V in a general edict of 1537. Nonetheless a promissory note did involve, like any credit operation, an element of risk. Many bearers of such notes transferred them to their own creditors for settlement. They would add a note of assignation at the foot or on the back. There could easily be a large number of such assignations, with all the doubts that the debtor's solvency might arouse. A further edict of 1541 stipulated that the acceptance of the assignment must remain optional and that if the final debtor defaulted, the earlier ones were to be held responsible. This provision prompted widespread use of assignation (in 1585 it was considered to be the normal method of settling commercial debts in Antwerp) which survived throughout the following century in both parts of the Low Countries, although the chains of debtors which developed continued to arouse the bitter resentment of creditors who wanted to get their money back.

Until the 1560s the bill of exchange was only used among the merchants of southern Europe and those of the Low Countries who had business with them. Their negotiation was the chief purpose of the Bourse at Antwerp, as it had been earlier in Bruges. It probably spread through the development of the Piacenza fairs, which became a sort of financial dependency of the Antwerp market and constituted a link in financial transactions between the Low Countries and Italy. The bearer clause and assignation to third parties had been carried over from the promissory note to the bill of exchange, to which the edicts of 1537 and 1541 also applied. The custom arose in Antwerp of noting on the back of the bill of exchange the name of successive beneficiaries: the modern practice of endorsement had come into existence, and was used in Antwerp and Amsterdam from the early seventeenth century onwards, becoming general after 1640. From there it went to Italy in the last quarter of the century.

The Bank of Amsterdam's monopoly obliged men to deposit there any bill of exchange valued at more than six hundred florins. No merchant with any pretensions could avoid opening an account to cover the bills he would draw. The money thus deposited increased the stock of coinage in the bank which amounted to 925,560 florins in 1610 (after a single year's activity).

It reached a peak in 1645, with 11,840,000 florins, of which 11,228,000 belonged to third parties, and the figure in 1670 was 5,367,000, of which 4,840,000 represented deposits. The authorities, despite their hostility to the changers, could not prevent them from taking deposits, and had to accept this in 1621, although they received for the bank the privilege that its deposits could not be distrained – a guarantee that gave it a considerable advantage in the competition. The facilities that financial organization had provided in Bruges had now reappeared, after lapsing for a century, in Amsterdam.

The bank and the Amsterdam changers also met the market's credit requirements. The Church's prohibition of usury still hampered credit in Antwerp. On several occasions scrupulous merchants there had consulted renowned canon lawyers as to the morality of interest. A decree of Charles v's in 1540 did, however, legalize a practice that had presumably been current for many years among merchants, and allowed a maximum interest rate of 12 per cent. The loans issued by the Fuggers against individual deposits, at 9 per cent per annum, circulated in Antwerp after 1546, and twenty years later third-party investment in the merchant houses at 12 per cent per annum was quite widespread. In the last quarter of the century the della Failles also accepted deposits to increase their working capital, and thus allowed a wider public to place its capital at the service of trade, and to take some profit from it. The constitution of large trading companies in the United Provinces meant that there was direct participation by shareholders of all social types, while the changers also took up the practice of their Bruges predecessors and authorized overdrafts for their clients. Although the Bank's statutes forbade it from opening commercial credits, it had granted advances to the East India Company by 1615. The small interest these loans brought in, successively lowered from 6.25 per cent to 3.5 per cent per annum, shows how much capital a perfected financial technique could make available on the Dutch market. The Bank of Middelburg also extended credit, though on a lesser scale, to the two India Companies.

The mobility of commercial capital also increased because of the development of discounting. The earliest instance of this in the Low Countries occurred in 1536 in a promissory note payable at the Antwerp fairs. It became increasingly popular, chiefly for the encashing of deeds payable at a relatively distant date, and especially with promissory notes, since the term of bills of exchange was usually short and they needed discounting to a much lesser degree. Such discounting was forbidden anyway, according to the Antwerp laws recorded in 1569 and 1608. However, in March 1560 some bills were being discounted that were payable in the May at the Besançon and Lyons fairs, and in 1600 they were being discounted at a rate of 1.5 or 2 per cent. The practice appears to have been less current in Amsterdam, perhaps because of the small interest rates, but by the mid-seventeenth century it became very popular (probably in imitation of the goldsmith bankers of London who had borrowed the technique from Antwerp).

Personal credit continued to be supplied by 'Lombards' in the sixteenth century. In 1540 in the hope of halting their exploitation of public poverty, Charles v limited the interest they were allowed to take to 33 per cent, and it was reduced to 21 in 1600. Since 1525 many towns had been establishing interest-free loan banks, on the Italian model, but they had soon had to surrender to reality and charge a small interest to survive. At the instigation of Wenceslas Coberger, all private pawnshops were closed in 1618 and replaced by a network of public ones, established in all large towns in the Catholic Netherlands. Coberger took over their management and, since he was also a talented architect, designed buildings in a baroque style to house them. Many may still be seen.

Despite the persistent opposition of some merchants to the principle of loans, the public pawnshops lent on security at a rate first of 15 per cent, then 12 per cent in 1620 and 10 per cent in 1635, with the help of capital mainly subscribed by ecclesiastics and religious institutions. But these funds were too great a temptation for the public authorities who were always short of money. After 1625 the Brussels government raided them a great deal, and Coberger himself did so for money to drain the Moëres in 1620–2. Many loans soon turned out to be irrecoverable, and the pawnshops had to raise their rates again in 1652 to 15 per cent. The Liège region soon adopted Coberger's scheme for its own pawnshops.

The abolition of ecclesiastical charitable institutions in the Reformation created a void in the United Provinces. Many towns sought to fill it by setting up municipal lending banks. The main one, the *Bank van Leninge* in Amsterdam, was founded in 1614. Not surprisingly in this case, the merchants' interest was not over-looked for, apart from private credit, it was also empowered to lend to merchants, although the abundance of capital in the town soon made such advances unnecessary. In Rotterdam, however, they persisted. The initial capital had largely been supplied by the local *wisselbanken*, and they continued to advance money as re-quired by the lending banks, at least the one at Amsterdam, until about 1640, sometimes to the detriment of their own liquidity. When the United Provinces were invaded by the French, in 1672 the lending banks of Rotterdam and Middelburg had so little cash in hand that they were unable to pay back the *wisselbanken*, which had to face considerable withdrawals.

The financial embarrassment of the authorities worsened during this period. The public credit market was still dominated, in the later fifteenth century, by Italian firms, chiefly Florentine ones such as the Gualterotti and the Frescobaldi. It was deeply perturbed by the political troubles and the economic crisis that they caused in the 1480s. The rates of interest on government loans rose from about 19 to 29 per cent between 1480 and 1486, and in 1490 money was so dear that Maximilian of Habsburg had to resort to the expedient of buying goods on credit and selling them for cash, which could mean forfeiting as much as three-quarters of the purchase price. His credit returned to its normal rate of 20 per cent only after his victory over the rebels in 1492. Thereafter, however, the money market altered fundamentally. There was a temporary setback in Italian trade that had built up a large balance in Bruges, and the town, though in decline, kept its great financial market until about 1515 by virtue of tradition and the modest require-ments of the treasury before then. But when Charles v came of age and succeeded to Spain in 1516 and to the Empire in 1519, an era of wars began that cost enormous sums and lasted for the next two centuries.

The money for this was supplied by Antwerp. The exports of the great firms of southern Germany, the Fuggers, Höchstetters, Imhofs, Tuchers, Welsers and others, had allowed them to build up considerable funds for which they needed a use. When loans turned out to be profitable, they extended their financial dealings at the expense of their trade in general. The Fuggers, for instance, built up their loans in the Low Countries from 111,000 florins in

1527 to 1,122,000 in 1546 and to 2,160,000 in 1560. Other firms followed, some Spanish, but most Italian, among whom the Genoese were supreme, with the Grimaldi, Centurioni, Fornari and Cattaneo families and others: Genoa had entered the orbit of Spanish power and specialized in organizing credit for it. Apart from the Genoese, other Italians entered the Antwerp capital market, for instance the Bonvisi of Lucca and the Affaitadi of Cremona, who estimated in 1570 that Spain owed them 727,000 florins. Some financiers native to the Low Countries, such as Peter van der Straten, who had been a broker before entering high finance, or the Schetz family, who had grown rich in trading calamine and spices, played a secondary part.

Antwerp became an important capital market. From 1515 to 1550 Charles v's debt there rose from about 10,000 florins to 500,000, and by 1556 had climbed to 7,000,000. Other means were available to him. When credit was too tight, or needs too large, he could increase his income by selling or leasing parts of the domain. Moreover, the Antwerp market did not dominate his finances for he took three times as much from Castile. When Philip II succeeded, however, he at once named Gaspar Schetz his representative or factor, at a salary of three hundred florins and a commission of 0.5 per cent on new, and 0.25 per cent on renewed loans. Of course, it was not only to the Habsburgs that Antwerp supplied funds. The king of Portugal also borrowed, through his factor, on future sales of spices, and his debt in Antwerp amounted to four million florins in 1542, and six million in 1552. Henry VIII of England could not get sufficient funds at home, and began to borrow in Antwerp in 1544; when Mary Tudor died in 1558, she owed 400,000 florins. The English crown also maintained official factors at Antwerp, the famous Sir Thomas Gresham holding the office between 1551 and 1574. Elizabeth I wished to free herself from the Antwerp market, however, and entrusted Gresham with the establishment in London of a similar one. Political tension between England and Spain brought English loans in Antwerp to an end by 1568.

The loans were most often made through bonds that would fall due at the next fair or the one after, but they were regularly renewed from fair to fair at current market prices. As the princes' credit suffered from their reputation for financial irresponsibility, and even from their very omnipotence – what could be done against them if they defaulted? – lenders covered themselves by linking their loans with lucrative commercial deals, for instance a monopoly in the purchase of goods, or some profitable public function like a tax farm. Often they wanted personal guarantees. The Portuguese factor guaranteed his king; the Privy Councillors or the Fellowship of Merchant Adventurers, the English Crown; high officials or the Knights of the Golden Fleece the Habsburgs. Through such guarantees, the interest rate for the government of the Low Countries fell, on the eve of the Dutch Revolt, from 20 per cent to 12 per cent.

The government also borrowed a great deal through intermediaries. The *rentmeestersbrieven*, bonds issued by the receivers-general, were particularly appreciated in the Low Countries. These men were actually businessmen whom the government entrusted with the management of provincial finances, and they enjoyed personal credit. Until about 1540 it was usual to append to their bonds a formal promise by the sovereign, though later that was regarded as superfluous. Sovereigns of the Low Countries also continued to borrow, for their own purposes, on the credit of the large towns which were subject to collective responsibility for communal debts. The towns issued perpetual annuities in their own names for one or several lives, at only 6.25 per cent or 10 per cent. Nine-tenths of Charles v's debt was composed of such transactions at one time, and in 1526 annuities issued by the town of Antwerp on behalf of the government amounted to 400,000 florins.

Antwerp's capital market collapsed shortly after the middle of the sixteenth century. Spain, crippled by debt, declared bankruptcy in 1557, as did France, and Portugal in 1560. Almost every twenty years thereafter, until 1647, the Spanish Crown repeated this move. At this time bankruptcy meant converting the immense floating debt into perpetual annuities at 5 per cent. This was considerably below the agreed rate, and, worse still, the operation immobilized the loan capital indefinitely. Moreover, the first bankruptcies occurred shortly before the trade crisis in Antwerp, so that the market could no longer count on the usual injections of new money. The receivers-general stopped their payments, and the towns no longer issued annuities on the government's behalf; many merchants failed. Philip II's credit in the Low Countries was ruined.

To find means, which the Dutch Revolt made particularly necessary, *asientos* were issued, i.e. transfers from Spain to the Low Countries, ultimately repayable by the crown in Spain from the proceeds of American silver. The sum was usually advanced by Genoese bankers whose power was now at its height. Sometimes the need for money was so pressing that the governors-general in Brussels had to conclude an *asiento* of their own, submitting it later for Madrid's approval. Between 1567 and 1632 Madrid sent 505,000,000 florins there for the armies, largely through *asientos*. Thanks to these, Antwerp sustained some financial activity, even between 1576 and 1585 when it joined the rebel side. The great losses that the Genoese *asiento*-dealers suffered in the Spanish bankruptcies of 1627 and 1647, and the substitution of French for Spanish influence in Genoa, forced them to abandon their role in these dealings, and it fell increasingly to bankers of Amsterdam, reconciled with Spain after Westphalia.

The war of independence also forced the Dutch to incur large debts, despite the subsidies paid to them by England and France. They used the traditional method of bonds issued by the Estates-General, the Estates of the various provinces and the receivers-general of these provinces. As military operations went in their favour, their loans became easier to remit and by the early sixteenth century their interest rates had fallen from twenty per cent, where they had stood when the issue was in doubt, to six per cent. Their prosperity made capital abundant, especially in Holland, which succeeded in converting its debt into five per cent bonds in 1644, and even to four per cent bonds in 1655. The public debt of the United Provinces differed from that of almost all other European countries in that it was consolidated. For the most part it consisted of annuities, life or redeemable. Several times the authorities reduced their debt by redemption, but each war in which the Republic was involved increased the debt again.

The *Wisselbank* of Amsterdam had a share in public credit quite early on. When the province of Holland was in financial difficulty in 1624, it asked for assistance from the towns, and Amsterdam raised its part of this loan (229,000 florins) from the bank's deposits. The capital was never paid back, although interest on it continued to be paid until the end of the eighteenth century. Similarly in 1650 the town advanced two millions to the Stadholder William II, partly from the bank's deposits. The construction of the New Town Hall, the present-day royal palace, which was built in 1648–65 was partly financed by these funds. In 1663 the treasury of Amsterdam's debt to the bank stood at over two millions, but the town had never benefited from the bank's profits, which were left to accrue and constituted an asset of over 1,700,000 florins.

The United Provinces soon began to export capital. In 1613 the Estates-General agreed to a loan for Gustavus Adolphus, who would repay it in copper for the Dutch arms industry. In 1618, however, Dutch businessmen took over this debt, on the same conditions for repayment. The chief ones were Louis de Geer and his brother-in-law, Elias Trip. The Elector of Brandenburg, and James 1 and Charles 1 of England also approached Holland for loans. During the English Civil War (1642–9) Queen Henrietta Maria pledged the crown jewels as security for a loan of 300,000 florins which she obtained from the municipal lending bank of Rotterdam; shortly afterwards came the first Danish loan on the Amsterdam market, and in 1659 the Emperor followed, with a loan from the town repayable in supplies of copper and mercury. Amsterdam thus became the chief market for this metal, as for so many other goods. In 1667 it was Spain's turn to join the clients of what had now become the greatest money market in Europe, where many states, lacking money or a satisfactory credit structure, came to supply their needs.

While the financiers in Amsterdam lent abroad, a great many individuals subscribed to loans issued on other markets, chiefly in London, which gave interest rates of nearly twice the current ones in the Republic. The English Civil War bred an insecurity that led rentiers to repatriate their money in quantity, and this probably made possible the conversion of the Holland bonds in 1644. Investments abroad were to win favour again after economic conditions had worsened, when industrial and commercial investment declined in appeal and fixed rates became preferable. Growing political stability also made such investment safer.

PART FOUR

Towards a New Equilibrium *1670–1800*

1 Population

The population of both the United Provinces and the Spanish
Netherlands ceased to grow in the second half of the seventeenth
century. The wars at the end of Louis XIV's reign caused severe
damage in the Belgian provinces and since 1635 the country had
been prey to French invasion; but the Nine Years War (1688–97)
and the War of the Spanish Succession (1701–13) not only lasted
longer but were also waged on a much larger scale. In the
southern provinces, which became the battlefield of Europe in the
full sense of the word, any passage of troops left destruction and
famine in its wake, and often their sequel, epidemics, especially in
the countryside abandoned by migrants who kept the towns at
their earlier levels of population. The castellany of Ypres,
threatened by its own situation on the border, lost between 19
and 25 per cent of its population in the Nine Years War, while the
Furnes region, which was also in an exposed situation, declined
from 29,000 in 1688 to 21,000 in 1697, after which there was a
recovery, revealed in the baptismal registers of parishes. This was
interrupted by the great famine of 1709 and again in the 1720s;
only around 1750 did the population return to its level of a
century before.

However, it would be misleading to believe that war was the
chief cause of the population's decline. In the area of Alost, births
had been falling since 1665, and the population decreased from
about 94,000 to some 84,500 before rising again in the decade
1706–15. Elsewhere the birthrate fluctuated between 1650 and

1710. This pattern was not peculiar to the Catholic Netherlands. It was also true of the United Provinces, which had generally avoided the horrors of war. In the Noorderkwartier in Holland, between the IJ and Alkmaar, the population steadily fell after 1650, the decline accelerating after 1700, with an overall fall from over 200,000 to about 130,000. Other areas of the province are thought to have stagnated at best between 1670 and 1750. Friesland, a largely rural area, is believed to have declined from about 170,000 around 1650, to some 135,000 in 1744. Some regions did stand out as exceptions. In Overijssel the population rose from 71,000 in 1650 to 122,400 in 1748 and in the Veluwe from 40,700 in 1650 to 54,200 in 1749. It is worth noting that both underwent considerable industrial development in this period.

The chief reason for such widespread decline appears to be the depression of agriculture in general and grain prices in particular. This brought land clearance, which might have catered for the needs of a growing population, to an end and the lack of employment was reflected in the postponement of marriage, perhaps even in a rise in the number of confirmed bachelors and voluntary contraception.

Apart from war, taxation also contributed to rural poverty. In this respect the great-power policy of the Dutch imposed heavy burdens. In Holland land tax was based on a survey of land made in 1632, and took 20 per cent of the net return. However, owing to high agricultural prices, these returns were at their height at that time and the tax, which was regularly increased by 50, 100 or even 200 per cent after 1680, became an increasingly heavy load as prices fell. In one polder of the Noorderkwartier where stock was raised, taxes and expenses for maintaining the drainage system took the equivalent of 400,000 pounds of cheese in 1681 when the fiscal exemption came to an end. In the 1720s the burden was equivalent to 784,000 pounds, and if prices improved later on, it was only because cattle plague had made cattle scarcer. Friesland was in a similar situation. Direct taxes took between 16 and 25 per cent of the gross income of agriculture. In a village of northern Brabant, south of Dordrecht, the land tax in 1750 represented about 17 per cent of expenses, to which payments for the polders had to be added: they were certainly not negligible. The poor maintenance of the dykes, owing to the depression, allowed storms to breach them more often than before, and finally worms began to eat into the wood which supported the dykes after 1731, and a great deal of money had to be spent on replacing it by stone struts.

The economic crisis in agriculture – which affected the whole of Europe – inevitably had a secondary influence on economic activity in general since the rural outlets were so important. It had a fatal effect on industry and the towns that lived mainly from it. They could not offer many openings to countrymen seeking a livelihood, and the influx of rural immigrants declined. In Holland the only town to rise in population was The Hague, thanks to its position as capital and residence of the Stadholders. The Hague is thought to have increased from 19,500 in 1667 to 29,500 in 1732. Amsterdam apparently reached its peak at 217,000 inhabitants around 1680. In Rotterdam the decline in baptisms between about 1690 and 1745 suggests a fall from 51,000 to 44,000. Other towns suffered more than this. Leyden remained at its peak of 60,000 for some twenty years until about 1685, and had fallen to 35,000 by 1750. In Haarlem the 32,500 of 1707 already marked a probable decline and by 1748 had fallen to 26,800. The five-year average of baptisms registered at Delft declined from 878 in 1681–5 to 456 in 1746–50. The province of Holland thus seems to have had only about 783,000 inhabitants in 1750 – some 100,000 less than in 1680.

The demographic picture was no more favourable in the other provinces. The little Frisian ports of Harlingen and Sneek fell from 8,800 to 7,100 and from 4,400 to 3,700 respectively between 1689 and 1744. Kampen, Deventer and Zutphen shared in the rise of Overijssel between 1675 and 1764, though less than the countryside and country towns. In northern Brabant, Bois-le-Duc owed its recovery (from some 9,000 to over 14,000 between 1665 and 1747) to the revival of its role of intermediary between the United Provinces and the Spanish Netherlands after the Peace of Westphalia, and in the Veluwe the small boroughs with handicrafts were the only ones to rise between 1650 and 1749. In the Belgian provinces, Antwerp fell from 67,000 in 1699 to 42,600 in 1755; Bruges from almost 37,500 around 1700 to 27,800 in 1748; Ghent from about 50,000 in 1690 to 42,700 in 1730; Louvain from 15,800 in 1670 to 14,400 in 1760; Malines from about 24,100 in 1680 to 19,300 in 1740.

At this time a change occurred in the Austrian Netherlands,

coinciding with a new turning-point in economic conditions, which once more illustrates the close relationship between economic development and population. The recovery occurred first of all in the countryside with the revival of agricultural prices; and moreover peace was only disturbed there after 1713 by the War of the Austrian Succession, in which the French occupied the Austrian Netherlands and the southern fringes of the Republic between 1744 and 1749. While Antwerp and Louvain still suffered decline, the population of Brabant rose overall from 373,200 in 1709 to 447,300 in 1755, and went up to 618,400 at the census of 1784, which indicated a rise of 65.7 per cent, and a growth rate of 0.875 per annum over seventy-five years. The birth rate recovered everywhere after 1706–15; in the Alost region, for example, the population doubled over eighty years to 172,000.

The towns of the Austrian Netherlands also benefited from the clear economic improvement after the middle of the eighteenth century, and made good their population losses. In Brabant, between the censuses of 1755 and 1784, Antwerp rose to 51,000, Louvain to 20,800, and Brussels, now the country's largest town, and stimulated by its position as seat of increasingly centralized government, from 57,900 to 74,400. In Flanders, Bruges contained 31,300 inhabitants in 1796, Ghent 51,300 in 1784 and some little towns appear to have risen throughout the century, e.g. Saint-Nicolas from 6,200 in 1698 to 10,600 in 1794.

The United Provinces presented a more varied pattern. The Veluwe, with 65,800 inhabitants in 1795, had an annual growth rate of 0.42 per cent in the second half of the century; the countryside of northern Brabant grew by 0.45 per cent per annum between 1766 and 1805; Friesland grew by 0.31 per cent, and had 157,000 inhabitants in 1796. By contrast Overijssel, the industry of which had developed, gained 12,000, or only 10 per cent, between 1748 and 1795, and Holland apparently stagnated after 1750. The rural population south of the IJ may have risen slightly, although it is questionable, but the decline north of that river appears to have continued. As to the towns, the 215,000 inhabitants counted in Amsterdam in 1798 suggest long-term stagnation. The number of baptisms in Delft also remained low in the second half of the century, whilst Leyden and Haarlem continued to decline, with 31,000 and 21,200 inhabitants respectively in 1795. Rotterdam, on the other hand, was flourishing. Its annual baptisms rose and indicated a population, by 1795, of 57,500, perhaps a reflection of the economic growth of the hinterland on the Meuse and Rhine. Its neighbour, Schiedam, rose by more than half between 1747 and 1795, from 6,000 (almost the same as the census of 1622) to 9,100, probably because of the progress of the local gin industry. The Hague went on growing, to some 42,000 in 1795.

As in other countries, the governments of the Low Countries decided to take a general population census at the end of the eighteenth century. In 1784 the Brussels government estimated the population of the Austrian Netherlands at 2,273,000, which was probably accurate to within 5 per cent. The still independent principality of Liège was not included; its population has been estimated at 350,000 people. The area roughly corresponding to modern Belgium and Luxembourg must thus have had a good 2,600,000 inhabitants, a quarter of today's population. The Batavian Republic, which succeeded the United Provinces, had 2,078,000 in 1795–6, or barely 15.3 per cent of the present-day Dutch population.

Holland had been for many years one of the most urbanized of European regions, and this was still more the case in the seventeenth and eighteenth centuries. According to the census of 1795, 59 per cent of the people dwelt in towns as against 54 per cent in 1622. Elsewhere, although the towns kept up in numbers, their share declined because the countryside experienced a population explosion. In Overijssel the urban share declined from 42.5 per cent to 34.8 per cent between 1675 and 1795; in Austrian Brabant from 26 per cent to 23 per cent between 1755 and 1784. However, there was still a large-scale flight from the land. In 1771 no less than 43 per cent of Alkmaar's population came from elsewhere. In the same period 29 per cent of the families that were given charity in a Catholic parish of Rotterdam had come from northern Brabant. In a metropolis such as Amsterdam, up to 75 per cent of the men who contracted marriages were immigrants.

The migrants did not, of course, all come from the nearby countryside. The great Dutch cities, especially Amsterdam and Rotterdam, and the Republic in general attracted a great many half-starved Germans throughout the seventeenth and eighteenth centuries, mainly from the bishoprics of Münster and Osnabrück, eastern Friesland and Oldenburg; they have left their mark in many of the surnames in today's Netherlands. 27 per cent of the poor of the same parish in Rotterdam in the second half of the eighteenth century were Germans. Apart from such permanent settlement, there was a large-scale seasonal migration from Germany. The *Hollandgänger*, who came to work at hay making, the harvest or peat cutting, were unpopular with the common people of the region, who felt their livelihood was threatened by the low wages accepted by the Germans. Besides, a great many pedlars, also German, competed in the retail trade and excited resentment.

The arrival of French Huguenots in the United Provinces in the later seventeenth century was somewhat analogous to that of the Belgian refugees a century before, although the scale was smaller. As the Protestants' situation in France deteriorated, some of them decided to emigrate and they were attracted to the United Provinces both by the prosperity and the position of Calvinism as the established religion. Local and provincial authorities, motivated by religious solidarity or economic interest, helped expert artisans to set themselves up, and offered them tax concessions and similar favours. Between 1681 and 1684 Amsterdam took in over two thousand of them. The revocation of the Edict of Nantes in 1685 gave a greater stimulus to the emigration, and the Republic was among the countries that profited most. Some Irish Catholics sought refuge in the Spanish Netherlands after the disaster of the Boyne in 1690, and soon became integrated with the lesser nobility comprising government officials; there were also some Scottish refugees in Holland after the failure of the Jacobite rising in 1745. In both cases the numbers were small.

It does not seem that many people left the Low Countries at this time. Rich or poor, the Dutch could hardly have found better conditions anywhere else. After 1750 some five thousand recruits did leave the Belgian provinces for Austrian agricultural colonies in the Banat of Temesvár. People who left for the overseas colonies usually did so only temporarily, except in the case of the Cape of Good Hope, where the favourable climate enabled a small permanent colony to develop, among them Huguenots, whose surnames have since become quite widespread, and Germans, for whom the Republic had been a first stage on the way abroad.

The limited amount of emigration meant that the level of population was determined essentially by natural factors, i.e. birth and death. The birth rate, though always high, tended to fall. In the administrative district of Furnes it oscillated around 50 per thousand in the first half of the eighteenth century, and 40 per thousand after 1750, while the villages of North Holland had an average of 39 per thousand in 1742 and between 31 and 32 per thousand in 1809. There was a similar pattern in many towns, although the figures were lower: in Antwerp the birth rate rose from 29.17 per thousand in 1699 to 33.13 in 1755, and fell back to 27.66 in 1784. In a parish in Ghent it declined from 35.76 per thousand in 1681 to 31.4 in 1765 and rose, for the whole town, to 38 in 1784, a level almost attained by Brussels in 1755.

The birth rate naturally reflected crises of all kinds. Famine would cause an immediate decline in the number of marriages and hence of legitimate births, though it is also clear that in the famine of 1740 at Liège and Louvain illegitimate births did not increase, as usually happened elsewhere in such conditions. Perhaps contraception had now become more widespread, especially when there was insufficient food, and in any case there would be an increase in miscarriages in such periods, because of the consumption of blighted grain; and the typhus or syphilis accompanying troop movements usually had the same effect. Still, when the crises passed, the postponed marriages could take place, and the birth rate rose temporarily above the average.

Apart from such short-term factors, progress in contraceptive techniques may have had some effect in the long-term decline of the birth rate. It was also influenced by the composition of the age-pyramid, for a high birth rate would first increase the lower levels of the pyramid, so there would be many women of below child-bearing age and births, though rising in absolute terms, would decline as a proportion of the population. The village of Krommenie on the Zaan had 41 per cent of its inhabitants under twenty in 1742, and the equivalent figure for a group of villages west of Ghent in 1796 or 1798 was 45.5. However, the proportion fell to 32 per cent in the borough of Maaseik and in Malines, for places that were regional centres, even if they were quite small like Maaseik, always had a large number of adult immigrants who worked as artisans, in trade or in administration.

It seems that the age on marriage was quite high. As the population grew, there were problems for young couples who were setting up, especially in the countryside, for the large amount of available labour depressed wages and prevented or delayed the foundation of new homes. In 1795, in Lede, near Alost, only 7.77 per cent of the married men and 12.14 per cent of the married women were under thirty, and married people made up an astonishingly low proportion of the population – hardly more than 30 per cent in Antwerp in 1755 or in Malines, or west of Ghent, or in Lede at the end of the century. There were a great many children and young people, but life-expectancy was not high. As a result of the many early deaths, there were large numbers of widows and widowers: they formed 6.71 per cent of the adult population of Antwerp in 1755, and the equivalent figures for the borough of Geel in the Campine and for the Alost area in 1795 were respectively 6.23 per cent and 6.76 per cent. 4.06 per cent of Malines's population in 1796 was made up of widows, for whom the chance of remarriage was slight, especially if they had children.

The limited duration of many marriages, infant mortality and the prevalence of celibacy all explain why the average number of people per household was so low – 3.92 in The Hague in 1674, 3.04 in Antwerp and 3.2 in Brussels in 1755, 3.54 at Malines in 1796 – although a household often included three generations living under one roof, as well as domestic servants. The figure was higher in the countryside, in general about five, although here too the household included servants and farm girls. Half of the farms in the Veluwe and Overijssel employed wage-labour in 1748–9, usually people under twenty, and such labourers made up 12 per cent and 14 per cent of their respective populations. In Friesland the equivalent percentage was 10.7 in 1746. The hard agricultural work meant that there would be at least as many men involved as women.

It was different in other rural areas, where a preference for stock-raising or the small size of farms made the work easier. In the countryside of the Noorderkwartier and the Alost area, the number of servants fell to 5 per cent, and a large majority of them were women. In the Frisian towns domestic servants were on average 6 per cent of the population, 6.4 per cent in Malines in 1796, in Antwerp and Brussels 8.2 and 10 per cent respectively in 1755. There would usually be three female for every male servant. This makes the urban demography of the *ancien régime* easier to understand: the numerical balance of the sexes, which was about equal in the countryside, tipped heavily in the women's favour in the towns. In Brussels in 1755 they were 56.5 per cent of the population; in Antwerp 58 per cent; in 1796 in Malines as much as 59.5 per cent. In the age group nineteen to twenty-four, to which many female servants belonged, the female preponderance in Malines was as high as 63.5 per cent. The large numbers of domestic servants were a typical feature of the old order.

The death rate was high and death came early. Around Furnes death rates were more than forty per thousand between 1690 and 1730, with a peak of fifty-seven per thousand in 1693. The rate then fell, stabilizing at about twenty-eight per thousand after 1760. It was slightly lower than this in the Alost region, but higher (though improving) after 1740 in North Holland. Infant mortality remained a terrible scourge but it, too, was declining. In two villages near Furnes before 1755, 8.6 per cent of new-born children died within one month, 24.6 per cent before reaching one year, and 35.5 before the age of thirteen; after 1755 the figures were respectively 7.9, 22.3 and 30.3. In some villages of the Noorderkwartier the number of children dying in their first year rose to 37.4 per cent in the first third of the eighteenth century, while 45.7 per cent died before the age of five, and only 51.8 per cent reached the age of twenty. In other cases a good half of the children would die before the age of twelve, and their life expectancy at birth was apparently only twenty-three years. Here, too, there was a perceptible improvement during the second half of the century, which did much to raise the population.

Dysentery still caused great damage. It is said to have carried off about a tenth of the Flemish rural population between 1676 and 1678, and it raged again between 1779 and 1785 and after 1790. However, the instance of the Belgian monasteries (see page 138) suggests that after a decline in the average age on death (from 53.7 years in the second half of the seventeenth century to 52.8 years in the first half of the eighteenth) there was a rise to 55.6 years between 1750 and 1789. These figures do include monks born in the exceptionally bad years 1680–1719, who had an average age on death of 51.9, whereas those born between 1720 and 1750 lived on average to the age of 56.8 years, and a group of soldiers in the Austrian army, born in 1730, had an average age on death of fifty-six years and eight months. It is the case, of course, that these figures apply to men who were sheltered from dearth and whose diet was not only copious but also healthy and well balanced, so that they were better able to resist disease. But in any case agricultural changes in the eighteenth century, and especially the introduction of potatoes for popular consumption, banished the spectre of famine for a great many people in all classes of society.

2 *Agriculture and Fisheries*

I THE YIELD OF AGRICULTURE AND STOCK-RAISING

Except in Holland, the polders of which were mainly pasture, cereals still predominated. Among the bread grains, rye kept its lead, which had grown because of the popularity of gin, for which it was a main ingredient. Even peasants who grew wheat did so mainly for the market, and themselves ate bread made from rye or some other inferior grain. In time of famine rye flour was often mixed with oats or barley, which were not usually regarded as bread grains, or even with beans or peas.

Although no wheat at all was grown at Lichtervelde, south of Bruges, in 1968, more wheat bread seems to have been eaten there than hitherto. Perhaps the fall in the price of cereals until the middle of the eighteenth century stimulated such consumption, although it is worth mentioning that wheat imports from the Baltic to the United Provinces did decline once prices rose again. Wheat being about half as much again in price as rye, white bread bore in Holland the revealing name *heerenbroot* ('gentlemen's bread') and in Leyden it was even called 'professors' bread'. Holland, favoured by Amsterdam's position vis à vis the European grain market, was far in the lead as a consumer of wheat, which accounted for 53.3 per cent of the cereals consumed in the rural areas, and 64.2 per cent of those eaten in the towns. In 1782–6 the average annual consumption of cereals in Amsterdam was estimated at 21,000 tonnes, 16,000 (76.2 per cent) of those being wheat. The demand made peasants in Zeeland turn their fields mainly over to wheat, whereas rye led everywhere else, except in the Ardennes and neighbouring regions, where spelt was still grown.

Consumption of bread was high. At Lichtervelde in 1693 the daily need of the population was estimated at 800 grams of rye, although by 1785 the figure for the Austrian Netherlands had fallen to 0.58 litres. In Groningen consumption of rye seems to have fallen between 1742 and 1774 from 600 to 400 grams per day, and for the whole of Holland in 1798, needs were reckoned at 325 grams per head per day. Bread was gradually being replaced by other foodstuffs, however – buckwheat, for instance. Possibly it was the rise in cereal prices after 1750 that stimulated the consumption of buckwheat, for even in Holland in 1798 it amounted to 17 per cent of the cereals consumed (however inaccurate it may be to class it as a cereal). It was even imported from the Antwerp Campine and the Waasland. By the end of the *ancien régime*, it had replaced peas and beans in the ordinary diet.

This diet underwent a fundamental change with the introduction of the potato. It had been known as a botanical curiosity since the late sixteenth century, and was cultivated in kitchen gardens around Nieuport by the mid- 1620s, having arrived, perhaps, from England, where it was already popular, through Carthusian refugees who had set up a monastery nearby. It was cultivated in the open fields in west Flanders by 1670 at the latest, and spread from there to Flemish Zeeland in the late 1690s. It went on to Brabant, and appeared in the islands of Zeeland in the 1730s, around Utrecht in 1736, in Overijssel in 1746, near Venlo in 1755 and in Friesland in 1761. It arrived in Luxembourg at the end of the seventeenth century, having come from Alsace, and it reached the kitchen gardens of Namur and Hainault in the 1710s. Potatoes were grown in the open fields there twenty years later.

Its progress was obviously fostered by the high cost of grain in times of famine, especially in 1740 and more consistently after mid-century. It was originally a poor man's food, and was taken up by the rich only after 1780. The very novelty of the potato was an encouragement, for it was not affected by the tithe levied on cereals, and this caused a great deal of generally unsuccessful litigation. It was also unaffected by the excise on grain milling, and people were not slow to discover that, for a given surface of land, it could provide almost twice the nutritive value of grain. Its introduction constituted a decisive improvement in the masses' diet, quite apart from the better balance that its abundance of vitamins provided. By the 1740s it was cultivated on a large-scale in Northern Brabant: in a village north of Breda only two farmers in any one year would be growing potatoes, but each one gave over to the crop an average of 1,200 *ares*. At the same time, four farmers in five would be growing potatoes in villages in Flanders, but only on fifteen *ares* in each farm, and only for their family. It was not until the end of the century that large-scale commercial cultivation became widespread in the Austrian Netherlands, and whereas in Holland quantities of potatoes were marketed in the towns from the middle years of the century and took over from the traditional hotpot of beans, peas, turnips and cabbages in most ordinary households, it became general in the Belgian provinces only by the end of the *ancien régime*.

Merely by reducing the peasants' requirements of grain, the potato made increased cereal production for the market possible, and stimulated the formation of a market economy. The land released by the cultivation of potatoes permitted greater commercial exploitation of grain, and the Low Countries became less dependent on foreign foods. For the first time since the Middle Ages, the Belgian provinces managed, despite their larger population, to meet their own needs as far as grain was concerned, and even to export it. Cash crops were stimulated by the greater firmness of their prices, while grain had been harmed by the long-term crisis, and as economic conditions improved they benefited from the extra land that potato-growing made available. Certainly when cereal prices were at their best, peasants were tempted to increase their grain-production. Thus, in the Zeeland islands, northern Brabant and Flanders flax, still the chief industrial crop, gained ground until about 1750, but it declined thereafter in Overijssel when the area shifted to cotton manufactures. It probably also declined in Flanders when the government put pressure on prices in 1765–6 by forbidding the export of linen. Among the oleaginous crops, rape seems to have spread much more widely in the Austrian Netherlands at the end of the eighteenth century. In this period, the country deserved the sobriquet 'the hop garden of Europe'; in good years, the Alost region alone would produce 3,600,000 pounds of hops. Tobacco spread from the Dendre area, where even in 1703 so much of it had been grown that it was taxed. It was especially profitable for small farms, because of the good returns offered by labour-intensive crops. While the United Provinces mainly produced snuff, the Austrian Netherlands' tobacco was better and was used for smoking. The American War of Independence interrupted imports of American tobacco, and the consequent price rise gave the tobacco growers high hopes, but when peace returned, tobacco growing went back to earlier levels.

The acquisition of culinary skills in wealthy houses stimulated the development of many market gardens. The masses ate vegetables essentially for their nutritive value as before, but the rich ate finer vegetables that were lower in calories. Beginning in the later seventeenth century, the *Westland* south of The Hague, which specialized in such vegetables, appears to have pioneered greenhouse production in Europe. In the eighteenth century, brussels sprouts and chicory became common, and it was discovered that the root of the latter could be a substitute for coffee. As interest in agronomy increased, the first experiments in fruit growing resulted in the production of several still-familiar varieties of apples and pears. It also stimulated the cultivation of flowers and trees. The urgent industrial need of firewood caused a considerable amount of reafforestation, and the nobles tried to improve their lands, especially the newly cleared ones, by planting conifers and oak trees.

Moreover, although the woods remained open to pasturage, for instance in the Ardennes, their gradual exhaustion and an acknowledgement of the harm that cattle caused them led to stricter regulation of their use. Other methods of feeding herds had to be found, especially when the low price of grain caused an increase in stock-raising, which became more profitable than grain. Since the second half of the seventeenth century fodder crops had been much improved. Before clover meadows had been left alone for several years, the weeds gradually taking over. Now clover was grown as a secondary crop, mixed with grain or flax, and after the harvest of the crop it could grow freely until the autumn of the following year and be repeatedly mown. This biennial cultivation, which probably began in the Waasland, soon spread to the rest of Flanders and Brabant, though with greater difficulty in the Walloon provinces, where the persistence of common pasture made secondary cultivation difficult. After 1730 the authorities began sporadically to exempt arable land from the laws regarding common use, but it was only with the legislation of the French Revolution that the peasant could deny his pastures to the community. If secondary cultivation of clover became extensive in the Netherlands only in the nineteenth century, fodder beets had been brought in from Germany and were grown almost everywhere by the later eighteenth, although the Belgian provinces used it on a large-scale only in the following century.

The delay in turning arable land into artificial meadow was caused, in the case of Holland, by the humidity of much of the land there, which had been under grass for years. In North Holland Jan Kops, the commissioner for agriculture, noted in 1800 that in many villages there were hardly any fields. In the Pays de Herve, meadows replaced fields in the second half of the seventeenth century because of the low price of grain. Moreover, stock-raising left more time than agricultural work did for rural handicrafts, and pasture was not liable to tithes, and so the peasants' costs were less. On the other hand, pasture was reconverted into arable land in Friesland after 1750 to take advantage of the recovery in grain prices.

There was of course another reason for this. Since the later seventeenth century, the animal stock had been frequently decimated by epidemics. One occurred in 1681 in Brabant and Flanders, but those of 1713–20, 1744–54 and 1768–86 were more widespread and deadlier. Cattle plague, brought from Germany by the thin cattle that were imported for fattening, carried off 61,000 beasts in Friesland in 1714, 110,000 between November 1744 and August 1745, and 98,000 from May to December 1769, by which time the province had only 160,000 left. Holland had 225,000 adult beasts in 1769, but 160,000 died in 1770, and losses had exceeded 400,000 by 1784. Two villages in Overijssel had lost 1,838 out of 2,062 and 816 out of 839 respectively in 1714.

The remedies applied turned out to be futile until 1769 and 1770, when the Brussels government forced owners of contaminated stock to slaughter all their cattle, even apparently healthy beasts, to burn the manure, straw and hay piled up in the barns, and to bury the ash as well as the cadavers. They were compensated for loss. The system seems to have worked well and aroused considerable interest abroad, especially in France and Hanover. The United Provinces did not adopt it, perhaps because it was too costly, but a peasant in Groningen discovered, early in the 1770s, that innoculation of the calves of cured cows could make them immune. Vaccination was henceforth successfully used. After each wave of the disease efforts were made to replenish the stock. The number of cattle in Austrian Brabant was estimated at 300,000 around 1770; in Overijssel at 72,700 in 1800. In one part of this province it had risen by 60 per cent since 1739. Consumption of beef or veal and butter was estimated in Holland in the later eighteenth century at forty-seven and forty grams per head per day respectively, but we do not know how far this was true of the country as a whole.

Animal epidemic caused a further conversion of pasture into ploughland, but it could equally be turned over to other animals. The horse, for instance, probably thrived. The poor soils of Overijssel, earlier overpopulated with horses, still had sixty-four for each hundred cultivated hectares in 1812. Horse breeding was probably stimulated both by the intensification of agriculture and by the growth of the military strength of the neighbouring lands: they bought remounts from Friesland and the Austrian Netherlands, which exported 13,600 in 1772. Pig breeding (which is said to have developed in Overijssel) supplied pork for the poorer households. Daily consumption of pork in Holland in the later 1790s was twenty-eight grams per head, but it was higher in the northern part of the province, the poorest, where the figure was thirty-five grams. Since the seventeenth century pig farming had, however, been forbidden on the small farms of Flanders and Brabant, so as to prevent the damage caused by the wandering pigs the peasants could not feed on their own lands. Sheep may have temporarily replaced cattle on grasslands during plague years, but sheep raising was in decline, and so was bee keeping, although every year many hives were still taken to orchards when the trees bloomed or to heaths. Moreover, sheep rearing and bee keeping were affected by the shift to more intensive agriculture, which reduced customary rights and turned the commons and other uncultivated land into ploughland.

2 CLEARANCES AND TECHNICAL PROGRESS

The long-term crisis had not favoured clearances which were expensive and which seemingly offered only modest profits. In Overijssel less than nine hundred hectares seem to have been claimed for cultivation between 1682 and 1749. The growing population there sought its livelihood in industrial labour, which paid better than agriculture. When conditions improved, and agricultural prices rose, there was more reason for clearances. The annual average for lands cleared for cultivation in the United Provinces rose to 717 hectares in the years 1765–89 as against 456 in the preceding hundred years. In 1761 the town of Groningen resumed drainage of the peat bogs, which had ceased in 1651. Even so, one-third of the Republic's land was not in use in 1795.

In the Austrian Netherlands the government went ahead with clearances energetically from 1755 onward. It ordered the cultivation of common lands, first in Hainault and then in the Campine and Namur, and it exempted reclaimed land from taxes and tithes. To raise their income, landowners responded enthusiastically to this encouragement, as for instance the Duke of Arenberg in Flanders or the Premonstratensian abbeys in Brabant. However, the attack on uncultivated land worked to the detriment of small farmers, for whom the commons were indispensable as grazing for cattle and hence for manure. They were also victims of measures restricting grazing on stubble and in the woods. The Austrian government did not much bother with individual problems of this kind, however: they considered intensive agriculture the surest way of raising the national income and were not much concerned about how this was distributed. Nevertheless, collective rights were a long way from disappearing in the Belgian provinces by the end of the old regime, and the Kingdom of the Netherlands attacked the problem seriously only in the following century.

Intensive cultivation was essentially concerned with crop rotation. Whereas England gradually abandoned fallow and demonstrated to continental agronomists the crop rotation she had herself borrowed from Flanders, continuous working of the land now became general in that very province and spread from there to the sandy soil of the Antwerp Campine and northern Brabant. Usually it spread most rapidly among the small farms, those directly farmed by their owners, or lands that belonged to various proprietors and from which rents and taxes were due whether they were cultivated or not. The large farms, the taxes on which were proportional to the yield, had not the same interest and were slower in adopting new methods of crop rotation. Until the latter half of the eighteenth century their leases sometimes even obliged them to retain the fallow period, but it was gradually given up in

Hainault and disappeared in Friesland, at that time an area of large farms, because of the stimulus of high agricultural prices. Elsewhere the time between fallow periods was extended, as for instance in the Liège district of Hesbaye or among the alluvial lands of Zeeland and northern Brabant, where fields were henceforth left fallow every six or nine years. Cultivation of potatoes, rape or clover, which had the advantage of giving nitrate to the soil, took the place of fallow periods, but these were maintained in the poorer soils of the Walloon area, in the two Limburgs and the eastern regions of the United Provinces, in the absence of eager markets.

Owing to the more abundant yields of fodder crops, cattle could not only be increased in number, but could also be kept in the byre permanently so that no manure would be lost. Similarly at night the sheep would be put in a pen under the open sky, which would often be shifted around to fertilize the various parts of the natural meadows, the *triches* of the Walloon area, before they were cleared, or the fields before they had clumps of grass spread over them. Marl was now hardly used at all as fertilizer, as stocks of it were running out, but in the polders mud taken from the dykes at their annual dredging was scattered over ploughed land. Austrian Flanders imported large quantities of peat ash, liquid manure, sewage and rape cakes from the United Provinces and French Flanders.

Tilling of the soil was also helped by the improvement of agricultural implements. Early in the eighteenth century in Brabant the wheel of the plough was replaced by a mobile foot, the height of which could be regulated according to the desired depth of the furrow. Moreover, the ploughshare and the mould board were joined in a single, concave piece. The 'Brabant', which was light in build and did not drag on the soil, needed only limited traction, two horses at the most for the heaviest soils. This was the prototype of the modern plough throughout the West. It was introduced to England by James Small, to France by Mathieu de Dombasle (1777–1843) and to Germany by J. N. Schwerz (1759–1844). A new type of harrow, used in Flanders in the eighteenth century, made possible the retraction of the teeth according to the amount of hoeing that was needed. The fields were levelled with heavy wooden or stone rollers or, in clearances particularly, a sort of large wooden spade pulled by horses. In the peat colonies around Groningen five or six parallel furrows would be traced by little boards attached to a beam, after which seeds would be slipped through a cow's horn sawn off at the tip. This was replaced around 1780 by a funnel, the outlet of which could be regulated according to the size of the seed. For the harvest the long-handled sickle, which could be more easily handled than the scythe and was better adapted to the irregularities of the strips, finally prevailed in Flanders and the Campine. In Friesland and the Groningen area in the eighteenth century threshing was carried out by a heavy conical block turned on a pivot by horsepower. The winnowing mill, borrowed by the Dutch from China, was used after 1727 on the Austro-Dutch border in Brabant.

Besides improved tools, better seeds could also increase the yield. It was customary in the United Provinces in the later eighteenth century to forestall diseases of wheat by treating the seeds with lime, salt or saltpetre. In the first potato blight in 1779, the authorities of the castellany of Oudenaarde imported American plants; and selected Virginia and Maryland tobacco plants were introduced and distributed to planters in the Austrian Netherlands. It would be interesting to see statistics regarding such advances, but there is little information on this topic for the Belgian provinces in the eighteenth century, and not much more for the Republic. Probably the Frisian yields of 1771 – 28:1 for wheat, 48:1 for rye, 33:1 for barley and 25:1 for oats – were exceptional, occurring as they did on rich lands, but yields of 8–10:1, 13–20:1, 10–16:1 and 14–20:1 for the four cereals respectively were normal around 1800 on land of average quality, and were higher than those of other countries. Contemporaries were conscious of the advances made in agriculture in the Low Countries, as can be judged from the attention paid to it in travellers' accounts of the second half of the eighteenth century, and especially from the studies made there by foreign agronomists, for instance J. N. Schwerz, a founding-father of the science in Germany and author of the useful *Anleitung zur Kenntnis der belgischen Landwirtschaft* (three volumes, 1807–11).

Stock-raising had not progressed as far; interest in horse breeding preceded interest in the others. After 1610 Friesland supervised the quality of stallions and the example was followed, after 1767, first in Brabant and then in Namur, Flanders and Luxembourg. The castellany of Alost even set up a stud-farm in

1718, and that of Ghent in 1754, with stallions from Friesland, Hanover, Holstein and Denmark; but the attempts were short-lived. The central government maintained another from 1768 to 1781, and bought stallions in England, where Bakewell's 'black horses' had been cross-bred with Frisian stock to give better draught horses; these stallions may have given the race its definitive character. Another aim was to provide cavalry remounts and to reduce imports of saddle and coach horses. Some agronomists tried to improve sheep cross-breeding with Spanish merinos, and they recommended more rational ways of bee keeping; however, if cattle plague did give rise to veterinary experiments and research, the improvement of cattle was the result more of better feeding than of considered, selective breeding. The cross-breeding was still largely left to chance, and there was always considerable variety in the herds.

The yield of cow's milk was modest. Lactating cows supplied only from four to five litres a day on average on Frisian farms in 1760 – no more than two hundred years previously. At the time between 27.5 and 32 litres of milk were needed for a kilogram of butter. At least there had been some progress in churning. In 1660 churning was done in Holland with the aid of a horse-driven mill, the rotation activating a vertical plunger. In Flanders a hundred years later a dog would be used for this purpose, working from the inside of a treadmill fixed against the farm wall, so that its movement worked the plunger.

3 LANDOWNERSHIP AND PEASANT CONDITIONS

Farms naturally varied in size a great deal. Arable farms were usually smaller than those given over to the stock-raising. Around 1800 in the region of today's Netherlands, the former had on average sixteen hectares, the latter about sixty. Poor soils normally demanded larger areas for their very extensive agriculture and stock-raising. South of the Sambre and Meuse trench, the greater part of the cultivated land was occupied by large holdings, of between 40 and 160 hectares. The system of land tenure also played its part. Many circumstances could influence the division of private property, but for centuries the entailed properties survived intact. In the Liège Condroz the only two farms with several hundred hectares belonged respectively to the Knights of Malta and the St Hubert's Abbey. Moreover, the commons increased the usable acreage of farms. There were, however, tiny farms that could not support the farmer, and those farmers lived at least partly as labourers in the service of larger farmers, or as artisans.

Eighteenth-century agronomists often discussed the respective advantages and disadvantages of small and large farms, especially in the Austrian Netherlands. Advocates of the former praised the care that could be brought to cultivation in small farms, and stressed their role as suppliers of poultry, eggs, dairy products, etc., to the weekly urban markets. The more there were, the more households would be set up, and the more children born. Supporters of large farms pointed out that their general costs were lower, that they were better suited to progressive experimentation, that their yield could be stocked to await higher prices and finally that their high rents would be accessible to only a small minority of farmers, so that a balance between supply and demand would prevent them from rising. Of the two arguments, the authorities preferred the first in this period of population growth. In 1767 the authorities of Hainault limited the size of farms to ninety hectares, although the edict may never actually have been applied. Similar edicts planned for Brabant and Namur never saw day, and in 1788 there were complaints that the extreme subdivision of land in the Campine was making its farms quite unprofitable.

Farms of small or medium size were usually directly farmed. Peasant property, apart from commons and land attached to seignorial domains, made up 46 per cent of the land in Liège just before the French conquest and 29 per cent in Hainault, but in the sandy region of Flanders it could be up to 85 per cent, and in a village of the Liège Campine as much as 92 per cent. The expropriations carried out in Brabant between 1698 and 1788 for roads or canals reveal lower figures there, but still between 9 and 23 per cent. Peasant property tended to increase after 1750, owing to the prosperity that came with the rise of agricultural prices, though it often grew only through loans and mortgages. Clearances could help to extend it, as in Overijssel between 1601 and 1751.

The small peasant proprietor frequently increased his farmland by renting. In two villages south of Alkmaar in Holland 62 per cent of the farms were cultivated by the owner himself in 1812, and 16 per cent partly. They amounted to 48 per cent and 34 per cent of the arable land respectively. By contrast Heemskerk still further

E.H.—9

south included only twenty-seven peasants among 137 proprietors of arable land, and their share was less than 27 per cent. Peasant property was markedly less extensive around 1700 in Friesland than it had been two centuries before, and declined until the mid-eighteenth century, when the turning-point in conditions reversed the tendency. In fact the other classes had considerable holdings in most areas. Entailed property made up 17 per cent of the land in Liège but rose to 31 per cent in the Hesbaye district there and sometimes even 50 per cent on the lower Sambre. In Brabant the many abbeys and charitable institutions of the towns, rich in the past, owned between 30 and 50 per cent of the land, but their share declined to 16 per cent in Hainault, 7 per cent in eastern Flanders and to only 3 per cent in the Pays de Herve. There was hardly a village in the Belgian provinces where clergy, church or parish charitable institutions did not own some land. It was rare for these to be farmed directly, as was done by needy priests of the Pays de Herve, where the Abbey of Val-Dieu gave up using agricultural labourers in 1759. As entailed property was exempt from civil taxes, in 1753 Maria Theresa obliged institutions that held such property to amortize it, i.e. pay a lump sum that was relatively high in lieu of taxes. The sale of the properties of some poor monasteries to meet this edict hardly changed the distribution of landed property, any more than the abolition of the contemplative monasteries by Joseph II in 1783. Their property passed on to a 'religious fund' instituted as a source of charitable assistance, but it was usually quite modest.

The nobility of Liège and Hainault owned a quarter of the rural property, that of Brabant and Flanders one-tenth, although there was, of course, a great deal of local variation. To a much greater degree than was true of the lands owned by other classes, their property included woods, vestiges of conditions that went back to medieval times and a sign of the taste for hunting that was one of the nobility's privileges. A few noblemen with an interest in agronomy tried to exploit their own lands, usually with considerable losses. In reality the well-off families of the Austrian Netherlands had succumbed to the blandishments of court life in Brussels and even Vienna, and they only seldom visited their country properties.

The village notables, stewards, notaries, *rentiers*, etc., also had landed property, but the urban bourgeoisie owned a great deal more, especially in regions of high urbanization. If they owned less than 12 per cent of the land in the principality of Liège, the figures were 30 per cent in Hainault and between 23 and 38 per cent in Brabant, where the bourgeoisie invested more in land, sometimes quite distant, as they had less opportunity to invest it in trade or industry. The area for investment in property did not extend beyond a radius of thirteen kilometres around Antwerp, but citizens of the town possessed between 45 and 69 per cent of the land there, the Brussels bourgeoisie 33 to 43 per cent within a radius of sixteen kilometres, and the townsmen of Louvain up to 47 per cent within a radius of twenty-five kilometres. Up to 83 per cent of the lands of a village situated five kilometres from Malines were owned by town dwellers. Bourgeois property was of course more mobile than that of the privileged classes. Many citizens sold their land once the rise in prices after 1750 increased its value, and it was chiefly from this source that the peasants were able to buy property. However, the sale of property belonging to dispossessed religious communities and to emigrants after the French conquest resulted in a large shift of property from the church and the nobility into bourgeois and peasant hands. In the department of Jemappes, today's province of Hainault, sales amounted to almost 43,000 hectares, a good 11 per cent of the total surface. Three-quarters of it went into townsmen's hands, the rest to peasants. In Friesland, too, a good 79 per cent of the confiscated ecclesiastical lands, sold off in the second half of the seventeenth century, went to the petty nobility or the bourgeoisie.

Share-cropping, which was in any case limited to backward regions, was declining. The fall in agricultural prices before 1750 helped to persuade farmers to abandon it. It was still used by some ecclesiastics and noble families to guarantee provisions, but if the land was too distant from the monastery or castle, they would commute the share into its cash value or instruct their steward to sell their share of the harvest. South of the Ruremonde and probably also in Liège Condroz, share-cropping was limited in the late seventeenth century to cattle, and the harvest went wholly to the share-cropper. A lease for a fixed rent, determined in advance, finally became the normal system for renting land. The rise in prices impelled owners to stipulate rents in goods or the cash value of an agreed quantity of grain in the latter half of the eighteenth century.

Moreover, farm rents strongly reflected the agricultural cycle. South-east of Ghent they declined after 1665 with a break in the 1680s, and had fallen by the end of the century by 80 per cent; around Bruges the fall was confined to 30 or 40 per cent. Sometimes land could not be leased at all in times of military occupation. Although grasslands generally did better in this respect than arable land, since dairy products fell less in price than grain, the rent of pasture south of Alkmaar declined by 55 per cent between 1655 and 1715. If in the Austrian Netherlands farm rents recovered shortly after 1713 as peace returned, by the mid-eighteenth century they were still lower than a hundred years before by a third, a half and sometimes more. In Holland they were even lower. They recovered as conditions improved, but less in Holland than in Flanders and Brabant, when quite often lands doubled or even trebled in rented value within a few years. This distinction between the United Provinces and the Austrian Netherlands was apparently caused by a smaller population and the heavier burdens on Dutch agriculture.

Besides general taxes on goods, the peasant was often subjected to taxes on plough horses and horned animals, sometimes to taxes on certain crops, and almost always to a land tax. It was divided among the various parishes and lordships according to frequently outdated registers and this caused innumerable complaints from communities that felt themselves to have been harshly rated. After 1750 the Austrian government made a determined effort to reform these registers. A local one fixed the share of each farm in the same area. In Holland and the other provinces of the Republic, the tax burden certainly fell more heavily than in the Belgian provinces, for a great-power policy was very expensive and the United Provinces had always fought shy of taxing trade too heavily, and so fell back on taxes on property. Even when shorn of a political role, they still had to carry a heavy debt that was a considerable burden, and despite reductions later on, it was only after 1770 that the rise in prices gave real relief.

The polder regions of the United Provinces were also severely affected by the rise of taxes due to the *Wateringues*. The tithe still had to be paid in both Protestant and Catholic parts of the Netherlands, but in the Protestant areas they were paid to the administration, usually the provincial governments, which were the legal successors of the dispossessed religious institutions. Beneficiaries of tithes tried to subject new crops to the same terms as the cereals they had earlier taxed, but this was resented, generally successfully, and particularly in the Austrian Netherlands. Of feudal rights no more survived than anachronisms and some corvées in the Walloon area and the eastern lands of the Republic. After 1775 the government permitted the redemption of all quitrents and services due on the land, but these seem to have been so negligible that the peasants involved hardly responded to the encouragement. Joseph II abolished what remained of serfdom in 1781. The Estates of Overijssel, lords of 168 serf families, allowed them to commute their obligations into rents in 1662, but in 1678 had to diminish considerably the rate at which the obligations were estimated. A supporter of Enlightenment found hardly any support among the peasants when he demanded the abolition of seignorial rights in Hainault around 1768. In 1795 the French government applied the abolition of 'feudalism' and tithes to the Belgian departments. The Batavian Republic, which was proclaimed that same year, also abolished serfdom but retained certain seignorial rights which to some extent have survived, more or less symbolically, and it also permitted the redemption of tithes. They disappeared completely from Dutch law only in 1907.

4 FISHERIES

On the North Sea coast innumerable fishermen beached their small craft every day and peddled their catch around the neighbourhood, or had their family do it. The Zuiderzee fisheries were showing signs of exhaustion. Holland agreed, first with Guelders in 1682 and then with Overijssel in 1698, to forbid the use of very fine nets, but the chief cause of the difficulty of fishing in these waters was an increase in their salinity that made them inhospitable to the usual fauna. By contrast, anchovy and herring fisheries were stimulated – a smaller herring than the one in the North Sea, but still good for salting. Eel was caught near the river mouths and on the lakes, particularly the Frisian ones, and to some extent exported. In 1765 the Austrian government subsidized oyster beds at Ostend.

The great herring fisheries remained based at Enkhuizen and the mouth of the Meuse, where they had moved from Rotterdam and Schiedam, which had become too expensive with the rise of trade and industry, to less urbanized centres such as Vlaardingen and Maassluis. But its golden age was over. Colbert's protection-ism closed the French market after 1664, and the concessions obtained by the Dutch in later treaties did not prevail over cor-ruption at the level of customs officers. After 1750 the Austrian Netherlands, Denmark and Prussia also adopted mercantilist policies. Competition was becoming keener. England, Scotland and Norway now took the opportunities offered them by the great spawning grounds off their coasts, and Sweden benefited from a return of spawning herring to the coasts of Scania. The Austrian government had granted privileges to a fishing company at Nieuport in 1727, though it did succumb eventually to the protectionism of the markets that had been envisaged. The traditional fishing centres in Holland managed to arrange the pro-hibition of casking on trawlers at sea, on the pretext that the herring was inferior. They were in mortal fear of the appearance of an international herring market in Hamburg and got the Estates-General to forbid the Dutch to unload herring there. Finally, to complete the picture, European consumption declined as potato and meat took the place of bread and herring in the diet of the people. Although taxation of marketed herring was abolished in 1750, the number of *buizen* or herring boats in Hol-land fell from 225 in 1756 to 140 in 1761. The grant of subsidies, following the example of Zeeland, after 1775 caused the number to rise to about two hundred, a quarter of them based on Enkhuizen and the rest on the Meuse ports.

Cod fishing off Iceland, which made use of many herring boats outside the spawning season, had at first developed well. Vlaardingen and Maassluis had some fifty trawlers there in 1687 and 143 in 1768. Seventeen were based elsewhere but fell victim to a rapid decline, with increased foreign competition and the closure of foreign outlets. The Nieuport company had also taken up cod fishing, and other enterprises established later at Ostend or Bruges were protected by the Austrian government, which pro-hibited foreign cod in 1785. By 1786 the United Provinces boasted only fifty-eight Icelandic fishermen, and the situation could not be made good even by the grant of subsidies after 1788.

The number of whalers (246 in 1684) grew to a peak of 257 in 1721, though there was great variation in the interval, owing to the fluctuation of yields and the dangers involved: many ships were sunk on icebergs in the Arctic, and this discouraged shipowners in the following season. At times, almost half of the whaling boats were stationed at Zaandam and the nearby villages. Early in the eighteenth century, the rarity of the whale in north-European waters forced the whalers to hunt in the Davis Strait. The number of catches went down from five per whaler between 1665 and 1705 to three and a half in the first half of the eighteenth century. The harpooned whales were also usually smaller than before, an unavoidable consequence of their gradual extinction. The quantities of oil produced reflected this, falling from an annual average of 38,820 barrels in peace-time between 1681 and 1701, to 20,760 between 1705 and 1747. After 1750 whaling also had to face keener competition. England recovered the place it had held two centuries before, while Norway, Russia, Bremen and Hamburg, and even the United States of America, appeared in strength in Arctic waters. The quantity of oil boiled in the United Provinces declined further, to 14,670 barrels per annum between 1749 and 1780, 5,000 from 1780 to 1789, when the Anglo–Dutch war paralyzed the fishing industry, and 3,000 in 1790–9. The annual average number of whalers fell from 165 between 1750 and 1760, to hardly forty-five by the end of the century, despite subsidy after 1777. During the war with England, reality had to be faced. Shipowners were permitted to sell their whalers abroad and their crews were allowed to go with them for the duration of hostilities. Many probably never returned.

The crew of a whaler was on average about forty men, and at its peak the whole fleet thus provided a living for about ten thousand sailors. They were ill-paid, and a great many of them had to be recruited from the German North Sea coast and islands. Despite their low wages, the length of the venture and the size of the ships required large investment. The decline of whaling did not only cause heavy losses for the shipowners; it also had repercussions, like the decline of fisheries overall, for many of the auxiliary and processing industries. It contributed to the general economic decline of the Republic.

3 Industry

I THE FOOD INDUSTRY

A great many workers were needed in the food industries. In each village there would be at least one miller, who would sometimes be paid with a share of the grain he ground (one-sixteenth in the Veluwe in 1805). In the Zaan region the number of mills fell from fifty-three in 1630 to forty-seven in 1731 and forty-one in 1795, perhaps because of the gradual substitution of potatoes for bread. In 1811 there were 7 bakers per thousand inhabitants in the towns of Holland; in those of the Veluwe, 6. In the villages, the figures were respectively 5.4 and 3, and in Overijssel in 1795, 2.3. Most peasants baked their own bread but others, and even town-dwellers, provided their bakers with grain. Moreover, peasants still came to sell their bread at the weekly market in the neighbouring town. The authorities supervised the weight and quality of this basic food. The villages of the Zaan, Wormer and Jisp, had specialized in the making of ship's biscuit, and seventy-five bakeries were involved in the trade in 1648. Later the industry moved to Amsterdam and nearby villages in the province of Utrecht where taxes were not so heavy.

The towns and the highly frequented routes had an extra-ordinary number of taverns. Brussels seems to have had one for every twenty houses in the eighteenth century, Malines 3.6 per thousand inhabitants in 1724, as did North Holland in 1811; Overijssel had 3 per thousand in 1795, the Veluwe 8 in 1749 and the Bois-le-Duc region 19 – perhaps the backwardness of the area invited alcoholism. In Louvain 339 litres of beer were drunk in

1775, and 271 in 1785; in Namur, which was a garrison town, twelve litres of spirits per head per annum were consumed. The great breweries of Holland's ports, which sometimes had their own malt beer factory, delivered these supplies to the ships. In 1660 they were able to prevent a reduction of excise taxes on wine which might have led ultimately to a reduction in the consumption of beer. The syndicate, which survived until the end of the eighteenth century, also opposed the importing of yeast or its manufacture by distilleries.

In the Austrian Netherlands Louvain was becoming the chief centre of Belgian brewing after the mid-eighteenth century, as it has remained since. The modest growth of output in the previous two centuries accelerated, quadrupling between 1750 and 1785 when 234,000 hectolitres, or 80 per cent of the output, were sold outside Louvain. Not far from there the village of Hoegaarden, an enclave of Liège in Brabant with some two or three thousand inhabitants, marketed beer illicitly in Austrian territory, practically tax-free. In 1727 it had 110 brewers, and 155 after 1750, mostly peasants. If each village had at least one small brewery, often attached to an inn, in the towns the large enterprises dominated. In Louvain in 1723 only two of forty-nine breweries produced more than 3,000 hectolitres per annum, 11 per cent of the beer made, but in 1795 the figure was twenty-eight out of forty, and they produced 91 per cent of output. Beer was being challenged by other beverages, however: coffee, tea, chocolate and especially spirits. The decline in the number of brewers in the Veluwe from at least sixty-eight in 1749 to twenty-three at most in 1807 must have been partly caused by this.

Dutch distilling probably owed its existence to French mercantilism. The United Provinces had prohibited the import of French brandy in 1671 as a reprisal. Consumption shifted to grain spirits. Schiedam, one of the few towns in Holland to experience any real increase in population in the eighteenth century, became a centre of the industry because of the lower wages and transport facilities available at the nearby port of Rotterdam. It had thirty-four distilleries by 1700, 121 in 1730 and 122 of the two hundred in Holland in 1771. Its gin was known all over the world, and was exported in great quantity. The armies of the Dutch Republic spread the taste for it when they fought in the southern provinces during the wars with Louis XIV. The low price of grain there persuaded the government to abandon its opposition to distilling in 1705. Today's province of East Flanders had 181 distilleries and Brabant two hundred by 1795. Many peasants boiled the must in their farms using rudimentary techniques less expensive than in Holland. The draff that was left after distilling could be used to feed more and fatter animals. Rural distilling, therefore, was favourably regarded by agronomists and the government also profited from the excise taxes they levied on it. This was why provinces and towns established distilleries, and the Austrian government itself had a factory at Warneton on the Lys, at the French frontier, so as to profit by smuggling – which amounted to 2,500 hectolitres in 1782.

Although distilling was among the rare industries in the Republic to develop, mercantilism affected its imports of raw sugar from the French and English West Indies. The number of refineries in Amsterdam fell from sixty in 1661 to about twenty by 1700, but rose again to ninety (out of a total of 145 throughout the country), because of the development of plantations in Java, Surinam and the Dutch West Indies. The small refineries in these places marketed their output in the colonies themselves; those in the Republic could profit, despite competition from Hamburg, from rising consumption in Germany, as well as from the favourable excise concessions that they were given in the Austrian Netherlands by the Treaty of Utrecht, to the detriment of the sugar industry in Antwerp. Maria Theresa repudiated these obligations in 1749 and supported the new refineries in Brussels and Ghent. General protectionism in Europe precipitated a crisis in the Dutch industry which could only be solved by protectionism, subsidies, for instance, for imports of raw sugar between 1776 and 1781 and in 1786–7. They managed to keep at least the Rhineland market.

Salt refining did not have any smoother a path. In 1659 France had subjected raw salt to the famous export tax of fifty *sous* per register-ton, which hit foreign shipping, although in fact the tax was reduced by half three years later. Portuguese salt went mainly to England after the Methuen Treaty of 1703. The Baltic countries, the main outlets for Holland's and Zeeland's salt refining, took more and more from elsewhere, although the Dutch fleet was still used for transport. In 1699 the fleet even managed to have a limit set on the subsidies demanded by the salt refiners from the

Estates-General. The refiners finally kept only the home market after the opening of the new salt-mines in Alsace and Lorraine, and the establishment of refineries in the Austrian Netherlands (seventy-four by 1764) ended their commercial predominance in their own hinterland.

Dutch oil refining did better, especially in the Zaan. The industry used forty-five windmills there by 1630, and there were 140 in the eighteenth century. By 1800 annual output was between 12,000 and 18,000 barrels of oil, 60 per cent of Holland's output, and they also produced between 20,000 and 28,000 tonnes of oil-cake. Oil was one of the few industries not to develop much in the Austrian Netherlands, either for reasons of quality or because the price was too high. In Flanders and Zeeland rape was pressed, and there were complaints against the export of the native produce.

2   TEXTILES

After its peak around 1665 Leyden declined spectacularly. England was very successfully producing cheap cloth made of native wool and after 1650 Leyden, unable to compete, developed her own cloth, woven from Spanish wool, trusting in the incontestable superiority of its technique. However, economic conditions did not favour expensive items, especially when Colbert's France and other countries blocked exports. As foreign outlets were closing down, the cloth had to be sold on the home market, and there was a return to cheaper goods. Their share in the total output, 17 per cent around 1700, rose to 85 per cent in 1795; but in the interim the amount of cloth produced fell considerably, from 85,000 pieces in 1703 to 72,000 in 1725, 54,000 in 1750, 41,000 in 1775 and 29,000 in 1795.

This fall naturally damaged the industries that were related to cloth. The fifteen windmills of the Zaan that had assisted fulling in 1700 declined by two-thirds by 1768; in that year, Amsterdam had only fifteen dye-works, and at Leyden itself only five of the twenty-nine dye-works that had existed early in the century still functioned in 1790. Foreign, especially English, custom had gone. Elsewhere the wool industry was also undergoing a profound crisis. The town of Haarlem sold off its fulling mill and cloth hall in 1721. Ypres's efforts to revive its cloth trade by hiring Dutch artisans failed. In Bruges the drapers begged the magistrates in 1698 to force the town's ecclesiastics to wear clothing of local manufacture. Bruges say weaving did somewhat recover when it adopted processes developed by Liège and Aachen, and rose again to a peak of 6,660 pieces in 1740, but then fell into depression. The luxury cloths produced by Ghent and Bruges in the seventeenth century were damaged in the eighteenth by embargoes and foreign competition.

Despite relatively casual organization, all of these industries suffered from excessively high costs. Owners therefore tried to lower wages as far as they could. The wages of Leyden weavers, who were well-paid, declined between 1650 and 1700 from seven to four or four and a half florins per week. A large reserve army of unemployed, kept at starvation level, maintained wages at their low level. The workers became rebellious and were vigorously repressed by the authorities. After a weavers' strike in 1701 four ringleaders were hanged and six others were flogged at Leyden. In times of crisis only rural industry managed to profit. In 1741 wages at Tilburg were only half, and at Verviers only one-third, of wages in Leyden. Moreover, northern Brabant now became entirely independent of the employers in Holland; Tilburg therefore stood ready to assume Leyden's heritage in the nineteenth century, as capital of the Dutch wool industry.

The victory of Verviers over Leyden was also complete. The Austrian government taxed imports and transport of cloth from Verviers, which was in Liège territory, very heavily to support its own subjects in nearby Limburg, but the Verviers manufacturers smuggled on a large scale and eluded such measures by opening branches of their firms in Austrian territory. They won a great advantage when Liège abolished her duty on Spanish wools in 1754. The Brussels government, anxious to extend the traffic of Ostend, taxed wool arriving by other routes, and this increased costs at Eupen and other centres in Limburg which had hitherto, like Verviers, received their wool from Amsterdam via the Meuse.

Verviers' industry was subject to a process of concentration promoted by large investment that prefigured the Industrial Revolution. Except for spinning, which was always carried out by the abundant labour supply that became available in the economy of the nearby pastoral villages, all its work was done at Verviers itself, including dyeing, which before 1765 had gone to Leyden, Antwerp and sometimes Eupen. Concentration affected particularly the structure of the enterprises. Independent artisans gradually disappeared, and workers were grouped in the owners' shops. As far as weaving, still largely a domestic industry, was concerned this type of organization had not made much impression, but it was common among fullers and dyers, and became the rule for washing, shearing and carding. Many artisans became mere sub-contractors and even wage earners. Of the 204 drapers known in 1744-5, 174 produced less than ten pieces per annum, but between 1780 and 1789 six workshops produced from 30 to 76 per cent of the annual average of 72,350 cloths subject to tax (as against 19,000 forty years before), and the largest one alone produced almost one-third in 1782. By 1806 there were only 106 factories.

The cloth trade of Verviers owed its growth partly to the arrival of Dutch entrepreneurs and workers who had abandoned their declining country. Three hundred of these workers were recruited in 1718 to set up the royal works at Guadalajara in Spain, much to the disquiet of the Estates-General, who feared for their Iberian markets. In 1751 they forbade emigration by artisans. For a century Dutch artisans had been invited everywhere to found or develop industries, but now British mechanics, heralds of the Industrial Revolution, took their places. By 1777 two of them, the Thompsons, set up a spinning factory for wool and cotton in one of the suburbs of Rotterdam, on behalf of a local merchant. It closed after two years, probably for lack of capital. William Cockerill was hired by an industrialist from Verviers in 1799, and this marked the beginning of mechanization in the Belgian departments of Revolutionary France, confirming the lead of Verviers.

The United Provinces, a country of sailors, eagerly bought knitted woollen goods, which were also exported. But the decay of the fisheries and foreign prohibitions caused depression in the eighteenth century, both at Leyden and in the province of Groningen, where the labour force the industry employed fell from eight thousand in 1765 to two thousand around 1800.

The linen industry reached its height around 1650. At Haarlem, the bleaching and twisting of thread, which was imported from Flanders, England, Ireland and even Silesia, gained a European reputation. By contrast, weaving was already suffering from competition in the countryside of Brabant and, as the economic crisis began, the finishing in Haarlem of linens from Helmond and Eindhoven made them too expensive. Half of the four hundred looms weaving white linen at Helmond disappeared in the 1650s. Even the extension, in 1692, of free-entry rights to unbleached linen to Holland, which half-finished woollens had enjoyed since the middle of the century, was not enough to revive the trade, and by 1800 it had practically disappeared. The production of blue and white check linen to which artisans had turned, and which employed up to seven hundred looms at Helmond in 1758, had also been ruined forty years later.

Despite the obstacle of French and English protectionism and the competition of these countries on the Spanish market, linen industries of the Belgian provinces kept their lead over the Dutch. The Spanish Bourbons' mercantilism could not meet the needs of their land. In France an efficient smuggling operation, encouraged in the eighteenth century by the Austrian government itself, brought in a great deal of linen. It was said to account for 100,000 pieces in 1780, or twice the official imports. Since the mid-seventeenth century there had been attempts to make Flemish linen independent of Dutch bleaching. The increase of tariffs on unbleached foreign linen, decreed by the Dutch in 1693 as a counterpart to the franchise extended to such linen from northern Brabant, promoted this tendency. A large bleaching works was opened in 1700 at Borgerhout near Antwerp, and others followed under the Austrians. They also treated linen from French Flanders and Hainault, although the French prohibited bleaching abroad. As English linen was now bleached in Ireland, and Westphalian linen at Bielefeld, the Haarlem works increasingly lost their clients, and only eight such works remained by 1789.

It was discovered around 1700 in the Lille area that running water was more suited to the retting of flax than stagnant water, and the Flemish linen industry began to make use of this discovery. However, protests of fishermen at the pollution of the Lys forced the artisans to carry on the retting in ditches fed by the river but cut off from it. Spinning and weaving spread in the countryside, especially around the lower Dendre, where new markets were opened at Alost and Grammont. In the latter town sales rose from 9,800 pieces in 1651 to 59,800 in 1700; and in 1689 sales in Ghent were estimated at 100,000.

The Westphalian linen which passed through on its way to be

dyed in Holland had encouraged the poverty-stricken Twente population in the seventeenth century to work linen commercially. In 1700 Almelo had about twenty linen merchants buying the villagers' produce or putting out the work to other villagers. The linen was bleached, less thoroughly than in Haarlem, in the local meadows. Because of their low prices – which were a consequence of starvation-wages – they sold well until 1725 when the general economic crisis coincided with a shift of the labour force. In the seventeenth century, four hundred looms in Amersfoort annually produced some 49,000 pieces of fustian and bombazine from Westphalian or Overijssel linens mixed with cotton imported through Amsterdam. In 1728 the linen merchants of Enschede, discontented with measures taken by Amersfoort, obtained from the province of Overijssel a decree favouring the manufacture of bombazine, which henceforth gave the linen weavers of the Twente a new livelihood. Enschede took the place of Almelo as industrial capital of the area, particularly once its cotton goods became fashionable as the growing India trade popularized calico in Europe.

Calico was soon imported undyed and was finished in Europe, sometimes in printing workshops that had been converted for the purpose. Calico printing works were opened in Amsterdam after 1678 and became a speciality there, since, contrary to the experience of France and England, the wool and linen industries did not manage to stop them from growing. They rose to a peak of eighty in number before high production costs and the gradual closing of markets ended their prosperity. There were only eight left by 1800. The fustian industry also existed in Ghent and Bruges, where around 1727 it produced 22,000 pieces annually. The fate of a calico printing works founded in Brussels in 1675 is unknown. Others appeared in the eighteenth century – in 1753, the Beerenbroek company, which was given a monopoly for twenty-five years, established itself at the gates of Antwerp. It employed 576 workers, and produced up to 74,000 pieces annually, thanks to the very advanced methods of labour division. When the monopoly ran out many other printing works were also set up, but most of them succumbed after the annexation by France, which had a superior industry.

The cotton industry experienced the first effects of the Industrial Revolution. In 1776 a machine to finish linen and cotton was smuggled into Ghent from England. The mechanical spinning works at Rotterdam had worked more cotton than wool, and after it had closed down the Thompson brothers went to the assistance of a manufacturer in Utrecht who at once installed waterframes, hardly ten years after Arkwright's discovery of them. In 1799 the factory succumbed to the difficulties of the times, and probably also to excessive wage costs, the common disadvantage of Dutch industry. However, the war did not prevent Liévin Bauwens from setting up in 1798 the first mechanical cotton spinning factory of the Belgian departments in his native Ghent, the future Belgian Manchester. The Dutch cotton industry was to be mechanized only after the Belgian Revolution of 1830.

Many women were still employed in the Belgian provinces in domestic lace making. In 1764 between 10,000 and 12,000 women were said to be engaged in this craft in Antwerp (where it was described in 1738 as the 'chief trade' of the town), compared with between 9,000 and 10,000 in Brussels, and 4,500 at Malines. The merchants passed on orders to small entrepreneurs who employed women at such low wages that they were often in debt for money or food. The fine, light quality of the lace made extensive smuggling possible, and it defeated English and French efforts at protection.

The production of velvet and silk flourished late in the seventeenth century in Amsterdam, Haarlem, Utrecht and Antwerp, because fashion dictated the use of these fabrics rather than cloth, and this helped to attract Huguenot immigrants to the United Provinces. Amsterdam took the raw silk from Italy or, through the India Company, from Bengal or the Far East. Silk of the finest quality came from Persia, either through the Levant or via Russia, which permitted the transit of goods in 1675 while the war with France was making Mediterranean shipping difficult. This route remained open until 1734. The cocoons were emptied by cheap labour – young girls of pauper families in Amsterdam in 1682, orphans in Antwerp, old people, unemployed soldiers in peacetime, and rustics. In 1682 an Amsterdam merchant invented a twining machine driven by a water-mill on his country estate near Utrecht. By 1700 others with up to 150 spindles, and worked by horse-mills, were in use. Mechanization concentrated this process in workshops, but weaving was still domestic. Often the workers did not own their tools: in Antwerp, where there were

330 looms in 1689, 290 belonged to twenty of the two hundred masters in the guild. The dyeing of silk was usually done by artisans who dyed other textiles as well.

In the eighteenth century the contraction of the Republic's trade also affected the silk industry, and the closer relations of England and France with the countries that produced raw silk caused imports to dwindle. Although the Austrian Netherlands tried to limit the disadvantages that Antwerp faced because of its dependence on the silk market in Amsterdam by forging direct links with the East, their silk goods suffered also from the closure of export markets. In 1738 the silk industry in Antwerp, which was among the town's main industries, employed 750 twisters, 1,700 weavers and 290 makers of ribbon and borders. By 1778 a muslin factory recently established at Ghent had some fifty looms working.

The velvet factories of Utrecht and Naarden kept up quite well and exported to places as far away as India, but their output was now less fashionable than silk for furnishings. Moreover, the use of wallpaper limited that of tapestry, especially as the French workshops were now producing papers of the highest quality. Carpets became fashionable, however. The rich imported them from the East, but after 1752 they were manufactured out of cow hair for less wealthy households, especially at Hilversum, where the number of such workshops rose from forty-two in 1772 to seventy-six in 1796.

3   METAL AND COAL

Attempts to reduce costs stimulated the upper Belgian iron foundries, even though by modern standards they were still modest. In 1764 the largest of them had only forty-four workmen, and most had only seven or eight, but the small owners, unable to invest enough, had increasingly to give way to nobles or wealthy commoners for whom the title of forge master was often a springboard into the aristocracy. The growing use of iron persuaded them to build more powerful blast-furnaces, and in many cases to pursue economic integration: they would either rent or buy a mine, woods and a forge to work the cast iron. There were some illustrious instances – the dukes of Arenberg themselves exploited the lead mines at Vedrin near Namur.

The nail-making industry, still the chief rural industry in

Wallonia, remained the chief market for cast iron. In 1740 the number of nail makers was estimated at 15,000 around Liège, where large nails were produced for the Dutch shipyards, and as many on the Sambre between Charleroi and Namur. Like the mercantilists of neighbouring countries, who opposed the import of foreign nails, the Brussels government supported its nail industry against Liège's competition. Several times customs wars cut off the nail makers from their suppliers of cast iron or coal; Liégeois nail makers were driven to emigrate to England and Spain, especially to the duchy of Nassau, where they restored the nail industry that had been ruined by the Thirty Years War. To prevent their artisans from leaving for Austrian Namur or Luxembourg the Estates of Liège set up a Company of Nail Makers in 1743 which, in exchange for a monopoly of manufacture and for rebates on export excise, guaranteed a living wage to its workers. It soon collapsed in internal dissension, but a similar company, set up in 1770, functioned until the French conquest. The arms industry of Liège, especially the light firearms industry, took advantage of the wars of Louis XIV. During the Wars of the Spanish Succession the United Provinces ordered 15,000 muskets there, and Prussia 18,000 in 1713, as well as 16,000 pistols. Annual production was reckoned in 1730 at 240,000 firearms. These orders were placed with the arms manufacturers and paid for per piece by export merchants who supplied the raw materials. As only the smallest amounts of iron ore were used, Guelderlanders attempted to make arms and kitchen utensils in 1689 and again in 1754, but without much success. The Estates of Holland opened a gun foundry at The Hague in 1779, and St Hubert's Abbey also opened one, too, in the hope of profiting from the American War of Independence. It managed only to ruin the community.

In the eighteenth century a blast-furnace needed 140 hectares of forest to fuel it in one year. The principality of Liège alone had thirty such furnaces. For this reason after about 1770 many efforts were made to use coal to cast the ore rather than the now very expensive charcoal. Baron d'Huart in Luxembourg, and J. P. de Limbourg, a doctor, at Theux-lez-Spa, produced coke using Abraham Darby's invention, but it was not of good quality, and it was only after 1830 that coke foundries spread in Belgium. Iron working did, however, stimulate coal mining: new mines became very common, and the old ones were deepened, in the Liège basin, to an average of 220 metres and sometimes even 320. In the Mons basin the figure was seventy metres, but costs remained high as the number of shafts had to be increased in order to solve the ventilation problem.

The men of Liège were famous as experts in pumping and Louis XIV even engaged one of them to construct a hydraulic machine at Marly and another for the conduits and fountains of Versailles. But some mines needed more sophisticated techniques of drainage than human strength or horse-power could support. A mine in Liège was the first to lay in a 'fire pump' in 1720, barely fifteen years after Newcomen had invented the machine, and others were employed in the Charleroi coal basin around 1725 and at Mons in 1734. By 1767, however, there were still only about ten of them because mechanization demanded high investment and markets were contracting, especially that for coal from Hainault when the French market was closed. This closure and the technical problems helped to ruin several mines, the number of which fell at Quaregnon-lez-Mons from forty-two in 1630 to twenty by 1710 and eight in 1742. The same factors caused a shift towards wealthy shareholders. Of the eleven partners in a mining company set up at Houdeng in Hainault in 1685, eight belonged to the nobility or the wealthy bourgeoisie and the three others would today be described as engineers rather than miners.

4   OTHER INDUSTRIES

Coal from Liège increasingly took the place of wood or, in the towns of Holland, peat which was becoming rare and expensive: the local peat-fields were exhausted and were now no more than the extended lakes so characteristic of the modern countryside. By contrast, peat extraction did go on in the eastern provinces except in Groningen, where there was not enough left. Overijssel produced between 124,000,000 and 173,000,000 turves annually in the eighteenth century. The brick works used a great deal. The use of bricks and tile instead of wattle and thatch for walls and roofs now occurred in the countryside as well. The different provinces of the Republic used fiscal devices to protect their own brick manufacture. In 1728 Holland gave tax privileges to the brick works recently established along the Waal and the IJssel, and these gradually won the lead over the Dutch market they have kept ever since. In the Belgian provinces only those of the Rupel reached beyond their local market, even though the coal they used cost too much because of transport problems and taxes.

In Gouda eighty pipe makers had set up a syndicate in 1660 to secure good prices. After 1686, since they objected to the taxes they had to pay in Amsterdam, they organized weekly sales at Gouda itself. Their clay pipes were known throughout the world and enjoyed a golden age until the mid-eighteenth century. In 1740 Gouda itself contained 374 manufacturers, most of them small masters subcontracting for the twenty-nine large ones who alone had the ovens. Most of the active population – some four thousand men and three thousand women – were employed in this trade. After about 1750 it suffered from the competition of manufacturers closer to the kaolin deposits: by 1789 there were only seventeen factories left at Gouda, and in 1806 only eleven.

Delft pottery began to decline in 1720, and accounted for only ten workshops by the end of the eighteenth century. It fell victim to European competition in porcelain. Although some fine crockery was wrongly described as porcelain, Europe really only imported it from China and Japan until about 1710 when the Far Eastern secret was made known in Saxony, and porcelain spread from there. Factories were opened in Tournai in 1752 and in Weesp, near Amsterdam in 1757. Others were established later elsewhere, and they hired artisans who had worked at Meissen, Sèvres, Chelsea, etc. According to a custom widespread elsewhere, the governor-general, Charles of Lorraine, and many members of the great nobility in the Austrian Netherlands founded private porcelain works, which proved ephemeral because their goods could not match the quality of the great foreign workshops. Only the Tournai works, with over four hundred craftsmen in 1781, enjoyed real prosperity.

Fine glass making in the Low Countries lost its lead around 1675 to England, where a clearer glass was obtained by mixing lead and sand. Around 1700 Bohemia and Germany invented engraving by wheel rather than by diamond, and although the Netherlands glass industry soon adopted the technique, Bohemian and German goods remained cheaper. Common glass kept its market better. A bottle factory established with government support at Ghlin-lez-Mons produced 150,000 bottles in 1763. Window glass, which was now clearer because of high-temperature coal furnaces, gained in popularity, especially after the introduction of cylinder blowing, which probably came from Swabia to Charleroi about 1727. It made possible the production of cheaper and larger panes.

The Antwerp diamond cutters recovered somewhat after the mid-seventeenth century, but in 1738 the 180 masters of the guild were complaining about the competition they faced from non-affiliated suburban artisans. The Amsterdam diamond cutters, many of them Jews, worked in complete freedom and were famous throughout Europe for the perfection of their skills. In 1764 the Estates-General, fearing it might harm the market, rejected the Sultan of Turkey's request for an expert diamond cutter. Around 1750 some six hundred families lived from diamond cutting in Amsterdam, and the trade was also practised in Rotterdam.

Antwerp and Amsterdam also remained famous for their printing. Antwerp retained its speciality, religious literature, and the United Provinces, where there was considerable intellectual liberty, printed Pierre Bayle's *Nouvelles de la République des Lettres* (1684–7) and *Dictionnaire* (1697) and the Huguenots' *Gazette de Hollande*, which was smuggled into France. Books were also smuggled into France from the Austrian Netherlands, the principality of Liège and the duchy of Bouillon (which had become a miniscule independent state in 1678), with the tacit support of the authorities who had been won over to the Enlightenment. Editions of Voltaire, Rousseau and the *Encyclopédie* were printed.

The paper industry profited from the Netherlands publishing industry, especially after a high tax was imposed on French paper in reprisal for Colbert's tariffs. By 1650 some forty small works, each with five or six workers, had been set up in the Veluwe along the small tributaries of the Rhine or the IJssel which supplied water-power. There were 170 of them by 1700, and 130 still in 1750. In some villages they employed up to 20 per cent of the working population. Another centre developed in the Zaan, where larger works employing forty or fifty workers used windmills: the number of 'paper mills' rose from five in 1650 to about forty after 1730. As the stagnant water was not suitable for production of fine pulps, they at first produced wrapping paper, particularly for the sugar refineries of Amsterdam and the linen workshops of Haarlem. After 1670 pure water was drawn from deep wells and the Zaan's output included writing and printing paper. It rose from 20,000 reams per annum around 1650 to 160,000 around 1780. The supply of rags, 90 per cent imported ones, caused some concern because of the mercantilism of other countries. The Austrian Netherlands, for instance, attempted to develop their own paper industry. But the higher quality of Dutch paper preserved a large market for it, if need be through smuggling. The quality was partly a consequence of the invention of the 'Hollander' which tore up the rags in running water with knives mounted on rollers.

The Veluwe processed locally-grown tobacco, but in the sea ports the finer varieties imported from America were processed – especially in Rotterdam which was well placed both for English supplies and for the Rhenish market. Over fifty shops employed some three thousand workers in this industry by 1750. However, Amsterdam had by then only ten manufacturers of rolled tobacco as against thirty around 1720. Many of the manufacturers had left the town because of the excessive wages and had gone to the Zaan in particular, where they could use windmills. The authorities were concerned at the competition of Bremen and Hamburg and at attempts by the Austrian Netherlands to reduce their dependence on the north for this commodity.

In the Zaan, the industrial quarter of Amsterdam until the Industrial Revolution, the number of windmills grew from 128 in 1630 to 584 in 1731. In 1795 482 remained and were used for milling and oil extraction, the manufacture of snuff (which occupied twenty-five windmills in 1731 and thirty-two in 1795) and paper. In 1630 only one had been used to grind logwood or brazil-wood for dyeing, but there were about twenty in 1731 and 1795. Most were used for sawing wood: fifty-three in 1630, 256 in 1731, 144 in 1795. The trunks, beams and planks imported from the Baltic, Norway or the Black Forest were used in the building industry or by Amsterdam joiners, whose products, like Antwerp's, were exported throughout Europe. The Zaan's shipyards were still more famous. Whereas after 1650 England and France developed their own, Spain and the Scandinavian countries remained loyal clients of Holland. In 1708, 306 merchant and war-ships were being constructed simultaneously on the Zaan. It is well known that Peter the Great, wishing to study ship building, chose Zaandam as his first stop on his western journey in 1697: it is less well known that he was disappointed at its pedestrian ways. The lead in this field was in fact gradually passing to England and France, which applied the advances made in navigational science in their shipyards. The decline of fisheries and Dutch trade, together with the more peaceful course of European affairs which limited the losses caused by war, all cut the orders received by Dutch shipyards. Those of the Zaan were also affected by the silting up of the river, which hindered the construction of large ships at a time when tonnage was still rising. Such ships gradually disappeared after 1750. By 1790 not even five ships were launched annually, and by 1804 none at all.

To serve the sail making industry, which was complementary to shipbuilding, four windmills treated hemp for canvas in the Zaan in 1630, thirteen in 1731 and twelve in 1795. In some villages more than a third of the population was employed in this trade, which shared the fate of the shipyards as it had to face competition from cheaper Russian sailcloth. Dutch production is thought to have fallen from 60,000 pieces around 1730 to 28,000 around 1770. Rope manufacture was equally hard-hit. Everywhere economic nationalism prompted foreign markets to free themselves from Dutch industrial predominance.

4 Trade

Certain data provide figures for the volume of the Republic's foreign trade in this period, although great caution is needed. Contemporaries reckoned that the return of 'convoy taxes' reflected only a quarter of the real commercial traffic. Indeed, the five Admiralties of the Republic which levied the customs connived in varying degrees at smuggling, on the instruction of their provincial authorities which wanted to attract as much trade as possible. In the Admiralty of Zeeland smuggling may even have reached the figure of 80 per cent. It has been estimated at 40 per cent for Amsterdam and 30 per cent for Rotterdam. The same reservations can be applied to accounts of the movement of trade at Amsterdam and Rotterdam which have survived for certain years. We know after 1784 what the tax return was on goods sold by weight in Holland, which covered almost all foreign and internal trade, and we also know the volume of trade through the port of Amsterdam after 1643 and through Rotterdam and other places at the mouth of the Meuse after 1716. The uncertainties of these sources are compounded by others. A portion of Dutch trade normally went directly from one foreign port to another, even, in wartime, under foreign flags, without figuring in the statistics mentioned above. Ostend, especially, provided an alibi for part of the Dutch merchant marine during the Republic's intervention in the American War of Independence of 1780–4. Finally although convoy dues were fixed, fluctuation in prices could invalidate comparisons over time.

With all these qualifications, and with prices based on those of 1790, Dutch trade, excluding that of colonial companies, has been estimated to have been between 300,000,000 and 400,000,000 florins per annum at its peak around 1650. By 1675 a serious crisis brought it down to between 125,000,000 and 175,000,000, after which it recovered to between 275,000,000 and 300,000,000, by 1700. It fell again until 1720, then rose with some hesitation to between 250,000,000 and 270,000,000 by 1750, stagnating there until about 1790 except for the paralysis of wartime in the years 1780–4. The entry of the Batavian Republic into the French orbit in 1795 caused a new collapse. It finally destroyed the structures that in former times had influenced the rise of Dutch trade.

If these indications are accurate, the eighteenth century must have been a period of absolute decline. This chapter will trace the gradual erosion of the United Provinces' commercial hegemony and their loss of their role as intermediary, which increasingly passed to the English. Even the Austrian Netherlands, formerly an important hinterland for Dutch commerce, gradually liberated themselves from Dutch dominance.

2 THE BALTIC, RUSSIA AND SCANDINAVIA

The Baltic's links with Europe greatly increased, yet the Dutch share seriously declined. The annual average of passages through the Sound rose from 2,160 in the 1660s to 8,015 in the 1770s, the last decade for which the tolls were published, but the Dutch share, rising from 1,353 to 2,216, declined in proportion by almost half, from 52.9 to 27.7 per cent. Moreover, increasing amounts of Dutch shipping arrived in the Baltic under ballast – up to seventy per cent in the 1770s. From about 1725 a growing proportion of shipowners preferred to station their ships elsewhere than in Holland where life was too expensive, and which sometimes accounted for barely one-third of the Dutch passages through the Sound, the others coming mainly from Friesland and Groningen.

The volume of cereals, the cargo of half of the Dutch ships that passed through the Sound, declined from 111,000 tonnes per annum on average between 1651 and 1700 to 63,600 between 1701 and 1750. Europe's population and consumption had declined, whereas grain production had risen in many areas, and potatoes and American rice entered the market. Dutch imports did rise to 113,900 tonnes per annum between 1757 and 1780, probably because of the increase in the population. Rye accounted for only 70 per cent in the years 1661–80 as against 86.5 per cent hitherto, and if 83 per cent of this cereal had left the Baltic in Dutch ships between 1660 and 1720, the figure after 1760 was only 55 per cent. Wheat was gaining as a European bread grain, but it may be that the United Provinces lagged behind the improvement of living-standards in Europe, for only 55 per cent of the Baltic wheat left in Dutch ships in 1780 as against 95 per cent in 1660; and besides, voyages straight to southern Europe, which had been exceptional before 1740, were now more frequent, to the detriment of the Amsterdam grain market.

As for timber exports, Finland, which had hardly been used before 1700, had overtaken Sweden, Livonia and Courland by 1730. Her exports rose from just below 1,500,000 logs in the 1660s to 37,000,000 in the 1770s, but the share of Dutch shipping in its transport – two thirds until 1750 – fell thereafter by half. Holland, the main market (77 per cent in the 1680s) lost the position to England after 1770. Yearly exports of iron from the Baltic amounted to 42,665 tonnes in the 1660s and 541,750 in the 1770s, almost entirely from Sweden until about 1720, but later from Russia too, which gradually took the lead. Of that 56 per cent was shipped by the Dutch in the 1660s, but England had cornered the shipping by the 1670s, while the rise of the Swedish fleet reduced the Dutch share to 3.4 per cent in the 1770s. The Republic had imported between a quarter and a third of Baltic iron between 1671 and 1730, but took only 7 per cent in the 1770s. England, where shipbuilding had been vastly encouraged by the Naviga-tion Acts, took the lead from the Dutch here as well, as she did with imports of sail canvas, produced cheaply in Russia and Prussia.

Trade in other fields illustrated the decline of the Dutch Republic. Because of its economic recovery, salt consumption in the Baltic rose from 40,000 tonnes per annum in the 1660s to 70,000 in the 1770s, but Dutch skippers did not even carry 40 per cent of it after 1750 as against the 74 per cent of the 1660s, and the Republic's refineries, to which those of the producing countries were now preferred, accounted for only 2 per cent in the 1770s as against 19 per cent in the 1660s. The shipping and trading of herring had almost been a Dutch monopoly in the Baltic (with 90 per cent of transport and 81.4 per cent of trade respectively of the

5,800 tonnes that was carried through the Sound annually in the 1660s, but now the Dutch accounted only for 20 per cent of its transportation and 17.5 of the trade.

The United Provinces were the natural outlet to the sea for Rhine wines. In the 1660s the Baltic countries took 32,000 hectolitres per annum, 95 per cent of which was imported on Dutch ships and 90 per cent by Dutch merchants. By the 1770s consumption had dropped to 13,000 hectolitres. The Dutch share in transport fell to 44 per cent, because of Swedish, Danish and German competition, and in trade to 66 per cent as German merchants of the North Sea ports entered into competition. In the meantime demand for wine favoured the French and southern growths. In the seventeenth century they had reached northern Europe via the Dutch staple, but a century later the Dutch share in such trade was quite insignificant.

Imports of cloth to the Baltic were double the figures for the 1660s by the 1770s – 71,200 pieces per annum. The Dutch share reached its peak in the 1680s with 42,400 pieces, two-thirds of the total, and was still over half with 25,300 until the 1730s when the lead went to England. The Dutch share was only a quarter by the 1770s – 17,400. Dutch ships carrying the cloth accounted for about half until the 1730s, and then the English again took over, so that by the 1770s the Dutch share was below one-fifth. In the 1660s Amsterdam had supplied Baltic customers with almost half of the silk and cotton they needed, but after the 1730s they bought it directly from the Mediterranean. 1,500,000 of the 1,800,000 pounds of colonial goods entering the Baltic had some from Holland during the 1660s, and under the Dutch flag, and yet, though there was spectacular growth in such consumption, Dutch commerce and shipping enjoyed only a modest profit from it, since the 5,000,000 pounds sent from the United Provinces and the 7,400,000 carried on Dutch ships made up only 15.5 per cent and 23 per cent respectively of the total, 324,000,000, that passed through the Sound in the 1770s. By the 1670s England and France, now reaping the fruits of their colonial endeavours, increased their trade and Hamburg also rapidly extended its market.

Apart from cod and timber, Norway exported copper at the end of the eighteenth century, but could not afford to import much. The Danish company which monopolized Iceland's economy lacked ships and frequently used Dutch ones in the seventeenth

century, which facilitated smuggling. The growth of the Danish
fleet and English competition put a stop to this in the eighteenth
century. Despite the rapid rise of St Petersburg, founded in 1703,
with a brilliant court that provided Dutch exports with an eager
market, commerce with Russia still went on through the White
Sea. The Anglo-Russian treaty of 1734 and the enormous development in trade and shipping in the Russian Empire ended the
Dutch economic preponderance there.

3   CENTRAL AND WESTERN EUROPE AND THE
    MEDITERRANEAN

In the seventeenth century the Dutch had also dominated commercial relations with Bremen and Hamburg, the gateways to a
hinterland that was recovering from the devastation of the Thirty
Years War. More than half of the merchants of Hamburg in 1665
were agents or associates of Dutch firms. However, in the
eighteenth century they developed a market of their own for
herring, whale oil, tobacco, colonial goods and the Hungarian
copper which could not be sent to Amsterdam during the War of
the Austrian Succession of 1740-8. The reduction of tariffs
furthered this growth, and caused much concern in Amsterdam.
The United Provinces imported 3,400,000 florins' worth of goods
from Bremen and Hamburg in 1753 and 5,300,000 in 1790, and
exported 5,100,000 and 7,600,000 respectively, but since prices
had doubled in the interval the actual volume of the trade,
carried in 1785 by seven hundred coastal traders, was declining.

The Rhine opened up extensive markets for the Dutch, and its
proximity to the Danube also made accessible the Habsburg
monarchy. Exports from there to the Netherlands rose only
slightly, from 5,000,000 florins in 1753 to 5,300,000 in 1790, and
the rise in prices in the interval again meant a real decline. A company set up at Calw in 1755, licensed by the Duke of Württemberg
to export 3,500 pine trunks to Holland annually, was active for
thirty years. Rhine wines did not have the same popularity as
before; but exports from the Republic rose from 11,150,000
florins' worth in 1753 to 29,100,000 in 1790, particularly because
of increased German consumption of colonial goods. They made
up 70 per cent of the total in 1790 as against 14 per cent in 1753.
This advance also contributed to the strengthening of Amsterdam's position in Dutch commerce generally to the detriment of

Rotterdam. In 1790 Amsterdam's share was 63.6 per cent as against about half in mid-century.

A further privileged hinterland of the United Provinces were the Austrian Netherlands. However, cloth from Verviers and Limburg was to a large extent marketed directly by its producers at the Frankfort fairs, from where it went on via Vienna and Trieste or Venice towards Constantinople and Smyrna, or through the prospering fairs of Leipzig towards Breslau and Poland or Königsberg and Russia. The Republic also received a great deal from the southern provinces: after Belgium was annexed to France, 'French' exports of woollens suddenly rose from 38,000 pounds in 1789 to 257,000 in Year v (1796–7) and even 945,000 in Year viii (1799–1800).

However, after about 1750 the Austrian government successfully tried to escape from the thrall of Dutch trade. The value of commerce in the areas of the Dutch Admiralty of the Meuse and that of Zeeland, on which most of the Dutch customs offices on the border between the two countries depended, declined from 74,000,000 florins to 52,000,000 and from 15,000,000 to 9,000,000 respectively between 1749 and 1751. The Brussels authorities had carried out costly work on the port of Ostend, and it paid off in the Anglo–Dutch War of 1780–4, when most of the trade between the enemy countries went on through Ostend. In the two years 1764–5 only 818 ships had used the port, but in 1780 there were 1,560, in 1781 2,892, and in 1782 2,562.

The Treaty of Breda in 1664 had maintained the Dutch right to handle goods in transit which arrived by the great rivers that flowed into the sea in the Republic. Still, in the long run, the Navigation Acts severely damaged the intermediary role of the Dutch in trade and shipping from the Continent, although their application suffered from the inadequacies of the English merchant fleet. Even in 1721 there were more Dutch ships involved in Anglo–French trade than British ones. The programme of the Navigation Acts was, however, gradually put into effect. The decline of Holland's role emerges from examination of the origins of goods registered by the customs of the Admiralty of Amsterdam. Whereas the countries immediately bordering on the United Provinces accounted for 29.3 per cent of the total (136,700,000 florins) in 1753, their share rose to 43 per cent (out of 178,000,000) in 1790. British trade and shipping even entered the Dutch continental hinterland through the German North Sea ports and Ostend.

This rivalry could not jeopardize the increasingly close relations between England and the Dutch market itself. While English customers still turned to Amsterdam, Dutch merchants found in London, thanks to the spread of English colonialism, a supply of foreign goods which now overshadowed that of Amsterdam. British industry also took a lead that the Industrial Revolution only confirmed. In the eighteenth century cheap Irish linen, for instance, competed with Flemish linen, not only on export markets but in the Austrian Netherlands themselves. If for centuries the British economy had depended on deliveries from the Low Countries, in the early eighteenth century it was Great Britain that assumed the dominant role in the flourishing trade between the two countries. In 1784, although peace was not signed until 20 May between the United Provinces and Great Britain, 1,300 ships sailed from England to Holland whereas only 1,740 altogether sailed from German, Polish, Russian and Scandinavian ports.

In 1659 Colbert imposed on foreign ships a due of fifty *sous* per register ton both on entry and on departure, to combat Dutch commercial supremacy. It was as premature as the English Navigation Acts. With only five or six hundred ships of her own, France could not dispense with the three thousand Dutch ones. After 1662 the due was levied only on departure, and reduced to half for salt exports. On the other hand, although at the end of each of their wars with France the Dutch could get a reduction in the protectionist tariffs imposed after 1664, Dutch merchants still suffered from the vexations of the French customs officials. French trade and industry, especially colonial trade, reduced France's dependence on the Dutch market as they developed. Dunkirk, when it was annexed by France in 1668, diverted a large part of Flemish trade to the detriment of the Dutch ports, particularly after the grant of customs privileges from 1688. Around 1650 the United Provinces are estimated to have exported to France 21,500,000 *livres'* worth of goods, and imported 15,700,000; in 1779–80 the balance of trade had reversed, and Holland now exported 24,400,000 *livres* and imported 34,200,000. French protectionism seems to have harmed the southern provinces of the Low Countries, too, and their trade balance was apparently even worse, although there was, of course, an immense amount of smuggling, especially of linen and lace. The Eden Treaty of 1786 opened France to British linen and coal, whereas earlier she had taken up to 80 per cent of her coal of Hainault. Belgium only took her place in this market after twenty years of integration with France.

Trade with Spain, on the other hand, left the Low Countries a sizeable positive balance. Five or six ships in the 'Flanders convoy' left Dunkirk for Cadiz every year until Dunkirk was annexed by France, when Ostend took over. In 1780 twenty-four ships sailed from there to Spain, which imported Flemish or Dutch linen intended especially for the colonies. The high tariffs were soon evaded because of the officials' corruption, which even Charles III in his reforms could not stamp out. Common resistance to Louis XIV under William III of Orange gave the Dutch a status more privileged than that accorded to the Spanish Netherlands. However, the accession of the Bourbons in Spain in 1700 benefited France, and the Treaty of Utrecht gave the colonial *asiento* to Great Britain. By 1750 the Republic had lost its lead in Spanish trade. In 1681 it had been estimated that some two hundred Dutch ships went to Spain every year, and in 1794 the Dutch ports registered 191 arriving from there. Since the Methuen Treaty of 1703, Portugal had been in England's economic orbit.

Although the approaches to Gibraltar and the Mediterranean were infested with pirates from the Barbary Coast, Dutch merchants did buy skins and leather in Morocco, at Mogador and Safi. They also visited Marseilles and Italy, although her economic decline now limited the volume of her trade. Dutch deliveries of Baltic grain, for instance, which were inevitably expensive, went down except in times of famine. The Republic's ships were to a large extent expelled from the Mediterranean during the wars with France between 1672 and 1713. Apart from the French, the English were also taking over. About fifty Dutch ships had anchored off Smyrna in 1681, but by 1760–2 only sixty-nine did so in thirty months. However, a colony of Jewish, Greek and Armenian merchants, which had existed in Amsterdam since the mid-eighteenth century, gradually took the initiative in Dutch–Turkish trade and gave it some life, although at the cost of a reduction in the Republic's foreign trade. The authorities also rejected the request of some merchants to forbid residence by Turkish subjects, fearing that they would merely go to Hamburg and make it still more competitive.

4 COLONIAL TRADE

The India Company developed its trade with Asia until about 1725, when some forty of its ships returned annually to Holland, as against about thirty fifty years earlier. Despite a temporary recovery in the 1760s, the number gradually fell to less than twenty after the war of 1780–4. It is true that, with an average displacement of between eight hundred and one thousand tonnes instead of some three hundred, as with the ships working European routes, they contributed 4 per cent of the Republic's freight trade by 1700, and 10 per cent of the value of its commerce. Average sales by the Company, which amounted to 8,800,000 florins around 1650, rose to 20,000,000 per annum in the eighteenth century until the outbreak of the Anglo–Dutch War. They recovered somewhat after this event, to 15,500,000 in 1795, when the French invasion cut off Amsterdam from the colonies – though again the rise in prices in the meantime should not be forgotten in this context.

Anxiety to eliminate competition had induced the Company to extend its direct administration or protectorate in Indonesia since the mid-seventeenth century. It had a virtual monopoly of cloves, nutmeg and mace from the Moluccas, and of Ceylon's cinnamon, which made up a quarter of its sales in Europe. Pepper represented only 11 per cent of such sales by the end of the eighteenth century, compared with 33 per cent in 1650. The market was dominated by the English after their great conquests in India. Javanese sugar also suffered from the cheapness of the West Indian product. The decline of these two items was made up by trade in coffee and tea, which were sold after the mid-seventeenth century in cafés and tea houses in the great cities of Europe and were consumed in private homes in the eighteenth century. The Company imported coffee from Arabia after 1663 and grew it in Java in 1699, the first cargoes reaching Holland in 1712. It obtained tea from Chinese merchants visiting Batavia and then imported it directly from Canton on its own ships after 1728. Coffee and tea made up a good quarter of its sales in the eighteenth century.

From China it also imported porcelain, often baked according to models sent from Europe, armorial china, for example, as well as woven silk and raw silk. This also came from Persia and India. The fashion for calico in Europe stimulated trade with India after

1675, and the share of textiles in the Company's deliveries rose from 24 per cent in 1670 to 43 per cent in 1700. It then fell until 1730 because the English gradually took over the India trade and because the declining Dutch silk industry needed less raw silk. These Company purchases were paid for, as before, in precious metals, partly from the profits of the large-scale sales of spices and sugar in Asia herself: almost a third of the spices from the Moluccas were marketed in Asia. When Japan forbade silver exports in 1668, and gold exports in 1672, more had to be sent from Europe, and the Estates-General permitted the export of 336,000,000 florins' worth of these precious metals between 1701 and 1780.

The Company's revenue had been almost wholly absorbed by military efforts between 1650 and 1685, but they bore fruit: for fifty years the Company dividend was never less than 20 per cent annually, and double that figure between 1715 and 1720. Thereafter reduced profits brought down the dividend to 15 per cent between 1737 and 1748; it rose again to 20 or 25 per cent from 1749 to 1757, and declined again to 15 or 12½ per cent until 1781, after which there were no further dividends. Many contemporaries and, later, historians ascribed this decline to corruption, but other chartered companies did no better. The Company's agents could export modest quantities of goods on their own account but they also smuggled on a considerable scale. To stop this, in 1743 they were permitted to take a share of their own in trade between Indonesia and China, and soon a company was set up to market, in the Company's area, the opium obtained from Bengal. Corruption continued. A career in Indonesia, in whatever capacity in the Company, was regarded as a certain way of rapidly acquiring a fortune, and respectable families sent their black sheep there.

The chief reason for the decline of the Company's profitability was the size of the sums levied by the government and of those required for territorial extension. Never having increased its capital, the Company sought advances from the Amsterdam *Wisselbank* to finance its conquests and extend its trade. From 1676 it also borrowed from private individuals who gave it six-month deposits. Its debt, three-quarters of which was short-term, reached 30,000,000 florins in 1761. Energetic retrenchment brought it back to 20,000,000, but the defeat of 1784, which lost Negapatnam on the Coromandel coast to England, facilitated

English access to Ceylon cinnamon, and the opening of Indonesian waters to British shipping ruined the Company's monopoly in the Moluccas. Despite government assistance and support from Holland, the Company's situation worsened, and it was finally taken under control by the Batavian Republic in 1795 and abolished in 1798. It then owed 140,000,000 florins.

The Belgian provinces had not been left out of colonial trade. Their merchants largely evaded the Castilian monopoly, either by getting naturalization papers or by using a fraudulent intermediary among Seville merchants. In 1640, to the detriment of his Portuguese subjects, Philip iv permitted them to trade with the West Indies, though soon the revolution in Lisbon made this concession inoperable. A chartered company, set up in 1698 on his own account by Maximilian Emmanuel of Bavaria, governor of the Spanish Netherlands, was also unable to start trading, mainly because of opposition in the United Provinces, whose help he needed to obtain part of the Spanish succession. When the country fell under Austria through the Treaty of Utrecht, the prospects looked better: the Flemish coast might make some share in colonial trade possible, and Austrian 'Cameralist' writers, such as Becker and Hornigk, stressed its benefits. The China of K'ang Hsi did indeed welcome foreigners more than before, hoping to take advantage of rivalry among them, and the crisis of feudal anarchy that began in India on the death of Aurangzeb encouraged the nawabs to use European support against each other. Moreover, the speculation fever that reached its height in France with John Law's 'System' and in England with the South Sea Bubble, had its counterpart in the Austrian Netherlands. Enterprising shipowners sent ships in increasing numbers hither and thither throughout the tropics.

In 1723 the Brussels government regulated them by setting up the 'Imperial and Royal India Company', commonly called the 'Ostend Company' after the home port of its ships, although two-thirds of its capital of 6,000,000 florins (75 per cent of it paid) had in fact been subscribed in two days in Antwerp. The company was given a monopoly of colonial trade in the Austrian Netherlands for thirty years, with the usual rights of sovereignty. It traded only with India and China, the nine ships loading tea, silk and porcelain at Canton between 1724 and 1729 bringing in a profit of 7,000,000 florins, although the six that visited the six factories it opened in the Ganges delta brought in only 1,138,000. The United Provinces and England were concerned at the competition this meant for them, for the new company's share of European tea imports rose to 28 per cent between 1721 and 1730, and they exploited the political difficulties of Charles vi, who wanted to get their support for Maria Theresa's rights to the Austrian succession. He was made to suspend the monopoly of the Ostend Company in 1727, and to abolish it in 1731. In 1729–31, however, the Company sent seven ships to the East under other flags, refusing in 1728 to merge with the Danish Altona Company. It invested its capital in various foreign colonial companies and elsewhere, and gave out 166.16 per cent dividends before being liquidated in 1774. A year later Antwerp businessmen subscribed 824 of the 1,000 shares of the Trieste and Fiume Company that was given a monopoly for the hereditary lands of Austria, but it took only a small part in the colonial trade and soon went over to refining sugar imported by others.

On the route to the Indies, Mauritius, from which the Dutch Company took ebony and sugar cane, was occupied by the French in 1712, but at the Cape of Good Hope, where Huguenot refugees planted vines and raised stock, the white population rose in prosperity, from about six hundred in 1685 to 11,000 or 12,000 in 1795, besides ten thousand slaves from Africa and Asia. The Dutch factories on the Gold Coast and in Senegal were under the West India Company and when it was liquidated in 1674, another was founded with the same name and a small capital of 600,000 florins. The shareholders of the earlier company were permitted to subscribe through their own shares, which were accepted at 15 per cent of their face value, but the new company had to take over the debts of the earlier one (they were reduced from 6,000,000 to 1,800,000) and from the start it had the same problems to face. Even the slave trade was wide open to smuggling: in 1734 it was made entirely free, in exchange for compensation payments.

Dutch slave ships had a large share in the *asiento*, the monopoly of slave imports to Spanish America. From 1684 to 1687 Balthasar Coymans of Amsterdam leased it, and others invested capital in the Genoese, Portuguese or Castilian *asientos*, or they supplied blacks. The Dutch slave merchants provided 8,000 of the 20,000 slaves imported annually to America around 1700 but the grant of the *asiento* to the English between 1713 and 1750 was fatal to them. Whilst the trade developed more than ever before, their share fell to 6,300 slaves out of 70,000 in 1770, and to about 4,000 out of 100,000 after the war of 1780–4, naturally to the detriment of all the industries that made goods for barter, such as weaponry, metalware, cloth, glassware and spirits. The trade had its chief bases in Zeeland, first at Middelburg and later at Flushing. The 'Trading Company' at Middelburg loaded 31,000 blacks in 101 expeditions from 1732 to 1795, and 27,345 of them reached America – losses that seem less heavy than those of competitors. In 1767–8 Middelburg fitted out ten slave ships, Flushing eighteen, Amsterdam and Rotterdam four each; between 1783 and 1790 Amsterdam equipped eighteen, Rotterdam two, and both Zeeland towns together, thirty-one. Despite the high price of slaves and the proceeds of freight brought back from the New World, the costs of the trade caused losses for almost half of the expeditions of the Trading Company and left it overall only a small profit of 3 per cent per annum. The Austrian Netherlands had only a small part of the trade, generally for other countries. A ship's captain, Ignace van Alstein, from Ghent, for instance, took part in the slave trade on behalf of Nantes in the second half of the eighteenth century.

Because of the monopoly, only the possessions of the West India Company were officially open to Dutch commerce in America, but the favourable situation of the Leeward Islands as regards the Spanish and Portuguese possessions allowed them to live from exporting salt to Holland as well as from contraband trade with these possessions. Curaçao, where sugar cane was cultivated only temporarily, was the main centre until the Treaty of Utrecht transferred supremacy to British-ruled Jamaica. St Eustace had exceptional prosperity as a relay post for smuggling between Europe and the rebellious British colonies of North America until it was sacked by the British in 1781. The Dutch American colonies took their food supplies from these British ones. The independence of the United States created high hopes in Europe, but it rapidly became clear that they would continue to trade with London rather than Amsterdam. Holland did benefit from emigration to the new republic, however, and four-fifths of the ships bringing immigrants (mostly German) to Philadelphia from 1727 to 1775 left from Rotterdam. Although a consul was appointed to Philadelphia between 1783 and 1790, the Austrian

Netherlands' hopes of extending their American trade were also disappointed.

In 1667 an expedition from Zeeland had conquered Surinam from the English: the Estates of Zeeland ceded it in 1682 to the local Chamber of the West India Company. Unable to exploit it, the Chamber at once set up the Surinam Company in association with the city of Amsterdam and a nobleman from Holland, Cornelius van Aerssen van Sommeldijk, each taking one-third. Van Aerssen's heirs made over their share to the others in 1770. The Company retained the slave trade, but opened up the land to Dutch commerce for everything else. The establishment of Portuguese Jews expelled from Brazil by the Inquisition and of Huguenots brought by Van Aerssen, whose wife was a French Protestant, encouraged the development of the plantations. Further west Essequibo and Berbice had been exploited by Zeeland planters since the early seventeenth century. After a French attack in 1712, bankers from Amsterdam took a major share in the property of the Van Pere family and set up the Berbice Company. The fifty plantations of Surinam in 1682 grew into two hundred on Van Aerssen's death in 1688, four hundred in 1740 and 614 in 1793. There were 125 in Berbice and some two hundred in Essequibo. In 1794 Amsterdam imported 18,000,000 pounds of sugar, as against 7,600,000 in 1759, and between 14,000,000 and 15,000,000 pounds of coffee, first planted there in 1712. Cocoa was grown after 1685: Amsterdam received 600,000 pounds of it in 1759, and much more by the end of the century. Guiana also exported indigo and cotton (110,000 pounds to Amsterdam in 1759). Tobacco was given up after mid-century because of English competition. At this period about thirty ships came to Amsterdam every year from Guiana, and others, in unknown numbers, went to the ports of Zeeland.

However, the prosperity was largely illusory. The plantations were periodically raided by the 'forest negroes' (*bosnegers*), slaves who had fled to the virgin forest because of ill-treatment. The rise in the prices of colonial produce extended the plantations, and, in the end, over-production weakened the market. The planters financed this growth by loans and were heavily in debt. The price of slaves also rose. To reduce the burden, the Estates-General suspended the right of the West India Company to import them in 1789, at the planters' request. This finished the Company. Only rarely had it managed to issue dividends, always modest, and it could keep its African factories only by loans (in 1784 it owed 4,000,000 florins) and by government subsidy. Its monopoly was not renewed in 1791, at its term. Four years later Guiana fell to England, and this severed links between the Dutch colonies and their motherland.

5 THE STRUCTURE OF COMMERCE

The external trade of the Low Countries was based on a network of markets for collection and distribution where town and country traded in their particular products. Such trade was limited in the economically backward parts of the countryside, such as the Ardennes or the Drenthe, the inhabitants of which, having little to sell, were not able to buy much either. But wherever there was intensive agriculture or a commercialized rural artisanate, the old tendency to autarchy gave way to integration within a much larger economic framework. Internal trade must have progressed considerably by the end of the *ancien régime*; the subject would repay research.

In the seventeenth century a more distinct hierarchy of wholesale and retail merchants appeared. Wholesalers became a true commercial aristocracy, and sometimes even became aristocrats. They held public offices in the large towns, for which they often trained themselves in law. These dignities tended to become a professional career in themselves. The more or less legitimate profits that exercise of power could provide attracted candidates from the merchant class and gave them, through the income from their offices, riches that compared very favourably with the earnings of others who stayed as merchants. Millionaires were still quite rare in the seventeenth century, but there were many more in the eighteenth, especially in Amsterdam. 12,650 Amsterdam families supplied roughly half of the receipts from the income tax levied in Holland between 1742 and 1753, and about one hundred of them were assessed for an income of 16,000 florins or more. A good third of these lived from trade or industry, and the rest were either property owners or magistrates.

Whatever the source of their income, this class lived in opulent style. Theirs were the houses that still adorn the *grachten* of Amsterdam and the old quarters of Antwerp, Ghent and Bruges. In the seventeenth century they would be furnished with solid chests, cabinets and armchairs, and in the eighteenth with graceful commodes, delicate stools and porcelain. There were collections of masterpieces of painting and sculpture, and in the Century of Enlightenment this class shared a passion for music and built up large libraries of the fashionable classics. With their armies of domestic servants, they kept elegant carriages, and led a very active social life, both in their town houses and in the country seats where they would spend the summer season. Besides business matters, they would discuss and prepare at length the weddings of their children, and would usually try to find a marriage partner for them among the families of business associates or the hereditary or professional aristocracies, who often sought a rich match for their children.

Specialization also increased, certainly in Holland in general, and particularly in Amsterdam, distinguishing large-scale commerce and industry, insurance and banking, even within large-scale commerce. Like the English general merchants, some businessmen were essentially importers, either on their own account or on commission from foreign correspondents. They would keep to within fixed geographical limits, and hence dealt in a certain type of ware. A second set of merchants, the *tweede hand* ('second hand') ones, specialized not by area but by type of goods, which they stocked in warehouses, sorted and released according to demand. Alternatively, although the distinction was frequently blurred, wholesalers could be exporters to various regions within a given geographical area, most often on commission. There were complaints in Holland in the second half of the eighteenth century that trade on commission was weakening the backbone of the national mercantile class, and this was said to be causing the decline of Amsterdam. The real cause was the economic emancipation of other countries and the rise of competing markets, and in any case this was accompanied by the development of the financial role of Amsterdam, which will be discussed below.

The various exchanges were the central nerves of trade. The Amsterdam Exchange led, and its rates extended far beyond the Netherlands. Its list of current prices in the later eighteenth century covered more than seven hundred articles. These could be inspected in warehouses, many of which have survived in Amsterdam's architectural heritage, but men increasingly negotiated with reference to standard qualities or samples, which was not without risk in an era when communications were slow and delivery dates long. Forward sales for a fixed term in the future were being concluded in the early seventeenth century, though only for speculative purposes, and with no intention of delivery. Thus, in 1636–8 there was notorious speculation in tulips and hyacinths. Flowers were very much in vogue, and prices of bulbs rose. The bulbs were then sold, by men who did not have any but promised to acquire some, to other men who did not have any money but who thought they could get some by selling the bulbs at a profit later on. The market collapsed. A real futures market, dealing in long delivery dates, did emerge for some articles by 1700.

The many auxiliaries of large-scale commerce, brokers, shipping agents, insurers and the like, also became more specialized, as did retail trading, at least in places where there was a large enough population to maintain a shop that sold goods of a limited nature. Since the guilds allowed only their masters to sell the goods of their trade in the town, traders in goods from elsewhere had often to be grouped in a guild of mercers, which had a purely commercial and not an industrial function. Growing commercialization certainly gave prosperity to owners of shops that catered for the comfortable middle class. It was better educated and more sophisticated than before, and now it claimed a share of power. It opposed the patrician oligarchy in the United Provinces, Joseph II's enlightened despotism in the Austrian Netherlands and that of the prince-bishops in Liège, and became politically active in the Dutch Patriots' movement in 1787, and the Brabantine and Liège revolutions of 1789. After these movements had failed, some of them collaborated in setting up the new order that emerged with the Batavian Republic and the French conquest in Belgium.

Apart from the world of maritime trade, weekly markets and fairs, retaining their independence of the local guilds' monopolies, still played an intermediary role, between town and country. They were especially useful in gathering the output of rural handicrafts, for instance Flemish linen, which was also collected by itinerant dealers going from house to house. Pedlars were still very common, not only in the countryside, where they made up for the lack of shops, but even in the towns, where shopkeepers vainly and often protested against their competition as they attracted trade with their varied, picturesque cries.

5 *Economic Policy*

I INDUSTRIAL POLICY

Contrary to a general belief, the United Provinces did have a measure of protection for their industry. It was, however, less than elsewhere in Europe. The wealth built up in the Golden Age may have delayed recognition of the extent of the crisis, and in any case it came later than in other countries, only in the last third of the seventeenth century. Moreover, the political and economic structure made strict protection impossible. Holland, which brought the Republic almost 60 per cent of its income, had a preponderant influence, and its attitude was largely determined by wealthy Amsterdam, where the mercantile voice, hostile to protectionism that would have reduced imports, counted for more than any other. Even an industrial entrepreneur like the draper, de la Court, in Leyden felt in 1669 that the country's prosperity came essentially from the profits of commerce, and that imports should not be cut by high tariffs.

Aid to industry was therefore for many years a matter for local or regional authorities. On the arrival of the Huguenots, who had been encouraged to come because of Calvinistic sympathies with the persecuted, for instance, the States of Holland exempted refugees from all taxes for twelve years. In 1682 Amsterdam put 240 orphans from its homes at the disposal of the silk manufacturer Pierre Baille. But such intervention seems to have been neither frequent nor lengthy. Perhaps the gradual shift of the bourgeoisie of Holland to investment in annuities distracted attention from the industrial crisis, for not until the economic decline had accelerated was interventionism more favourably regarded in the Republic. The new spirit was displayed in 1749, when the export of tools to which certain industries owed their fame was prohibited; in 1751, when skilled workers were forbidden to emigrate; and in 1753 when all civil servants were forced to dress in Dutch cloth. This last measure was not, presumably, very effective. Certain activities were subsidized – the herring fisheries first, at a local level, in the town of Flushing in 1754. The Estates of Zeeland extended these subsidies to all of their subjects involved in fisheries in 1759, and those of Holland followed suit in 1775. The Economic Section (*Oeconomische Tak*) of the 'Scientific Society of Holland', founded in 1777, recommended resolute mercantilism as the way to restore prosperity, but as its members also promoted profound political reforms, the ruling oligarchy ignored the advice.

Mercantilism had a stronger pull in the Belgian provinces than in the Netherlands. Industry had greater economic importance there than commercial interests, and monarchical power was better suited to silence complaints from interested parties there than in the Republic where there was no well-founded central authority. It even took over the monopolies granted by some of the towns a century before. In these cases, a particular enterprise would be given a monopoly of manufacture, either for all the Belgian provinces or for one of them. Following the example of other towns, the Brussels government gave tax concessions from 1664 and advances to cover initial costs from 1676, while after 1682 manufacturers were permitted to take wood for nothing from the domain forests. These grants were especially numerous in the mid-eighteenth century: the 226 that were given from 1749 to 1763 to new factories included customs privileges, interest-free loans from the government and sometimes even permission to use cheap labour from the prisons or orphanages. Rewards were offered to inventors. However, physiocratic principles, which opposed interventionism, gradually defeated mercantilism after 1765, and the physiocrats were supported by tax officials concerned at the Treasury's failure to collect enough taxes, or its shortfall from losses on rash projects. The grants became rarer as the country's economic progress made public intervention less necessary.

The grants, which freed their beneficiaries from guild obligations, had often been opposed by the traditional monopolists of these guilds. The guilds, under the pretext of safeguarding the quality of output, often opposed technological change, either through a stubborn lack of imagination or because its adoption would be too costly. They often tried to eliminate competition among themselves by rotating the work or distributing raw materials equally among their members, or by limiting the number of workers and the tools that each member might have. They limited access to the mastership, and even the companionship, by increasing charges or by insisting on the severest tests of skill for entry, and since only the sons of masters were exempt, more and more guilds became hereditary fellowships, whether formally or informally. In the eighteenth century all of the butchers of Ghent belonged to six families, one of which had sixty, and two others forty-seven, of the 116 stalls in the *Grande Boucherie* ('Butchers' Hall') of the town in 1791. The number of brewers there fell from fifty-five to seven between 1645 and 1787. The hold of the guild system on the urban economy had actually grown since the Middle Ages. In the large towns, the emergence of new skills within a single trade had sometimes caused the division of existing guilds, and often industries which had been free to start with turned into guilds. In secondary centres some trades had become large enough to do the same. The first guild privileges for these were granted at Arlon in 1722 and Neufchâteau in 1729.

Around 1760 the guilds' economic Malthusianism persuaded the Austrians to attempt reform. The government did not dare attack them directly, and the draft edict which an over-zealous official prepared in 1784 to abolish them (following the example of Turgot at Paris in 1776) was never published. As the guilds had the right to seats in the councils of many of the towns, the abolition would have raised the question of representation in government. Moreover, if they were to be abolished, who would take over their substantial debts? The government could not do much: it forbade all sumptuary expense, here and there merged guilds that had similar trades, and abrogated restrictions on the number of apprentices and companies in Luxembourg in 1771 and in the whole country in 1775. The discontent that these reforms aroused contributed to the outbreak of the Brabantine revolution in 1789. In the Austrian restoration of 1790 they were repealed, but after the French conquest the guild system in Belgium was suppressed in 1795 through the Le Chapelier Law. The Dutch guilds had never had the same vigour, but abolition in the United Provinces as well was proposed in 1779 by a reforming advocate of Enlightenment. It was decided upon by the Batavian Constitution of 1798, but in view of its unpopularity the communal authorities were allowed to restore the guilds in 1801. They were finally abolished only in 1818, by the government of the new kingdom of the Netherlands.

Since the Middle Ages guild masters working for the local market had usually been independent artisans, but those who supplied large-scale commerce were in effect wage-earners usually distinguished from their fellows only in ownership of their tools. The number of wage-earners increased with industrialization and the advance of rural handicrafts. Their concentration in workshops, in industries with relatively complicated equipment, gradually made the factory worker, as a social type, more numerous. The condition of the wage-earner seems to have worsened throughout this period. In times of crisis the employers would cut wages and, although the price of essential foodstuffs declined, purchase taxes would reduce the advantage wholly or in part. When conditions improved in the Austrian Netherlands life would become more expensive, but the growth of population caused the supply of labour to rise faster than the number of jobs available.

Pauperism was therefore very widespread, despite the charitable institutions, old and new. Since 1654 the town of Amsterdam had put beggars to work in a public workshop, where the unemployed could also find employment. This example, like the *hôpitaux généraux* in France and the workhouses in England, was widely imitated. For a brief time there was some thought in the Austrian Netherlands of using the central prisons, which had been put up for Flanders in 1772 and for Brabant in 1779, as workhouses, but then there was a return to the principle of assisting paupers by providing work for them at home. The bodies instituted in several towns for the distribution of alms and maintained by subsidy from the authorities did not have enough funds, and they were also opposed by the church which claimed its own rights to organized charity. Joseph II's plan to centralize such efforts by devoting to them the income of the contemplative monasteries he had abolished in 1783 failed in the face of the public disorders that produced the Brabantine revolution.

2 COMMERCIAL POLICY

Since the seventeenth century the authorities had been intervening in the economy more deliberately and systematically, employing the methods of commercial policy which had hitherto been applied only in exceptional circumstances. The United Provinces prohibited imports of English cloth in retaliation to England's protection of her own finishing industry, and it was exceptional that the Dutch should have carried on this prohibition after the protection had ceased – indeed, the prohibition was even extended to cloth from other countries in 1651, a concession to the drapers of Leyden unusual for the times, in view of the preponderance of Amsterdam's merchants who resented any restriction of the volume of trade. It came about, perhaps, because the merchants believed that Holland's traditional finishing trade had to be safeguarded, whereas imports of unbleached cloth and re-exportation after finishing would not really decline. Reprisals against French mercantilist measures, however, were abandoned after each of the Franco-Dutch wars. The Estates-General preferred to maintain their trade, if not extend it, by means of commercial treaties.

Imports and exports were, of course, often subject to customs dues in the Republic, but in general these were purely fiscal in character and remained low. They were levied by the different Admiralties and the income went to the navy. Its expenses in the war with Cromwell's England prompted the Republic to increase the dues in 1652, theoretically by a third, in fact by an average of 22 per cent, and to levy dues on tonnage and convoy. In 1649 a tax on Baltic navigation was introduced, when a treaty with Denmark replaced the Sound tolls with a lump sum. It was not abolished even when the tolls were restored five years later, and the new rates levied in 1652 also remained in force. The deterioration of economic conditions soon after these increases in cost made them particularly burdensome, especially since the dues were levied at specific rates. Grain exports were affected by the considerable fall in prices. The depression damaged Zeeland, which gathered an appreciable share of its revenue from agriculture, and the province managed to obtain the levy of an import tax on cereals in exchange for the abolition of export duty at the request of the merchants of Amsterdam. Import taxes on animal products were introduced between 1671 and 1691, and confirmed the shift of Dutch commercial policy towards a measure of agricultural protection.

Since the mid-seventeenth century, the Spanish Netherlands had also experimented with how far licences could act as a stimulant for the economy. Although there were protests from trading circles in Antwerp (illustrated by their representatives' attitude to the vote of taxes in the Estates of Brabant) Flanders was a vigorous advocate of the new ideas, especially in connection with textiles after the French tariffs of 1664 and 1667 threatened to shut off the French market. The Spanish Netherlands tariff of 1670 was a protectionist measure for their trade with France, except for a few years when Philip v, Louis xiv's grandson, governed the country. The province of Luxembourg, isolated by the territory of Liège, acquired a special and more liberal arrangement in 1671; and the tariff applied to Liège, the United Provinces and England, which was decreed at Brussels in 1681, was also more moderate in character.

The governor, Maximilian Emmanuel of Bavaria, hoped to inherit the Spanish Netherlands when the Spanish succession fell vacant, and wanted to promote their prosperity. With his chief minister, Count Bergeyck, he consulted the chief industrial centres in 1699. The Perpetual Edict that emerged was a highly mercantilist document. It tried to hinder exports of raw materials and imports of manufactured goods, encouraging exports of the manufactures and imports of raw materials instead. In 1700 the Dutch and English, whose help was necessary if Maximilian Emmanuel's political ambitions were to be fulfilled, demanded the withdrawal of the measures affecting them. From 1703 they occupied the Belgian provinces during the War of the Spanish Succession, and demanded relief from the tariff of 1680. Moreover, under the terms of the Treaty of Utrecht, Austria, the new mistress of the country, had to consolidate the tariff, i.e. promise not to alter it without their consent. This consent was, of course, withheld and the Austrian Netherlands were thus even more under Anglo-Dutch commercial influence than before. After the War of the Austrian Succession, however, they were freed from this obligation in 1748, and were at last allowed to apply measures of protection. Maria Theresa did not abolish the 1680 tariff at once, but instead gradually changed one clause after another until there was a virtual prohibition on imports of manufactured goods or exports of raw materials. She did the same with regard to France and other countries. These gradual changes circumvented excessive objection from merchants threatened by a decline in the volume of trade or from consumers faced with rising prices, and also deflected violent reprisals from abroad. Joseph ii favoured the export of agricultural goods but he, too, protected industry, even more energetically than his mother had done. The rapid changes in Belgium's political status between the Brabantine revolution and the French conquest, though, left little time for much alteration in this respect.

In the meantime, the economic crisis had lent greater urgency to demands for protection in the United Provinces. The new tariff of 1725 was a compromise between the wishes of large-scale commerce and agricultural and industrial interests. It abolished or reduced the surtaxes levied in 1652, and tended towards more flexible taxation by replacing the flat-rate dues by *ad valorem* ones, which gave some relief. On the other hand, it upheld or even increased import taxes on the chief products of agriculture and fisheries. As far as industry was concerned, especially the *traffics*, the tariff hardly affected imported raw materials, while it harmed exports; it had the reverse effect on finished goods. The hoped-for recovery did not materialize, and there was an increasing conviction that more profound economic changes were needed.

In 1751 William iv submitted his famous Proposition to the Estates-General. It had been drawn up by representatives of the mercantile class, who believed that the rise of Hamburg was a product of its low taxes, and aimed to convert the Republic as a whole into a free port where raw materials and half-finished goods could be entirely liberated of import duties, while manufactured goods finished there would be exempt from export duties. Tariffs, even prohibitions, would apply to products consumed domestically. To stimulate transport, the system applied to the Belgian provinces since 1688, by which only one duty was payable (whichever was the higher), on exit or entry, was to be generalized. The reduction in customs revenues was to be offset by more effective suppression of smuggling. This, and the influence of particular interests, was a major cause of the Proposition's failure. Smuggling had become so widespread that most merchants preferred high duties, ineffectively levied by corruptible officials, to a general franchise. The opposition of Zeeland, where tolerance of smuggling had developed into a sort of provincial economic policy, was especially violent. William IV's sudden death some months after the Proposition had been tabled removed the only support that might have put it through, and the debate ended. Men made do with ad hoc measures for industries in difficulty. These steps towards protection were measures against the all-important priority of foreign trade that remained the Republic's official policy.

Despite its modest area and population, the principality of Liège also used the right to one-sixtieth of the value of imports and exports, on which its customs system was built, as an instrument of economic policy, although initially it had existed purely for fiscal purposes. Throughout the eighteenth century this mainly involved protecting Liège's industries against measures taken by Brussels to help Limburg draperies or the metal industries of Namur and Luxembourg; in the repeated trade wars between the Austrian Netherlands and Liège, she used prohibitions or tariff increases as weapons, so that the term 'one-sixtieth' was quite without significance in many cases.

3 TRANSPORT

The Low Countries had a network of excellent rivers for the transport of goods, and there were also the canals created for the drainage of the polders and for the peat-fields. Flat-bottomed boats could navigate these, at least between the villages and nearby towns. Some towns even had canals dug to improve their communications. Ghent and Brussels, for example, excavated canals from the mid-sixteenth century onwards in the direction of the Western Scheldt and the Rupel respectively, and Groningen dug one in 1598 which led to the mouth of the Ems. Louvain constructed a canal to Malines in 1750, to facilitate the transport of its beer and the coal needed for brewing it, and to attract traffic between the sea ports and Germany or Lorraine, for which there was keen competition between the United Provinces, Liège and the Austrian Netherlands.

Plans for a water-way system that went beyond a purely urban network had been cherished in the Belgian provinces since the 'closing' of the Scheldt. The canals of Flanders did not meet such hopes because of the high transport costs caused by the unloading on which the Ghent and Bruges skippers insisted, and other dues. In 1700 it apparently cost ten times as much to send a bale of wool from Ostend to Brussels as along the 'closed' Scheldt. Ghent and Bruges had, shortly before, opposed a plan for a canal from Antwerp to the coast through northern Flanders, and they did so again after 1750. The junction at Bruges of the canals for Ostend and Ghent, and the latter canal's junction with the Lys at Ghent could even, with 'cuttings', be used by small ships bound for Ghent and then Antwerp. But the authorities' efforts to stop the compulsory transshipments failed as long as the skippers' guild persisted. At Ostend work on the port enabled it to play a temporary role in European trade during the Anglo–Dutch War.

Schemes for a canal between Antwerp and the middle Meuse and Rhine continued into the eighteenth century. A similar plan, of 1699, for a canal between a Brabantine tributary of the Scheldt and the middle Meuse or the middle Sambre was not carried out, although its construction would have meant that river transport of coal, iron, lime or stone from the Walloon area could have avoided the long detour of the lower Meuse across Liège and the Republic. The Dutch objected, and Maximilian Emmanuel depended too far on their political support to ignore such objections.

Canals suited transport of all fragile goods as well as bulky ones. It was not even much slower than carting, for on the roads, pitted with ruts, horses could only walk. Even travellers, unless they were in a hurry, preferred the amenities of water-borne travel to the bumping of a carriage or the fatigue of the saddle. Since Roman times the main streets of the towns, and sometimes the approaches to them beyond the walls, had been reinforced with cobblestones or gravel, but sooner or later travellers would come upon earth tracks, where dust and mud alternated according to the season. The central government had assisted the local authorities in building roads, following a French example (that instituted under Philip v, after 1704). The Austrians maintained this system, often delegating the maintenance work to provincial authorities which sometimes organized the work as corvées imposed on the villages lining the new highways, though more usually they farmed out the work. Memories of this, which was reinforced by the grant of taxes to be levied at turnpikes on the roads, have been reserved in many place-names.

Good highways, therefore, linked the chief towns of the

Austrian Netherlands at the end of the *ancien régime*. Their combined length was 2,500 kilometres, and they were of a density without rival in Europe. Liège also did well, with her 360 kilometres of paved road. One of the chief roads, from Liège to the Dutch border, was meant to divert traffic between the sea and Germany towards Liège, a consideration that led the Brussels government to create the Louvain canal. In the Republic road building remained a matter for local and provincial authorities, and in 1795 there were only four hundred kilometres of highway. Bois-le-Duc, Eindhoven and the Estates of Holland had failed, one after another, in efforts to build the extension of the road from Liège. The stretch between Bois-le-Duc and the frontier was only finished in 1818.

Other survivals of the medieval economy continued to block the free circulation of goods. Circumstances facilitated the ending of venerable staples in the Belgian provinces. Since the sixteenth century the Bruges staple really mattered only in connection with the import of Spanish wool destined for Lille, and there was, in any case, a great deal of smuggling. After France annexed Lille in 1668, Bruges had to give way in order to prevent the diversion of traffic to Dunkirk, now French, or the Dutch port of Sas-van Ghent, and permitted it to come through Ostend or Nieuport in return for a due. In 1664 the Ghent grain staple was confined to exports of native grain, which occurred only after very good harvests. As the staple dues made the grain too expensive for foreign marketing, it fell into disuse.

The multiplicity of tolls also disrupted trade. By 1614 Antwerp had purchased exemption for its subjects from all government tolls, in exchange for a lump sum; Brussels did the same in 1648 and Malines in 1718. After 1687 Bruges often suggested their abolition pure and simple, in exchange for a customs surtax, but the opposition of the already-exempted towns, and the consolidation of customs dues between 1713 and 1748, prevented this reform from being executed. Similar projects of Joseph II's, who also thought of buying out all municipal and individual tolls, were no more successful than this, and they vanished only after the French conquest. The greater decentralization of power in the United Provinces meant that such reforms were even less likely to succeed, and obstacles to free circulation survived virtually intact there until the end of the *ancien régime*.

6 Money and Finance

I MONEY

Since 1647 Spain had sold her silver from the New World in Amsterdam. The Dutch monetary authorities tried, as in the past, to keep silver for their own coinage, part of which was used as payment in lucrative trade. At the authorities' instigation, the Estates-General decreed that only two-thirds of the silver could be sold freely. During the second half of the seventeenth century the English were able to get from Amsterdam 7,000,000 or 8,000,000 florins' worth of the metal annually, in the form of coins or otherwise. But resources of silver were declining, while the growth in Asian trade both of the Republic and other European countries required more and more of it, so that prices rose. Monetary reform in 1659 produced a prohibition of silver exports, though it was lifted after a year because of protests from merchants. The quota reserved to the Mint was, however, raised to half, in 1690. When the Dutch fought Philip v in the War of the Spanish Succession, the interruption of the supplies of silver prompted a new embargo on exports in 1701, except for trading money, for which merchants had to prove their need. Fears that silver supplies would be inadequate turned out to be unfounded, and the prohibition was ignored even before the war ended. It was not revived until the end of the century.

Thus, the silver stock nearly always met the needs of Dutch coinage, and if there were sometimes problems in the circulation of coins, that was because of the persistent infiltration of debased coins from the Spanish Netherlands, which forced the Dutch ones out of circulation. These inferior coins could not be excluded by modifications in the rate of exchange, which the Estates-General made periodically, and in 1659 the authorities resigned themselves to declaring parity – the new *rijksdaalders* of fifty *patards*, and ducats of sixty-three *patards*, which were chosen as the standard, were even slightly lower in alloy than the similar coins of the Belgian provinces. However, the hoarding caused by the rise in the price of silver, and exports of silver for purposes of trade once more caused a shortage of good coins around 1670. The country was invaded by base money of poor alloy, and the ordinary people, who were paid in debased coins at their nominal value, became annoyed at this rise in their cost of living: indeed, the lessees of the various mints outdid each other in producing debased coinage because it gave them large profits. The small coins of Zeeland were of such inferior quality that the Estates of Holland had to forbid circulation of them in their province. In 1681 Holland attempted to get a sound coinage by resuming, after a gap of 150 years, the striking of florins and by creating three-florin coins, but this was a failure, because the metal rose in price.

At the instigation of the Estates of Holland, and perhaps also to still the discontent of the Dutch forces fighting in the Nine Years War, William III used his authority in 1694 to force the towns that had kept their minting rights and had seriously abused them to give them up in exchange for an annuity; he also subjected the provincial mints to strict control by the federal government. The inferior coinage was withdrawn or stamped with a lower value, and from then on minting was uniform throughout the Republic, where the florin piece finally became a common monetary standard and a real coin.

The Spanish Netherlands suffered from a further difficulty in that they were repeatedly occupied by foreign soldiery in the various wars. The reform of 1659 had conferred on Dutch coins a lower intrinsic value but, even so, they were spread by soldiers fighting in alliance with Spain against Louis XIV, and, to satisfy wartime political ends, had to be accepted at par after 1676. In 1689 Maximilian Emmanuel of Bavaria had to devalue the coinage of the Belgian provinces. France then brought in her own coins, which were deliberately over-valued, and they caused all other coins in the lands she occupied to be hoarded and withdrawn from circulation. When Philip V inherited the Spanish Netherlands, he aligned their coins with those of depressed France and here, too, the coiners made vast profits by producing base money. After the cession of Namur and Luxembourg to Maximilian Emmanuel, from 1709 to 1713, he filled his coffers by marketing massive quantities of small coins (*liards*), at a profit of 22 per cent, in the provinces occupied by England and Holland which the Dutch had integrated into their own monetary system.

In the first half of the eighteenth century the discovery of large gold deposits in Brazil reduced the value of gold against silver. The conversion rates were sometimes revised only after long delays, silver money was withdrawn from circulation, and the mints did not strike new coins because they would be too expensive. The deflationary effects of this money shortage also help to explain the economic stagnation of the Netherlands and Europe as a whole. Since the Treaty of Utrecht had broken the Austrian Netherlands' political link with Spain, the regular despatch of funds through Madrid to pay the troops had ceased, and there was a serious lack of silver. The Brussels government could only attract foreign coins, especially French ones, by over-valuing them, and in mid-century French coins made up the bulk of the coins in circulation in the Austrian Netherlands, particularly as they were spread around by a new French occupation in the War of the Austrian Succession. The English blockade of Spain had more or less completely stopped Castilian silver exports to the Republic, and thus brought monetary confusion to a peak there as well.

The shortage of silver coins and the delay in adjusting their value against that of gold ones caused an extraordinary rise in the proportion of gold coins in circulation. It had traditionally been small: gold coins, together with large silver coins, had essentially served to meet the balance of trade, especially the adverse balance of the Republic with the Baltic, Russia and the Levant. They were also hoarded, or could be used as a reserve on a long journey. Early in the Austrian period gold was estimated at only one-fifth of the monetary stock of the Belgian provinces. John Law's monetary experiment prompted considerable exports of gold from France to the Low Countries, but the over-valuation of the French gold *louis* by 50 per cent meant that incredible amounts of counterfeit *louis* were manufactured in both parts of the Low Countries, and they restored a large amount of the lost gold, giving the counterfeiters enormous profits. During the War of the Austrian Succession, silver became so rare that even wages had to be paid in gold, with all the inconvenience this caused when small purchases were involved. As there had been a delay in adapting conversion rates, many gold ducats that had been earlier exported to the Baltic had returned from there to be changed at the official rate against silver, and silver had been withdrawn from circulation. The profit on the deal was all the greater since most of the coins, having suffered the usual fate of coins in the past, had come back clipped. Oddly enough, although in the Dutch Republic a greater uniformity of the coinage had been achieved with the use of screw-presses instead of hammers to strike the coins, the custom of milling them to curtail this abuse was not introduced until 1749. The Spanish Netherlands had combined the two developments since 1685.

Just after the War of Succession, in 1749, the Austrian government in Brussels failed in an attempt to settle the monetary troubles. A second effort succeeded in 1755, however, because the tension of the precious metals market had finally been relieved. The decline of Brazilian gold production and the discovery of new silver deposits in Spanish America balanced the value of the two metals and facilitated normal coining. The Austrian Netherlands' money stock, estimated for 1749 at some 45,000,000 florins, or twenty-two per inhabitant, seems to have doubled to thirty-nine per inhabitant in 1779. The United Provinces were also able to issue more coins, and this was not irrelevant to the improvement of economic conditions there after 1760. But the war of 1780–4 hindered trade with Great Britain, from where they had obtained a great deal of their silver and gold, and shortly afterwards the political crisis of 1787 again gave rise to hoarding – and all of this contributed towards the economic crisis in which the old regime ended.

The coins of the Brussels government circulated only to a limited extent in Luxembourg, Limburg and the lands east of the Meuse, which were isolated from the other provinces by foreign territory. Like many princes of the Rhineland, the prince-bishops of Liège tried constantly to attract good coins from the Habsburg mints in exchange for base ones. French coins, which were also of lower quality, were more usual than native ones in Luxembourg, Hainault and Namur, and special measures and dispensations from the official rates frequently enacted on behalf of these frontier provinces. The integration of the Belgian departments into the French monetary system after the Revolution was in no way a rupture, in matters of coinage, for much of the country.

The Dutch monetary reform of 1659 set an official stamp on the new distinction between real money and money of account. The *wisselbanken* were statutorily required to assess their coins at their former official values, without taking into account any alterations that may have happened in daily life. Since in effect these coins no longer circulated at their official values, the official rates gradually became a unit of account, distinct from the actual values of the coins in circulation, and in 1638 the term 'bank money' appeared, in contrast to 'current money'. The decree of 1659 officially recognized this money of account and formally equated the new *rijksdaalder* with forty-eight former 'heavy' *patards* and the new ducat with sixty of them, i.e. at a premium of 5 per cent above 'current money'. In fact the premium, subject to the law of supply and demand, oscillated thereafter, mainly around 4 per cent, and in the scare that followed the French invasion of 1672, it even changed temporarily into a discount of between 4 and 5 per cent, although it returned to its usual level once the danger was over. The bank's own abuse of credit caused a more serious discount to emerge around 1789.

The business world of the Spanish Netherlands was closely involved with the Dutch financial market, and regularly conducted its financial dealings through the banks of Amsterdam, on which it drew or cashed bills of exchange. Accordingly, the 'bank money' of the United Provinces had its equivalent, *wisselgeld* or 'exchange-money' in the Belgian provinces, and was used in the accounting of large-scale commerce. The Dutch coins were taken at parity in the Spanish Netherlands after 1676, so that the rate became officially identical in the two countries; but with the semi-official devaluation of 1689, *wisselgeld* was related to the earlier parity and it remained in use as a unit of account in business matters. Its relationship with the current coinage of the new type was fixed at twelve old to thirteen new, but this changed in the first years of the War of the Spanish Succession as the French monetary standard was brought in, and it was finally stabilized at six to seven until the end of the old regime.

2 FINANCE

The monetary role of the *wisselbanken* was facilitated by their credit dealings. In 1683 the Amsterdam bank was authorized to accept coins as security from individuals, who would then receive a small interest of between an eighth and a half of 1 per cent, for a sixth-month period. They would be given a receipt in 'bank money', which could be negotiated, and at the term of the transaction, the credit could either be renewed or the coin removed. The bank also accepted ingots after 1763. These facilities helped trade in precious metals which prospered, whereas other sectors of trade suffered from the structural crisis. They may even have delayed the process of economic decline.

They also increased considerably the bank's holdings of metal. In 1683 these amounted to 7,600,000 florins, a sum rarely attained since the bank started. It fell below this figure only in 1709 and 1712, years of war, and kept up, year in, year out, at a much higher level until the war of 1780–4. Its annual average, 11,665,000 florins in the 1690s, rose to 17,200,000 in the 1730s and 18,900,000 in the 1770s. There were peaks of 26,800,000 in 1721 when John Law's 'System' caused French coins to flood into Amsterdam, and 30,835,000 in 1764 when the banks of Amsterdam, damaged by the financial crisis of the previous year, received considerable support from their English colleagues, who had an interest in their survival. Contemporaries, who judged from the Republic's prosperity and the solidity of the Bank of Amsterdam, imagined that its funds were much greater. In 1750 the French economist Melon estimated that it had 400,000,000 florins, which, because of the secrecy involved, could not be challenged. The bank, with its great deposits of coins from everywhere, was a reserve for the monetary circulation of all Europe, and became a regulating force. It could be drawn upon in times of scarcity and when there was an excessive supply of money, coins could be frozen there so that a decline of the exchange rate, and hence a rise in prices, could be forestalled.

The services offered by the bank also brought it clients. The number of account holders depended to some extent on business conditions. Since the opening of the Amsterdam *wisselbank*, the number had risen constantly, to 2,012 in 1661. In the next twenty years it went down slightly, to 1,946 in 1681, but the fall was only temporary, for between 1691 and 1741 the figure was generally above 2,500, with a peak, for reasons explained above, of 2,918 in 1721. Then it fell to around the 2,200 mark until 1771. In 1796 there were 1,543 account holders. During the French invasion of 1672, depositors had rushed to convert their accounts into coin. The panic had soon subsided when men saw that the bank could meet their demands, but the banks of Rotterdam and Middelburg, which were short of ready cash because of the granting of excessive credit, temporarily closed. After 1683 account holders at the Bank of Amsterdam gradually stopped demanding payment in specie, for the expenses involved in paying cash were such that it was easier simply to shift money from one account to another. When John Law left Amsterdam, he did not manage to obtain the balance of his account at the bank in cash.

The *wisselbanken*, especially Amsterdam's, had a not-inconsiderable role in merchant banking as well. The merchant banks' specialization was not always absolute, except in the cases of a few firms dealing in the great centres of Dutch trade; in most of them, there was, rather, an emphasis on one particular activity, and differences between such banks became increasingly blurred as the influence of the great commercial centres declined. The private banks were complementary to the public ones. The 'cashiers' of Amsterdam, for instance – there were fifty-four in 1775 – gave cash in exchange for 'bank money' after the *wisselbank* had practically ceased to convert it into coinage. Moreover, they negotiated bills of exchange at a discount. Dutch international exchange was, however, much more regular than before and, thanks to the role of the *wisselbank*, did not have an equal outside the Republic, for it could draw on vast stocks of specie to transfer coins abroad in case of tension on the exchange markets. This greatly assisted Amsterdam in becoming the chief exchange market of Europe. Almost always bills of exchange used to pay for large transactions, especially those drawn on the Belgian provinces, went through Amsterdam, although Antwerp still had something of a role as a financial centre. If Amsterdam in 1634 had officially registered a rate of exchange with twelve other towns, a century later the figure was twenty-five, and the quotation on Amsterdam was, until 1763, the only one that Russia used.

The private banks, especially in Amsterdam, developed commercial credit with their system of acceptances: they allowed their clients to draw bills of exchange on them, without immediate cover, and guaranteed payment with their signature, in the expectation of cover when the bill fell due. These transactions, the origin of which is not clear, seem to have been widespread early in the eighteenth century, and they grew remarkably thereafter. Bills were accepted without difficulty, for a commission of a third or a half of 1 per cent of their total, from natives and foreigners from countries that still lacked capital but could make profitable use of Dutch cash. This cosmopolitanism worked in some measure against the Dutch market and even foreign trade, particularly as the bankers were not unhappy if traffic went directly between producer and consumer, by-passing the Republic. Some traditionalists felt that this financial activity was not sufficient compensation for the decline of trade.

Acceptances practically ended the use of credit issued on the security of goods, unless debtors of doubtful solvency were involved, or precious metals in the *wisselbanken*. The Amsterdam Lending Bank ceased to advance money in this way after about 1680, its Rotterdam counterpart after 1700. The Middelburg Bank offered substantial, and often unsecured, credit to the Chamber of Zeeland and the West India Company, and was involved in its fall in 1674. Thereafter, the Dutch *banken van leninge* restricted themselves to individual credit. The Belgian provinces' public pawnshops encountered increasing difficulties. Louis XIV's conquests had deprived them of some of their agencies, but had not lessened their financial burdens. After 1720 they had to suspend interest payments on their capital; the government continued to borrow from them, at a better rate than could be obtained on the money market, and in 1730 owed them 2,000,000 florins. Their position improved only after 1752, when the Austrian authorities intervened and stopped using the pawnshops' funds.

The *wisselbanken* confined their commercial credit to the colonial companies. The interest rate in Amsterdam for advances to the local Chamber of the East India Company was 4 per cent in 1665. It declined to $3\frac{1}{2}$ per cent in 1685 and then to $2\frac{1}{2}$ per cent in 1723, where it stayed for many years, never rising again beyond $3\frac{1}{2}$ per cent. The Company's debt remained small until about 1720 and, since at the time the hope was to liquidate it altogether, it was sometimes excluded from the balance sheet, or entered only partially. It rose above a million florins only eleven times before 1711, in which year it reached more than two millions for the first time. Afterwards, as business grew in volume, and as the same care was no longer taken to repay advances quickly, the Company's debt rapidly rose. A first record was reached in 1743, at 7,100,000 florins, paid off in eight years, but thereafter a constant Company debt became the rule. It amounted to 2,600,000 florins on the eve of war in 1780, and two years later stood at 7,650,000 florins, for without colonial goods it could not be repaid. The town of Amsterdam stood guarantor.

The bank's position worsened after the establishment of the *Stadsbeleenkamer* at Amsterdam in 1782, which gave loans on security of goods or bonds to merchants of the city who were in difficulties because of the war, and got a capital of 500,000 florins (increased to two millions in 1785) from the bank. The *Kamer* continued in peacetime, and the bank raised its credit to over 3,500,000 florins in 1790. The India Company was able to borrow from it on top of its debts to the bank, so that, for the first time in its history, the bank's credits were appreciably larger than its capital assets. Its liquid assets, which had always been about 100 per cent before 1780, fell to 40 per cent in 1785 and less than 25 per cent in 1789. This became public knowledge, and confidence in the bank collapsed. Bank money fell below the value of current money.

Since the beginning, the *wisselbanken* had also had a share in public credit. In 1685 the town of Amsterdam owed almost three million florins to the local bank. It decided to reduce this debt by means of the reserve which had accrued as a result of the policy of depositing, rather than spending, the bank's profits; the debt fell to 635,000 florins. Thereafter it remained small, and sometimes even non-existent, never rising above 1,500,000 florins until the difficult years of the Anglo-Dutch War in 1780–4 and the ensuing political troubles, which caused it to rise to 2,360,000 florins. Amsterdam drew from the bank's funds not only the capital for the *Beleenkamer* in 1785, but also its share of a loan to the province of Holland. The debt to the bank was liquidated in 1791, by means of a forced loan, and advances from this source were used only on a small scale thereafter.

The French declaration of war and the invasion of 1795 changed public caution into panic. The holders of accounts withdrew their money in precious metals, and the bank's position became impossible. When the old Republic came to an end, the position of the town itself, its guarantor, was just as difficult, and the extent of the problem was painfully revealed to the public by the authorities of the new Batavian Republic. Not surprisingly, a loan launched in 1796 to refloat the bank was a resounding failure, and its credit was restored only in 1802 when a forced loan refurbished its metal assets to some extent. It led an unimpressive existence thereafter, and was liquidated in 1820. The Rotterdam bank, which had always cut a modest figure by comparison, also extended considerable credit, both to importers of German linen and to the local Chamber of the East India Company. It experienced the same troubles as Amsterdam, and closed its doors in 1812. The Middelburg Bank had been especially bold in its credits, both to the Zeeland Chambers of the two Companies and to individuals, because Zeeland lacked commercial capital. With credits at 2,100,000 florins in 1791, it had only 28,000 florins in liquid assets. The province of Zeeland, the town of Middelburg and the Companies were unable to repay, and the bank collapsed in 1794.

Since the seventeenth century, the United Provinces had been lending increasing sums to other European powers. The first-class international role that the Dutch had played until the end of the War of the Spanish Succession was illustrated by the large subsidies they provided for their poverty-stricken allies, and their armies' military activities. Besides, modern ideas of government, which spread to all backward countries in Europe, created needs for capital that could not be satisfied at home. These foreign loans carried an interest of at least 4 or 5 per cent, always higher than the rates of $2\frac{1}{2}$ or $3\frac{1}{2}$ per cent of public funds in the Republic. Understandably they became the favourite investment of Dutch capitalists, to which the decline of trade and industry in the Republic was not unrelated, since the size and frequency of the loans exceeded the financiers' own resources, however great they might be. Some banking houses made a speciality of issuing loans to the public. The firms of Clifford and Hope, both of British origin, Deutz, Pelz, Fizeaux and Grand, and Neufville and de Smeth were among the best-known names in European high finance, and the luxurious life-style of their directors placed them in the first rank of social and public life of Holland. George Clifford, for example, had a country estate near Haarlem; he kept a zoo, as well as a botanical garden, rich in exotic plants, which was managed by Linnaeus from 1735 to 1738.

The first issue of foreign loans occurred in Amsterdam in 1695, at the instigation of the banker, Jan Deutz. Emperor Leopold borrowed 1,500,000 florins on the security of the mercury mines at Idria, in Slovenia, for which the Deutz house acted as agent. In 1700 other imperial loans were floated, this time on the security of the copper mines in Hungary, but the rebellion of Ferenc Rákóczy (1703–11) interrupted the metal supply that had enabled Deutz to meet the interest. The loans secured on mercury also proved troublesome to the issuing bank, because mercury was imported by the British East India Company and the abundance of it on the European market was such that prices collapsed and Deutz's sales no longer sufficed to meet the interest. The Estates-General forbade foreign loans in 1713 ostensibly because of the risks involved, although in reality they probably did so to make things easier for themselves on the capital market.

The prohibition became a dead letter quite soon. By 1716 Emperor Charles VI was able to launch a new loan, albeit on stringent conditions, in view of the appalling state of Habsburg credit: it was floated at 92 per cent, at 8 per cent interest, a true yield of 8.7 per cent. Thereafter Charles had to pledge the tax revenue of Silesia, and when after 1737 it was no longer enough, that of Bohemia as well. Some of these loans also benefited from guarantees given for political reasons by the Estates-General. In 1700 Bavaria had to pledge the crown jewels to get a loan, and in 1735 Denmark pledged the customs receipts of Bergen in Norway.

However, the states gradually restored their finances, and enough confidence was generated for such pledges no longer to be required. The hereditary lands of Austria henceforth regularly paid interest and amortized the capital on term; their debt to the Dutch amounted to 90,000,000 florins in 1784. Russia under Peter the Great had failed to get loans from Amsterdam, but she obtained her first loan there in 1769 and thirty years later owed 88,000,000 florins. Many German princes turned to the Dutch money market, and after 1775 French ministers also approached it to get money to effect the reforms for which their own country could not supply loans at a reasonable price. They also used Amsterdam to support their American allies in the War of Independence. By 1782 the future President, John Adams, who was then plenipotentiary of Congress in the United Provinces, acquired the first American loan in Amsterdam, and by 1796 the total American foreign debt ($12,000,000) had been issued in Holland. When the Batavian Republic became linked with revolutionary France, however, the capital market began to dry up.

That of the Belgian provinces was much smaller in scale, but it also grew and modernized in the eighteenth century. The policy of public works, for instance, led the Brussels government and the provincial administrations to issue forced loans through bankers of Antwerp and Brussels, where the local authorities' money requirements contributed to the development of the financial market. A total of 111,000,000 florins was lent in this way in the last forty years of the Austrian regime. The bank of Viscountess de Nettine in Brussels, the government's treasurer, played an important part in this, subscribers being particularly attracted by lottery bonds. By the end of this period the Belgian market was taking its first share in international financial activity, and the Antwerp banker, de Wolf, issued a loan on behalf of Catherine the Great in 1788.

The loans of the Austrian Netherlands were not large enough to absorb all of the local capital available. Their subjects subscribed to many loans for the hereditary Habsburg lands, issued through the Bank of Vienna, and they became in the end the chief investment of Belgian *rentiers*. In the eighteenth century investment became highly cosmopolitan. Flemish and Brabantine capitalists participated in loans issued in Amsterdam, Hamburg and Paris, although French loans suffered from the disorder of the royal finances and even their capital was reduced several times after mid-century. A large number of Dutch subscribers invested in British state bonds in London, where the rate was higher than in Amsterdam. Moreover, the guarantees given by Parliament from 1692 onwards concerning the National Debt made it seem exceptionally safe. By 1737 Dutch capital on loan to England was estimated at £10,000,000, and the Walpole administration did not dare convert the Debt for fear that any reduction in interest rates would make the Dutch lenders sell their bonds and take their money home, which would have caused a collapse of the financial and currency markets.

Dutch investment in British funds reached its peak between 1740 and 1780. Frequent wars made immense demands on the

British government, and exhausted native resources, and at the same time investors were less attracted to the Republic. In 1776 Lord North believed that the Dutch accounted for 43 per cent of the National Debt, or £59,000,000. The Prussian minister at The Hague thought in 1782 that the figure was 25 per cent, or 400,000,000 florins. British defeats in the war against the American rebels caused some anxiety in the Republic, however, and Holland's entry into the war in 1780 cooled the Dutch public's interest in Consols still further. On occasion the Dutch would subscribe to other state loans issued abroad, but such investment remained modest in comparison with those in British funds. They did not recover their former levels when peace returned.

There were other tempting investments at this time. Since early days company shares had been a popular investment in the Low Countries, and this was especially true from the later seventeenth century onwards. There was no great distinction made between foreign and national companies. For instance, the capital of the Ostend Company was subscribed within two days in 1723 on the Antwerp Exchange; Antwerp capital had a large share in the St Ferdinand Company which was constituted at Seville in 1749 to trade with the Spanish colonies in America, and also in the Prussian companies that were set up at Emden in 1750 to trade with China, and in 1753 to trade with Bengal. It also took an interest, sometimes through Dutch bankers, in shares or loans to the Danish, Swedish, Dutch and English colonial companies, and to the Bank of England. The bourgeoisie of Antwerp figured among the subscribers of the ill-fated Asiatic Company of Trieste in 1781, together with some of the greatest names of the Austrian and Belgian aristocracy, including the Chancellor, Kaunitz, and Joseph II himself.

Dutch interest in private business abroad, especially in England, was no less than in public funds. When the Bank of England was founded in 1694, out of almost 1,300 shareholders, it had only twenty whose names were unmistakably Dutch, but by 1726 the registers of shareholders contain over two hundred surnames beginning with 'van'. The Dutch public shared in the frenzied speculation in the English South Sea Company, a single Amsterdam notary registering, between January and August 1720, over two hundred transactions in its securities. In 1772 Dutch interest in the English East India Company was estimated at 40,000,000

310 / Part Four: Towards a New Equilibrium

florins. Throughout the eighteenth century Dutch money was also lent on mortgage to England and helped the English economy to advance. This caused a certain amount of resentment in the Republic, especially because the income from the money was reinvested in England, to the considerable profit of her economy. Much of this investment was placed through brokers in London who had continual links with the United Provinces, from where bankers sent the capital. Some of the brokers were of Dutch origin and became integrated into wealthy English mercantile circles or even, in the case of the van Necks of Rotterdam, who were the chief figures of the Dutch colony, into the British aristocracy. Others, who descended from Huguenots or Sephardic Jews, worked essentially for their co-religionists in Holland.

Dutch capitalists also played a remarkable role in financing the economy of the colonies. During the sugar and coffee booms, planters from Dutch Guiana and other colonies in the West Indies borrowed to increase their plantations. They turned first to individuals and then to the Deutz Bank, which issued the first loan in 1752, secured by plantations in Surinam. There were later loans, and by 1775 it was estimated that this colony alone accounted for 50,000,000 or 60,000,000 florins' worth of loans. But the excessive credit caused over-production and falls in price, which ruined many planters and inflicted heavy losses on investors. After 1780, even before American independence was secure, the American dream raised high hopes in the United Provinces. Their commercial expectations were not fulfilled, and vast investment went instead into the construction of canals and speculation in land, encouraged by the settlement of the virgin lands of the West. Investment in America, whether in public funds or private companies, appears to have reached 34,000,000 florins in 1794.

Although the Republic had lost its lead in world trade, it none the less remained the chief financial power in the world. In 1782 van de Spiegel, Pensionary of Holland, was certainly underestimating when he recorded that Dutch investments abroad amounted to 475,000,000 florins, 280,000,000 of which were in England and 140,000,000 in the colonies. A more accurate figure of 1,500,000,000 has been suggested. These investments brought increasing returns, and a French diplomatic agent wrote in 1799 that, before the Batavian Revolution, the Republic annually received from abroad between 50,000,000 and 60,000,000 florins. The share of landed property and Dutch securities in the great fortunes of more than 90,000 florins (which were liable to estate duty in Amsterdam) declined from 80.2 per cent in 1740 to 60.4 per cent in 1780; the proportion of British securities rose in the same period from 17.7 per cent to 27.1, and of other investment abroad from 2.1 per cent to 12.5 per cent.

The Amsterdam Exchange was thus not a financial centre for the United Provinces alone; other European exchanges acted to a large extent as branches of it. Until about 1670 the value of only the shares of the two Dutch India Companies had been quoted daily, apart from quotations of commodities. The loans floated in 1672 to meet the wartime expenditure caused by the French invasion were the first public funds to be quoted. In the later seventeenth century the public debt of the Estates-General, provinces and towns of the United Provinces were joined first by British public funds and the shares of large companies, and then by less celebrated enterprises (excepting the short-lived bursts of speculation, for instance Law's 'System' or the South Sea Bubble). In 1750 there were daily quotations for twenty-five Dutch public funds, the securities of three Dutch and three English companies and thirteen foreign loans. In 1796 the quotations included only public funds, ninety-six in all, of which fifty-seven were Dutch. The colonial companies established in the Republic had recently been wound up, while the Revolutionary government had repudiated the debt of the French monarchy, and the Batavian Republic was at war with England. It was obvious, now, that fixed-interest stocks, in terms of volume, had taken a lead over company shares.

However, it appears that most of the transactions on the Exchange involved companies. The clients of the Exchange consisted to a large extent of speculators who were not much attracted to public funds, with their relatively stable rates. Speculators were involved in futures of certain commodities, and also, from the moment of the East India Company's constitution, in its shares: the vast operation undertaken by Isaac Le Maire in 1609 to undermine their value was probably the first such operation in financial history. It caused the first ban on dealings in futures of commodities or securities, a ban frequently repeated and never successfully enforced. As the shares of the new West India Company of

1674 were never quoted in futures, unlike those of its predecessor, the shares of the great English companies became, like those of the Dutch East India Company, a favourite object of speculation in the eighteenth century, and this occasionally happened with other securities as well.

The exchange techniques of Amsterdam are known to us chiefly through descriptions left by Joseph de la Vega (*Confusión de Confusiones*, 1688) and Isaac Pinto (*Jeu d'actions en Hollande* which was written in 1761–3 and published in 1771). The custom, at first irregular, of settling accounts in futures deals monthly, on a special day of *rescontre*, became general between 1650 and 1680. By Pinto's time, the *rescontre* fell quarterly. Any profit, the result of a rise in prices in the interim, would then be cashed in, or a loss, caused by a drop in prices, paid for, unless there were a request for settlement to be postponed until the next *rescontre* in exchange for a bond made out to the vendor, the rates of which varied according to the market. Unless catastrophic events caused extraordinary variations in the quotations, speculators were thus able to negotiate large sales or purchases with no more than a small fraction of the capital involved. So many people were involved in exchange transactions that the area reserved for dealings in securities was no longer adequate and business had to be transacted in nearby cafés. By 1612 Amsterdam had three hundred brokers, with six hundred employees. Sephardic Jews, at first few in number, rose in this profession after 1650 and increasingly dominated it in the eighteenth century by virtue of their links with their fellow Jews in other countries.

The excesses of speculation in 1720, both in Paris and London, spread to the United Provinces and not only affected the shares of the Mississippi Company, the South Sea Company and others earlier quoted at Amsterdam, but also created many new companies, the product, all too often, of fantasy. The lure of easy profit tempted all classes of society, even the artisans, who abandoned their workshops to become shareholders. The writer, Isaac Pinto, a qualified observer, estimated the total of such issues at 1,100,000,000 florins. After only a few months the collapse of shares in the South Sea Company in London immediately affected Amsterdam, caused in turn the collapse of almost all of the new companies and on all sides provoked ruin and mistrust. Finance did not recover until after 1725.

A new stock exchange crisis in 1763 was provoked by the inflation of bank credit. To satisfy the financial needs of their governments during the Seven Years War, the bankers of the states at war, especially those in Germany and Sweden, had recourse to the credit of their colleagues at Amsterdam, who extended it without restriction by discounting bills of exchange. When the war came to an end, they could only be nominally covered by new drafts on third parties, who paid in the same way, for the debtor countries lacked specie and their balance of trade, normally favourable as regards the Republic, had been adversely affected by their military expenditure and the decline of their productivity during the war. Finally the drop in prices when peace was restored made many businesses vulnerable. In July the Neufville Bank and one other, which had been particularly imprudent in its handling of bills of exchange, went bankrupt. Although there was support from London houses interested in the retention of Dutch credit in England, more than thirty banking and merchant houses were dragged down. The storm passed quickly enough; trade recovered by the end of the year, and the exchange market the following year. None the less, Amsterdam had lost its absolute dominion over Russian affairs because of this, and it was on this occasion that Russia instituted relations with other financial markets. The stock exchange recovered after 1765.

The recovery did not last. The rise of shares in the English East India Company, which had become the unchallenged mistress of its colonial domain since the Treaty of Paris in 1763, had raised the quotation, both in London and in Amsterdam. This time the rise turned out to reflect false hopes: the fall of colonial prices put trade into depression and the planters of Surinam, suffering also from a revolt among their slaves, could not pay the interest on their loans. Six months after London had experienced a series of bankruptcies, the Clifford Bank, one of the most respected in Amsterdam, went the same way at Christmas 1772, with debts of five million florins. Many others followed, although help was once again offered by London and Hamburg, and although the municipal authorities set up a temporary support fund. Recovery was slower than in 1763, and began only in 1774. The absence of a clear division between banking and trade, and the lack of proper deposit banks and a discounting institution now turned out to be disastrous, for the Amsterdam financial market could not resist squalls in the new conditions of commerce. Its isolation in the Revolutionary period finally confirmed London's lead, for that city was better equipped, and acquired unchallenged priority in European and world finance in the nineteenth century.

Speculation shared its hazards with insurance. The insurance of commodities, its oldest function, tended in the eighteenth century to develop its own form of enterprise, in which merchant houses, abandoning their earlier practice of underwriting policies ad hoc, now did so permanently. The risks inherent in such operations made it desirable for them to establish limited companies. An insurance company established in Rotterdam in 1720 was one of the only companies to survive the collapse of speculation in that year; the 'Imperial and Royal Insurance Chamber' set up in Antwerp in 1754 with a capital of two million florins (a quarter of which was paid up), did between seven and eight million florins' worth of business annually and even, with increased premiums, 15,000,000 florins' worth during the Seven Years War and 18,000,000 florins' worth in the American War of Independence.

Other insurance companies were founded in Amsterdam in 1771 and 1772, and in 1782, during the trading boom at Ostend, an Insurance Company for Austrian Flanders was established there. Even before the constitution of limited companies, Amsterdam assumed a European role in the field of shipping insurance during the eighteenth century, in particular because of low premiums, which in turn were a reflection of the abundance of capital in the town and the practice of reinsurance, which dates, apparently, from the second half of the seventeenth century. There was even insurance against risks in wartime; the premium for an unconvoyed voyage between Holland and the Levant rose to 25 per cent during the War of the Spanish Succession. However, Amsterdam's position as the centre of European insurance was challenged, after the middle of the eighteenth century, by Hamburg and especially by London, which began at this time to assume an international role in this field as well.

In the interim the principle of insurance had been extended. In 1663 oil boilers in the Zaan concluded the first known contract for mutual insurance to cover their tools and production against fire-risk; in the eighteenth century, damage to property was specifically included in policies. Thereafter fire insurance for private dwellings was regularly underwritten. The Rotterdam Insurance Company issued such policies, on a somewhat modest scale, and another company was established in Amsterdam. Insurance against fire was only fully developed at the end of the eighteenth century, together with life insurance, which had been no more than an occasional phenomenon since 1700. The entry of the Batavian Republic into the orbit of France had slowed down trade, and consequently transport insurance. New areas for investment emerged which employed capital that business conditions would otherwise have left idle – capital that the Dutch people had inherited from a period of economic domination in the world that had now vanished for ever.

Conclusion

As we conclude this account of a thousand years of economic and social history, some effort should perhaps be made to summarize and assess the contribution of the Low Countries to the development of European civilization.

From the beginning the Low Countries had been one of the main centres of population growth on the Continent. They were thus among the first territories to experience a revival of town life – which had been almost extinct in the early centuries of the Middle Ages – and, soon thereafter an exceptional degree of urbanization. Overall their population increased enormously, although the increase was interrupted, as it was everywhere in Europe, by the depression of the later Middle Ages, and then, in the Belgian provinces in the sixteenth century, by the calamities of the religious wars. The massive emigration caused by these was greatly to the advantage of the host countries, especially the Dutch provinces. The growth in population was interrupted once more, again as happened elsewhere in Europe, during the second half of the seventeenth century. It recovered in the eighteenth century in modern Belgium, but the United Provinces did not begin to advance before the end of the *ancien régime*.

The powerful demographic pressure in the Low Countries was responsible in many ways for economic progress. As far as agriculture was concerned, the need to obtain subsistence for a rural population that was expanding considerably at the height of the Middle Ages encouraged the extensive clearance of land. The creation of polders, through the drainage of the coastal areas of the Low Countries, had its counterpart in land clearances in other regions of the country. Moreover, considerable peasant emigration from the Low Countries was important to the colonization of eastern Europe and its integration into the community of European civilization. At the same time, the most developed regions of the Low Countries sought to increase their yields by applying more advanced agricultural techniques. They provided these regions with the highest yields in Europe, and the Low Countries thus became the cradle of the agricultural revolution of the modern era. The techniques were borrowed by England and then transmitted by her to agronomists on the Continent.

The Low Countries were able to assume this role because of the early emancipation of their rural society from the manorial system, brought about by the migration of peasants in the Middle Ages towards both new countries and the reviving towns. The towns' development manifested itself in outstanding industrial and commercial growth. The Low Countries were Europe's chief manufacturer of textiles until the seventeenth century. In the Middle Ages cloth from Flanders and Brabant dominated the market; in the seventeenth century Leyden took the lead. From the sixteenth century onwards the linens of Flanders were renowned for their quality. With their exports of silks and other luxury textiles, the Low Countries also disseminated the sumptuous tastes popularized by the Renaissance. The people of the Walloon regions, the main centre for brass making in the Middle Ages, were probably the initiators of new methods that gave a decisive stimulus to iron working, and they shared with England the role of pioneers in coal mining. This aggressive development of the export industries soon established a capitalist system in the Low Countries which extended further and further.

Industrial development was indeed, from early times, the basis for brisk foreign and domestic trade. In the areas bordering on the Atlantic and the northern seas, the Low Countries were able to promote the rise of a commercial economy, and from the thirteenth century on, the chief markets for pan-European trade – Bruges, Antwerp and Amsterdam – grew up there. The rise of Amsterdam in particular was foreshadowed by the maritime enterprise displayed by the Hollanders who, by the end of the Middle Ages, dominated Baltic shipping. The requirements of this trade soon led them to other shores. As the refugees from the Belgian provinces had given new life to the export industries, so the arrival of merchants from Antwerp opened up new areas to Dutch trade and forged its links with the Mediterranean and the colonial world. After the Golden Age in the seventeenth century, competition from other countries, especially England, gradually reduced the world market of Amsterdam, the final collapse of which was caused by the troubles that preceded the end of the *ancien régime*.

Large-scale international trade had early on fostered the growth of a money market. Bruges, Antwerp and Amsterdam successively became the great centres for public and commercial credit, and learnt from Italy the most sophisticated techniques in finance then known. Amsterdam became a capital market of such importance that the wealthy classes of the Dutch Republic, disappointed at the decline of its trade and industry, damaged these further by investing increasingly in funds. The Belgian provinces, on the other hand, experienced an emergent mercantilism in the eighteenth century which caused a revival vigorous enough to reduce the gap between them and their prosperous northern neighbours that had grown since their separation in the sixteenth century. The Belgian provinces were preparing to become, in the nineteenth century, the cradle of the Industrial Revolution on the Continent.

Glossary of Political Events

768–814: Reign of Charlemagne.

810–1006: Norman invasions.

843: Partition of the Carolingian Empire; the territory west of the Scheldt, soon to be known as Flanders and Artois, under western Frankish (later French) suzerainty; Lotharingia, east of the Scheldt, becomes part of Germany after 880.

End of ninth century; tenth century: Formation of feudal principalities – west of the Scheldt, Artois and Flanders; east of the Scheldt, Lotharingia split up into Brabant, Hainault, Namur, Luxembourg, Limburg, Guelders, Utrecht, Holland, Zeeland.

Fifteenth and sixteenth centuries: Most of the feudal principalities united under the House of Burgundy, succeeded after its extinction (1482) by the Habsburgs: Flanders (1384), Namur (1421), Hainault, Holland, Zeeland (1428), Brabant and Limburg (1430), Luxembourg (1443), Friesland (1524), Utrecht and Overijssel (1528), Groningen and Drenthe (1536), Guelders (1543). Only Liège remains independent.

1555: Abdication of Charles v; the Low Countries under the kings of Spain.

1568–1648: Eighty Years War: Declaration of Independence of the United Provinces (1581); Twelve Years' Truce (1609–21).

1578–85: Spanish reconquest of the Belgian provinces, the 'Spanish Netherlands', roughly south of the present Dutch–Belgian border.

1598–1621: Belgian provinces granted independence from Spain under Archduke Albert and Archduchess Isabella; after Albert's death, a return to Spanish rule.

1602: Foundation of the Dutch East India Company: conquers territories in Indonesia and elsewhere in Asia and in Africa (until 1798).

1621: Foundation of the (first) West India Company: territorial conquests in America and Africa (until 1791).

1648: Treaty of Westphalia; the independence of the United Provinces recognized; the *de facto* 'closure' of the Scheldt henceforth enforced by treaty.

1652–4, 1665–7, 1672–4: United Provinces at war with England.

1659–97: Franco–Spanish wars result in loss of some of the Spanish Netherlands and formation of the present frontier between France and Belgium.

1701–13: War of the Spanish Succession: Peace of Utrecht (1713); the Spanish Netherlands transferred to the Austrian Habsburgs.

1780–4: Fourth Anglo–Dutch War.

1787: Patriot movement in the Dutch Republic.

1789–90: Austrian Netherlands independent after the Brabantine revolution.

1790: First Austrian Restoration in the Austrian Netherlands.

1792–3: First invasion of the Austrian Netherlands by the French.

1793–4: Second Austrian Restoration in the Austrian Netherlands.

1794: Second French invasion in the Austrian Netherlands; annexation to France until 1814.

1795: Fall of the old Dutch Republic; Batavian Republic set up (until 1806); the Kingdom of Holland 1806–10; annexation to France 1810–13.

Map 1. The Netherlands. In both maps the modern coastline is given and no attempt has been made to indicate the relative size of the towns, due to the many changes in both the coastal shape and the size of the towns over the period 800-1800.

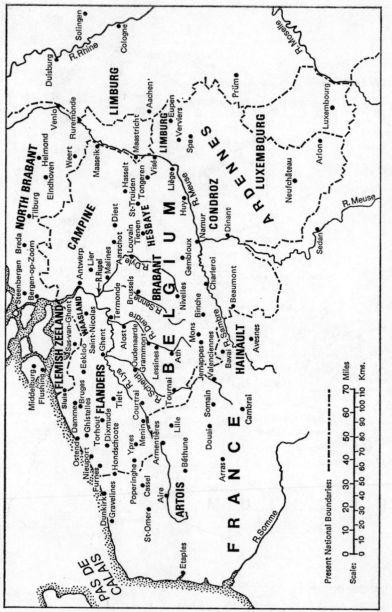

Map 2. Belgium, Luxembourg and northern France.

Select Bibliography

Treatises on the general history of the Low Countries, or of their present components, the Netherlands, Belgium and Luxembourg, devote some attention to economic and social subjects, particularly:

P. J. Blok, *Geschiedenis van het Nederlandsche volk*, 4 vols (3rd edn, 1923–7).

H. Pirenne, *Histoire de Belgique*, 7 vols (1900–32). Dutch translation: *Geschiedenis van België*, 4 vols (1954–6).

J. A. van Houtte, J. F. Niermeyer, J. Presser, J. Romein, H. van Werveke (eds.), *Algemene Geschiedenis der Nederlanden*, 12 vols (1949–58).

P. Weber, *Histoire du grand-duché de Luxembourg* (1949).

They can be supplemented by bibliographies, for example: H. de Buck, *Bibliografie der geschiedenis van Nederland* (1968). H. Pirenne, *Bibliographie de l'histoire de Belgique* (3rd edn, 1931).

New publications are reviewed or listed regularly in the periodicals *Bijdragen voor de Geschiedenis der Nederlanden* (until 1969), *Bijdragen en Mededelingen betreffende de Geschiedenis der Nederlanden* (from 1969 on), *Economic History Review* (since 1956), *Revue belge de philologie et d'histoire*, and *Revue du Nord*.

All books and articles on economic and social history subjects quoted below have bibliographical lists or footnote references.

I. GENERAL ECONOMIC AND SOCIAL HISTORY

W. J. Alberts and H. P. H. Jansen, *Welvaart in wording. Sociaal-economische geschiedenis van Nederland van de vroegste tijden tot het einde der middeleeuwen* (1964).

J. L. Broeckx, C. de Clercq, J. Dhondt, M. Nauwelaerts (eds.),

324 / *Select Bibliography*

Flandria Nostra. Ons land en ons volk, zijn standen en zijn beroepen door de tijden heen, I (1957).

J. A. Faber, 'Drie eeuwen Friesland. Economische en sociale ontwikkelingen van 1500 tot 1800' (thesis, Utrecht, 1972); also in: *A.A.G. Bijdragen*, 17 (1972), 2 vols.

H. Hasquin, *Une mutation: le Pays de Charleroi aux XVIIe et XVIIIe siècles. Aux origines de la révolution industrielle en Belgique* (1971).

T. S. Jansma, *Het vraagstuk van Hollands welvaren tijdens hertog Philips van Bourgondië* (1950).

N. W. Posthumus, *Inquiry into the Prices in Holland*, 2 vols (1946–64).

B. H. Slicher van Bath, 'Economic and Social Conditions in the Frisian Districts from 900 to 1500', *A.A.G. Bijdragen*, 13 (1965), 97–133.

B. H. Slicher van Bath, *Een samenleving onder spanning. Geschiedenis van het platteland van Overijssel* (1957).

A. M. van der Woude, 'Het Noorderkwartier. Een regionaal historisch onderzoek in de demografische en economische geschiedenis van westelijk Nederland van de late middeleeuwen tot het begin van de negentiende eeuw' (thesis, Utrecht, 1972); also in *A.A.G. Bijdragen*, 16 (1972), 3 vols.

J. G. van Dillen, *Van rijkdom en regenten. Handboek tot de economische en sociale geschiedenis van Nederland tijdens de Republiek* (1970).

H. van Houtte, *Histoire économique de la Belgique à la fin de l'Ancien Régime* (1920).

J. A. van Houtte, *Economische en sociale geschiedenis van de Nederlanden* (1964).

J. A. van Houtte, 'Onze zeventiende eeuw, ongelukseeuw?' (1953), reprinted in his *Essays on Medieval and Early Modern Economy and Society* (1977), pp. 109–42.

R. van Uytven, 'La Flandre et le Brabant, "terres de promission" sous les ducs de Bourgogne?', *Revue du Nord*, 43 (1961), 281–318.

R. van Uytven, 'Politiek en economie: de crisis der late XVe eeuw in de Nederlanden', *Revue belge de philologie et d'histoire*, 53 (1975), 1097–1149.

R. van Uytven, 'Sociaal-economische evoluties in de Nederlanden voor de Revoluties', *Bijdragen en Mededelingen betreffende de Geschiedenis der Nederlanden*, 87 (1972), 60–93.

H. van Werveke, 'Beschouwingen over het economisch leven in de Zuidelijke Nederlanden tijdens de XVIIe en de XVIIIe eeuw', *Bijdragen en Mededelingen van het Historisch Genootschap*, 61 (1940), lxxxii–c.

C. Verlinden (ed.), *Documents pour l'histoire des prix et des salaires en Flandre et en Brabant*, 4 vols (1959–73).

P. Weber, *Histoire de l'économie luxembourgeoise* (1950).

2. POPULATION

M. A. Arnould, *Les dénombrements de foyers dans le comté de Hainaut, XIVe–XVIe siècles* (1956).

W. Brulez, 'De diaspora der Antwerpse kooplui op het einde van de 16e eeuw', *Bijdragen voor de Geschiedenis der Nederlanden*, 15 (1960), 279–306.

A. Cosemans, *De bevolking van Brabant in de XVIIe en XVIIIe eeuw* (1939).

J. Cuvelier, *Les dénombrements de foyers en Brabant, XIVe–XVIe siècles* (1912).

J. de Brouwer, *Demografische evolutie in het Land van Aalst, 1570–1800* (1968).

J. A. Faber, H. K. Roessingh, B. H. Slicher van Bath, A. M. van der Woude, H. J. Van Xanten, 'Population Changes and Economic Developments in the Netherlands: a Historical Survey', *A.A.G. Bijdragen*, 12 (1965), 47–110.

M. Hélin, *La démograbie de Lièhe au XVIIe et XVIIIe siècle* (1963).

A. M. van der Woude, 'De omvang en samenstelling van de huishouding in Nederland in het verleden', *A.A.G. Bijdragen*, 15 (1970), 202–41.

H. van Werveke, *De curve van het Gentse bevolkingscijfer in de 17de en 18de eeuw* (1948).

H. van Werveke, *Demografische problemen in de Zuidelijke Nederlanden, 17e en 18e eeuw* (1955).

J. Verbeemen, 'De werking van economische factoren op de stedelijke demografie der XVIIe en XVIIIe eeuw in de Zuidelijke Nederlanden', *Revue belge de philologie et d'histoire*, 34 (1956), 680–700, 1021–55.

3. AGRICULTURE AND AGRARIAN SOCIETY

H. Blink, *Geschiedenis van den boerenstand en van den landbouw in Nederland*, 2 vols (1902–4).

J. de Vries, *The Dutch Rural Economy in the Golden Age, 1500–1700* (1974).

F. L. Ganshof and A. Verhulst, 'Medieval Agrarian Society in its Prime: France, the Low Countries and Western Germany', *The Cambridge Economic History of Europe*, I (2nd edn, 1966), 291–339.

L. Genicot, *La crise agricole du bas moyen âge dans le Namurois* (1970).

L. Genicot, *L'économie rurale namuroise au bas moyen âge*, 2 vols (1943–60).

M. K. E. Gottschalk, *Storm Surges and Riverfloods in the Netherlands*, 2 vols (1971–5).

Landbouwgeschiedenis (1960).

P. Lindemans, *Geschiedenis van de landbouw in België*, 2 vols (1952).

J. A. Mertens and A. E. Verhulst, 'Yield Ratios in Flanders in the

Fourteenth Century', *Economic History Review*, 2nd Ser. 19 (1966), 175–82.

W. J. Sangers, *De ontwikkeling van de Nederlandse tuinbouw tot het jaar 1930* (1952).

B. H. Slicher van Bath, 'The Rise of Intensive Husbandry in the Low Countries', in J. S. Bromley and E. H. Kossmann (eds.), *Britain and the Netherlands* (1960), 130–53.

A. E. Verhulst, *Het landschap in Vlaanderen in historisch perspectief* (1966); French translation: *Histoire du paysage rural en Flandre* (1966).

4. FISHERIES.

C. de Jong, 'Geschiedenis van de oude Nederlandse walvisvaart, I' (thesis, Tilburg, 1972).

N. Gottschalk, 'Fischereigewerbe und Fischhandel der niederländischen Gebiete im Mittelalter' (thesis, Cologne, 1927).

H. A. H. Kranenburg, 'De zeevisscherij van Holland in den tijd der Republiek' (thesis, Rotterdam, 1946).

5. INDUSTRY AND TOWN LIFE

P. Bonenfant, 'Hôpitaux et bienfaisance publique dans les anciens Pays-Bas des origines à la fin du XVIIIe siècle', *Annales de la Société belge d'histoire des hôpitaux*, 3 (1965).

P. Bonenfant, *Le problème du paupérisme en Belgique à la fin de l'Ancien Régime* (1934).

F. Breedvelt-van Veen, 'Louis de Geer, 1557–1652' (thesis, Utrecht, 1935).

E. Coornaert, 'Draperies rurales, draperies urbaines. L'évolution de l'industrie flamande au moyen âge et au XVIe siècle', *Revue belge de philologie et d'histoire*, 28 (1950), 59–96.

E. Coornaert, *Un centre industriel d'autrefois. La draperie-sayetterie d'Hondschoote, XIVe–XVIIIe siècle* (1930).

J. Craeybeckx, 'Les industries d'exportation dans les villes flamandes, particulièrement à Gand et à Bruges', in *Studi in onore di A. Fanfani*, IV (1962), 413–68.

C. H. de Jong, *Oud-Nederlandse majolica en Delftsch aardewerk, een ontwikkelingsgeschiedenis van omstreeks 1550–1800* (1947).

G. de Poerck, *La draperie médiévale en Flandre et en Artois. Techniwue et terminologie*, 3 vols (1951).

P. J. Dobbelaar, 'De branderijen van Holland tot het begin der 19e eeuw' (thesis, Utrecht, 1930).

J. E. Elias, *Geschiedenis van het Amsterdamse regentenpatriciaat*, 2 vols (1923).

G. Espinas, *La draperie dans la Flandre française au moyen âge*, 2 vols (1923).

F. L. Ganshof, *Over stadsontwikkeling tussen Rijn en Loire gedurende de Middeleeuwen* (1941); French translation: *Etude sur le développement des villes entre Loire et Rhin an moyen âge* (1943).

A. Gillard, *L'industrie du fer dans les localités du comté de Namur et de l'Entre-Sambre-et-Meuse de 1345 à 1600* (1971).

J. Hollestelle, *De steenbakkerij in de Nederlanden tot omstreeks 1560* (1961).

P. Lebrun, *L'industrie de la laine à Verviers pendant le XVIIIe et le début du XIXe siècle. Contribution à l'étude des origines de la Révolution Industrielle* (1948).

P. Moureaux, *Les préoccupations statistiques du gouvernement des Pays-Bas Autrichiens et le dénombrement des industries dressé en 1764* (1971).

H. Pirenne, 'Les anciennes démocraties des Pays-Bas' (1910); reprinted in his *Les villes et les institutions urbaines* (5th edn, 1939), I, 143–301.

N. W. Posthumus, *De geschiedenis van de Leidsche lakenindustrie*, 3 vols (1908–39).

J. J. Reesse, *De suikerhandel van Amsterdam van het begin van de 17e eeuw tot 1813*, I (1908).

S. C. Regtdoorzee Greup-Roldanus, 'Geschiedenis der Haarlemmer bleekerijen' (thesis, Amsterdam, 1936).

E. Sabbe, *De Belgische vlasnijverheid*, 2 vols (1943–75).

E. Sabbe, *Histoire de l'industrie linière en Belgique* (1948).

E. Scholliers, *Loonarbeid en honger in de XVe en XVIe eeuw te Antwerpen* (1960).

Z. W. Sneller, 'De opkomst der Nederlandsche katoenindustrie', *Bijdragen voor vaderlandsche geschiedenis en oudheidkunde*, 6th Ser., 4 (1926), 237–74, and 5 (1927), 101–13.

Z. W. Sneller, 'De opkomst van de plattelandsnijverheid in Nederland in de 17e en 18e eeuw', *De Economist*, 78 (1928), 691–702 (reprinted in *Economisch-Historische Herdrukken. Zeventien studiën van Nederlanders* (1964), 117–27; French translation: *La naissance de l'industrie rurale dans les Pays-Bas aux XVIIe et XVIIIe siècles*, in *Annales d' histoire économique et sociale*, I (1929), 193–202).

A. K. L. Thijs, *De zijdenijverheid te Antwerpen in de zeventiende eeuw* (1969).

A. van Braam, *Bloei en verval van het economisch en sociaal leven aan de Zaan* (1944).

J. A. van Houtte, 'Gesellschaftliche Schichten in den Städten der Niederlande', *Untersuchungen zur gesellschaftlichen Struktur der mittelalterlichen Städte in Europa* (1966), 259–76; reprinted in his *Essays*, pp. 227–48.

J. A. van Houtte, 'Die Städte der Niederlande im Uebergang vom Mittelalter zur Neuzeit', *Rheinische Vierteljahrsblätter*, 27 (1962), 50–68; reprinted in his *Essays*, pp. 203–26.

J. C. van Loenen, 'De Haarlemse brouwindustrie voor 1600' (thesis, Amsterdam, 1950).

L. van Nierop, 'De zijdenijverheid van Amsterdam historisch geschetst', *Tijdschrift voor Geschiedenis*, 45 (1930), 18–40 and 151–72, and 46 (1931), 28–55 and 113–43.

R. van Uytven, 'De Leuvense bierindustrie in de XVIIIe eeuw', *Bijdragen voor de geschiedenis der Nederlanden*, 16 (1961), 193–227.

R. van Uytven, 'De sociale krisis der XVIe eeuw te Leuven', *Revue belge de philologie et d'histoire*, 36 (1958), 356–87.

M. A. Verkade, 'De opkomst van de Zaanstreek' (thesis, Groningen, 1952).

C. Wyffels, *De oorsprong der ambachten in Vlaanderen* (1951).

J. Yernaux, *La métallurgie liégeoise et son expansion au XVIIe siècle* (1939).

6. TRADE AND TRANSPORT

H. Ammann, 'Die Anfänge des Aktivhandels und der Tucheinfuhr Nordwesteuropas nach dem Mittelmeergebiet', in *Studi in onore di A. Sapori* (1957), I, 275–310.

R. Bijlsma, *Rotterdams welvaren, 1550–1650* (1918).

C. R. Boxer, *The Dutch Seaborne Empire, 1600–1800* (1965).

H. Brugmans, *Opkomst en bloei van Amsterdam* (2nd edn, 1944).

W. Brulez, 'Anvers de 1585 à 1650', *Vierteljahrschrift für Sozial- und Wirtschaftsgeschichte*, 52 (1967), 75–99.

J. Craeybeckx, *Un grand commerce d'importation: les vins de France aux anciens Pays-Bas, XIIIe–XVIe siècle* (1958).

D. W. Davies, *A Primer of Dutch Seventeenth Century Overseas Trade* (1961).

R. Doehaerd, *L'expansion économique belge au moyen âge* (1946).

C. Douxchamps-Lefevre, 'Le commerce du charbon dans les Pays-Bas Autrichiens à la fin du XVIIIe siècle', *Revue belge de philologie et d'histoire*, 46 (1968), 393–421.

J. Everaert, *De internationale en koloniale handel der Vlaamse firma's te Cadiz, 1670–1700* (1973).

L. Genicot, 'Etudes sur la construction des routes en Belgique', in: *Université Catholique de Louvain, Bulletin de l'Institut de Recherches Economiques,* 10 (1938–9), 421–51, 12 (1946), 495–559, and 13 (1947), 477–505.

K. Glamann, *Dutch–Asiatic Trade, 1620–1740* (1958).

R. Häpke, *Brügges Entwicklung zum mittelaltedichen Weltmarkt* (1908).

J. Hovy, 'Het voorstel van 1751 tot instelling van een beperkt vrijhavenstelsel in de Republiek' (thesis, Utrecht, 1966).

T. S. Jansma, 'De beteekenis van Dordrecht en Rotterdam omstreeks het midden der zestiende eeuw', *De Economist*, 93 (1943), 212–50.

F. Ketner, *Handel en scheepvaart van Amsterdam in de vijftiende eeuw* (1946).

N. Laude, *La Compagnie d'Ostende et son activité commerciale au Bengale*, *1725–1730* (1944).

M. A. P. Meilink-Roelofsz, *Asian Trade and European Influence in the Indonesian Archipelago between 1500 and 1650* (1962).

M. A. P. Meilink-Roelofsz (ed.), *De VOC in Azië* (1976).

A. Michielsen, *De evolutie van de handelsorganisatie in België sedert het begin van de achttiende eeuw* (1938).

J. F. Niermeyer, 'Dordrecht als handelsstad in de tweede helft van de veertiende eeuw', *Bijdragen voor vaderlandse geschiedenis en oudheidkunde*, 8th Ser. 3 (1941), 1–36 and 177–222, and 4 (1942), 86–113 and 145–68.

E. Perroy, 'Le commerce anglo-flamand au XIIIe siècle: la Hanse flamande de Londres', *Revue Historique*, 252 (1974), 3–18.

H. Reincke, 'Die Deutschlandfahrt der Flandrer während der hansischen Frühzeit', *Hansische Geschichtsblätter*, 67–8 (1942–3), 51–164.

F. Rousseau, 'La Meuse et le Pays Mosan en Belgique: leur importance historique avant le XIIIe siècle', *Annales de la Société archéologique de Namur*, 39 (1930), 1–248.

H. J. Smit, 'Handel en scheepvaart in het Noordzeegebied gedurende de 13e eeuw. Bijdrage tot de kennis van de opkomst van den Hollandschen en Zeeuwschen handel', *Bijdragen voor vaderlandsche geschiedenis en oudheidkunde*, 7th Ser. 10 (1939), 511–72 and 197–220.

Z. W. Sneller, *Deventer, die Stadt der Jahrmärkte* (1936).

Z. W. Sneller, 'Handel en verkeer in het Beneden-Maasgebied tot het einde der zestiende eeuw', *Nederlandsche Historiebladen*, 2 (1939), 341–72.

E. Stols, 'The Southern Netherlands and the Foundation of the Dutch East and West India Companies', *Acta Historiae Neerlandicae*, 9 (1976), 30–47.

E. Stols, *De Spaanse Brabanders, of de handelsbetrekkingen der Zuidelijke Nederlanden met de Iberische wereld 1598–1648* (1972).

W. S. Unger, 'Bijdragen tot de geschiedenis van de Nederlandse slavenhandel', *Economisch-Historisch Jaarboek*, 26 (1956), 133–74, and 28 (1961), 3–148.

W. S. Unger, 'Middelburg als handelsstad (XIIIe–XVIe eeuw)', *Archief uitgegeven door het Zeeuwsch Genootschap der Wetenschappen* (1935), 1–173.

W. S. Unger, 'Een nieuw deel der Sonttabellen', *Tijdschrift voor Geschiedenis*, 55 (1940), 272–7.

W. S. Unger, 'De publikatie der Sonttabellen voltooid', *ibid.*, 71 (1958), 147–205.

W. S. Unger, 'De Sonttabellen', *ibid.*, 41 (1926), 137–55.

W. S. Unger, 'Trade through the Sound in the Seventeenth and Eighteenth Centuries', *Economic History Review*, 2nd Ser. 12 (1958–9), 206–21.

H. van der Wee, *The Growth of the Antwerp Market and the European Economy, Fourteenth–Sixteenth Centuries*, 3 vols (1963).

J. G. van Dillen, 'De Opstand en het Amerikaanse zilver', *Tijdschrift voor Geschiedenis*, 73 (1960), 25–38; (reprinted in his *Mensen en Achtergronden* (1964), 181–92).

J. A. van Houtte, 'Anvers aux XVe et XVIe siècles. Expansion et apogée, *Annales. Economies, sociétés, civilisations*, 16 (1961), 248–78 (reprinted in his *Essays*, pp. 143–79).

J. A. van Houtte, 'Déclin et survivance d'Anvers, 1550–1700', *Studi in onore di A. Fanfani*, 5 (1962), 705–26 (reprinted in his *Essays*, pp. 181–201).

J. A. van Houtte, 'The Rise and Decline of the Market of Bruges', *Economic History Review*, 2nd Ser. 19 (1966), 29–47 (reprinted in his *Essays*, pp. 249–74).

7. FINANCE

V. Barbour, *Capitalism in Amsterdam in the Seventeenth Century* (1950).

G. Bigwood, *Le régime juridique et économique du commerce de l'argent dans la Belgique du moyen âge*, 2 vols (1921–2).

E. Coornaert, 'Les Bourses d'Anvers aux XVe et XVIe siècles', *Revue Historique*, 217 (1957), 20–8.

E. E. De Jong-Keesing, 'De economische crisis van 1763 te Amsterdam' (thesis, Amsterdam, 1939).

R. de Roover, *The Bruges Money Market around 1400* (1968).

R. de Roover, *Money, Banking and Credit in Mediaeval Bruges. Italian Merchant-Bankers, Lombards and Money-Changers. A Study in the Origins of Banking* (1948).

F. P. Groeneveld, 'De economische crisis van het jaar 1720' (thesis, Amsterdam, 1940).

Z. W. Sneller, 'De Rotterdamsche Wisselbank, 1635–1812', *De Economist*, 87 (1938), 685–716, 808–40, 882–902 (reprinted in his *Rotterdams bedrijfsleven in het verleden* (1940), pp. 107–84).

J. G. van Dillen, 'De Amsterdamsche Wisselbank in de zeventiende eeuw 1609–1686', *De Economist*, 77 (1928), 239–59 and 349–73; reprinted in his *Mensen en achtergronden*, pp. 336–84.

J. G. van Dillen, 'Bloeitijd der Amsterdamse Wisselbank 1687–1781', in his *Mensen en achtergronden*, 385–415.

J. G. van Dillen, 'Ondergang van de Amsterdamse Wisselbank', *ibid.*, pp. 416–47.

J. G. van Dillen, 'De termijnhandel te Amsterdam in de 16e en 17e eeuw', *De Economist*, 76 (1927), 503–24; reprinted in his *Mensen en achtergronden*, pp. 466–83.

C. Wilson, *Anglo-Dutch Commerce and Finance in the Eighteenth Century* (2nd edn, 1966).

8. MONEY

V. Janssens, *Het geldwezen der Ooostenrijkse Nederlanden* (1957).

J. Nicolas, *L'argent des principautés belges pendant le moyen âge et la période moderne*, 2 vols (1933).

P. Spufford, *Monetary problems and policies in the Burgundian Netherlands, 1433–96* (1970).

H. E. van Gelder, 'Munthervorming tijdens de Republiek, 1659–1694' (thesis, Utrecht, 1949).

A. E. van Gelder and M. Hoc, *Les monnaies des Pays-Bas bourguignons et espagnols, 1434–1713* (1960).

Index

Aa, 25
Aachen, 36, 38, 41, 87, 132, 161, 183, 258
Aalsmeer, 148
Aardenburg, 100
Aduard, 60
Africa, 37, 101, 110–11, 175–6, 189, 197–8, 202, 281, 284
agricultural implements, 4, 5, 38, 71, 151, 244, 246; methods, 4, 70–1, 142, 145, 150–1, 243–5; yields, 3, 13, 71–2, 151–2, 254–6
Aire, 25, 83
Aleppo, 197
Alkmaar, 72, 144, 153, 228, 231, 247, 250
Almelo, 261
Alost, 25, 227, 230, 234–5, 239, 245, 260
Alps, 20, 101, 108, 181
Alsace, 238, 257
alum, 34, 169, 175, 180–1
amber, 96
America, 182, 201, 203, 212, 214, 240, 245, 264, 309; Spanish, 196, 202, 222, 281–2, 300
Amersfoort, 147, 171, 261
Amsterdam, 26, 45, 72, 96–8, 103, 114, 125, 130, 134–6, 141, 143, 154, 157, 160–1, 165, 168, 170–1, 173–4, 182, 184–7, 191–201, 206–10, 213–19, 222–3, 229–32, 237, 254, 256–8, 261–3, 266–8, 270, 272–8, 282–5, 287, 290–1, 301–9, 311–15
Ancona, 182
Andalusia, 100, 179–81

annuities, 55, 116, 221–2
Antwerp, 21, 23–4, 27, 33, 41, 62–4, 67–8, 73, 78, 83, 87, 104–9, 114–17, 119, 124, 126–7, 131–4, 136–7, 142, 157–8, 161, 164–6, 168, 170–91, 194, 196–7, 200, 204–9, 211, 215–22, 229–30, 233–5, 249, 256, 258, 260–3, 267–8, 280–1, 284, 292, 295–6, 303, 308–9, 314
Apeldoorn, 72
Appenines, 36
Aragon, 181
Archangel, 194
Arctic Ocean, 184, 252–3
Ardennes, 4, 15, 32–3, 46, 94, 144, 238, 240, 284
Armenia, 277
arms and munitions, 18, 41, 167, 192, 194, 196–7, 223, 264, 282
Arnemuiden, 109, 177–80
Arnhem, 24, 46
Arras, 25, 27–30, 34, 36–7, 42, 51, 53–4, 86, 115
Artois, 4, 32–3, 43, 53, 64, 67, 71, 82, 104, 137, 179
ash, see potash
Asia, 18–21, 33–4, 37, 100–1, 165, 171, 175, 197, 199, 200, 213–14, 262–3, 278, 281, 297
asientos, 222; colonial, 277, 281
Asti, 43, 55, 117
Asturia, 37
Ath, 85, 138, 147, 158, 162

332